Reference Books Bulletin, 1998–99

A compilation of evaluations
September 1998 through August 1999

*Prepared by the American Library Association
Reference Books Bulletin Editorial Board*

*Edited by Mary Ellen Quinn
Compiled by Michelle Kaske*

BOOKLIST Publications
Chicago 2000

Copyright 1996, 2000 by the American Library Association.

Permission to quote any review in full or in part must be obtained from the Office of Rights and Permissions of the American Library Association. Permission to quote a review in full will be granted only to the publisher of the work reviewed.

Library of Congress Catalog Card Number 73-159565

International Standard Book Number 0-8389-8104-6
International Standard Serial Number 8755-0962

Printed in the United States of America

Cover design by Jim Lange

Contents

- v   Preface
- vii   Reference Books Bulletin Editorial Board
- ix   Guest Reviewers

    Special Features
- 1   Encyclopedia Update, 1998
- 4   Electronic Encyclopedia Update, 1998
- 7   An Evaluation of Current World Atlases
- 11   African American Reference Books for Public Libraries
- 12   Patent and Trademark Resources

    Core Collections
- 16   The Sciences
- 18   Genealogy
- 20   SF/Fantasy Reference Sources

- 22   Another Look At . . .

    Featured Reviews and Reviews
- 24   Generalities
- 34   Philosophy, Psychology, Religion
- 41   Social Sciences
- 50   Business, Economics
- 52   Law, Public Administration, Social Problems and Services
- 56   Education, Communication, Customs
- 59   Language
- 61   Science
- 67   Medicine, Health, Technology, Management
- 74   Fine Arts, Decorative Arts, Music
- 79   Performing Arts, Recreation
- 83   Literature
- 92   Geography, Biography
- 99   History

    Indexes
- 112   Index to Type of Material
- 115   Subject Index
- 119   Title Index

Preface

Reference Books Bulletin, 1998–1999 is the 31st cumulative edition of *Reference Books Bulletin* (*RBB*) reviews, published from September 1998 to August 1999 in the magazine *Booklist*. In re-reading those issues, I was again impressed with the high quality of the reviews written by *RBB* Board members, as well as the alumni and contributing reviewers. Because the final product reflects the collaborative effort of the Board in making revisions most of our reviews are unsigned, but they are drafted by individuals from all walks of librarianship who bring a great breadth of knowledge, as well as excellent writing and analytical skills, to their work. Thanks go to all of *RBB*'s reviewers for making our jobs in reference and collection development a little easier.

Readers of this compilation should note that while it includes over 300 of *RBB*'s reviews of print, CD-ROM, and major online reference tools, it excludes other information, such as editor Mary Ellen Quinn's "News & Views" column (with updates on reference publishing), "Reference Books in Brief" (short summaries of new titles worth noting), and the "Fall Reference Preview." Also omitted here, due the volatility of Web site addresses, are our numerous reviews of free Internet resources. So, do not forget to check out *RBB* and *Booklist* every month for these valuable sections!

This year, as usual, *RBB* had a large number of lengthier, in-depth articles, which you will find listed in the "Special Features" section. In addition to our annual print and electronic encyclopedia updates, the "Another Look At" column, initiated last year to highlight reference standbys, continues its success with *Penguin Dictionary of Art and Landscape Architecture*, *New Book of Popular Science*, *Famous First Facts*, and *CQ Researcher*. I thank Barbara Bibel, Chair of the *RBB* Special Features Task Force, for her work in pulling together "Core Collections" on science fiction and fantasy, the sciences, and genealogy, and recommended African-American, patent and trademark, and world atlas resources, among other topics.

It has been a real pleasure to work again with *Reference Books Bulletin* editor Mary Ellen Quinn, who has done a wonderful job. Thanks too, to publishing assistant Michelle Kaske for keeping things organized, no mean task. As I final note, I would like to thank my colleagues at the Raymond H. Fogler Library of the University of Maine for their support.

Deborah Rollins,
Chair
Reference Books Bulletin Editorial Board
1998–99

Reference Books Bulletin Editorial Board

Deborah Rollins, Reference Librarian, Fogler Library, University of Maine, Orono, Maine, Chair.

Charlotte Decker, Librarian, Children's Learning Center, Public Library of Cincinnati and Hamilton County, Cincinnati, Ohio.

John Doherty, Undergraduate Reference Services Librarian, Cline Library, Northern Arizona University, Flagstaff, Arizona.

Nora Harris, Branch Manager, Fairfax Library, Fairfax, California.

Jeff Kosokoff, Electronic Resources Coordinator, John T. Richardson Library, DePaul University, Chicago, Illinois.

Christopher McConnell, Library, Dominican College, San Rafael, California.

J. Sara Paulk, Assistant Director of Public Services, Tifton-Tift County Public Library, Tifton, Georgia.

Randall Rafferty, Reference Librarian, Mitchell Library, Mississippi State University, Mississippi State, Mississippi.

Karen Reiman-Sendi, Social Work Library, University of Michigan, Ann Arbor, Michigan.

Cheryl Karp Ward, East Hartford High School, East Hartford, Connecticut.

Reference Books Bulletin Contributing Reviewers, 1998–1999

Donald Altschiller, Mugar Library, Boston University, Boston, Massachusetts.

James D. Anderson, Professor, School of Communication, Information, and Library Studies, Rutgers University, New Brunswick, New Jersey.

Susan Awe, Interim Director, Business and Economics, Parish Memorial Library, University of New Mexico, Albuquerque, New Mexico.

Barbara Bibel, Reference Librarian, Oakland Public Library, Oakland, California, Special Features Task Force, Chair.

Ken Black, Director of Teaching and Learning Technology, Dominican University, River Forest, Illinois.

Christine Bulson, Assistant Director for Reference and Circulation Services, Milne Library, SUNY Oneonta, Oneonta, New York.

Robert Craig Bunch, Librarian, Jones H.S. Library, Coldspring, Texas.

Jerry Carbone, Director, Brooks Memorial Library, Brattleboro, Vermont.

Ann E. Cohen, Assistant Division Head, Information Center, Rochester Public Library, Rochester, New York.

Sharon E. Cohen, Librarian, Children's Department, Westfield Memorial Library, Westfield, New Jersey.

Deborah Daniels, Fremont Elementary, East Syracuse, New York.

Donald Davis Jr., Graduate School of Library and Information Science, University of Texas at Austin, Austin, Texas.

Carole C. Deily, Reference Librarian, Plano Public Library System, Plano, Texas.

Marie Ellis, Librarian IV Emeritus, University of Georgia Libraries, Athens, Georgia.

Lesley S. J. Farmer, CSU Long Beach, Long Beach, California.

Jack Forman, Public Services Librarian, San Diego Mesa College Library/LRC, San Diego, California.

Elizabeth L. Fraser, Reference Librarian, Kanawha County Public Library, Charleston, West Virginia.

Rochelle Glantz, Coordinator of Libraries, Lexington Public Schools, Lexington, Massachusetts.

Susan Gooden, Librarian, Concord High School, Wilmington, Delaware.

Ruth M. Hadlow, Head, Children's Literature Department, Cleveland Public Library, Cleveland, Ohio.

Mary Ann Hansen, The Libraries, Montana State University, Bozeman, Montana.

Carol Sue Harless, Stone Mountain High School, Stone Mountain, Georgia.

Dona Helmer, College Gate Elementary School, Anchorage, Alaska.

Judith Higgins, White Plains, New York.

Robin Hoelle, Librarian, Badin High School, Hamilton, Ohio.

Patricia M. Hogan, Administrative Librarian, Poplar Creek Public Library District, Streamwood, Illinois.

Nancy Huntley, Director, Lincoln Library, Springfield, Illinois.

Jacqueline A. Jackson, Nelson Poynter Memorial Library, University of South Florida, St. Petersburg Campus, St. Petersburg, Florida.

Sally Jacobs, University Library Services, Virginia Commonwealth University, Richmond, Virginia.

Sarah Sartain Jane, Head of Collection Development, Lee County Library System, Fort Myers, Florida.

Lisa N. Johnston, Associate Director/Head of Public Services, Sweet Briar College Libraries, Sweet Briar, Virginia.

Rashelle Karp, Associate Professor, College of Library Science, Clarion University of Pennsylvania, Clarion, Pennsylvania.

Marlene M. Kuhl, Catonsville Library, Catonsville, Maryland.

Abbie Vestal Landry, Head of Reference Division, Watson Library, Northwestern State University, Natchitoches, Louisiana.

John C. Larsen, Baltimore, Maryland.

Jan Lewis, Coordinator of Instructional Services, Joyner Library, East Carolina University, Greenville, North Carolina.

Arthur A. Lichtenstein, Outreach Services Coordinator, Torreyson Library, University of Central Arkansas, Conway, Arkansas.

Marilyn L. Long, Palm High School, Salinas, California.

Kathleen M. McBroom, Media Specialist, Fordson Media Center, Dearborn, Michigan.

Josephine McSweeney, Professor and Reference Librarian, Pratt Institute Library, Brooklyn, New York.

H. Robert Malinowsky, Manager of Collection Development and Reference, University of Illinois at Chicago, Chicago, Illinois.

Arthur S. Meyers, Library Director, Russell Library, Middletown, Connecticut.

Carloyn M. Mulac, Assistant Head, Information Center, Chicago Public Library, Chicago, Illinois.

Elizabeth Nibley, Reference Librarian, American University Library, Washington, District of Columbia.

Jack O'Gorman, Reference Librarian, Roesch Library, University of Dayton, Dayton, Ohio.

Barbara O'Hara, Audorra Library, Philadelphia, Pennsylvania.

Mary Scott Patterson, Tippecanoe Public Library, Lafayette, Indiana.

Margaret Power, Depaul University Library, Chicago, Illinois.

Linda Loos Scarth, Reference Librarian, Busse Center Library, Mount Mercy College, Cedar Rapids, Iowa.

Diana Donner Shonrock, Science Librarian/Family and Consumer Science Bibliographer, Iowa State University, Ames, Iowa.

Esther Sinofsky, Coordinating Field Librarian, Library Services, Los Angeles, California.

Kathleen Stipek, Adult Services Librarian, Alachua County Library District, Gainesville, Florida.

Martin D. Sugden, Reference Librarian, Business, Science, and Documents Department, Jacksonville Public Library, Jacksonville, Florida.

Terri Tomchyshyn, Sales Consultant, RoweCom Canada, Ottawa, Ontario, Canada.

David A. Tyckoson, Head of Reference, Madden Library, California State University-Fresno, Fresno, California..

Sarah Barbara Watstein, Director, Academic User Services, VCU Libraries, Virginia Commonwealth University, Richmond, Virginia.

Ann Welton, Terminal Park Elementary School, Auburn, Washington.

Christine A. Whittington, Head of Reference, University of Maine, Orono, Maine.

Wiley J. Williams, Chapel Hill, North Carolina.

Special Features

Encyclopedia Update, 1998

It has been a year of changes since our last Encyclopedia Update, in the September 15, 1997, issue. For the most part, these changes have meant that the world of encyclopedias-as-books continues to shrink. Early in the year, Atlas Editions (formerly Collier Newfield, formerly P. F. Collier) sold the electronic rights to *Collier's Encyclopedia* to Microsoft. Although Atlas has retained the rights to the print version, it appears likely that the 1997 print edition of *Collier's* is the last one we will see. In June, it was announced that the Learning Company sold the print version of *Compton's* to Success Publishing Group, Ltd.; Success tells us that *Compton's* will not be printed in 1998.

Still standing are *Academic American Encyclopedia*, *Encyclopedia Americana*, and *New Book of Knowledge* from Grolier, and *World Book*, all of which are reviewed below. Also still among the living are *New Standard Encyclopedia*, published by Ferguson Publishing Co., who tells us that the 1998 *New Standard* will be available early next year, and the venerable *New Encyclopedia Britannica*, whose 1998 edition we reviewed in RBB March 1, 1998. Britannica, despite publishing the oldest and in some ways the most conservative of the print encyclopedias, has been in the forefront in terms of adapting to change. They were the first with an Internet-based version, and they have aggressively pursued various other opportunities offered by the Web. The latest is a new Web directory called eBLAST [http://www.eblast.com], which seems to be an enhanced version of their *Britannica Internet Guide* [RBB Mr 1 98]. Meanwhile, Britannica continues to look for new ways to market its print product. Most recently, they have announced a "Ready Reference" version of *New Encyclopedia Britannica* to be sold through bookstores. Consisting of the 12 volumes of the Micropedia, it will sell for a suggested retail price of $499.

Grolier and World Book also continue to explore new avenues for content delivery. At the ALA Annual Conference in June, World Book introduced its Internet-based encyclopedia, and Grolier showed off the latest addition to its Grolier Online family, *New Book of Knowledge Online*. RBB will be taking a look at both in the coming months. All of the encyclopedias reviewed here are now available as Web subscription products. Of course, we will continue to provide updates on CD-ROM encyclopedias as well; watch for our reviews of the newest versions beginning in the November 1 issue.

The pace of change in encyclopedia publishing has prompted the *Reference Books Bulletin* Editorial Board to ask ourselves whether the annual Encyclopedia Update in its present form continues to be a useful tool for our readers. We would be very interested in hearing from you about the kind of information you want us to provide regarding encyclopedias. Please e-mail your comments to me at mquinn@ala.org.

—Mary Ellen Quinn

Academic American Encyclopedia. 21v. 1998. Grolier, $725 (0-7172-2068-0). DDC: 031.

- *History*: The Academic American Encyclopedia (AAE), first published in 1980, is intended to be used by nonspecialist adults and students in the upper elementary grades through college.

- *Scope and Treatment*: There are approximately 30,000 entries in the 1998 edition, ranging from short paragraphs to multipage surveys. At 205,000 entries, the completely revised index has been increased by 2,000 access points. New contributors, who created new and replacement articles, include Kathryn Cullen DuPont, author of *The Encyclopedia of Women's History in America* (*feminism*); Lee Kogan, director of the Folk Art Institute (*folk art*); William A. Turnbaugh, professor of anthropology at the University of Rhode Island (*North American archaeology*); and Robert M. Veatch, professor of medical ethics at Georgetown University (*euthanasia, death and dying*). They and others join 2,680 authors whose affiliations are provided in volume 1. All of the longer articles and many of the short ones include brief bibliographies. Visual material in the form of 18,000 illustrations and 1,908 maps makes up approximately one-third of the set, adding information and interest to every page.

- *Quality and Currency*: There are 135 new articles in the 1998 AAE, of which 60 are replacement articles. The approach to thoughtful revision can be seen in *folk dance*. While the previous version of the article concentrated mainly on the forms of dance, costume, and accessories, in the revised article, Joann W. Kealiinohomoku (director, Cross-Cultural Dance Resources, Flagstaff, Arizona) discusses folk dance as a difficult concept that may be defined differently by scholars, countries, cultures, and the people who perform the dances. The distinction between first (functionally integral to their community) and second (recreational or theatrical, and less dynamic) existence dances is important. Although it may not be easy for a middle-school student to understand these ideas, there are ample cross-references to separate articles on individual dance forms (*hora*, *morris dance*) for younger users. Among other replacements are *Indians of North America, music and dance of the*; *psychology, history of* (with substantial room given to cognitive issues that have come to the fore in the late twentieth century); *archaeology* and related major articles; and *cardiovascular diseases*. Entirely new subjects this year include *Ebola virus*, *juggling*, *macrobiotics*, and *rope*. Some new biographical entries describe the lives of U.S. Secretary of State Madeleine Albright, UN Secretary-General Kofi Annan, the musical Carter family, British archaeologist Colin Renfrew, and golfer Tiger Woods. And, after her tragic death, Diana, Princess of Wales, has been given a separate entry this year.

  Maps for geological periods were revised, and those for the U.K. now show the new local government structure of unitary authorities. Of 26 map changes, 9 are entirely new city maps (*Hong Kong, Mexico City*). *Modern architecture* added a shot of the Guggenheim Museum in Bilbao, Spain, and *archaeology* added the Great Zimbabwe complex, epigraphy, radiocarbon dating, and the Lindow Man—just some of 166 new and revised color illustrations.

  In terms of currency, the AAE is usually right on top of things. Major revisions were done in 190 articles, concentrating on volumes 4, 6, and 8, with big topics such as *Canada*; *drug*; and *film, history of*; as well as updates to bibliographies. Another 2,500 articles were updated with small but important changes, such as the reclassification of the skunk in the family Mephitidae. In all, 16 percent of the text pages were revised, according to the editors. Although the 1997 Nobel Prize winners from October are not listed, death dates were added for Jacques Cousteau, James Stewart, and Mother Teresa, and August's devastating Montserrat volcano eruption and September's historic vote for an independent legislature in Scotland also made it into print. The glossary in *computer* now includes *newsgroup* and *search engine*. It is interesting to note that *tobacco* makes no mention of the alkaloid nicotine, described in the nicotine entry as extremely poisonous, nor does it recount June's tobacco company settlement or any of the recent (post-1992) political and legal wrangling surrounding this controversial topic.

- *Electronic Versions*: The CD-ROM version of AAE is known as *Grolier Multimedia Encyclopedia*. This year, there is a DVD version as well. *Grolier Multimedia Encyclopedia Online* is available as part of a package called *Grolier Online*, which also includes *Encyclopedia Americana Online* and, new this year, *New Book of Knowledge Online*.

- *Conclusion*: The 1998 AAE is an attractive, reliable, informative, and up-to-date encyclopedia that is well suited to its audience. It will be read and enjoyed by library users of all ages.

Encyclopedia Americana. 30v. 1998. Grolier, $995 (0-7172-0130-9). DDC: 031.

- *History*: Acquired by Grolier in 1945, the 168-year-old *Encyclopedia Americana* was the first general encyclopedia published in the U.S.
- *Scope and Treatment*: *Americana's* breadth and depth recommend it for grades 8 and up. Although international in scope, this encyclopedia is especially strong on U.S. and Canadian topics. There are approximately 45,000 entries. Volume 30, the index, contains approximately 53,000 entries. New among the 6,500 contributors this year are Paul Friedlander, California State University at Chico (*rock music*); Mitzi Myers, lecturer, English and writing programs, University of California at Los Angeles (*literature for children*); and Hunki Yun, associate editor, *Golf Digest* (*Woods, Tiger*). Contributors and their affiliations are listed in volume 1. Major articles can be quite long, providing more in-depth coverage than most other print encyclopedias. *Library*, for example, is more than 90 pages. There are approximately 23,000 illustrations, 20 percent of them in color.
- *Quality and Currency*: The encyclopedia underwent revision through November 11, 1997. This is the first year of a two-year transition to move "from a production cycle based on the publication of the print set to one that is more in keeping with . . . expanded capacity to publish electronically." This year's print edition contains 42 new articles, 22 replacement articles, and more than 2,000 major and minor revisions. There is more new and revised text than in previous years. Of the 91 new photographs, 68 are in color; of the 31 new pieces of artwork, 20 are in color. Although no new maps were added this year, 29 were revised. Overall, the print set includes more illustrations than the electronic versions.

  Literature was the focus in humanities this year. *Literature for children* has been "reconceived." *Literature* from the 1997 electronic version is now in the print set, as is *slave narrative*, which relates to a host of articles on African American writers. The article on romance does not reflect the huge market for series romances, such as Harlequins. New biographies cover Dario Fo (1997 Nobel Prize for literature), Chester Himes, and Jean Toomer.

  Revisions in the social sciences continue in the areas of law, politics, economics, society, and education. Political tables reflect the 1997 U.S. gubernatorial races. *United States: International Relations* and *United States: Modern Nation* include the past year's events. There is a new article on preschool education. New biographies include Madeleine Albright, Kofi Annan, and Tony Blair. Biographies on Bill Clinton, Newt Gingrinch, Jiang Zemin, and Mobutu Sese Seko were revised. In anthropology, *tool* and *Stone Age* were added to the print set. Revisions in area studies span the globe. *Hong Kong* was revised to reflect the shift from British colony to Chinese special administrative region. *China* was also updated to reflect the Hong Kong changeover. *Korea* includes the Hambro Iron and Steel scandal and the arrests, trials, and sentencings of former presidents Chun Doo Hwan and Roh Tae Woo. Over in Europe, revisions included the peace talks in North Ireland; earthquakes in Italy's Umbrian region; flooding in Poland and the Czech Republic; the referendum in Scotland to allow establishment of its own legislature; and the invitations to Poland, Hungary, and the Czech Republic to join NATO. In Africa, the key event was the overthrow of Mobutu in Zaire. Kabila changed the country's name to the Democratic Republic of the Congo, which caused 120 articles to be altered to reflect the change in nomenclature. Articles on the Americas reflect natural disasters such as the flooding in North Dakota, Hurricane Pauline that devastated Acapulco, and the volcanic eruption on Montserrat. The Canadian and Mexican elections are covered. Approximately 330 articles on U.S. cities were updated. The Middle East naturally focused on the stalled Israeli-Palestinian peace talks and the election of moderate leader Mohammed Khatami as president of Iran. Population statistics were updated for 1,378 articles, including cities and administrative divisions of the former Soviet Union, Germany, France, the Balkans, the Czech Republic, Slovakia, and China. Population figures for the U.S. are taken from the 1990 census, with no later estimates.

  In the arts, *architecture* and *rock music* were expanded and illustrated with color photographs. New biographies cover Milton Berle, George Lucas, Robert Mapplethorpe, Steven Spielberg, Martin Scorsese, Mae West, and Ellen Taaffe Zwilich. Deaths were noted in biographies of Rudolf Bing, Alexandra Danilova, Willem de Kooning, Roy Lichtenstein, Marcello Mastroianni, Robert Mitchum, Georg Solti, James Stewart, and Victor Vasarely. The life sciences saw the continued expansion of mammal articles, with emphasis on greater detail and consistency of presentation. Replacement articles include *enzyme*, *hormone*, *embryology*, and *genetic engineering*. In the physical sciences and technology, there is a program under way to add biographies of scientists in earth science, chemistry, mathematics, physics, and astronomy. This year's emphasis was earth scientists such as Mary Ann Anning, Friedrich Mohs, and Henry Darwin Rogers. Revised and new articles include *plate tectonic* and *radar*; both contain new artwork. The periodic table now reflects 112 elements, but not all the electronic articles on elements have migrated to the print set. The article on space exploration includes an overlay section on the space shuttle mission sequence, but the "space achievements" table still ends in 1992.

  The *Americana Annual* supplements the print set by recording each year's significant developments.

- *Electronic Versions*: Encyclopedia Americana is available in both CD-ROM and online versions.
- *Conclusion*: Encyclopedia Americana remains one of the most comprehensive general encyclopedias available. The electronic versions continue to be more up to date than the print set, and many articles appear there first. High-school, public, and academic libraries may want to consider an electronic version instead of the print set if currency is an issue. The print set may be a more economical choice depending on the student enrollment or number of patrons used for the online pricing structure.

The New Book of Knowledge. 21v. 1998. Grolier, $659 (0-7172-0529-0). DDC: 031.

- *History*: Published since 1911 for the home and school market, *The New Book of Knowledge* (NBK) is revised annually by staff editors and consultants who analyze curricular requirements of school systems across the country. The content of the 1998 edition was selected by educators and librarians conversant with the research needs of children and by a team of cultural specialists who considered the needs of users beyond the school and library setting. It continues to provide adults and children with information about subjects, with material to read aloud, and with games and activities on topics of interest to elementary and middle-school children and adults.
- *Scope and Treatment*: NBK is designed for elementary-through middle-school-age children, but it also has information of use and interest to adults. Although helpful for reports, this is an encyclopedia that is designed to be read and shared by families. For that reason, home schoolers might find this an extremely useful addition to their libraries. Many articles contain activity projects or examples of stories or poems written by the subject of the entry. For example, the article on Beatrix Potter contains an excerpt from her *Tale of Jemima Puddle-duck*, and the article on puppets contains instructions on how to make a hand puppet, a simple stage, and a marionette.

  The encyclopedia has approximately 9,243 entries. Each volume contains its own index on blue paper that is cross-referenced to the entire contents of the encyclopedia. The individual indexes are cumulated in an index of approximately 85,000 entries in volume 21. Among the 43 new contributors and reviewers to the NBK this year are Stephen Ambrose, author of *Undaunted Courage: Meriwether Lewis, Thomas Jefferson, and the Opening of the American West* (*Lewis and Clark expedition*), and Virginia Gobeli, National 4-H Program Leader (*Four-H*). Approximately one-third of NBK is occupied by illustrations, of which 90 percent are in full color.

- *Quality and Currency*: Substantial changes continue to be made in the content, design, and illustration of NBK as part of the overall major revision begun in 1992. A new editor in chief was appointed in January 1997. The 1998 revision covered more than 934 pages of text, but the most substantial changes were made in volumes H, L, O, and P. Among the subject areas receiving special attention are 7 states—Louisiana, Ohio, Oklahoma, Oregon, Rhode Island, South Carolina, and South Dakota—so that a total of 42 states now have the new format. Sixteen new biographical entries cover Neil Armstrong, John Glenn, Graham Greene, Ted Hughes, Anne Hutchinson, Aldous Huxley, and Pythagoras, among others. The 39 new articles include *abortion*, *fairies*, *Loch Ness Monster*, *Puritans*, and *pyramids*. Twenty-four articles were replaced or heavily revised, including *circus*, *heart*, *jazz*, and *locomotives*. An additional 34 were completely updated and substantively rewritten, and 257 articles received minor revision or updating. Fifty-six new maps replaced existing ones, 10 U.S. state population-density maps were revised to reflect the 1994 Census Bureau estimates. More than 547 new photographs and 131 pieces of color art were added to the set, and 116 new titles were added to the bibliographies in the separate "Home and School Reading and Study Guides." This volume also now includes 12 research activities keyed to the content in the encyclopedia. The bibliographies are up to date and indicate reading levels. The brief dictionary entries that used to appear on the blue pages preceding the index in each volume are gone, most having been absorbed into the main text.

NBK notes world events of 1997—the revision deadline extended into November of 1997 so that off-year election results, the 1997 Nobel Prize winners, and the results of the 1997 World Series could be included. Also included is information on the election of Tony Blair as British prime minister in May, the *Pathfinder* probe to Mars, and the deaths of Princess Diana and Mobuto Sese Seko. *Motion pictures* has a note on the death of James Stewart. The article on Hong Kong includes the information about its reversion to Chinese rule, and there is information about Madeleine Albright becoming secretary of state. Some postdeadline events that made it into the 1998 edition included the death of Sonny Bono and the outcome of Superbowl XXXII.

- *Electronic Versions*: An online version is new this year.
- *Conclusion*: The numerous color illustrations, timeliness, and large, nonthreatening typeface coupled with accurate, helpful information and interesting articles that can be used for elementary and middle-school reports make NBK a good purchase for both home and school use. It might also be useful for special-education and ESL students. The research activities in the "Home and School Reading and Study Guides" are both useful and interesting. The added bonus of selections from works by some of the biographees is a real plus.

The World Book Encyclopedia. 22v. 1998. World Book, $769 (0-7166-0098-6). DDC: 031.

- *History*: Published since 1917, *World Book* provides information in accessible form for homes, schools, and libraries. Although designed primarily for elementary- and secondary-school students, adults also find it useful. Librarians rely on it for quick answers to a wide variety of questions.
- *Scope and Treatment*: One of *World Book's* major strengths is its accessibility to users at all levels. Another is its excellent layout and visual presentation. Approximately one-third of the space is devoted to 28,000 illustrations, including maps, photographs, time lines, diagrams, graphs, and art. More than 80 percent are in color.

More than 3,700 scholars and specialists served as authors, authenticators, illustrators, reviewers, and consultants for this edition. Among the 57 new contributors this year are Roberto S. Goizueta, associate professor of theology at Loyola University of Chicago (*liberation theology*), Joseph M. Moran, professor of earth science at the University of Wisconsin (*climate* and *weather*), and Laurence Steinberg, professor of psychology at Temple University (*adolescent*).

World Book has approximately 17,000 articles, all of which are signed. Many articles, especially those likely to be of interest to younger students, are accompanied by study aids, which may include a list of related articles, an outline, study questions, and a list of additional sources that may be annotated. Longer bibliographies are divided by reading level. Volume 22, the Research Guide and Index, has more than 150,000 index entries and 200 reading and study guides that suggest paper topics and provide additional bibliographies. It also contains instructions for using the index and brief articles on writing papers, giving oral presentations, and doing research. The index provides access to illustrations, maps, overlays, and study guides. More than 5,000 *see* and *see also* references within the text make it easy for unsophisticated users to locate material without the index. Volume 1 contains general instructions on using the encyclopedia and lists the names and affiliations of all the contributors.

- *Quality and Currency*: *World Book* does an excellent job of staying up to date. The 1998 edition has 80 new articles. Fifty-five articles have been extensively revised, and more than 1,180 have been partially revised. Some 105 book lists, in addition to those in revised articles, have been reviewed and updated as necessary. One hundred thirty-three maps have been added or changed for this edition, and 250 new photographs, diagrams, or illustrations appear.

- Among the new articles are *colon cancer*, *domestic violence*, *Kristallnacht*, *obsessive-compulsive disorder*, and *pest control*. New biographies include entries for Kofi Annan, Shannon W. Lucid, Madonna, Jacqueline Kennedy Onassis, and Shaka. Extensively revised articles include *adolescent*, *concentration camp*, *Jerusalem*, *map*, and *weather*. Statistics are current. Figures for the U.S. include the 1990 census totals, 1998 estimates, and projections to 2003. Those for other countries include the latest available census figures, current estimates, and five-year projections. Awards lists and economic indicators are up to date. Such 1997 events as the election of Tony Blair as prime minister of Great Britain, Laurent Kabila's takeover in Zaire, and the reversion of Hong Kong to Chinese rule are covered. The deaths of Jacques Cousteau, Princess Diana, Willem de Kooning, Deng Xiaoping, Allen Ginsburg, James Michener, and Mother Teresa are noted. *World Book Yearbook*, an annual supplement, updates the encyclopedia.

- *Electronic Versions*: *World Book* is available on CD-ROM as the *World Book Multimedia Encyclopedia*. A Web-based online version is new this year.

- *Conclusion*: *World Book Encyclopedia* is an outstanding, beautifully illustrated, current general reference source for all age levels.

Electronic Encyclopedia Update, 1998

Except for updated information and a few new features, we don't see many changes in the new crop of CD-ROM encyclopedias. The ones we review here are *Compton's Interactive Encyclopedia, Encyclopedia Americana, Grolier Multimedia Encyclopedia, World Book,* and *Funk & Wagnalls Multimedia Encyclopedia,* the new kid on the block. Others were not received from their publishers in time for this issue, so we'll look at them at a later date. As in the past, *Encyclopedia Americana* is the only CD-ROM encyclopedia not to offer multimedia. On the other hand, *Americana* has the most sophisticated search capabilities. The others, which are marketed for the home as well as the library, offer lots in the way of cool features but keep their searches simpler.

This year's big news in electronic encyclopedias is the entry of *World Book* and *The New Book of Knowledge* into the online arena, joining *Britannica Online, Encyclopedia Americana Online,* and *Grolier Multimedia Online*. We hoped to include reviews of the online versions of *World Book* and *The New Book of Knowledge* in this update, but neither is quite ready for prime time. Watch for our reviews in upcoming issues.

Compton's Interactive Encyclopedia. CD-ROM. 1999. The Learning Co., deluxe ed., $39.99 (0-7911-3068-1). Networking available.

System requirements: Windows 95 *or higher,* 16 MB RAM, 15 MB *free hard disk space.*

Compton's Interactive Encyclopedia (CIE) was the first to integrate animation, sound, video, pictures, and text in a truly multimedia CD-ROM encyclopedia. The 1999 edition is currently available for Windows 95 on two discs. The encyclopedia can be installed in two ways, one requiring less hard drive space. A narrated Guided Tour is available to give users an overview of the encyclopedia's features and how to access them.

- *Content:* The CD-ROM contains the entire print set with updated information, and includes a dictionary/thesaurus. Double clicking any text will bring up the dictionary entry, which can easily be changed to the thesaurus entry. The CIE contains 41,224 articles, 413 tables, 16,125 pictures, 468 maps, 151 video clips, 713 sound clips (many of which are narrations to accompany pictures), and 4,061 Web links. There are more than 1,000 articles that do not appear in the print set, including those on dinosaurs, stars, and Caldecott and Newbery Medal winners. There are 1,045 articles that are new to this edition, including *Amistad; El Nino; Kwan, Michelle;* and *tamoxifen.* Updating was done to 340 articles and 44 tables. Many of the updated articles are those dealing with American colleges and universities, and types of snakes. The updated article on Bill Clinton primarily adds information on his 1997 State of the Union Address and on the Paula Jones case (to May 1997), although more current information is available through the Recent Events feature. The AIDS article includes the AIDS "cocktail," but the bibliography contains only resources from the early 1990s. *Ireland, Northern* includes the 1998 peace accord, but *Irish Republican Army* only goes up to 1997. Most of the updated tables, including sports championships and awards, include 1998 winners. Videos are, for the most part, sophisticated and informative. An Atlas feature contains physical, topographical, and historical maps. The World and U.S. History Timelines can appear on the screen together or separately, and the time scales can be changed to year, decade, or century. Clicking on an event will bring up the encyclopedia article or a quick-reference fact box.

  Among the special features are six Multimedia Explorations, which include Biomes, Space, and U.S. History; the Planetarium, in which the user can see the night sky from a selected city; Recent Events; On This Date; Exploring Questions, where answers to randomly selected questions are found in articles; and Picture Tours, which are random slide shows of all images. The Research Tools feature includes Topic Chooser; Word Processor; Dictionary/Thesaurus; Bookmarks; Report Starter; which helps students research and organize reports; and Presentation Maker, which helps the user create multimedia presentations. The Online feature, working with the user's Web browser, includes Electric Library and access to Compton's research team, which answers questions by e-mail. Monthly updates can be downloaded from the Web, and are necessary to keep the Recent Events feature current. A directory of available Web links includes the URL, age levels, and a brief summary of the site's content.

- *Access:* The encyclopedia can be searched by word using Boolean operators, or by browsing the A–Z list of titles, including all media, or by specific medium. Text, images, maps, and tables are printable or can be copied to a notepad or another word processor. A control bar with drop-down option menus appears on every screen, and many of the features also contain an appropriate task bar. Entire articles can be printed, or highlighted sections can be saved to a word processor and printed from there. Lists of bookmarks can be saved for future use. Since the basic text and many of the multimedia features are on both discs, occasional switching is not disruptive to use.

- *Conclusion:* CIE99 is an easy-to-use CD-ROM product that will appeal to upper-elementary and middle-school students. Its simple navigation and multimedia features are especially attractive. The Online features offer users access to updated information, though more current information in main articles and the bibliographies would be helpful.

Encyclopedia Americana. CD-ROM. 1998. Grolier, $179 (0-7172-3404-5). Networking available.

System requirements: For Windows CompLex 2 version: Windows 3.1 *or higher,* 4 MB RAM, 4 MB *free hard disk space.* For Windows CompLex 3 version: Windows 95 *recommended,* 16 MB RAM, 4 MB *free hard disk space.* For Macintosh: System 7.0 *or higher,* 2.5 MB *free RAM (in addition to RAM used by system),* 4 MB *free hard disk space.*

First released in 1995, *Encyclopedia Americana* on CD-ROM is available in Windows 3.1, Windows 95, and Macintosh platforms. If running on a Windows platform, either CompLex 2.5 or 3.0, a 32-bit architecture that enhances search capabilities, must be installed from the CD-ROM.

- *Content:* The CD-ROM contains the full text of the 30-volume 1998 print set plus additional articles not yet released in the print version. There are 76 new entries; the print set has 42 new entries. The electronic version now offers 1,689 illustrations and 830 maps. Maps are from the 1997 *Grolier Multimedia Encyclopedia*. The Middle East map seemed to have Jerusalem and Tel Aviv reversed. The reference shelf now includes *Merriam-Webster's Collegiate Dictionary* (10th ed., 1994), Helicon's *Chronology of World History* (1994), and Academic Press' *Dictionary of Science & Technology* (1996). There are replacement articles on the Newbery Medal and John Newbery, as well as a new article on the Caldecott Medal. Fourteen maps were revised to reflect the nomenclature change from *Zaire* to *Democratic Republic of the Congo*. There are more than 24 new articles on the arts that do not yet appear in the print set, including biographies of artists Jim Dine, M. C. Escher, and Niki de Saint Phalle, and an article on the Royal Academy of Arts. There is also a replacement article on the Beatles. Articles in the arts have 15 new bibliographies on architects, buildings, and places. Stephanie Lipscomb of the Art Institute of Chicago contributed new biographies in photography and a new article, *pictorialism*. The periodic table was revised to reflect all 112 elements.

  The Grolier Internet Index links the *Americana* CD-ROM to prescreened Web sites. Currently, more than 30,000 articles are linked to at least one Web site for a total of more than 120,000 links,

which are tested periodically for validity. An updated version of the Grolier Internet Index is posted online on a monthly basis, although sometimes updates are more frequent.
- *Access:* The CD-ROM offers comprehensive search capabilities, simple copying and printing options, and a quick note-taking system which may be disabled on network versions. A click on an icon allows users to switch sources on the Reference Shelf or take the self-guided Tutorial.

  One of two windows is used for searches. The Entry window allows a user to browse one index at a time. The Advanced Search window allows searches of more than one index at a time, as well as Boolean searches. The indexes are Article Title (the main index), Full Text, Bibliography, Contributor, Subject, Geography, Article Form, Date (only available in Advanced Search), and Maps. There is also a User Notes search capability if users' annotations are allowed. There are three steps in a search: specify which index to search; enter the search term or expression; run the search. A Speed Scroll feature moves the highlight bar to the closest word/expression match available as a search term is entered.

  Icons at an article's start indicate the presence of tabular material (tables and fact boxes), maps, flags, images, and World Wide Web links. Most articles have a table of contents window at the bottom of the article window itself. This window can be adjusted, as can the index and article windows. The Entry window can be positioned anywhere on the desktop; it retreats to the background when another window is active. Hypertext links cross-reference materials. Other features include wildcard searches and a link button to rapidly search other articles for the highlighted word.
- *Conclusion:* The *Encyclopedia Americana* on CD-ROM is a serious research tool. It delivers the depth and breadth for which this encyclopedia is known in a clear, easy-to-read layout. The various indexes and search features allow a multitude of access points to information and also encourage browsing. The continued improvements to tabular information, flags, and maps enhance the CD-ROM's usefulness. But, as in the past, this set is not aimed at those looking for a multimedia encyclopedia with an abundance of audio and video clips. Since the CD-ROM includes more material than the print set—and is cheaper—it should be considered for purchase over the print set where appropriate to a library's needs.

Funk & Wagnalls Multimedia Encyclopedia. CD-ROM. 1998. Versaware Technologies, Inc., 151 W. 25th St., New York, NY 10001. Scholastic ed., $29.95 (1-892653-04-4).

System requirements: Windows 95 *or* NT 4.0, 16 MB RAM (32 MB *recommended*), 100 MB *free hard disk space.*

The is the debut year for the *Funk & Wagnalls Multimedia Encyclopedia* (F&W). The product is easy to load. An online version is called *Funk & Wagnalls Knowledge Center.* A DVD version is also available. A Macintosh version will be available next year.
- *Content:* F&W is on a single disc and contains the complete text of the 29-volume *Funk & Wagnalls* print edition along with 50 video clips, 51 animations, 3,097 audio clips, and nearly 10,000 photographs, maps, and flags, for a total of more than eight hours of multimedia. Articles and media are updated on a monthly basis. Content seems to be fairly up to date. There are no Web links within articles.

  To expand the content, a unique online feature called the Versabook Library Builder allows the user to purchase and download additional electronic books, including titles such as *Merriam-Webster's Biographical Dictionary,* and *Oxford Dictionary of Art.* There is also a link (not available on the version viewed by the Board) to *Funk & Wagnalls Knowledge Center,* a Web site which features Reuters News Service, "interactive art exhibits, a classical music hall, a planetarium, a tour of the human body, a world atlas, a teacher's lounge, and a student chat room, all online."
- *Access:* Navigating F&W is easy. From the Main Menu, options are Book View, which lists the books in the user's personal *Versabook* library; Binder (a bookmark feature); Library, where users can organize their books; Versabook Bookstore, where users can purchase books online to add to their personal library; Media Gallery; Search; *Funk & Wagnalls Knowledge Center;* and Guided Tour, which presents an overview of the different features of the encyclopedia. The Search icon provides access to the encyclopedia content. Articles and media can be selected from a browse list. The user can also search by text, keyword, or topic. Options for text searches are titles of articles or media items, full text, and natural language. There are also advanced search and Boolean search options. A search for children's literature using a title-only search led to just one article, but 23 using full text (including articles on modern children's magazines and twentieth-century literary criticism), and 100 using natural language (including an article on Maria Montessori). Search results can be gathered together using the Binder icon and printed. A Related Articles icon provides cross-referencing. Versabook titles in the user's personal library can be searched with the same ease, either individually or in combination.
- *Conclusion:* F&W has a great deal of flexibility and features that will be sure to please users. For the cost, this is an attractive alternative to *Encarta*. The articles seem geared to school-age children and adults who are seeking basic information about a topic. The graphics are attractive and ease of navigation and searching will make this a product that school and general libraries will want to consider adding to their reference towers.

Grolier Multimedia Encyclopedia. CD-ROM. 1999. Grolier, deluxe ed. $59.99 (0-7171-3415-0). Networking available.

System requirements: For Windows: Windows 3.1 *or higher,* 16 MB RAM, *and* 10 MB *hard disk space.* For Macintosh: System 7.1 *or higher,* 5 MB RAM *(in addition to system memory),* 10 MB *free hard disk space.*

Published in various forms since 1986, the 1999 *Grolier Multimedia Encyclopedia* (GME) is based on the text of the *Academic American Encyclopedia* (AAE), with additional text and multimedia content that have expanded its size to two CDs for the deluxe edition under review here. A DVD version is also available.
- *Content:* GME contains more than 36,000 articles, but also has online links to another 22,000 articles from the more in-depth *Encyclopedia Americana Online* and the children's *New Book of Knowledge Online,* both of which are published by Grolier. In a way, the user is getting the text of three encyclopedias for the price of one. Also included are illustrations unique to the CD-ROM edition, sounds, an atlas, videos and interactive features, 360-degree panoramas, a yearbook with coverage through April 1998, and guided tours. One of the most useful features of GME is the Online Knowledge Explorer, which appears next to the text of an article when there are new, updated, or additional articles, as well as related Web sites.

  GME is visually appealing, thanks to more than 15,000 illustrations, including photographs, graphics, drawings, and reproductions of paintings and other art. There are also 163 videos, including seven "multiplex videos" exploring topics such as twentieth-century world leaders and engineering feats. The atlas, with 1,200 maps, uses a drill-down feature to allow the user to go quickly from large to small areas of countries or states. Individual political and thematic maps are also linked directly from articles, so the user does not have to go to the atlas as a separate search. For this year's GME, maps showing features of major ocean floors have been added. Multimedia maps and essays on wars and other topics illustrate events in history. Animations (e.g., *catapult, plant osmosis*) are used when motion adds to understanding of an idea. One hundred 360-degree panoramas of places such as Times Square and Portage Glacier, Alaska, are a fun new feature that will certainly attract attention, although their informational value may be less than other parts of the encyclopedia. Interactivities involve the user in things like the solar system, ecological habitats, and parts and processes of the human body. Users are prompted for disc 2 when a video or interactivity is chosen.

  Other features include guided tours, grouping articles and media that fit into categories such as For the Fun of It and Steeped in Time, which are further subdivided. One of the divisions of For the Fun of It is Name That Life-Form, with links to articles about dozens of oddly named creatures such as clethra, asity, and gavial (good for your next Scrabble game). More than 15 hours of audio give us a taste of bird songs, animal noises, national anthems, speeches, and examples from numerous composers. Time line graphics are divided into countries and world areas, with colorful graphics and text that link to major events and ideas. For more, one can view a detailed list of significant events by clicking on a year, and can get articles related to that entry by clicking on any item in the list. A dictionary is always available for use in defining any highlighted word. An interesting and educational feature is the inclusion of the *New York*

Times Book of Questions and Answers, for which users must register, although access is free.

The Online Knowledge Explorer (OKE) links to Grolier's Internet resources, including articles from the publisher's other encyclopedias, as noted above, and Web sites that have been selected by editors. The OKE links appear in the lower left area of an article's text frame. By this means, updates for current political figures and issues are always just a click or two away; for instance, from the article on Bill Clinton, one can go directly to CNN/Time's *AllPolitics* Web site to find the latest on the Starr Report. One can also read a Clinton online article update that is current through May 1998. It would be nice if such articles were dated. There are 22,000 article links to approximately 5,600 Web sites.

- *Access*: Searching is easy. Options include browse by entry word, and simple or Boolean word searching. Searches can be limited to all or individual media types (e.g., videos, sounds) or to broad categories of information (e.g., visual arts). In addition, information type (articles, gallery, atlas, guided tours, etc.) may be selected from the outset through the buttons in the window header. A Results list is displayed in a frame that takes up the left third of the viewing window. The article frame on the right has an icon that may be clicked to view text only, as well as one that allows the user to find a keyword within the article, much like that found in a Web browser. This frame also shows tabs that link to related articles, media, and maps. Text and pictures are easily copied, pasted, printed, and saved to Notepad, which is included, or other programs. Articles may be marked and grouped in named files for future reference.

- *Conclusion*: Although the print set will remain a standard for many libraries, and GME is also available as a Web subscription, the CD-ROM has the best of both, plus additional multimedia content. With the increased information capacity that comes from linking to Internet updates and Web sites, the 1999 *Grolier Multimedia Encyclopedia* is a reliable, current, and fun resource for schools and libraries that serve students from the middle grades through adult patrons.

World Book. CD-ROM. 1999. World Book, deluxe ed., $69.95 (0-7166-8462-4). Networking available.

System requirements: Windows 95, 98, or NT 4.0 or higher, 16 MB RAM, 39 MB free hard disk space.

First published in 1990 as *World Book Information Finder*, this encyclopedia has evolved into its current form, combining *World Book's* high-quality content with excellent multimedia features that contribute to understanding the text. It is easy to install using standard Windows protocol.

- *Content*: The deluxe edition is on two CD-ROMs. The first disc contains all the articles from the print encyclopedia, the 225,000-entry *World Book Dictionary*, maps, illustrations, sound clips, short multimedia segments, and Homework Wizard features. This disc can stand alone and is available separately as *1999 World Book*. The second disc has extended multimedia features such as interactive simulations, longer videos, and animations. Users are prompted to change discs when necessary.

The multimedia version of *World Book* has more than 8,000 illustrations, including 800 full-color printable maps especially designed for electronic use. The print edition has 28,000 illustrations. The multimedia version has several features that enhance the visual portion of the work. Bubble View allows users to explore 360-degree views of places such as the Brooklyn Bridge, Mount Rushmore, and the Louvre. New this year, Cyber Safari, a joint venture with the San Diego Zoo, takes users on tours of several habitats, letting them learn about various animals while seeing and hearing them. Film clips of various environments such as the Great Barrier Reef, and historical events such as Hitler's rise to power provide greater contact with the subject matter. Animations of scientific concepts demonstrate the immune system in action and the measurement of blood pressure, while interactive experiments allow users to understand concepts such as buoyancy and the laws of momentum.

Around the World is an atlas with many useful features. By clicking on a continent on the introductory world map, users can view increasingly detailed maps of countries, states, provinces, or cities. The Overlay Controls button allows selection of political information, population density, average January or June temperatures, average yearly precipitation, agriculture and fishing, mining and manufacturing, terrain, and economy. There are also links to relevant articles, related maps, and photographs. A distance calculator opens both a globe and a flat map. One can select two locations, mark them on the maps, and find the distance between them.

World Book is known for being up to date. Since the print and electronic editions have different release dates, one may be more current than the other at various times of the year. The CD-ROM contains more than 1,800 articles that are not in the print set. Among these are individual entries on all of the first ladies of the U.S. There are also many biographies of actors, athletes, writers, singers, and other entertainers not found in the print set, among them Barry Bonds, Garth Brooks, Jodie Foster, Audrey Hepburn, and John Travolta. The Update Now feature available on the deluxe edition provides monthly article updates, a list of major news events, and new Web site links. It also enables users to download articles from *World Book* archives dating back to 1922.

- *Access*: Searching the World Book is both quick and easy. Users can browse the entire encyclopedia, the media features, or What's New, which contains the article What's Happening. This article changes each month and does not require an online connection. The text can be searched by either topic or keyword using Boolean and proximity operators and truncation if desired. When an article is chosen, it appears along with Article Outline, Related Info: CD, and Related Info: Online buttons displayed at the top. Choosing Article Outline causes an outline to appear in a box on the left side of the screen. Users can scroll through the outline to a specific section, click, and go directly to that part of the article. Choosing the Related Info: CD option brings up a list of hyperlinks; there are also hyperlinks within the article text. Related Info: Online provides access to more than 5,000 non–World Book Web sites. Audio and video clips and photographs are accessed by clicking on appropriate icons within the text.

In addition to printing, copying, highlighting, and notepad options, the menu bar has new Homework Wizards features accessed from the Tools menu. These include Report Wizard, which walks students through the process of doing research and writing a report; Chart Wizard, which makes and prints charts and graphs; Timeline Wizard, which creates and prints custom time lines; Quiz Wizard, which allows students to create and take three types of quizzes; and Web Page Wizard, which lets users create and post up to three linked pages on the World Wide Web.

Time Frame allows users to locate information related to a specific date. It can search by year, decade, century, millennium, or era in either B.C. or A.D. If desired, users can limit a search to specific categories such as humanities, industry/technology, or life sciences.

- *Conclusion*: The 1999 *World Book* is an outstanding resource. It contains accurate, current information that can be updated instantly, multimedia features that are very useful, and tools that are true learning aids. Libraries with sufficient hardware should add it to their collections.

An Evaluation of Current World Atlases

by Christine Bulson

World atlases have been a basic reference source for centuries. They are a unique and necessary reference tool for graphically depicting the world to answer the question "Where is it?" Since 1990, when RBB last surveyed the field, there have been changes in the world, new atlas publishers have appeared, others are no longer in existence, and the technology used for publishing maps and atlases has improved. CD-ROM atlases are gaining popularity as reference tools.

The basic elements that are needed in the best world atlases are a large and detailed index in combination with maps that are accurate, clear, and comprehensive. Additional criteria for evaluating atlases include currency, format, legends, scale, special features, and the balance of coverage.

This review concentrates on world atlases suitable for high-school, public, and academic libraries, published from 1996 through the fall of 1998 and still in print. Not included are pocket-size and children's atlases. Two standard atlases, MacMillan's *Book of the World* and *The Times Atlas of the World*, were not available in their newest editions in time for this review; they are discussed on p.10. Also on p.10 we highlight two CD-ROM atlases that might be competitive with print atlases in school and public libraries. Although their maps are generally not as detailed as those found in print atlases, CD-ROM atlases are popular because of their searching and printing capabilities, multimedia features, and Internet links.

CD-ROM atlases often require equipment that may not be affordable or available in all libraries. Online map sites are increasing, with the *Perry-Castaneda Library Map Collection* of the University of Texas one of the most popular. These sites may in time rival a print atlas, but currently the lack of clarity, slow loading time, and printing problems make online map sites not a first choice to answer an atlas question. Even with up-to-date equipment, the majority of reference librarians still choose a print atlas to quickly answer basic geographical questions.

The print atlases discussed below are rated as ★★★, ★★, and ★, with ★★★ being the best. All libraries should own at least one of the three-star atlases. The annotations elaborate on the strong points of each. Two-star (★★) atlases are a notch down from the best. They may be smaller, less expensive, and are not as comprehensive. One-star (★) atlases are suitable as supplemental resources in medium-to-large reference collections, and good choices for the circulating collection. They may be elementary in nature and not comprehensive, or may not be completely current.

Price was one consideration in the ratings, but librarians and patrons need quality, not mediocrity. As with many products, atlases that are comprehensive, clear, and accurate are usually expensive. You get what you pay for!

The author believes the most important consideration in an atlas is the number of entries in the index, and whether places appear in both the index and on a map. The atlases discussed in this survey were put to the test by choosing 13 places throughout the world and checking in each atlas for an entry in the index and a location on a map. The test locations were Al, Norway; Anif, Austria; Canyon de Chelly, Arizona; Democratic Republic of the Congo (formerly Zaire); Dorloo, New York; Hong Kong as part of China; Ita, Paraguay; Lamu, Kenya; Mendocino, California; Ter Apel, The Netherlands; Victor, Montana; Wahroonga, Australia; and Yakutsk, Russia. The percentage of hits is included in the evaluations; for example, 54 percent of the 13 test locations were found in both the index and on a map in *Hammond Atlas of the World*, so that atlas has a 54 percent hit rate. Readers may approach an atlas expecting that all the index entries will be found on a map, and all the locations indicated on maps will be found in the index, but this is not necessarily the case.

Other considerations in the evaluation of atlases may depend on the personal preference of the user. Is a grid location preferable to the longitude/latitude indication in the index? What area of the world should be first in the atlas? The classic arrangement begins with Europe and ends with South America, but many U.S. atlases begin with North America. Are thematic maps (maps that cover specific topics, such as industry, land use, or population) important? How much encyclopedic material is necessary? What statistics are useful? The person choosing an atlas must consider all of these questions. The evaluations that follow will help librarians choose world atlases that best meet their preferences and their library's budget.

Three-star (★★★) atlases

All of the atlases in this group are at least 18 x 12 inches in size, have more than 30,000 entries in the index, and cost more than $50. Each has unique features that may make it a first choice for a particular library. *Atlas of the World* (Oxford) is the only atlas that uses 14 colors depicting elevation. The detailed maps of cities including Baltimore, Havana, Jakarta, and Vienna are also a plus. *Hammond Atlas of the World* (published by the grandson of Caleb Stillson Hammond, who founded the company in 1900), provides relief maps of continents that are photographs of 3-D models showing contours of the land. *Macmillan Centennial Atlas of the World* is the second of the four atlases in the Macmillan atlas program (*The Book of the World*, discussed on p.10, is the first). All use the resources of the Bertelsmann Cartographic Institute and each contains fantastic satellite photography. People familiar with maps that are included in *National Geographic* magazine will recognize the maps in the National Geographic Society's atlas, where satellite images of the continents are a very attractive feature. Rand McNally advertises its 25th anniversary edition as the most popular atlas in its class. Even with a price of $150, this is the best choice for libraries that can afford spending more than $100 on one atlas.

Atlas of the World. 6th ed. 1998. 304p. Oxford, $75 (0-1952-1464-1).
Hit rate: 62 percent.

Oxford is the U.S. publisher of this atlas, originally published in England. It contains 176 pages of world maps, 66 city maps with a separate index, and a 75,000-item main-entry index. That the city index is separate is a minor flaw. Introductory material consists of 48 pages of text, charts, graphs, and photographs of atmosphere, climate, population, wealth, etc. An interesting depiction shows the urbanization of the world from 1850 to 2000. Scale is displayed prominently at the top of each page, since various scales are used throughout the book. The 14 colors used for elevation make it easy to locate entries. The index uses page numbers and grid squares, but latitude and longitude are also included. Libraries that own the fifth edition (1997) may choose not to buy the sixth since there are few changes—16 added pages of world maps and an updated index.

Hammond Atlas of the World. 2d rev. ed. 1998. 312p. Hammond, $69.95 (0-8437-1172-8).
Hit rate: 54 percent.

This second edition has 167 maps on 216 pages, plus 62 city maps and an index with 110,000 entries. Following introductory material there are double-page spreads of the world depicting global standards of living, energy, agriculture, climate, and environmental concerns. The primary map section begins with a photograph taken from the *Galileo* spacecraft of both the Earth and Moon from 3.9 million miles away. Superimposed on the picture is a quotation from Galileo: "Facts which at first seem improbable will stand forth in naked and simple beauty." The computer-generated maps have beautiful tints of colors and shadings combining elevation and political features. They are arranged by continent beginning with Europe. Maps of cities and urban areas are inset adjacent to the country maps, which results in some country maps being split across different pages. Maps of Central America and the Caribbean Islands are outstanding. The statistical information placed just before the index includes major ship canals, dimensions of the earth, and population of countries and major cities. The only criticism of this atlas is that it uses red print in the index and statistical section, which may make them difficult for some people to read. For this reason, libraries may prefer to choose another atlas from the ★★★ group.

Macmillan Centennial Atlas of the World. 1996. 520p. Macmillan, $175 (0-02-861264-7).

Hit rate: 46 percent.

Although this atlas has the lowest index entry/map location hit rate, the 32 pages each of satellite photography and city maps, 64 pages of U.S. and Canadian maps, 224 pages of world maps, a 150,000-entry index, and the promise of a second edition in 1999 make it competitive as a ★★★ atlas. The maps of the Aleutians, Arctic Islands, Greenland, and Barren Grounds are more detailed than those in any other atlas. Libraries that have this beautiful volume should be satisfied; those that don't own it should wait for the second edition.

The National Geographic Atlas of the World. 6th ed., 2d. rev. 1996. 269p. National Geographic, $100 (0-7922-3036-1).

Hit rate: 77 percent.

The introduction to this atlas provides a great quotation from Gilbert Grosvenor, the first president of the National Geographic Society: "A map is the greatest of all epic poems." The satellite images that precede each section of this atlas are certainly beautiful epics. There are nearly 150,000 entries in the index, and on 172 maps, including one foldout map of the political and physical world. For each continent there are two pages of maps and information on population, resources, environment, land use, and transportation. Following these are two-page spreads for both the physical and political maps of the continents. The supplementary material in this atlas includes a number of pages on the geology of the earth as well as a detailed discussion and depiction of the solar system. There is also encyclopedic material for countries (not all of this is current) and U.S. states. Readers of *National Geographic* will no doubt select this atlas as their first choice.

New International Atlas. Rev. ed. 1998. 560p. Rand McNally, $99 (0-528-83808-3).

Hit rate: 92 percent.

The 25th edition was published in 1994 and revised in 1998. It is the only major atlas that provides all its text in five languages (English, French, German, Spanish, and Portuguese). A glossary at the end of the volume provides terms used on the maps in the five languages. The 259 maps are divided into five separate series, from the equivalent of an area seen from 4,000 miles in space to an area as small as a city. A unique feature of Rand McNally's candidate for a top atlas is the shade relief that gives a 3-D impression. There are 160,000 entries in the index, with longitude and latitude used as the key for location. State and country are only listed in the index if there is more than one place with the same name. There are 65 city maps, but the detail of the city maps in Oxford's *Atlas of the World* is superior. There is some overlap in the city maps of these two atlases but maps of Lagos, Manchester-Liverpool, Taipei, and Saigon are found only in *New International*. The beautiful maps of the 25th edition, the highest index/map location hit rate, and a reasonable price for a top-of-the-line atlas make this one of the best.

Two-Star (★★) Atlases

Centennial World Atlas. 1998. 224p. Hammond, $45 (0-8437-1150-7).

Hit rate: 46 percent.

This appears to be an abridged version of *Hammond Atlas of the World*. It is almost the same trim size, but with 90 fewer pages and a significantly smaller index (60,000 entries compared to 110,000). Many of the maps are identical but some have more vivid color. The index uses blue print for the page/grid system, compared to red print in the more comprehensive atlas. For libraries that don't own *Hammond Atlas of the World* as their ★★★ choice, this a good ★★ atlas.

Concise Atlas of the World. 4th ed. 1997. 264p. Oxford, $45 (0-19-521370-X).

Hit rate: 46 percent.

Here is a smaller version of the publisher's *Atlas of the World*. It has some of the same thematic maps, city maps, and statistics. U.S. maps begin the volume and have a separate index; the 14 colors used to depict elevation in the world maps section are not included in the U.S. section. The world maps section encompasses the U.S., making the separate U.S. map section seem unnecessary. The 40,000-entry main index provides grid location as well as longitude and latitude. This would make a good circulating atlas—or add another $30 and buy *Atlas of the World* with larger maps and greater definition.

DK World Atlas. 1997. 338p. DK, $60 (0-7894-1974-2).

Hit rate: 62 percent.

DK is a new name in atlas publishing, and they have produced a good product in their first attempt. There are 220 pages of maps with 80,000 entries in the index. Whereas maps in the three-star atlases generally cover two-page spreads in full, some of the DK maps cover less than 75 percent of available page space. The rest of the space is filled with text, small color photos, charts, and smaller thematic maps. There are foldout maps of Canada, the U.S., Japan, Southeast Asia, and the Pacific. Almanac-type information is included for the 192 countries of the world—for example, calorie consumption and ethnic mix. There is a useful glossary of more than 400 technical and geographical terms. With lots of information in addition to maps on each page, this is a good choice for high-school and small public libraries.

Macmillan World Atlas. 1996. 415p. Macmillan, $59.95 (0-02-862244-8).

Hit rate: 46 percent.

Planet Earth Macmillan World Atlas. 1997. 415p. Macmillan, $34.95 (0-02-861266-3).

Hit rate: 46 percent.

The third and fourth atlases in the Macmillan series are almost identical in content. *Planet Earth* is smaller (9 x 12 inches) compared to *Macmillan World Atlas* (11 x 14). There are more satellite photographs in *World Atlas*, but the maps and index (105,000 entries) are the same in each volume. Viewing the atlases side by side, the metropolitan areas in *Planet Earth* appear more cluttered. For libraries considering these two atlases, it is tempting to purchase the cheaper *Planet Earth*. However, the clarity of the larger-size maps in *World Atlas* is a real plus. A new edition of *World Atlas* is promised for late 1999.

Portrait World Atlas. 1998. 224p. Rand McNally, $39.95 (0-528-83995-0).

Hit rate: 62 percent.

This may be considered a successor to Rand McNally's *Today's World* (see ★ entries). It has the same trim size, a few more pages of maps (144 compared to 128), but fewer entries in the index (50,000 instead of 52,000). Its strength is that it utilizes digital cartography with new elevation data that provide shaded colors, similar to that in *Premier World Atlas* (see ★ entries) and *New International Atlas* (see ★★★ entries). The "portrait" part of the volume is 12 pages of photographs and text of natural wonders—mountains, canyons, reefs, deserts, etc. Although it is limited in supplementary material (there is no indication of world time zones, for example), this new atlas is a good, basic, reasonably priced source.

Reader's Digest Illustrated Great World Atlas. 1997. 288p. Reader's Digest, $40 (0-89577-988-9).

Hit rate: 54 percent.

Reader's Digest commissioned Rand McNally to supply 81 maps for its *Illustrated Great World Atlas*. The maps are not as clear as those Rand McNally uses in its own publications. The first quarter of the volume is entitled "Story of the Earth" and describes the weather, geology, oceans, etc., with photographs and text but very few maps. There are 40,000 entries in the index, with a grid system for location. In a narrative section on "Nations of the World," countries are grouped by area rather than alphabetically. This atlas is not as current as other atlases in the ★★ group; Democratic Republic of the Congo is still listed as Zaire. It may be useful in libraries that need encyclopedia material as well as maps.

The Times Atlas of the World Second Family Edition. 1997. 143p. Times, $39.95 (0-8129-2949-7).

Hit rate: 62 percent.

Times Books, which is a division of Random House, should get the award for the most confusing atlas title. *Times Atlas of the World Second Family Edition* is the revised and updated edition of *The New York Times Atlas of the World*, which was a condensed version of the seventh edition of *The Times Atlas of the World Concise Edition* (1995). This new edition continues to use the digital mapping of the eminent cartographers Bartholomew and Son, which provides the maps for the more comprehensive *Times Atlas*. There are 45,000 entries in the index, with 96 pages of maps plus 46 city maps. The city maps are excellent, with many streets and buildings included. Caracas and Jerusalem have downtown city maps that are unique to this atlas. The double-page spread of physical maps of continents includes sidebars of geographical statistics such as major islands, rivers, and mountains. The encyclopedic information at the beginning of the volume is so concise as to be almost useless. The detailed city maps and a reasonable price make this a good choice as a supplementary atlas.

One-Star (★) Atlases

Cartographic Satellite Atlas of the World. 1997. 152p. Warwick, $35 (1-895629-99-3).

Hit rate: 38 percent.

The Canadian publishers describe the maps in this atlas as "fifty-one full color satellite maps . . each interpreted and enhanced with elevation data and overlaid with cartographic detail." The introduction describes the process of satellite mapping, and the results are then illustrated with seven full-page satellite photographs of different areas of the world, including Lake Ontario, the Bosporus, and Hong Kong. The maps are really relief maps with national boundaries, major cities, rivers, mountains, and oceans overlaid. The choice of major cities is interesting—in New York, Endicott (population 13,500) is on the map but Binghamton (population 53,000) is not. Maps appear very uncluttered. The vibrant colors, simplified format, and use of new technology make this an appropriate additional purchase for school libraries.

Concise Atlas of the World. 1997. 90p. National Geographic, paper, $25 (0-7922-7120-3).

Hit rate: 38 percent.

Compared to other atlases in the ★ category, this contender from National Geographic has the advantage of size. The dimensions are equal to that of the more comprehensive *National Geographic Atlas of the World* and other atlases in the ★★★ category. All the maps in the *Concise Atlas* are reprinted from the parent volume. However, there are only continent maps, with the exception of the U.S., which does rate an individual map. Country information is on pages adjacent to the continent maps, and there are two pages of geographic comparisons—earth extremes, metric conversion tables, etc. Fans of large maps will get this for a quarter of the price of the parent atlas, but may be disappointed in the lack of individual country and state maps.

Encyclopedic World Atlas. 4th ed. 1997. 264p. Oxford, $45 (0-19-521369-6).

Hit rate: 38 percent.

Encyclopedia information is more prominent than maps in this atlas. The maps are based on those in the publisher's *Atlas of the World* but are limited to continents and countries. Coverage of the U.S. is particularly weak, with just a U.S. map and a small map of the northeast. There is no map of Antarctica. The index contains 25,000 entries with no state designation for U.S. cities unless there is more than one city with the same name. The thematic maps of the world and continents, combined with the country essays, will make this a supplementary resource in reference collections.

Hammond Citation World Atlas. Rev. ed. 1998. 328p. Hammond, paper, $19.95 (0-8437-1295-3).

Hit rate: 62 percent.

The introduction notes that this atlas "is organized to make the retrieval of information as simple and quick as possible." This may be possible if the country where a city is located is known, since there are indexes for each map and no comprehensive index. It is curious that the individual indexes do not include all entries that are included on the maps. The physical maps in the atlas appear to be identical to those in *Hammond Atlas of the World*, but are smaller and have less definition. The U.S. is emphasized, with a double page for most states, but only major roads and rivers are noted. Since the percent of entry/map locations is good, and the price is very affordable, this is a possibility for circulating collections.

Premier World Atlas. 1997. 248p. Rand McNally, $15.95 (0-528-83894-6).

Hit rate: 38 percent.

Another entry from Rand McNally, this one is aimed at the beginning geographer. The first four pages describe maps and atlases and how to use them. A photo essay of two pages for each continent is very elementary—large print, and a box with facts and figures. The section that follows contains two-page spreads of the political and physical aspects of the world, and then regional maps. The last map section contains a full page for each of the Canadian provinces and U.S. states. Rhode Island is as big as Montana! The index has 45,000 entries and uses what the editors call a "bingo key" for location, which is really just a grid system. Affordably priced, this is a good choice for an additional atlas in school and small public libraries. The ★ rating is assigned primarily because of the atlas' elementary nature and lack of depth.

Reader's Digest Bartholomew Illustrated Atlas of the World. 3d rev. ed. 1997. 184p. Reader's Digest, $24 (0-89577-937-4).

Hit rate: 46 percent.

This Reader's Digest atlas uses maps from Bartholomew, similar to those in *The Times Atlas of the World Second Family Edition*. However, there are fewer maps and index entries, the colors of the maps are significantly darker, and they are not as up to date (Zaire and British Hong Kong are listed). On the plus side, introductory material for each continent is presented attractively. This feature, combined with serviceable maps, makes this a possible supplementary volume in school or small public libraries.

Today's World. 1997. 192p. Rand McNally, $29 (0-528-83871-7).

Hit rate: 46 percent.

Today's World, with the dimensions of large, ★★★ atlases, concentrates on all-purpose maps that are marked with political, topographic, and natural features. As a revision of a 1993 edition, this atlas lacks the digital technology that provides the color shadings for elevation that more recent Rand McNally atlases have. There are 52,000 entries that may be found on 128 pages of maps. With no extraneous material and a reasonable price, this could be a suitable supplementary "maps-only" atlas for circulating collections or for very small libraries.

The World Book Atlas. 1997. 192p. World Book, $49 (0-7166-2699-3).

Hit rate: 54 percent.

Some of the introductory material is reprinted from *Goode's World Atlas* (19th ed., Rand McNally, 1995), and most of the rest of the volume is appropriated from Rand McNally's *Cosmopolitan World Atlas* which was not rated here since it is out of print, with no plans for reprinting or revision. *The World Book Atlas* is current as of 1997 and has more than 52,000 entries in the index, but there are no thematic maps and the detail of many area maps is weak.

Delorme Enters the World Atlas Market

Eartha World Travelog. 1998. 168p. DeLorme, paper, $19.95 (0-89933-264-1).

The publication of *Eartha World Travelog* coincides with the completion of the largest rotating globe in the world, named Eartha, that is located in the DeLorme headquarters in Yarmouth, Maine. Although not a true world atlas, this new resource from the well-known mapmaker provides cutout maps of all countries of the world and 120 inset maps of world urban areas. The maps, taken from satellite imagery, show physical features, political boundaries, major roads, railways, and airports. Boxes around the perimeter of the maps give basic information on food, activities, climate, languages, population, currency (including availability of ATM machines), and transportation (national airlines and major airports) for each country. The index contains only 15,000 place names but the entry/map location hit rate is as good as some of the ★★ atlases. The use of blue and light gray print for page numbers and longitude/latitude in the index may be difficult to see and confusing to read for some people. This inexpensive atlas will not withstand heavy use but will be enjoyable for library users who are tourists or armchair travelers.

Two Great Atlases

The Book of the World. 1999. 560p. Macmillan, $465 (0-02-865368-8).
The Times Atlas of the World Ninth Comprehensive Edition. 1994. 392p. Times, $175 (0-8129-2077-5).

The new editions of *The Book of the World* and *The Times Atlas of the World* were not available in time to be included in this survey. Both atlases are expensive but worth the cost. The second edition of *The Book of the World* is scheduled for January 1999 publication. The 10th edition of *The Times Atlas* was to be published in August 1998, but has been postponed until the fall of 1999.

Reviewers described the first edition of *The Book of the World* as massive and grand. It is a beautiful 18-pound atlas with 264 pages of maps produced by the Bertelsmann Cartographic Institute, an index of more than 100,000 entries, and 24 full-page satellite photographs of the Amazon, the Grand Canyon, and other major geographic features. For this world atlas survey, the publisher supplied advance information and two signatures of maps from the second edition. The information indicates that the atlas has been updated, with name changes, and Hong Kong included as part of China. However, the maps on the two signatures that were seen are identical to the first edition. It is recommended that libraries that own the first edition wait for reviews before ordering the second, which will have a price of $465. Those without the first edition should certainly consider purchasing the second edition, assuming it is as grand as the first.

Since it was first published in 1967, *The Times Atlas of the World* has been considered a top reference source as well as an excellent atlas. The ninth edition continued this tradition with a 200,000-entry index/gazetteer, 123 double-page maps of continents and countries, and almost 50 pages of thematic maps. Librarians and atlas lovers await with anticipation the 10th edition of this great resource.

The Best Atlases on CD-ROM

Microsoft Encarta Virtual Globe. 1998. Microsoft, $54.95 (1-5723-1777-9).

Hit rate: 100 *percent.*

Rand McNally New Millennium World Atlas Deluxe. 1998. Rand McNally, $66.95 (0-5285-2054-7).

Hit rate: 92 *percent.*

Both of these CD-ROM atlases, compatible with Windows 95 or NT, have a very high entry/map location hit rate, with the *Encarta Virtual Globe* having a perfect score. However, on U.S. maps *Encarta* includes tiny hamlets and towns that no longer exist, and fails to list larger villages. *Encarta* is easy to use and contains a lot of encyclopedic information as well as maps. In viewing a map there is an option to learn about the land and climate, society, animals, and sights and sounds of the country. Maps may be viewed as political, physical, satellite, natural, or outlines. Statistics are available but are no more up to date than those in print atlases. The definition and color in the maps are not equal to most print atlases. Other features include links to the Internet and a choice of seven "World Flights," where the user is flown over the terrain.

The developers of the *New Millennium* identified specific criteria that their atlas should meet. The criteria include accuracy, detail, quick place location, and a fun experience. Most of these criteria were met. There are a few mistakes in accuracy—one town in New York is misplaced by around 50 miles. The maps load quickly, so entries are on the screen in a very short time. There are several "fun experiences," including a good selection of music, photographs, and statistics; links to the Internet; and the ability to customize maps. The clarity and color of the majority of maps are superior to those in *Encarta*, but not up to the standards of a ★★★ print atlas. The 65 city maps are excellent, with points of interest and hotels indicated.

There are advantages and disadvantages in these two CD-ROMs, but the *New Millennium* is the first choice. Even with the pace of technology, print atlases may be one of the few reference resources where print is still preferable to CD-ROM. High-school, junior-college, and public libraries may find that CD-ROM atlases are good teaching tools, but the print atlas remains the first choice of the majority of reference librarians.

Christine Bulson is Assistant Director for Reference and Circulation Services, Milne Library, SUNY Oneonta, and a former chair of the *Reference Books Bulletin* Editorial Board.

African American Reference Books for Public Libraries

by Nora Harris

Black History Month comes only once a year. But questions about African American literature, biography, history, art, and science come every month. The following titles will form a good basic collection of resources that will be useful throughout the year.

The African American Almanac. 7th ed. By L. Mpho Mabunda. 1997. 1,270p. Gale, $165 (0-8103-7867-1).

A standard reference source for decades under a variety of names (*The Negro Almanac, Reference Library of Black America*), this is the place to find information about the history and culture of African Americans, as well as speeches, documents, and numerous illustrations. A glossary, a bibliography, and a subject index are included.

African American Quotations. Ed. by Richard Newman. 1998. 520p. Oryx, $49.95 (1-5735-6118-5).
Contemporary Quotations in Black. Ed. by Anita King. 1997. 160p. Greenwood, $39.95 (0-3132-9122-5).
My Soul Looks Back, 'Less I Forget: A Collection of Quotations by People of Color. Ed. by D. Winbush Riley. 1995. 496p. Harper, paper $15 (0-0627-2057-0).

Locating quotations can be a frustrating experience. These three resources, all with a slightly different slant, can make the job easier. The Newman book includes more than 2,500 quotations from more than 500 persons but does not cite the sources of the quotations. Name and occupation indexes and a subject index are included. The King book is arranged by last name of the speaker, an improvement over her *Quotations in Black* (1981), and includes quotations by Africans such as Nelson Mandela. There are more than 1,000 quotes, each with a citation, and keyword and subject indexes. The Riley book has a broader scope, including all persons of color, and has keyword and speaker indexes, as well as a bibliography. If there is room for just one, the King book would be it, but having all three will provide complete coverage.

Dictionary of AfroAmerican Slavery. Rev. ed. Ed. by Randall M. Miller and John David Smith. 1997. 912p. Praeger, paper $35 (0-2759-5799-3).

Three hundred articles, exploring the history of slavery in the U.S. from the first English settlement to the post–Civil War period, delve into all of the aspects of slavery. Written by subject specialists, each entry includes a selected bibliography. The editors have also added a comprehensive bibliography, grouped by thematic subject and keyed to topics treated in the text. This should be the starting point for any research on the topic of slavery.

The Norton Anthology of African American Literature. Ed. by Henry Louis Gates Jr. and Nellie Y. McKay. 1996. 2,665p. Norton, $59.95 (0-3930-4001-1).

This complete resource covers all forms of African American expression, from the oral tradition to the modern novel. Split into sequential sections, each begins with an overall essay and includes brief profiles of each of the 120 authors. There are indexes for names, titles, and the first lines of poems. A time line and selected bibliographies are also included. For many students, this will be the resource of choice for literary research.

Notable Black American Women. Ed. by Jessie Carney Smith. 1992. 1,134p. Gale, $80 (0-8103-4749-0).
Notable Black American Women: Book II. Ed. by Jessie Carney Smith. 1996. 775p. Gale, $80 (0-8103-9177-5).

Notable Black American Women profiles 500 women from a variety of fields. A continuation rather than a replacement, *Book II* contains biographical information on 300 additional women. There are bibliographies for each subject, and each volume has a list of women by occupation. *Book II* also has cumulative geographic and subject indexes for all 800 women.

The Oxford Companion to African American Literature. Ed. by William L. Andrews and others. 1997. 866p. Oxford, $49.95 (0-1950-6510-7).

Students looking for information about characters in novels, stories, or plays; students seeking biographical information; students attempting to understand topics as broad as the novel or as narrow as a stereotype will find it here. Plot summaries for 150 books, and profiles of more than 400 authors, plus an index, extensive cross-references, and bibliographic references at the end of each entry, make this a resource that will be used over and over.

The Schomburg Center Guide to Black Literature: From the Eighteenth Century to the Present. Ed. by Roger M. Valade and others. 1996. 545p. Gale, $75 (0-7876-0289-2).

There has been an explosion of information about African American literature, and this guide from New York Public Library's premiere site for African American research can help students to find what they need quickly. There are biographical, thematic, and subject topics for the more than 500 authors and the more than 450 works, and a chronology and a subject index are included.

Statistical Record of Black America. 4th ed. Ed. by Jessie Carney Smith and Carrell P. Horton. 1996. 1,064p. Gale, $109 (0-8103-9252-6).

A wealth of statistical information makes this an essential resource for research on African American life, including household characteristics, educational status, and labor and employment demographics. A detailed table of contents and an alphabetical index assist researchers.

Timelines of African American History: 500 Years of Black Achievement. Ed. by Tom Dale Cowan and others. 1994. 368p. Berkley, paper $16.95 (0-3995-2127-5).

This book covers five centuries of African American history year by year. Comprising more than 1,500 entries, the work profiles people and events in all areas of African American life. It includes an index of names, brief biographies, and excerpts from speeches.

Nora Harris is Reference Librarian, Marin County Free Library, San Rafael, CA.

Patent and Trademark Resources

by Nancy Adams

Patented life-forms, trademark infringement, copyright in the online environment—intellectual property is one of today's hottest topics. Two areas of intellectual property, patents and trademarks, are of special interest to small-business owners and inventors plus others who seek such information for historical research, educational purposes, or just curiosity's sake. This article highlights some of the best print and electronic resources available, for libraries of all types.

The subject of patents and trademarks is fascinating and complex, and sorting out patents from trademarks and other types of intellectual property protection, such as copyright, can be confusing. It's easy for librarians to feel lost in the intellectual-property environment. They may get requests from inventors who are trying to gauge the patentability of their inventions or small-business owners who seek to know whether their proposed trademarks are "free and clear." Incorrect information or an ineffective search can lead to legal or financial repercussions for these individuals.

Librarians who get requests for patent and trademark information should remember that a specialized, free resource exists for these and all types of related questions: the local area Patent and Trademark Depository Library (PTDL). The U.S. Patent and Trademark Office (USPTO) has set up a network of information centers in public and academic libraries across the U.S. and Puerto Rico. PTDLs maintain a core collection of the print and electronic resources that are required for doing a complete U.S. patent or trademark search, as well as a staff of librarians well versed in the complexities of this type of information. Many PTDLs own copies of patents dating back to 1790 and other related historical materials. Referrals are welcomed. Call 800-PTO-9199 or 703-308-HELP for the location and phone number of the nearest PTDL, or visit the Web site [http://www.uspto.gov/web/offices/ac/ido/ptdl/ptdlib.htm].

For this article, patent and trademark resources have been grouped into two lists, and items are loosely ordered in terms of their importance so that librarians building collections in these areas can work their way from the top of the lists down. The most important source, the U.S. *Patent and Trademark Office Homepage*, is shown first on both lists—and it's free.

Patents

The U.S. government has been in the patenting business since 1790, when the first U.S. patent was granted to Samuel Hopkins for a new method of manufacturing potash, a soap-making ingredient. American ingenuity has continued unabated since then, and the milestone of the six-millionth U.S. patent will be reached in the near future. Most of these patents have been granted for new processes, machinery, goods, or compositions of matter ("utility" patents), but ornamental designs for manufactured articles ("design" patents) and new varieties of plants can be patented as well.

Patents can be thought of as a contract between an inventor and the U.S. government. In return for protection from others making, selling, or using the invention without permission for a set time period, the inventor agrees to disclose details on the invention to the general public. Usually this is a pretty good deal for both parties, but sometimes inventors choose not to divulge any details on their product, keeping it as a trade secret. Trade secrets are another form of intellectual property, of which perhaps the most famous example is the formula for Coca-Cola. Had it been patented, patent protection would have expired long ago and the formula would be public knowledge.

The patent number is the magic key to the patent information system. Because patent numbers are often found on manufactured objects, collectors often use patent numbers to find information relating to a particular antique object. Once the patent number is identified, an entire copy of the patent is easy to obtain. This can be done by first using the chart "Issue Years and Patent Numbers" at the USPTO Web site [http://www.uspto.gov/web/ofices/ac/ido/oeip/taf/issuyear.html] to find out how old the patent is. The full text of patents issued later than 1976 can be found at the USPTO Web site. Patents issued earlier than 1976 might be found at a local library or ordered from a document delivery service such as the one offered by the USPTO, which sells complete copies of any patent for $3.

U.S. Patent and Trademark Office Homepage. [http://www.uspto.gov].

Specific information about the patent and trademark application process is located here. Highlights include online pamphlets such as *Basic Facts about Trademarks* and *General Information Concerning Patents*, downloadable forms and instructions for patent and trademark applicants, fee information, a searchable database of registered patent attorneys and agents, and links to the home pages of other governments' patent offices. A mother lode of interesting statistical information can be found by following the links to the USPTO's Technology Assessment and Forecast Program pages, which have full-text reports on patenting trends.

The main reason why the USPTO Web site should be bookmarked, though, is that free trademark and patent databases are maintained there, allowing access to vital information not available anywhere on the Web until recently. The USPTO's patent database allows searching and viewing of full-text U.S. patents issued since 1976. Images of the patents were added in March, but viewing them requires plug-in software that can display TIFF (Tagged Image File Format) images; the Web site contains a link to available free sources of the software. The entire text, or fields such as inventor name or patent number, can be searched. Inventors who try to find related patents by searching for text words should be advised that this method does not provide comprehensive results. Referral to an area PTDL is recommended for people who need to perform these preliminary patent searches.

IBM Intellectual Property Network. [http://www.patents.ibm.com/ibm.html].

This patent database is similar to the USPTO's patent database, described above, with two advantages: no plug-in software is needed to view the images, and it includes European patents and World Intellectual Property Organization (WIPO) patent applications. Drawings and text are scanned in, so viewing by modem can be quite slow. This database has records for U.S. patents issued since 1971, although there are many gaps in the 1971–1975 range. Text-word searches will search fields such as title, abstract, and claims of the patent, not its full text.

Patent It Yourself. 7th ed. By David Pressman. 1998. 496p. Nolo Press, $44.95 (0-87337-469-X).

This resource goes a long way toward demystifying the patenting process. Aimed at the do-it-yourselfer market, it delineates every step in the process, from preliminary search to maintaining the patent after issue. The first chapter is an excellent reference for basic questions about patents, such as what can and cannot be patented and the difference between patents, trademarks, copyright, and trade secrets. Several chapters guide the inventor through the application-writing process, and others discuss marketing, licensing, and dealing with the USPTO. The text is clearly written with very little legalese, and the layout is visually appealing. Beware of outdated information contained in the discussions of electronic resources, however: the current edition makes no mention of the USPTO Web patent database and describes another Web database that is no longer available.

Patent Searching Made Easy: How to Do Patent Searches on the Internet and in the Library. By David Hitchcock. 1999. 256p. Nolo Press, $24.95 (0-87337-476-2).

Before embarking on the patent-application process, inventors usually do a preliminary patent search to uncover any patents that are similar to their own ideas. Based on the results of the search, an inventor makes decisions on whether to pursue a patent, modify the idea, or abandon it entirely. This book thoroughly explains how to search for previously issued U.S. patents, using resources available on the Internet and at PTDLs. The author does not oversimplify the search process or give the false impression that a comprehensive search can be done using Internet resources alone. The explanations are helpful for both computer expert and "newbie."

African-American Inventors Database. [http://www.detroit.lib.mi.us/glptc/aaid].

The Patent and Trademark Office does not collect personal information from inventors other than name and address, so information such as the sex or race of patentees is difficult to find. However, relying on published, verified sources for their information, librarians at the Detroit Public Library's Great Lakes Patent and Trademark Center have created a very useful database of African Americans who were issued a patent for their inventions. Each record contains the name of the inventor, the patent number and title, and, in some entries, a brief note about the invention. Search the database by name or by keyword or link to a complete list of the inventors and their patents. A bibliography is included. More than 800 entries are in the database. For additional information on African American patentees, including drawings and text from their patent applications, see the Web site *The Faces of Science: African Americans in the Sciences* [http://www.lib/lsu.edu/lib/chem/display/faces.html], produced by librarians at Louisiana State University.

A History of the Early Patent Offices: The Patent Office Pony. By Kenneth W. Dobyns. 1997. 249p. Sergeant Kirkland's, $29.95 (1-887901-13-2).

Abraham Lincoln was the only U.S. president who was a patentee (no. 6,649, for inflatable bellows that helped to buoy a boat over shoals). When the government began issuing patents in 1790, Secretary of State Thomas Jefferson served as a patent examiner. The Confederacy had its own patent office. These and many other facts can be found in this book, which relates a detailed history of the U.S. patent system from 1790 through 1900. It contains colorful stories of patent office personalities and is a good source of information about famous early patentees and their patents. Appendixes include a list of all known patents issued by the Confederate Patent Office and examples of Confederate and pre–Civil War U.S. patents. A bibliography and index are included.

Subject Matter Index of Patents for Inventions Issued by the United States Patent Office from 1790–1873, Inclusive. 3v. Ed. by Mortimer D. Leggett. 1976. Ayer, $173.95 (0-405-07737-8).

Thanks to the Internet, information on U.S. patents from the mid-1970s to the present is easily accessible, but information on earlier patents is a different matter. This three-volume set, a reprint of an 1874 work compiled by a patent commissioner, lists all early patents for inventions, from *abdominal supporter* to *zincing iron*. Inventor name and place of residence, date of issue, and patent number are given for entries that are listed alphabetically by subject matter. Nineteenth-century terminology is used, so be creative when thinking of words to express the subject of interest. The third volume also contains a list of goods for which trademarks were registered, along with company name, date, and registration number. Keep in mind that collector's encyclopedias and guides often include information on patents for inventions relating to specialized and everyday technology such as guns, telephones, and kitchen implements.

Historical First Patents: The First United States Patent for Many Everyday Things. By Travis Brown. 1994. 224p. Scarecrow Press, $41.50 (0-8108-2898-7).

Like *Subject Matter Index of Patents for Inventions Issued by the United States Patent Office*, this book contains information on early patents but gives more detailed information on famous inventions. More than 80 inventions are discussed, including a brief history, biographical information on the inventor, patent number, and excerpts from the text of the patent.

Official Gazette of the United States Patent and Trademark Office: Patents. Periodical. U.S. Government Printing Office, $92/yr. (SuDocsNo. 703-033-00000-8).

This journal, published every Tuesday, contains a record of all patents that are issued each week. Arranged by patent number, each entry contains basic information such as the inventor name and place of residence, assignee, and date of filing. Every entry lists at least one "claim" (a precise statement describing a specific aspect of the invention, for which patent protection is sought). Most entries also include a line drawing or diagram of the invention. Each issue also contains an alphabetical index of the week's patentees and a list of patent numbers arranged by patentee's state of residence.

Many libraries receive the *Official Gazette* through the Federal Depository Library Program. A back file is especially helpful for inventors doing preliminary patent searches. They can use this resource to look up numbers of patents (generated in the first part of their search) that are similar to theirs in terms of subject matter. Based on the information they find, they may decide that the complete patent is worth a closer look. Because it traces the history of American ingenuity, the *Official Gazette: Patents* is a treasure trove for antique buffs seeking information on historical patents or researchers needing a primary historical source.

National Inventor Fraud Center, Inc. By Martin Neustel [http://www.inventorfraud.com].

The patenting, marketing, and licensing process can be complex, and some inventors turn to "invention marketing" companies for help. Some of these are aboveboard, but others may use unscrupulous tactics that waste inventors' time and money. This Web site, maintained by a registered patent attorney, outlines warning signs and contains data on the success rates of specific companies. Neustel provides information to help the inventor in decision making yet he does not use the Web site to market his own services.

Trademarks

The concepts of trademarks and copyright are easily confused. *Trademark* and *copyright* both refer to the protection of intellectual property such as words and images, but a trademark is the use of these words or images to identify the source of a good or service. Sometimes, a trademark is the most valuable property a company owns. Not only can words, slogans, product and brand names, and logos be protected as trademarks, but other so-called devices can be registered as well. These include the shape or design of the product or packaging, sounds, and the characteristic color or fragrance of a product, among other features. Well-known examples of these include the NBC "chimes," the pink color of Corning insulation, the architectural shape of Pizza Hut restaurants, and the shape of Pepperidge Farm Goldfish Crackers.

Trademark disputes are judged on the legal test of "likelihood of confusion to the consumer," which asks whether a reasonable person would confuse the goods or services of one provider with those of another, based on the trademark. Recent trademark litigation illustrates this, such as the suit in which a fish-shaped cracker made by Nabisco was deemed a trademark infringement on Campbell's Soup Company, makers of Pepperidge Farm Goldfish Crackers. For words used as trademarks, problems may arise not only if two trademarks sound or look alike but if they have similar meanings, such as "White Mountain" and "Mont Blanc."

When filing a trademark application, potential registrants must specify what types of goods or services for which they will be using the trademark. Usually, protection is limited to the goods or services specified, but this can be extended to other goods or services, especially for very famous marks. For instance, naming a mattress store "McSleep" or a pet store "Pets R Us" would be very foolish, because of the proposed marks' high similarities to the marks of commercial giants McDonald's and Toys R Us.

U.S. Patent and Trademark Office Homepage. [http://www.uspto.gov].

When contemplating the use of a new trademark, one should first ask whether the mark is already in use or is registered at the federal

Sources for Patent Searching

The subject of patent searching is not immune from the common myth that "it's all on the Internet." Using the free Web U.S. patent databases on the Internet, many would-be patentees will do a quick keyword search or two, find nothing of interest, and continue with the patenting process, assuming that they have done a complete search. But it's not that easy! Inventors who need to do a preliminary patent search must be informed that they should search by patent classification code, not keyword, to uncover all patents in their field of interest. This method requires the use of several tools that are not yet on the Web.

There are other reasons why a comprehensive search is usually impossible on the Web (at least, for free). For many subject matter areas—especially the "low-tech" kinds (mousetraps or eating utensils, for example)—early patents are a vital source of information and are used by U.S. patent examiners to assess the "novelty" of a patent application. However, patents issued before the 1970s are not currently freely available on the Internet. Also, foreign patents and nonpatent literature are also used by U.S. patent examiners to assess the novelty of an idea. The Web is a poor source for this information as well.

An area PTDL has all the tools necessary for doing a comprehensive search of previously issued U.S. patents. The following bare-bones list of search tools is provided for those who, for curiosity's sake or convenience, would like to do a patent search at a library other than a PTDL. Many libraries receive these publications through the United States Federal Depository Library Program. Other resources described in this article explain how to use these tools to generate a list of patent numbers in the field of interest. A complete copy of the patent can then be retrieved from one of the Web databases described here, from a library that owns copies of patents, or from fee-based document delivery services such as the USPTO's patent copy service.

- **Index to the U.S. Patent Classification.** 1998. 262p. U.S. Government Printing Office, $22 (SuDocs No. 903-006-00042-1).

  A keyword guide to the patent classification system.

- **Patents ASSIST:** Full Text of Patent Search Tools. DVD-ROM. U.S. Patent and Trademark Office, $200/yr. (Product Code EIP-2030P-CD).

  Contains the *Manual of Classification*, similar to a "Library of Congress" system for patents, and *Classification Definitions*, which are the accompanying "scope notes."

- **Patents BIB:** Selected Bibliographic Information from U.S. Patents Issued 1969 to Present. DVD-ROM. U.S. Patent and Trademark Office, $300/yr. (Product Code EIP-2040P-CD).

  Retrieves titles and patent numbers for patents issued from 1969 to the present, searchable by keyword or class/subclass.

- **Patents CLASS:** Current Classifications of U.S. Patents. DVD-ROM. U.S. Government Printing Office, $300/yr. (Product Code: EIP-2050P-CD).

  Searched by the class/subclass of interest, it retrieves patent numbers for patents issued from 1790 to the present.

---

or state level. As of mid-1998, the U.S. Patent and Trademark Office Web site provides access to federal trademark records, free of charge. By searching for a word or phrase, the trademark database retrieves records for federally registered active trademarks or proposed trademarks that are pending registration. Information includes the trademark owner's name, address, date of registration, description of the good or service for which it is used in commerce, and an image of the logo, if any. As always, users should be aware of the limitations of the database, as summarized on the opening screen. Searching for features of an image is possible but requires the use of trademark design codes, which can be obtained through a PTDL. Contact the PTDL in your area for tips on effective searching using the database.

The site also contains general information about trademarks, downloadable application forms and instructions, and information on fees. The online *Trademark Manual of Examining Procedure* is a good reference for specific questions on the trademark application and examination process. Application forms that can be completed and submitted online are also available.

Trademark: Legal Care for Your Business and Product Name. 3d ed. By Kate McGrath and Stephen Elias. 1997. 352p. Nolo Press, $29.95 (0-87337-396-0).

Applying for a trademark is not quite as complicated as applying for a patent, but choosing a strong trademark is nonetheless an important decision for anyone providing a good or service. This book, written for the small-business owner, describes the process of trademark registration from start to finish, including strategies for choosing a strong mark and avoiding weak or ineligible ones. The book was written before the federal trademark database was available at the USPTO Home Page, but the authors give good advice on what to look for during a trademark clearance search. Trademark issues relating to Internet domain names are addressed, as well as what to do in the case of trademark infringement.

State Trademark Agencies and Databases. [http://members.tripod.com/~whitemj/statetm.htm].

Registering a trademark for protection throughout the entire U.S. is a function of the U.S. Patent and Trademark Office, but each state also maintains its own trademark registry. Business owners who do not plan on doing interstate commerce sometimes only register their trademark within their own state. This site links to the agencies in each state that handle trademark matters and to searchable state trademark databases on the Web. Individuals considering trademark registration would do well to search for their proposed name in the federal trademark database and the state databases as well, because any previous users of a trademark (even if it was never registered) may have some claim to the mark.

Official Gazette of the United States Patent and Trademark Office: Trademarks. Periodical. U.S. Government Printing Office, $672/yr. (ISSN 0-16-009679-0). (SuDocsNo. 703-034-00000-4).

One of the last "stops" in the trademark application process is "publication for opposition," following which the public has 30 days to oppose a pending trademark before it is registered. The *Official Gazette: Trademarks* is the official vehicle for this public notice. The bulk of each weekly issue contains a record of all trademarks that are published for opposition, including the applicant's name, date of filing, and a description of the goods or services on which the mark will be used. Logos are included, as well as drawings for those trademarks that relate to the three-dimensional design or shape of an object (such as the shape of a bottle). Sorry, no scratch 'n' sniff for fragrance trademarks. Information on other types of office actions, such as trademark renewals and cancellations, is included. At the back of each issue is an alphabetical list of all business entities for which trademark actions were executed that week. The *Official Gazette: Trademarks* back file provides an interesting glimpse into trademark trends and corporate history throughout the decades.

Trademarks of the '20s and '30s. By Erik Baker and Tyler Blik. 1989. 144p. Chronicle Books, $14.95 (0-8770-1360-8).

Trademarks of the '40s and '50s. By Erik Baker and Tyler Blik. 1988. 144p. Chronicle Books, $14.95 (0-8770-1485-X).

Trademarks of the '60s and '70s. By Tyler Blik. 1998. 132p. Chronicle Books, $16.95 (0-8118-1698-2).

These three books offer an entertaining look at six decades of business logos and label design and consist mostly of illustrations, although some editorial comment is included. Even if *Official Gazette: Trademarks* is already available in a library, these books provide a more accessible and compact view of the visual history of trademarks.

Brands and Their Companies. 3v. 19th ed. Ed. by Donna Craft. 1999. Gale, $805 (0-7876-2290-7).

Not every trademark is registered. Although trademark registration confers certain legal benefits, those who use a trademark without registering it may have some common-law rights to the mark. A comprehensive trademark search, therefore, includes the investigation of Web sites, trade journals, phone directories, and other sources for any previous uses of the proposed mark. This reference work is a good place to start such a search because it includes many brand names that have never been registered as a trademark. Compiled from USPTO records, company literature, and trade journals, this set alphabetically lists word-based trademarks, with a description of the product or service and company name. The latter half of the publication contains company contact information, including Web site and e-mail addresses. The companion publication, *Companies and Their Brands*, lists manufacturers.

Nancy Adams is Patents and Trademarks Librarian, Science and Engineering Center, Fogler Library, University of Maine, Orono, ME.

The Sciences

Core Collections

The Sciences

by David Tyckoson

Reference Books Bulletin regularly features evaluative reviews of newly published reference sources. While we continue to keep reference librarians informed on new developments in reference publishing in both the print and electronic formats, we also want to occasionally remind you about those sources that form the heart of every reference collection. Beginning with this issue, RBB is starting a new series that will examine and rereview some of our old favorites. This series will help new librarians identify the most important sources in their collections as well as to alert experienced librarians to new editions or features of works that have been reviewed in the past. The criteria for works reviewed in these features are the following:

- Sources must be central reference works in the subject area.
- Sources must be appropriate for our audience.
- Sources must be currently available for purchase or license.

Core Collection reviews will appear on a regular basis, and each will be written by an RBB Board member or guest reviewer. Each review represents the opinions of an experienced reference librarian with a background in the subject field. Although such "best" lists can always be debated, we hope that you find these Core Collection reviews helpful in evaluating your own reference collections. Send your feedback to Mary Ellen Quinn, RBB editor, at mquinn@ala.org. We have chosen to compile a basic public library science reference collection for adults as the first in our series of Core Collections. The sciences have always had a certain mystique among librarians. Scientists use highly specific language and mathematical and numerical values or formulas, and discuss highly abstract concepts. Perhaps more importantly, few reference librarians are specialists in the sciences. Fortunately, publishers have produced many reference works that help reference librarians answer science questions. The sources on this list are intended to provide basic scientific information to a general adult audience. They cover a wide range of questions in the physical and life sciences. Medicine, technology, agriculture, and engineering are excluded, but may be the topics of future Core Collections.

The author of this first Core Collection is David Tyckoson. David has been a reference librarian for 20 years, having begun his career in a science library and later moved into general reference. He has a degree in physics and has been a science reviewer for RBB since 1984. He has also published a number of articles on reference services and was chair of the committee that developed the RUSA (Reference and User Services Association) Behavioral Guidelines for Reference and Information Services Librarians. —*Mary Ellen Quinn*

Encyclopedias and Dictionaries

McGraw-Hill Dictionary of Science and Technical Terms. 5th ed. Ed. by Sybil Parker. 1994. 2,200p. McGraw-Hill, $125 (0-07-042333-4).

Because science uses such specific and unusual terminology, a good dictionary is a necessity, and this is the best general science dictionary around. It provides short definitions and pronunciations for words and phrases used in all branches of science and technology. When terms have different meanings in different fields, the definition for each is given along with the field in which that definition is used. For example, the word *scaling* has eight different definitions in fields ranging from biology to graphics to nuclear physics. Illustrations are used to enhance the definitions for some entries. This dictionary is based on the terms found in the *McGraw-Hill Encyclopedia* (see below) and serves as a one-stop companion for the language of science. Like the *Encyclopedia*, it has been updated every five years and a new edition is due out in 1999.

McGraw-Hill Encyclopedia of Science and Technology. 8th ed. 20v. Ed. by Sybil Parker. 1997. McGraw-Hill, $1,995 (0-07-911504-7).

If you buy only one science reference source for your collection, this is the one to get. It provides authoritative articles on topics in all branches of science, from astronomy to chemistry to zoology. Entries range in length from a short paragraph to dozens of pages and are well indexed. Each entry is written with the nonspecialist in mind, explaining theories and results in such a way as to be understood by the general adult reader without skimping on scientific fact. No biographies are included, although the work of important scientists is mentioned within subject entries where appropriate. Updated every five years, this work is truly the heart of every science reference collection. Although it is also available in CD-ROM format, the print version is still easier to use and more accessible to most patrons and librarians. This title is expensive, but it is worth the price to be able to purchase a single source that covers all areas of science. Those libraries that cannot afford to purchase every new edition may wish to alternate purchasing *McGraw-Hill* with *Van Nostrand's* listed below.

Van Nostrand's Scientific Encyclopedia. 8th ed. 2v. Ed. by Douglas M. Considine. 1994. Van Nostrand Reinhold, $269.95 (0-442-01864-9).

Van Nostrand's is a shorter and not-as-useful competitor to the *McGraw-Hill Encyclopedia*. Like *McGraw-Hill*, it covers all fields of science from animal life to space exploration. Also like *McGraw-Hill*, entries are written with the nonscientist in mind and are approachable by the informed adult reader. Unlike *McGraw-Hill*, entries tend to be quite short and present fact more than theory. *Van Nostrand's* is a good place to look for quick facts, whereas *McGraw-Hill* will give more background material. However, *Van Nostrand's* is much less expensive and is a good purchase for small libraries that cannot afford *McGraw-Hill*.

Scientific Biography

American Men and Women of Science: A Biographical Dictionary of Today's Leaders in Physical, Biological, and Related Sciences. 20th ed. 8v. 1998. Bowker, $900 (0-8352-3748-6).

There are more practicing scientists today than throughout all of Western history, and they are almost all found in this work. *American Men and Women of Science* is the Who's Who of scientists, providing name, education, experience, and contact information. In addition to personal information, each entry provides the field of study and research interests, professional memberships, and awards received. Fax numbers and e-mail addresses are included when available. As in the *Who's Who* series, scientists provide this information themselves and a lack of response will result in only a very brief entry. However, most scientists desire to be included and will be found in this set. Updated every three years, this work is the first source to turn to for finding information on living scientists.

Dictionary of Scientific Biography. 18v. By the American Council of Learned Societies. 1981. Scribner, $1,600 (0-684-80588-X).

Scientists come in only two kinds—the living and the dead. This work is the definitive biographical source for scientists in the latter category. It contains scholarly biographies of scientists throughout history and from around the globe. Each entry provides not only the personal life of the scientist, but also a thorough discussion of his or her theories and scientific contributions. Entries range from a paragraph to hundreds of pages for the most important figures. Each entry includes a bibliography of the scientist's original writings and also refers the reader to other secondary and critical sources. Supplements appear irregularly to update the set with recently deceased scientists or with persons who had been missed in earlier volumes. Considering that the material in this publication will never become outdated, the high price can be justified for even a small library.

Physical Data

CRC Handbook of Chemistry and Physics. 79th ed. Ed. by David R. Lide. 1998. Annual. 2,480p. CRC Press, $99.95 (0-8493-0479-2).

As scientists have attempted to explain nature in a precise way, they have created a foundation of mathematical equations and experimental results upon which their theories are built. CRC Handbook of Chemistry and Physics is the best source for obtaining this data. From chemical elements to mathematical functions, this work provides the scientist with the fundamental constants of the universe. Although much of the work deals with chemical and physical data, it covers much more than just these two fields, including conversion factors, laboratory safety, geology, astronomy, and pure mathematics. Information is presented primarily in tabular form, requiring some understanding of science to interpret. Updated annually, this work remains the first choice of sources for scientific data—as it has for most of this century.

The Animal Kingdom

Grzimek's Encyclopedia of Mammals. 2d ed. 5v. Ed. by Bernhard Grzimek. 1990. McGraw-Hill, $525 (0-07-909508-9).

The best reference work on animals ever published was Grzimek's Animal Life Encyclopedia, which is now unfortunately out of print. Originally published in German, it was translated into English in the 1970s. Fortunately, the section on mammals has been revised and published under a slightly different title. This work is remarkable in its comprehensiveness and clarity. It includes lengthy entries for mammals found anywhere on the globe. Each entry includes a description of the animal's life cycle, geographic distribution, food systems, predators, and overall ecology. Magnificent color photos and drawings accompany each entry, as do a variety of maps, charts, and tables. Whether for a school report or a research scientist, this is the first source to use when seeking information on mammals. We hope that McGraw-Hill will revise and update the rest of the series in the near future.

The Plant Kingdom

New Royal Horticultural Society Dictionary of Gardening. 4v. Ed. by Anthony Huxley. 1992. Macmillan, $450 (1-56159-001-0).

There is no single reference work for plants that is as comprehensive as Grzimek's is for animals, but this one comes close. Although it concentrates on plants with some horticultural value, it includes the vast majority of the plants found in our daily lives. This work includes entries for almost 4,000 plant genuses from around the globe, indexed by both scientific and common names. For each genus listed, the work provides the history of its discovery, physical description, geographic range, and methods for cultivation. Common species names are also provided along with their distinguishing characteristics. Since the work is aimed at people who will be growing plants, subject entries are also provided for topics and important people in the field of gardening. A revised version focusing on North American plants, The American Horticultural Society A–Z of Garden Plants [RBB Ja 1 & 15 98], is also available. This edition is much less expensive but is also much more limited in geographic coverage. It would work well in smaller libraries.

The Mineral Kingdom

Encyclopedia of Minerals. 2d ed. William Lincoln Roberts. 1989. 979p. Chapman and Hall, $115 (0-412-07831-7).

This is one reference source that really rocks—since that is what it's all about. It simply lists and describes all known minerals found on the earth. For each mineral, the encyclopedia provides chemical formula, physical data, color and appearance, and geographic distribution. Color plates are provided for the most photogenic materials, with some others illustrated by black-and-white photos or crystal diagrams. Each entry includes a bibliographic reference to a source providing more information. This is the first place to turn for information on the third kingdom of the natural world.

Field Guides

National Audubon Society Field Guide Series. Knopf.
Peterson Field Guide Series. Houghton Mifflin.

Field guides were originally intended to be used by botanists, birdwatchers, herpetologists, and others to identify plants and animals in the wild. Each guide provides a directory to a particular type of plant or animal (reptiles, birds, wildflowers, insects, etc.) within a particular geographic region. For each organism, a description, habitat, range, breeding habits, and food sources are given. Field guides are known for the quality of their color illustrations. Since the illustrations were originally created for identification purposes, they provide the reader with a clear image of what the organism looks like and how it differs from similar species. The Peterson series uses artwork, while the Audubon series uses photographs. Both are equally spectacular. Since there are many volumes in each series covering a number of geographic areas, libraries may pick and choose those that are most useful to their own patrons. In many cases, libraries may wish to buy two copies of each—one for reference and one for the circulating collection. Field guides are some of the most economical science reference books.

David Tyckoson is Head of Reference at California State University–Fresno.

Genealogy

by Deborah Rollins

When a library patron stops by the reference desk and asks about the location of the "genealogy section," some librarians may cower and cringe, if only on the inside. The reason for this reaction? Genealogy reference differs from other reference work in that genealogy's first objective, the verification of information about individuals (e.g., birth, death, and marriage dates and places), must be accomplished through the use of original sources, which are not usually sitting on a shelf in the reference collection. Our role is to identify resources that will describe, locate, and assist in the interpretation and use of such sources. Although we can't look up a person's military records as easily as we can find an article on the Battle of Gettysburg, we should be prepared to point to a book or Internet source that will tell us and our patrons about such records and how to go about searching for them. The genealogy Core Collection includes some of the best starting places for both librarian and patron. The books may not all have been published in the last year or so, but the basic principles and materials of genealogical research have not changed. The Internet seems to have been made for genealogists, given the wealth of information on it that is by and for them. It's often a very good idea to connect with other people doing research on the same ancestral lines (why reinvent the wheel, or, in this case, the family tree?), and the ability to do has been greatly increased by Web site indexes and compilations of trees contributed by other researchers.

This collection of books and Web sites represents what any public or academic library would need to educate patrons on the genealogy research process and refer them to sources, institutions, and organizations appropriate for their needs. The next step in building a more comprehensive collection would be to buy from the lists in Elizabeth D. Moore's *Librarian's Genealogy Notebook* (see below) and to identify pertinent regional secondary and online sources.

Start with This

The Librarian's Genealogy Notebook. By Elizabeth D. Moore. 1998. 142p. ALA, $32 (0-8389-0744-X).

This accessible guide should be read by every reference librarian. Moore's description of the reference interview process for genealogical inquiries is short but covers all the important points. The answers to "who, what, where, when, why?" are what will determine how we assist the patron. Annotated bibliographies in the sections "General Books Most Libraries Should Own" and "Basic Genealogy Bibliography" will help fill in any gaps in the collection. Brief entries on record types (e.g., probate, cemetery, census, passenger lists) provide understanding of their use. Other sections cover libraries, publishers, book dealers, education, computer programs, periodicals, and more. Photocopies may be made of the appendix's 18 forms, including one for each U.S. census, if patrons have not brought their own record-keeping system.

Next Stop

Ancestry's Red Book: American State, County, and Town Sources. Rev. ed. By Alice Eichholz. 1992. 858p. Ancestry, $49.95 (0-9164-8947-7).

For each state and the District of Columbia, there is an overview of original and printed or microfilmed sources, as well as helpful hints on the idiosyncrasies of finding state and local records for that area. Charts for counties and towns give contact addresses, dates of formation, and beginning dates for records on marriage, birth, death, and land. Detailed state maps help locate place names.

Printed Sources: A Guide to Published Genealogical Records. By Kory Meyerink. 1998. 800p. Ancestry, $49.95 (0-9164-8971-X).

Companion to *The Source* (see below), which discusses original records and where to find them, *Printed Sources* is about materials (in print, microfilm, or electronic format) that compile original records or otherwise contain information about individuals and families. Among chapter topics are geographic tools; published vital, cemetery, probate, land, court, and legal records; ethnic, church, military immigration, and documentary sources; censuses and tax lists; county and local histories; compiled family histories and genealogies; medieval genealogy; and more. Each chapter opens with a list of key concepts and sources and closes with a selected, but extensive, bibliography of material for each state. Numerous visual aids in the form of charts, graphs, tables, and copies of pages from sources like government documents, gazetteers, and indexes add to the understanding of the text. A good example is the table "Information in Land Records," which shows how to use such data as place, price, previous owners, and 11 other variables to root out information on individuals. *Printed Sources* will get a lot of use in any library with genealogical or historical materials.

The Source: A Guidebook of American Genealogy. By Loretto D. Szucs and Sandra H. Luebking. 1996. 846p. Ancestry, $49.95 (0-9164-8967-1).

If you have *The Source*, you will be able to identify the appropriate resources for most of the genealogy questions that come in to the library. The detailed index has points of access for almost any question. Most chapters focus on types of records, such as birth, death, cemetery, census, church, land, military, and employment records, to name a few. An entire section is devoted to the discussion of ethnic origins, from general advice on researching immigrants to chapters on the special sources and research techniques for Native American, Hispanic, African American, and Jewish American family histories. If the patron wants to find documents on a Civil War ancestor, information about ships' passenger lists, or old maps that show the location of family homes, start here for an overview and list of suggested sources. Although it was published prior to the explosion of online genealogical data, librarians can use *The Source* as a way of navigating the information on the Web by identifying types of data, titles of resources, and appropriate agencies prior to an Internet search.

Additional Sources

Evidence! Citation and Analysis for the Family Historian. By Elizabeth S. Mills. 1997. 124p. Genealogical, $16.95 (0-8063-1543-1).

A kind of MLA *Handbook* for the genealogist, this style guide gives standard forms of citation with examples for different types of documents, including those found on the Web.

Genealogist's Address Book. 4th ed. By Elizabeth P. Bentley. 1998. 842p. Genealogical, $39.95 (0-8063-1580-6).

A handy reference for addresses and phone numbers most wanted by genealogists. Some entries give URLs, but a *Yahoo!* search will turn up Web sites quickly enough for those that do not. This is especially useful for directory listings for genealogical societies, adoption registries, immigration centers, genealogical software, publishers, preservation, and periodicals. The section on ethnic archives and organizations, organized by country and culture groups, will open whole new worlds of research and support for patrons. Although libraries and historical societies are included, more-comprehensive listings of these institutions may be found in *American Library Directory* (Bowker, annual) and *Directory of Historical Organizations in the United States and Canada* (American Association for State and Local History, 1990).

Genealogist's Companion & Sourcebook. By Emily A. Croom. 1994. 256p. F & W, $16.99 (1-5587-0331-4).

Unpuzzling Your Past. 3d ed. By Emily A. Croom. 1995. 180p. F & W, $14.99 (1-5587-0396-9).

Although these titles are not reference works in the usual sense, you may want to keep a copy of each on the reference shelves. Croom's writing is reader-friendly and is perfect "how-to" advice for the beginner. *Unpuzzling* comes first, with descriptions of the basics: finding and documenting census, birth, marriage, and death records. *Genealogist's Companion* follows, with supplemental and alternative information like city directories, cemetery records, and using specialized resources for tracing African American or Native American ancestors.

Genealogy Software Guide. By Marthe Arends. 1998. 269p. Genealogical, $24.95 (0-8063-1581-4).

Once they really get going, genealogists come to realize the importance of the computer in organizing their tree and related data files. This guide outlines the features, functions, and types of reports generated by 27 database programs for the PC (e.g., *Personal Ancestral File, Family Tree Maker*) and more than 40 utilities (such as programs that can be used to create a family tree Web page). Although almost all of the companies do have Web pages with data about their products, having all the information in the same format in this handy book makes comparisons easier to make.

Guide to Genealogical Research in the National Archives. Rev. ed. 1985. 304p. National Archives, $35 (0-911333-00-2); paper, $25 (0-911333-01-0).

Records on U.S. population and immigration, military service, and numerous other topics of interest to genealogists (e.g., land records) are kept at the National Archives. Limitations, indexes, varieties, format, and location of each record type are detailed.

Reading Early American Handwriting. By Kip Sperry. 1998. 289p. Genealogical, $29.99 (0-8063-0846-X).

If you have any original source documents in your library (e.g., census schedules on microfilm for your state or county or archival collections of manuscripts, letters, and diaries), this will be appreciated. In addition to a general discussion of older styles of letter formation, it also covers abbreviations, contractions, dates, and numbering systems. More than half the book contains facsimile reproductions of old wills, marriage records, military rosters, letters, and more, with typeset transcription of each item on the facing page.

Researcher's Guide to American Genealogy. 2d ed. By Val D. Greenwood. 1990. 623p. Genealogical, $24.95 (0-8063-1267-X).

Another standard, this is notable for its examples of typical research situations and problems, complete with tips on use and interpretation of data from different types of records.

U.S. Military Records. By James C. Neagles. 1994. 445p. Ancestry, $39.95 (0-9164-8955-8).

So many people are hunting for the war heroes in their family trees that this more-specialized guide will be a worthwhile purchase. Covers both federal sources in the National Archives and state-finding aids, records, and publications.

Deborah Rollins is Reference Librarian, University of Maine, Orono, Maine; and current Chair of the *Reference Books* Bulletin Editorial Board.

SF/Fantasy Reference Sources

By Richard Bleiler

This is RBB's second Core Collection of guides to genre fiction. The first, "Mystery and Detective Reference Sources," appeared in *Booklist*'s Mystery Showcase in the April 15, 1999, issue. The collection is appropriate for academic libraries and larger public libraries supporting research in the sci-fi and fantasy genres. Smaller libraries will also find useful titles here, depending on the level of sci-fi readership and fandom they serve.

Encyclopedias

The Encyclopedia of Fantasy. Ed. by John Clute and John Grant. 1997. 1,049p. St. Martin's, $75 (0-312-15897-1).
The Encyclopedia of Science Fiction. 2d ed. Ed. by John Clute and Peter Nicholls. 1993. 1,370p. St. Martin's, $75 (0-312-09618-6).

Many reference works surveying science fiction and fantasy have the word *encyclopedia* in their titles, but these two are genuine encyclopedias, containing well over 8,000 alphabetically arranged entries on all aspects of science fiction and fantasy: biocritical entries on the authors, critics, and artists; analyses of the magazines, journals, and specialty publishers; descriptions of the movies, television shows, and dramatic presentations; definitions of theoretical terms; and explanations of historical movements and figures. All entries are signed and are models of clarity and concision, useful bibliographies are provided, and cross-references abound. Indeed, entries in *Fantasy* are cross-referenced with relevant entries in *Science Fiction*. A CD-ROM version of *The Encyclopedia of Science Fiction* was published by Grolier in 1995; in addition to the text of the volume, it includes numerous illustrations, interviews, film clips, and photographs. Updates to *The Encyclopedia of Fantasy* and *The Encyclopedia of Science Fiction* are available through the home page of science fiction writer and editor David Langford at [http://www.ansible.demon.co.uk/].

Science Fiction and Fantasy Biobibliography

Science Fiction Writers: Critical Studies of the Major Authors from the Early Nineteenth Century to the Present Day. 2d ed. Ed. by Richard Bleiler. 1999. 1,009p. Scribner, $125 (0-684-80593-6).

The first edition of this work was published in 1982 and contained biocritical essays on 75 major writers of science fiction, from Mary Shelley to contemporary figures. The arrangement was broadly chronological. The second edition revises and updates the essays and bibliographies of the first edition and expands the coverage of the contemporary writers, offering 98 critical essays in all. The arrangement of the second edition is alphabetical, and although Jules Verne and Stanislaw Lem are among the authors profiled, the focus remains on Anglo-American writers.

St. James Guide to Fantasy Writers. Ed. by David Pringle. 1996. 711p. St. James, $140 (1-55862-205-5).
St. James Guide to Horror, Ghost & Gothic Writers. Ed. by David Pringle. 1998. 746p. St. James, $140 (1-55862-206-3).
St. James Guide to Science Fiction Writers. 4th ed. Ed. by Jay P. Pederson. 1996. 1,175p. St. James, $140 (1-55862-179-2).

These volumes provide biobibliographical profiles of approximately 1,400 authors. The majority tend to be Anglo-American writers of the twentieth century, but *Horror* contains entries for such early writers as Horace Walpole and Ann Radcliffe, and the fantasy volume profiles a number of fantasists of the nineteenth century. A typical entry opens with brief biographical information, followed by lengthy bibliographies of the author's work. Citations are arranged chronologically and are followed by a selective list of secondary works. An autobiographical statement is occasionally given, and each entry concludes with a signed article discussing the writer's works. The articles tend toward the appreciative rather than the critical, and there is an occasional problem of editorial balance, with some significant writers accorded less space than emerging or peripheral writers.

Supernatural Fiction Writers: Fantasy and Horror. 2v. Ed. by Everett F. Bleiler. 1985 1,169p. Scribner, $210 (0-684-17808-7).

A companion to the first edition of *Science Fiction Writers* (above), these two volumes contain 147 biocritical essays. Coverage begins with the writings of Apuleius and concludes with profiles of such contemporary fantasists as Ramsey Campbell and Stephen King. Each essay concludes with a bibliography. The arrangement of the volumes is broadly chronological by literary period, with essays offering discussions of "British Gothic and Romantic Writers" and "American Pulp Writers of the Circumbellum Period," to name but two; there are separate sections devoted to French and German fantasists. Though now somewhat dated in its coverage of contemporary (post-1960) writers, the essays on historical figures remain useful and helpful.

Reader's Guides

Anatomy of Wonder 4: A Critical Guide to Science Fiction. 4th ed. Ed. by Neil Barron. 1995. 912p. R. R. Bowker, $52 (0-8352-3288-3).

The fourth edition of a work first published in 1976, this volume annotates more than 3,000 works. The first section is devoted to fiction, the second to nonfiction, and each contains numerous subsections. The first four chapters offer a roughly chronological survey of the primary literatures, with each chapter opening with a lengthy historical and critical overview followed by an extensive annotated bibliography of the significant works; chapter 5 comments upon the science fiction written for young adults. Chapters 6–15 provide discussions of such topics as science fiction publishing and libraries, the merits of specific reference works, and research library collections of science fiction. The volume concludes with excellent indexes. AOW4 belongs in all academic and public libraries; it is unequivocally the best general reader's guide available. In 1990 Barron edited *Fantasy Literature: A Reader's Guide* and *Horror Literature: A Reader's Guide* (both Garland); though they are out of print, they remain valuable, and Barron is said to be readying second editions of both.

What Fantastic Fiction Do I Read Next? A Reader's Guide to Recent Fantasy, Horror, and Science Fiction. By Neil Barron. 1997. 1,679p. Gale, $95 (0-7876-1866-7).

Consisting of cumulations of data from Gale's *What Do I Read Next?* series, this guide lists and describes more than 4,800 works published from approximately 1989 until 1996. In addition to the standard bibliographical information (author, title, publisher), each entry lists (and provides indexes to) the series to which the work belongs (if any), followed by the story type, the major characters, the time period, locale, plot, and titles involving similar themes or written in a similar style. Though occasionally frustrating if one is attempting to locate the titles in a series that began prior to 1990, and irksome if one does not know the full series name, this is an extraordinarily helpful guide, one that belongs in all public libraries.

Bibliographies

The Locus Index to Science Fiction, with Index to Science Fiction Anthologies and Collections. CD-ROM. Ed. by William Contento and Charles N. Brown. 1998. Locus, $49.95.

From 1984 until 1991 *Locus Magazine*, science fiction's premier trade journal, published an annual volume entitled *Science Fiction, Fantasy,* and Horror: A Comprehensive Bibliography of Books and Short Fiction Published in the English Language, compiled by indexer Contento and Locus publisher Brown. This CD-ROM is the cumulation and continuation of those volumes, plus the electronic version of the two volumes of Contento's long out-of-print Index to Science Fiction Anthologies and Collections (G. K. Hall, 1978–84). Contento and Brown promise annual updates, and Contento's Web site at [http://www.sff.net/locus/0start.html] provides free access to the data on the CD-ROM and offers addenda. This product offers much that is completely inaccessible elsewhere.

Science Fiction: The Early Years. Ed. by Everett F. Bleiler and Richard Bleiler. 1990. 998p. Kent State Univ., $83.50 (0-87338-416-4).

This enormous annotated bibliography focuses on the science fiction written in English from the third century B.C.E. to 1930 or written in other languages prior to 1930 and since translated and published in English. The volume begins with a scholarly discussion of the history and motifs of premodern science fiction, after which are descriptions of the more than 3,500 novels, short stories, and dramatic works published prior to science fiction becoming a discrete genre. Indexes offer access by author, title, magazine, publication date, and motif and theme. A companion to E. F. Bleiler's now out-of-print Guide to Supernatural Fiction (Kent State Univ. Press, 1983), which describes 1,764 works published prior to 1960.

Science Fiction: The Gernsback Years: A Complete Coverage of the Genre Magazines Amazing, Astounding, Wonder, and Others from 1926 through 1936. By Everett F. Bleiler and Richard Bleiler. 1998. 730p. Kent State Univ., $65 (0-87338-604-3).

This provides summaries for each of the 1,835 stories in early American and English science-fiction magazines, several of them published by Hugo Gernsback (for whom the Hugo, science fiction's award of excellence, was named). The introduction discusses stories, authors, and readers and analyzes basic ideas and patterns. The annotations are arranged alphabetically by author, with many pseudonyms provided and much completely unknown biographical information revealed. In addition, there are histories and contents listings of the individual magazines, analyses of the illustrators and their illustrations, and several indexes, including an extensive motif and theme index.

Science Fiction and Fantasy Literature, 1975–1991: A Bibliography of Science Fiction, Fantasy, and Horror Fiction Books and Nonfiction Monographs. By Robert Reginald. 1992. 1,512p. Gale, $199 (0-8103-1825-3).

This volume and its out-of-print companion, Science Fiction and Fantasy Literature: A Checklist, 1700–1974, with Contemporary Science Fiction Authors (1979), document with admirable thoroughness an entire field. Indeed, if one held every work listed in these volumes, one would have a library of more than 37,000 works of science fiction and fantasy published in English in (predominantly) the U.S. and Britain between 1700 and 1991. The volumes are arranged alphabetically by author's or editor's name (when known) and by title when there is no author; pseudonyms are frequently identified at this level. Detailed bibliographic data are provided for each separately published work. Each volume includes a title, series, and awards index. All academic and public libraries with comprehensive literature reference collections should hold Reginald's volumes, but they should not discard E. F. Bleiler's long out-of-print Checklist of Science Fiction and Supernatural Fiction (2d ed., Firebell Books, 1978), for it cites a number of pre-1948 fantastic publications not listed by Reginald.

The Science Fiction and Fantasy Reference Index, 1878–1985: An International Author and Subject Index to History and Criticism. 2v. Ed. by Hal. W. Hall. 1987. 1,460p. Gale, $185 (0-8103-2129-7).

The Science Fiction and Fantasy Reference Index, 1985–1991: An International Author and Subject Index to History and Criticism. Ed. by Hal. W. Hall. 1993. 677p. Libraries Unlimited, $90 (1-56308-113-X).

The Science Fiction and Fantasy Reference Index, 1992–1995: An International Author and Subject Index to History and Criticism. Ed. by Hal. W. Hall. 1997. 503p. Libraries Unlimited, $75 (1-56308-527-5).

Critical information on science fiction and fantasy and its creators is available through most of the standard indexes, but Hall's works are far more comprehensive. These volumes reference more than 40,000 books, articles, essays, dissertations, news reports, and audiovisual items. Each volume contains two sections, an author index and a subject index. Citations are given in full in each section, with no abbreviations, and researchers will find that Hall's coverage of fanzines, little magazines, and international materials is unparalleled in its thoroughness. On the debit side, cross-references are occasionally inadequate, and Hall's choice of subject headings is occasionally frustrating. The volume covering 1985–91 is out-of-print, but the publisher tells us that a limited number of copies are still available.

Science Fiction, Fantasy, and Weird Fiction Magazines. Ed by Marshall B. Tymn and Mike Ashley. 1985. 970p. Greenwood, $105 (0-313-21221-X).

The history of American science fiction and fantasy is related closely to the history of its magazines, and this volume provides the histories and discussions of hundreds of genre magazines published between 1882 and 1983. Arrangement is alphabetical by title. The essays are written by experts and occasionally the editors themselves. Each essay concludes with two sections. "Information Sources" provides a bibliography listing secondary studies, index sources, the sources of genre-based reprints, and lists of the libraries in which runs of the magazine may be found; and "Publication History" lists the magazine's title and its changes (if any), its numbering system (if any), its publisher(s), its editor(s), its format(s), and its price(s). Separate sections list English-language anthologies, academic periodicals and major fanzines, and non-English-language magazines (by country); appendixes provide indexes by major cover artists and a chronology of the publication of the magazines. A lengthy bibliography and an excellent index conclude the volume.

Science Fiction, Fantasy, and Weird Fiction Magazine Index (1890–1997). CD-ROM. By William Contento and Stephen T. Miller. 1998. Locus, $49.95.

Stephen T. Miller is one of the great collectors of science fiction, fantasy, and weird fiction magazines, and with Contento he offers access to more than 50,000 stories appearing in more than 11,000 issues of 730 English-language genre magazines published between 1890 and 1997. Indexes offer access by magazine, author, title, and cover artists. Though this is a specialized product, it must be remembered that American science fiction came of age in the pulp magazines, and without an index such as this, the contents of these pulp magazines are forever inaccessible.

The Supernatural Index: A Listing of Fantasy, Supernatural, Occult, Weird, and Horror Anthologies. By Mike Ashley and William Contento. 1995. 952p. Greenwood, $195 (0-313-24030-2).

Compiled by noted scholar Ashley and indexer Contento, this index lists the contents of more than 2,100 volumes containing more than 21,300 stories by more than 7,700 writers, offering access by indexes for editor, book, author, story, and book contents. Entries in each section are gratifyingly thorough and helpful. The citations in the author index include information on the length and original source and date of each story, providing first book publication when original periodical publication dates are lacking. Coauthors are listed, anonymous and pseudonymous stories are cross-referenced, and special version notes identify versions of a story specific to a given book. Cross-references abound.

Richard Bleiler is Humanities Reference Librarian at the Homer Babbidge Library at the University of Connecticut. He has written several guides to genre fiction; future projects include a volume of biocritical essays on contemporary fantasy and horror writers.

Another Look At . . .

Another Look At . . .

The CQ Researcher. 1923–. Congressional Quarterly, $396 (ISSN 1046-2036). Online version, call 1-800-432-2250 ext. 279 for subscription information.

Frequently mentioned in RBB's recent survey of field-tested reference sources [RBB My 1 98], *The CQ Researcher* is celebrating its 76th anniversary this year. It was founded in 1923 as *Editorial Research Reports* by three newspaper correspondents in Washington, D.C., who recognized the need for reporters and editors to have access to reliable background information on issues of national interest. Typewritten on letter-size paper and issued in September 1923, the first report dealt with coal shortages caused by problems within the industry. Reports published during the next 12 months ranged in length from three to 20 pages and treated such topics as farm credits, prohibition, the Teapot Dome inquiry, and trade with Russia.

Although originally intended as a service for editors and publishers of newspapers and magazines, *Editorial Research Reports* attracted wider notice after *Public Affairs Information Service Bulletin* (now *PAIS International in Print*) began indexing it in 1926. As the reports became more extensive, libraries started to recognize the publication's potential as a timely and trustworthy source for patrons interested in contemporary affairs. By the mid-1930s, subscribers were receiving not only the weekly issues but also bound, six-month cumulations that contained retrospective subject indexes.

During its early decades, *Editorial Research Reports* focused primarily on national, political, and economic issues. Congressional matters received special emphasis, and reports covering the records and roll-call votes of each session of Congress were regular features. By the late 1940s, the scope had broadened to encompass emerging social problems and concerns in such areas as health, housing, crime, religion, education, and mass media. Following its purchase in 1956 by Congressional Quarterly, *Editorial Research Reports* dropped its reports on each Congressional session because similar coverage was provided by CQ *Weekly Report* (now CQ *Weekly*). In 1986, *Editorial Research Reports* was renamed *Congressional Quarterly's Editorial Research Reports*. Format changes during the following year led to a more attractive layout and a more effective use of maps, charts, and other graphics, which helped broaden the publication's appeal and made it more appropriate for use by high-school students.

Published under its present title since May 1991, *The CQ Researcher* continues to be an excellent resource for obtaining background information on topics of current interest. The equivalent of a small monograph, each signed report averages 12,000 words and conforms to a standard format that includes an introduction to the issues involved, historical background, a summary of the current situation, an analysis of the outlook for the future, and a two-part annotated bibliography. Additional features include a chronological chart, a section offering opposing viewpoints on a major aspect of the topic by two experts, sidebar articles, and a variety of photographs and other illustrations. Subscribers to the full service receive 48 reports a year, quarterly subject indexes, and an annual bound volume containing an index to issues from 1991 to date. Recent issues have focused on such diverse subjects as school violence, food safety, Social Security, coastal development, U.S.-Russian relations, patients' rights, evolution vs. creationism, and democracy in Asia. A CD-ROM version of *The CQ Researcher*, now available through SilverPlatter, debuted in 1996 [RBB My 15 96], and in 1998, CQ introduced a Web version as part of its CQ *Library* [http://library.cq.com], which also provides access to CQ *Weekly*. (Libraries can choose to subscribe to both or either of the Web versions of these publications, and cost is based on several factors, including size of the institution.) Containing the full text of all CQ *Researcher* reports published since November 1991, the Web site makes issues available 48 hours before they are published in paper format. This generally means that a report is accessible on the Web at least a week before its print counterpart is actually received by a subscribing library. The frames-based site is easy to navigate, and the search interface offers keyword and phrase searching with the ability to limit by date. Although no provision is made for controlled vocabulary subject searching, users have the option of downloading the latest subject index. In contrast to the print version, users cannot move through a Web issue page-by-page, but must select one section to view at a time (e.g., Background, Chronology, or an individual sidebar or chart). Beginning in July 1998, most photographs and other illustrations on the Web site are reproduced in color.

Long noted for its accuracy, objectivity, and almost uncanny timeliness, *The CQ Researcher* continues to fulfill the goal of its original founders. Moreover, it can serve a diverse range of users, from a high-school student preparing a speech or term paper to a journalism graduate student writing an editorial to practitioners in such fields as mass media, political science, health sciences, and education. Although many librarians view this title primarily as an indispensable source for information on contemporary affairs, its back volumes are equally valuable, not only for identifying what topics or issues were of interest during a particular year or era but also for documenting the historical development of major national concerns. —Marie Ellis

Famous First Facts: A Record of First Happenings, Discoveries, and Inventions in American History. 5th ed. By Joseph Nathan Kane, Steven Anzovin, and Janet Podell. 1997. 1,122p. indexes. H. W. Wilson, $95 (0-8242-0930-3).

It's surprising that this title, a classic in the reference byway of "firsts" compendiums, hasn't been updated in 17 years. Since the fourth edition came out in 1981, there have been other books of firsts, including *Historical First Patents* (Scarecrow, 1994), *Science and Technology Firsts* (Gale, 1997), and *Women's Firsts* (UXL, 1998), but Joseph Nathan Kane's *Famous First Facts* (FFF) is the granddaddy of them all.

According to the preface, Kane, a freelance journalist, spent the better part of 10 years traveling around the U.S., gathering facts for what was intended to be a history of American inventions. The first edition of FFF was published in 1933—somewhat grudgingly, by Halsey W. Wilson, "after receiving multiple requests for the book from reference librarians to whom Mr. Kane had shown portions of his manuscript." The book was so successful that it spawned a radio program entitled *Famous First Facts*, hosted by Kane in 1938several other reference standards, including *Facts about the Presidents* and *Facts about the States*.

With the fifth edition, FFF adds 1,000 new firsts and is extensively reorganized, making it much easier to navigate. Arrangement is now by broad subject category, from Agriculture to Writing Implements. Many of these categories are broken down into further divisions; Agriculture, for example, has 10 subdivisions, including Crops—Cotton; Flowers; and Livestock. Within this structure, individual firsts are arranged chronologically. The editors state that "much of the material in the previous edition was consolidated to make room for the events of the recent past." New firsts include *astronaut who was a mother* (1984), *round-the-world solo sailing trip by an African-American* (1990), *library to possess 100 million items* (1996), and *kosher cyber cafe* (1997). Almost half the volume is taken up by indexes. Instead of the extensive cross-referencing developed by Kane, there is a now a subject index, listing entries from *first abdominal operation other than a cesarean section* to *zoo with twilight conditions*. An index by years (from 10,000 B.C. to 1997), an index by days, a names index, and a geographical index have been continued from previous editions.

The publication of the fifth edition of *Famous First Facts* provides an opportunity to retire an aging reference classic in favor of a newer model. According to the publisher, FFF will also be available on CD-ROM and via the Web.

The New Book of Popular Science. 6v. 1998. appendix. charts. illus. index. maps. tables. Grolier, $259 (0-7172-1221-1). DDC: 500.

The New Book of Popular Science was first published in 1924 as the *Book of Popular Science*. A review appeared in the very first issue of RBB (called

Subscription Books Bulletin back then) in January 1930. That review concluded: "While a well-stocked library can have no actual need for this set, if picked up second-hand at a bargain its enjoyment by men and boys might justify the purchase. The experience in a small public library is that it has been used only for its pictures, although several junior and senior high schools report that it stimulated an interest in the study of science."

Since then, *The New Book of Popular Science* has become a standard science encyclopedia for young people (girls included) in the upper-elementary through secondary grades. We last reviewed it in 1992. With several other up-to-date, student-level science encyclopedias available, including *Macmillan Encyclopedia of Science* [RBB Ag 97], *UXL Encyclopedia of Science* [RBB My 1 98], and *World Book Encyclopedia of Science* [RBB Mr 15 97], not to mention the well-established *Raintree Steck-Vaughn Illustrated Science Encyclopedia* (rev. ed., 1997), we decided it was time for another look.

Perhaps we could call this *The New* (and Improved) *Book of Popular Science* to distinguish it from its predecessors, since the 1998 covers are unchanged from the 1996 edition. Inside, however, this standard reference for upper-elementary through high-school age has been updated in some important areas. Volume 4 (Plant Life/Animal Life) has been entirely rewritten and reorganized to reflect current scientific classification of bacteria, fungi, and algae. Ecosystems, paleontology, and scientific careers are included now, to reflect curriculum changes in many schools. Another change is the introduction of numerous sidebars on topics such as snakebites and zebra mussels. Volume 6 (Technology) has new material about computers and the Internet; the new Internet article is nine pages long and includes sidebars on interactive TV and copyright issues. There are major and minor revisions to other articles throughout the set, including the deaths of Carl Sagan and Jacques Cousteau, the cloning of Dolly, the development of HDTV, and updated statistics on recycling, cancer, heart disease, and organ transplants. There are nearly 600 new illustrations, almost all four color. The appendix lists Nobel Prize winners for 1996 and 1997.

Contributors to the 1998 edition include writers for scientific magazines and educators. Selected readings found at the end of each volume date mostly from 1992 through 1995, with a very few from the 1980s and some from 1997. According to the publisher, more than 75 percent of the selected readings have been replaced.

Will school libraries really need to order another set of six volumes for brand-new information in just one? The answer here is yes if your students do research on biomes, plants, animals, and careers, unless your budget allows essential purchases only. Public libraries, too, will want to provide patrons with the latest edition of this nontechnical, highly readable work. Though it does not match other sets in terms of visual appeal, it often provides more in-depth information, making it a good choice for older students at report-writing time.

The Penguin Dictionary of Architecture and Landscape Architecture. 5th ed. Ed. by John Fleming, Hugh Honour, and Nikolaus Pevsner. 1998. 643p. Penguin, $40 (0-670-88017-5).

Almost from the moment it was first published in 1966, *The Penguin Dictionary of Architecture* was a reference classic. This was due in no small part to the stature of its editors. Both Fleming and Honour are noted experts on architecture and design, but it was the distinguished architectural historian Sir Nikolaus Pevsner who really lent luster to the project. Born in Leipzig, Germany, in 1902, Pevsner fled to England when the Nazis came to power and eventually became art editor of Penguin Books. Between 1948 and 1974, Pevsner traveled throughout England, gathering material on every structure of architectural importance in every county, from great houses and cathedrals to factories, farms, and pubs; the result was the 46-volume series The Buildings of England, commonly known as *Pevsner*, which remains an important source of information about British architecture. In the midst of his perambulations, Pevsner also found time to collaborate on the first three editions of *The Penguin Dictionary of Architecture*. Although he died in 1983, eight years before the fourth edition appeared, his contribution is acknowledged by the fact that his name is still attached to the fifth edition, now called *The Penguin Dictionary of Architecture and Landscape Architecture*.

The new title reflects a more encompassing perspective. Though the fourth edition had entries on a few major figures in landscape, such as Lancelot Brown and Frederick Law Olmstead, these entries have been expanded; and entries for Gertrude Jekyll, Jens Jensen, Humphry Repton, and others have been added, as have entries for various related forms—*cemetery, theme park, promenade, roof garden, suburb*, to name a few. Content has expanded in other ways as well, demonstrating a more liberal view of what constitutes and informs architecture. There are new entries related to materials (*cement, marble, terracotta*); forms (*charterhouse, megalith, Quonset hut*); and systems (*air conditioning, elevator, escalator*). There are new entries for styles (*colonial revival, Mission style, Shaker architecture*) and movements (*constructivism, City Beautiful movement*). Current attitudes and trends are addressed in entries such as *barrier-free, computer aided design*, and *historical reconstruction*; and architects, including Spain's Santiago Calatrava and Japan's Shin Takamatsu, have been added. At the same time, there are now entries for individuals, such as seventeenth-century bricklayer Peter Mills and sixteenth-century master mason Jacob Wolff, who did important work back when the lines between architects and laborers were less distinct; and for those such as San Simeone architect Julia Morgan, overlooked in previous editions.

One of the most useful features of *The Penguin Dictionary of Architecture* has been its surveys of national architectures, and the country essays have been updated. Brief discussions of landscape architecture have been added to many. There are a few new national surveys, *Slovak architecture* being an example. The U.S. entry has not been substantially revised, but where it used to begin "The earliest permanent buildings were those erected by Spanish settlers" it now begins, "Apart from pueblos, the earliest permanent buildings. . ." This slight but important addition is indicative of another change in the fifth edition. In general, attention has been paid to widening the net to include more non-Western forms and terms—*caravanserai, chullpa, maidan, Seljuk architecture*, to name just a few. Still, the dictionary retains a British flavor, with terms like *intelligent building* instead of *smart building* and spellings like *shopping centre*.

In addition to all these changes, numerous entries have been expanded (among them *adobe, balloon framing, classicism*, and *mosque*); and many bibliographies have been revised. Architects who were once mentioned within the context of other topics now have their own entries, Frank Gehry being the most notable example. Finally, the drawings in the fifth edition are much crisper.

Guide to Reference Books (ALA, 1996) calls the fourth edition of *The Penguin Dictionary of Architecture* "an essential source," and no less can be said of the fifth.

Generalities

Featured Reviews and Reviews

Generalities

What Do I Read Next? Online. Gale, pricing starting at $495. (Last accessed September 15, 1998.)

What Do I Read Next? Online, part of GaleNet, combines the entries from Gale's *What Do I Read Next?*, *What Do Young Adults Read Next?*, *What Do Children Read Next?*, *What Do I Read Next? Multicultural Literature*, and *What Historical Novel Do I Read Next?* There are additional selections from contemporary mainstream and classic fiction, and popular nonfiction, for a database featuring more than 80,000 recommended titles. The main menu offers several ways to search.

In Help Me Find a Book, a patron enters a book title (or portion of one) and receives a list of all titles that fit the search. When a title is selected from the list, associated terms are displayed to help locate similar books. Genre Search allows patrons to explore the fantasy, historical, horror, mystery, romance, science fiction, and western genres. Pull-down menus help refine the genre searches. For example, fantasy can be refined to subgenres such as alternate world, gay-lesbian fiction, and time travel. Award Winners and Top Picks offer the search options Award Winners, Librarian Favorites, Expert Picks, and Bestsellers, with pull-down menus to further refine these categories. Award Winners include not only the more familiar awards, but also awards such as the Abbott Prize for Medical Writing and the Grand Prix de L'Imagianaire: Jeunesse. Librarian Favorites are lists ranging from 100+ *Favorite Romances* to *Weddings*. Expert Picks include numerous "best books" lists, from "10 Books of Social Concern for Journalists" to "YA Mind-Stretchers." None of the lists seem to be more current than 1995. Best-sellers include both Canadian and U.S. titles. There are also approximately 3,000 author biographies, with more to be added.

Who? What? Where? When? offers a Boolean search. Pull-down options for Who? include *1st grader, actor, alligator, cat,* and *zoo keeper*. What? ranges from AIDS (*disease*) to Zulu War. Where? allows the user to enter a locale. The When? pull-down menu covers everything from the conventional (*12th century*, 1815, 2950, *Age of Exploration*) to stardate 2323.23232323232323 1/2.

Author Search provides a list of titles by a favorite author. Title Search finds a book based upon exact title or part of the title, and provides brief information about that title. Custom Search finds appropriate titles by searching any combination of nine fields: author, title, genre/story type, subject, location, time period, character descriptor, character name, and full text. Searches can be restricted to fiction or nonfiction, and adult, young adults, or children's books. A Keeper List encourages the creation of a personal list of titles for review as the database is browsed. Special features include a Highlights area, with links to entries for new best-sellers, recent award winners, literary milestones, and titles related to events in the news. The Highlights area is updated every month, while the rest of the database is updated quarterly.

We looked at Alice Hoffman's *Turtle Moon* as an example of a title entry. Following a brief synopsis of the plot, information about the book is sorted into different categories: Major Characters, Age Range, Setting/s, Time Period, Awards, Librarian Favorites (lists on which the book has appeared), and Recommended Similar Titles. Awards, Librarian Favorites, and Recommended Similar Titles all provide links to other areas of the database. Users can access more links by selecting from a menu to find Books with the Same Topic, Books by the Same Author, and May We Suggest. . . The entry also provides a best-seller history for *Turtle Moon*, summarizing its appearance on such best-seller lists as the *Chicago Tribune* and *New York Times*. There are no links to reviews.

The database provides hours of browsing fun and is a definite help at the Readers' Advisory desk. It may also help in collection development, especially in genre areas. There are currently some slight problems, some of which have migrated from the print sets, and some of which are unique to the online version. An online resource should be up to date on award winners, yet the award lists seem to cover winners only through the early 1990s (the Highlights area does provide some more current information). In the romance genre, Betty Neels, a popular Harlequin Romance author, only has one book listed, which certainly won't satisfy her fans. The alphabetical pull-down menu for Who? has *slave* listed after *zoo keeper*. Not all the title entries are consistent in terms of the information they provide.

Public libraries that can afford it should certainly consider adding this database to their offerings. It is a definite advantage to have all the *What Do I Read Next?* volumes combined into a single interactive tool. There is a CD-ROM version, also updated quarterly, for a single-building price of $595. Print sources such as Libraries Unlimited's *Genreflecting* [RBB O 15 95] and *Teen Genreflecting* [RBB Ap 15 98] are still good alternatives for libraries with limited budgets.

World Book Online. Internet Database. 1998. World Book, visit [http://worldbook.com] for subscription information. (Last accessed April 2, 1999.)

Developed by the IBM Consumer Software Division, *World Book Online* is based on *World Book Multimedia Encyclopedia* [RBB N 1 98]. It offers access to more than 31,000 encyclopedia articles; 6,000 Web sites; 25,000 periodical articles; 800 videos, animations, and sounds; 100 three-dimensional bubble views; and 400 interactive maps.

Several features are accessible from the home page. In the navigation frame, Behind the Headlines lists current events, as well as events that are ongoing or recently past. Clicking one of these events leads to an article and links to related *World Book* content and Web sites. Today in History lists important events that happened on the day that the user has gone online. Monthly features include an in-depth look at a single issue and a calendar with important dates and birthdays. April's special feature was "Earth in the Balance," a collection of articles, multimedia, and Web sites compiled in recognition of Earth Day. The calendar included holidays and observances around the world (Arbor Day, Easter, Passover) with links to related encyclopedia content.

The menu bar at the top of the page offers several options. Around the World is an interactive atlas. The main screen is a map of the world. One can click on a continent to obtain a more detailed map. The navigation frame has a list of continents and oceans and a search box. Users can type in a country or click on a region to go to a particular map. Typing in *France* brings up a country map with a navigation frame that offers links to specialized maps showing population density, average January and June temperatures, economy, and average yearly precipitation. There are also links to related encyclopedia articles. The map of Israel has links to maps of Jerusalem, with a detailed map of the Old City, as well as links to maps of Lebanon, Syria, Jordan, and Egypt and articles on Haifa, Tel Aviv, Elat, Nazareth, and Beersheba.

The Zone offers a number of features: Back in Time, Homework Help, Monthly Features, Teacher Resources, and Throughout the Year. Back in Time allows users to search articles in the *World Book Yearbook* back to 1922. Clicking on a category (History, Humanities, Industry and Technology, Life Science, Physical Science and Mathematics, Sports and Recreation, or Social Science) produces a list of subheadings to refine the search. There is also a search box for entering specific subjects. These articles provide a glimpse of how a subject was viewed at the moment of discovery. Among the articles available are a 1922 entry on insulin and a 1948 account of the founding of the state of Israel. Homework Help derives from the index volume of the print set and offers help for doing research and preparing reports and oral presentations. It also provides Research Guides, which are the reading and study guides found in the print index. Monthly Features contains a collection of reports and in-depth articles on various topics, such as *The Quest for Women's Equality* (March) and *Cinquo de Mayo* (May). Teacher Resources offers links to lesson plans, professional development sites for educators, and other ways to incorporate *World Book* into classroom activities. Throughout the Year offers information on important dates and people who were born during the current month. Not all areas of The Zone are hyperlinked with the rest of the encyclopedia; it is not possible to go directly from the *Reformation* article, for example, to the *Reformation* research guide.

There are two types of searching available. Users may browse by category (life science, history, etc.) or alphabetically. Clicking on a subject will bring up a list of subdivisions. Clicking on a letter will lead to subdivisions within the alphabet. Users may also enter a term into the search box, which leads to a list of articles. Word searches all seem to be full-text searches. When we entered AIDS in the search box, the 50 top hits that were displayed included not only the article on AIDS, but also *hearing aid*, *children's literature*, and *aviation*. The advanced search mode, which allows the use of Boolean operators, wasn't much help. A search on AIDS AND *women* OR *drug abuse* brought up an odd assortment of material. The articles on AIDS and drug abuse were relevant; those on Shakespeare and painting were not, but they appeared because they contain the word *women*. Truncation is accepted in either the basic or advanced search mode. In advanced search, one can also limit the search to the type of material—articles, video, and so forth. There doesn't seem to be a list of content by media type, so it's not possible to identify all the animations, bubble views, or videos.

Once an article is chosen, the search term is highlighted in the text and the navigation frame offers an outline, media features, and related articles. Many articles also have buttons for related periodical articles and Web sites. The Related Periodicals button links to UMI's *Proquest Direct* for full-text articles, a very useful feature. We found links to 25 articles from *alligator*, several as recent as 1999. *World Book's* selection strategy for Web sites seems to be more inclusive than what the Board has seen in other online encyclopedias, leading to some sites that may not be useful for students. For example, one of the links in *Middle Ages* is to *Medieval Life*, a journal published in Great Britain; this site contains little more than information on how to subscribe.

Updated monthly, *World Book Online* is quite easy to use and has some interesting visual features, such as three-dimensional bubble views of the Brooklyn Bridge, the Eiffel Tower, and the Western Wall in Jerusalem. The anatomical drawings, such as views of the heart, are of good quality. The links to full-text articles are a definite strength. Searching, especially in the advanced mode, needs to be refined—there are too many irrelevant hits. This is a new product, so there are bound to be a few bugs. Given *World Book's* reputation for quality, it will improve. At this point, libraries that own the CD-ROM should stick with it. Those who want the convenience of online access should obtain price information and a trial password so that they can make an informed decision.

InfoTrac LifeCenter. Online database. Information Access, subscription and pricing information at http://library.iacnet/lifecenter. (Last accessed September 10, 1998.)

Hypertext comes to the world of personal and consumer decision-making. *InfoTrac LifeCenter* offers interactive access to an integrated tool that can help users make decisions about what to buy, how to take care of their cars, manage personal finances, or explore career options. With content from a panel of experts and some trade organizations and publishers, some full-text periodical articles, and interactive decision-making tools, *InfoTrac LifeCenter* was developed in collaboration with a number of public libraries. It is designed as a "self-service" tool to help patrons answer some of the questions that are common at public library reference desks.

InfoTrac LifeCenter has four main modules: Personal Finance, Auto, Jobs and Careers, and Consumer Purchases. More modules and more content within existing modules are promised for the near future. Each module is developed to a different level, and each contains a large amount of valuable information. "Source experts," such as syndicated career columnist Joyce Lain Kennedy, were commissioned to develop each module and to prepare and update articles and reports. All the modules have some "Interactive Tools," which are forms or sets of questions that walk the user through a variety of options, the end product being a summary or list of choices that match the user's responses. This is most effective when the topic is the choice of a product for purchase. In addition to the Interactive Tools, there are links to articles "from today's most respected publications," and links to relevant Web sites. The Web site links are well annotated.

The most efficient way to use the program is to choose one of the modules from the Main Menu, although there is also an option to search all the *LifeCenter* documents by entering key words. The Jobs and Careers module provides a good example of how the product works. From the main Jobs and Careers menu, the user is offered five choices—Explore Career Options, Find a Job, Land a Job, Know My Work Place Rights, and Choose an Interactive Tool. Each of the first four areas contains various subtopics. For example, there are three subtopics under Explore Career Options—Know Your Interests and Skills, Choose a Career, and Change Your Job or Career. Each of these is subdivided further into sections that contain original content as well as links to one or two journal articles, and hyperlinks to other relevant areas of the program.

Among the Interactive Tools in the Jobs and Careers module are Company Finder, Career Descriptions, Values Assessment Quiz, Resume Sampler, and Compensation Package Calculator. These tools can be accessed from a special Interactive Tools icon, as well as from the Jobs and Careers menu. Other icons provide links to information about the source experts, the Reference Shelf (selected articles from journals), and Help. A Retrieve icon leads to options for retrieving documents, including e-mail and Acrobat Reader. There is also a link to a "feature article," which on September 10 was a discussion of recent Supreme Court rulings on sexual harassment. The Find a Job area of the module offers links to "Best Companies" Web sites and "Hot Jobs" Web sites. Among the "Hot Jobs" sites are *Tomorrow's Jobs*, posted by *Occupational Outlook Handbook*, and 20 *Hot Job Tracks* from *U.S. News & World Report*.

While *InfoTrac LifeCenter* does pull together a large amount of very useful content, many libraries probably already own or can access a great deal of the information. Job hunters and people changing careers are well served by the print collections in most libraries. While the interactivity available here is useful, the original content adds up to one good book on the topic. Data come from widely available sources like *Occupational Outlook Handbook*, the Bureau of Labor Statistics Web site (*American Salaries and Wages Survey*. The basic information about companies is right out of Information Access' *Business & Company Profile ASAP* database. Similarly, the automobile pricing and specification information comes from the Automotive Information Center, which provides precisely the same information for free at its Web site at tion data come from another database that is free on the Web at

The Personal Finance module is like a hypertext version of any number of how-to books for managing finances. The advantage of this interactive module is its ability to respond to the user's needs and display only the information that is likely to be relevant. The tools it pulls together are certainly useful, but once again, many of them can be found elsewhere. MoneyMinded [http://www.monyminded.com/], Motley Fool [http://www.fool.com] and The-Street.com [http://www.thestreet.com/resources/index.html] are particularly good places to find similar tools..

For tips about maintaining and fixing a car, beginners will find much that is useful in the Auto module. Information Access has brought in content from Delmar, a leader in technical publishing for the automobile industry. However, the tips on researching and buying a car are a notch below the information in every April's issue of *Consumer Reports*. The other useful parts of the module, offering pricing information, access to classifieds, and a new car buying service, are either available for free over the Internet, or are simple links to other sites on the Web.

Perhaps least developed is the Consumer Purchases module, which allows the user to consider options for purchasing 10 different household products, mainly appliances. After choosing the general specifications, with some guidance, the user is presented with a list of matching products along with buying tips, reviews and articles, and worksheets for brand comparison. Conspicuously absent for now is information about televisions, VCRs, computers, and other electronics. Again, similar information is available for free on the Internet. The information in *Consumer Reports* is generally of a higher quality and reliability.

Overall, this is a highly useful tool that many public library users will find extremely helpful. The interface is very easy to use, and patrons with a basic familiarity with a Web browser will be able to jump right in and find what they need. The interactivity of the Web is exploited nicely, and the ability to retrieve entire sections within modules, while not yet fully functional, will allow users to easily take away the information contained in *InfoTrac LifeCenter* for offline reading. However, libraries considering purchase of the program should be aware that much of the actual content may already be available to their users.

The New Book of Knowledge Online. Online database. 1998. Grolier, call 1-888-326-6546 for subscription information. (Last accessed November 8, 1998.)

Based on the print version of *The New Book of Knowledge*, which has been published since 1911, *The New Book of Knowledge* (NBK) *Online* is the latest addition to the Grolier Online family of databases, which also includes *Encyclopedia Americana Online* and *Grolier Multimedia Encyclopedia Online* [RBB Ag 97]. Grolier is promoting *Americana* as the source for in-depth research, *Grolier Multimedia* as the source for quick reference, and NBK as the source for student reference*student* meaning primarily grade three through middle-school level. Subscription packages are available for all three databases, or for a combination of any two.

NBK *Online* has two main areas, Encyclopedia and NBK News. Selecting Encyclopedia from the main menu opens the Encyclopedia Home Page. From here, the user has four options: Search, Browse, Maps, and Help. An alternate way to search the database is by clicking on the lighthouse symbol that appears on every page; this takes the user directly to the Search screen. Search choices include natural keyword searches by full text or article title, refining a search using Boolean operators and wildcards, and limiting a search by selecting subject areas, such as Arts or Geography. Our full-text search for *space shuttle* yielded 28 hits, but was reduced to 12 hits when we checked the Technology subject box so that only technology-related documents would be searched. In Browse there are three options: Alphabetical Browse, Subject Browse, and Feature Browse. Feature Browse allows the user to browse the various special features that are some of the hallmarks of the print set—wonder questions, projects and experiments, and literary selections. The Maps feature is cumbersome. Instead of being able to access a map directly, users must navigate their way through a series of screens. Viewing a map of Miami, for example, requires going from the world map to a continent map to a U.S. map to a map of Florida. Coverage is inconsistent. Clicking on Miami leads to a map of the city with a link to the encyclopedia article, but clicking on Jacksonville leads only to an article, no map. The map of Chicago is out-of-date, showing the old location for the Museum of Contemporary Art.

Encyclopedia article elements vary, but may include photographs, artwork, maps, and flags, accessed from a toolbar at the top of the page. There may also be links to related articles, and to special features, such as fact boxes, activities, profiles of famous people, and literary selections. In addition, many articles have links to selected Internet sites recommended by the American Library Association. *Space shuttles*, for example, has links to six sites, each with a brief annotation and a reading level.

While encyclopedia content is updated quarterly, the other main area, NBK News, is updated weekly and features stories from six curricular areas: social studies, science and technology, animals and nature, arts and entertainment, and sports and recreation. During the week of November 8, the stories, called NewScoops, ranged from "hard news" (peace in Northern Ireland) to an article on Leonardo di Caprio, with links to pertinent encyclopedia articles. Archived news stories can be searched by subject area; the archives are naturally a bit thin now, but will certainly expand as time goes on. Users can do combined searches of encyclopedia articles and archived news stories by clicking on the lighthouse symbol.

NBK News is packed with special features. Fast Fact offers an informational tidbit. Word Challenge lists words from the week's stories; users are instructed to click on each word to get to the story in which it appears, and then to click on the word within the story to find a definition. There are six additional special features, two of which are featured on an alternating basis each week. During our review week, we found History Mystery, which offered information on the "other" Leonardo, Leonardo da Vinci; and Winners Circle, with a story on popular entertainers Brandy and Monica. Other alternating features include Earth Watch (environmental issues and activities), Wild Wonders (plants and animals), Time Again to Celebrate (special observances and occasions), and This 'n' That (miscellaneous topics). One of the unique characteristics of NBK is its interactivity, designed to meet the needs of teachers as well as students. Each NewScoop comes with a lesson plan that includes preview questions and printable follow-up activities. The extensive online teacher's guide provides numerous activities for using NewScoops across the curriculum, as well as for teaching Internet research skills.

An educational purpose combined with easy access, uncluttered screens, and lots of kid-friendly activities and features make NBK *Online* an attractive choice, especially for school libraries. In our review of the print version, we suggested that NBK might be a valuable resource for homeschoolers, and a home version of NBK *Online* will be available later this year.

History of the Internet: A Chronology, 1843 to the Present. By Christos J. P. Moschovitis and others. 1999. 312p. appendixes. bibliogs. glossary. illus. index. ABC-CLIO, $65 (1-57607-118-9). DDC: 004.67.

This work presents a readable history of perhaps the biggest technological phenomena of this century. The intent, according to the preface, is to weave "together . . . the many strands that make up the history of the Internet: technological, military, educational, corporate, and civilian." The chronology is current through the November 1998 announcement of America Online's plan to purchase Netscape. (To satisfy the curious, the year 1843 saw the publication of Ada Lovelace's *Sketch of the Analytical Engine*, a work that helped publicize Charles Babbage's ideas.)

Each of the first seven chronologically arranged chapters opens with five or six pages giving a descriptive overview of the span of years covered within that chapter, the work features year-by-year entries of key events. The descriptions are quite detailed compared to most chronologies, typically ranging from two hundred to more than eight hundred words per event. Because of the intertwining of the Internet with computers in general, *History of the Internet* can practically be considered a history of computing. Entries cover such topics as the invention of the transistor, the debut of the Macintosh, Usenet, and the first use of the term *cyberspace*. In addition to the chronology entries, there are several separate boxed entries in each chapter on such themes as "Biography," "From the Hacker File," "Media History," and "Netspeak." The various biographies feature a "who's who" of computing: Tim Berners-Lee, Bill Gates, Steve Jobs, and Mitchell Kapor, among others. The work's eighth chapter, "Future Trends," covers such topics as the Microsoft trial, advertising on the Internet, and Internet2. The work concludes with some statistical appendixes, bibliographies for each chapter, a brief glossary, biographies of the four authors, and a detailed index. Black-and-white photographs are scattered throughout the volume. The bibliographies are noteworthy for including recent works as well as historically significant works. Many entries in the bibliography, appropriately enough, are Web sites—with the caveat that the addresses are current as of January 1999.

There are places where the breezy style of the authors almost detracts from the information itself. A section heading in the introduction of chapter 2, for example, is titled "A *Sputnik* Cocktail: (Two Parts Stolichnaya and One Part Sour Grapes)." The lack of cross-references within the entries themselves is unfortunate. The 1998 entry *Linux Operating System Becomes a Cause Celebre*, for example, fails to refer the reader to an earlier entry, *Linus Torvalds Develops the Linux Operating System*, that appears in the 1991 section. One error was spotted—it is stated that the Yahoo! Web directory uses the AltaVista engine when in fact they switched to Inktomi in July 1998.

This work can justifiably find a home in the reference collection or in the circulating collection, because an interested layperson could read it cover to cover. Public, academic, and secondary-school libraries looking for a readable, nontechnical history of the Internet will want to purchase this reasonably priced volume. But do so quickly—the Internet is changing as this is written.

A to Zoo: Subject Access to Children's Picture Books. 5th ed. By Carolyn W. Lima and John A. Lima. 1998. 1,398p. indexes. Bowker, $65 (0-8352-3916-0). DDC: 011.62.

The new edition of *A to Zoo* lists more than 18,000 titles (4,000 more than the fourth edition) under more than 1,000 subjects. The format replicates those of earlier versions, with the goal still to facilitate the task of finding a picture book ("a fiction or nonfiction title with illustration occupying as much or more space than the text and with text vocabulary or concepts suitable for preschool to grade two") that fits a particular subject. An updated history of the picture book with recent sources and suggestions for further reading is found in the introduction.

The book is divided into five sections. The subject heading section contains an alphabetical list of subjects, with numerous cross-references and subheadings. The subject guide, arranged alphabetically, lists the picture books by author and title within subject categories. Entries in the bibliographic guide are alphabetically arranged by author (or title, if the author is unknown) and include title, illustrator, publisher, publication date, subjects, and ISBN (when available). Out-of-print materials are included, as many libraries still house such materials in their collections. Following the bibliographic guide is the title index, which includes an alphabetical list of all titles in this book, including the author's name followed by the page number of the listing in the bibliographic section. An illustrator index also gives titles and authors, followed by the page numbers in the bibliographic guide.

Comparable resources are Picture Books to Enhance the Curriculum [RBB Ag 97] and Adventuring with Books [RBB Ap 15 94]. Both provide annotations; Adventuring with Books also includes interest levels. Annotations are an asset in choosing a particular book, and the lack of them in A to Zoo limits its usefulness as a selection tool. However, Picture Books to Enhance the Curriculum has only 1,500 titles, and Adventuring with Books has 1,800. A to Zoo is by far the most comprehensive subject guide to picture books, and libraries that use it regularly will want the latest edition.

A Guide to Latin American, Caribbean, and U.S. Latino-Made Film and Video. Ed. by Karen Ranucci and Julie Feldman. 1998. 361p. bibliog. indexes. Scarecrow, $74.50 (0-8108-3285-2). DDC: 011.

This video guide was designed to expose U.S. audiences to films produced in Latin America by independent/national filmmakers and video makers. IMRE, the International Media Resource Exchange, has organized a Latin American Video Archive and Database, computerized information on more than 4,000 Latin American, Caribbean, and Latino film and video titles. They also created a reference and distribution service to assist users in locating and obtaining these titles. This volume represents the collective effort of educators, communications professionals, and arts programmers to evaluate materials from IMRE's list. The result is a directory of 445 films that are available for distribution in the U.S.

The guide is arranged by country with titles listed alphabetically. Each title entry provides the original title; English title where used; genre (animation, documentary, feature, etc.); language; if available in English or with subtitles; director; distributor; producer; names of evaluators; description of content; strengths and weaknesses; a section called "Introducing the Tape," to indicate what background information might be useful for U.S. audiences; suggestions for ways to incorporate the film or video into a course or class; suggested readings; and academic level, from elementary school to university, with "university" appearing most frequently. In some instances, complementary titles are designated. The evaluators are listed in the opening pages while indexes and a bibliography organized by countries, Argentina to Venezuela, complete the volume. The indexes are arranged by subject, distributor, and title.

This guide is easy to use and can be an aid to teachers and film students. Though designed primarily for those who would be using the films in an academic setting, the book would also be useful in academic and public libraries whose patrons desire more information on Latin American, Caribbean, and Latino film.

American Historical Fiction: An Annotated Guide to Novels for Adults and Young Adults. By Lynda G. Adamson. 1999. 416p. appendixes. indexes. Oryx, $49.95 (1-57356-067-7). DDC: 016.813.
World Historical Fiction: An Annotated Guide to Novels for Adults and Young Adults. By Lynda G. Adamson. 1999. 736p. appendixes. indexes. Oryx, $49.95 (1-57356-066-9). DDC: 016.80883.

Lynda Adamson has written several guides to historical fiction, including Literature Connections to American History, K–6 [RBB F 1 98], Literature Connections to American History, 7–12 (Libraries Unlimited, 1998), Recreating the Past: A Guide to American and World Historical Fiction for Children and Young Adults (Greenwood, 1994), and Reference Guide to Historical Fiction for Children and Young Adults (Greenwood, 1987). These two new volumes are updates of previous works, the fifth edition of Dickinson's American Historical Fiction by Virginia Brokaw Gerhardstein (1986) and World Historical Fiction by Daniel D. McGarry and Sarah Harriman White (1973). Adamson's volumes contain titles published since those previous guides appeared, including some published in 1998. However, she points out that she has not merely added more recent publications. Instead, she examined all the titles listed under Library of Congress catalog subject heading Historical Fiction, as well as several other headings, and selected review journals. She includes some titles that were left out of the previous guides. In addition, she includes titles that overlap with the previous guides but are classics, have sequels or prequels, or "contain settings rarely appearing in more recent historical fiction." Books selected for inclusion must have been reviewed, though this requirement was waived in the case of genres not receiving much critical attention, such as Christian fiction. Although the titles indicates that these volumes include works for young adults (meaning grades nine and up), this is somewhat misleading. Adamson includes only a small handful of works written specifically for young adults, preferring instead to use a symbol to indicate adult titles that young adults might also appreciate and enjoy.

Covering more than 3,300 works, American Historical Fiction is divided into 13 chronological periods from "North America before 1600" to "After 1976—the Late 20th Century," followed by five indexes: author, title, genre, geographic, and subject. Within the chronological sections, arrangement is alphabetical by author, with titles grouped alphabetically under their authors' names. Each title entry includes publication date, known reprints, number of pages, a brief descriptive annotation, setting, character, plot, sequels, and genres. Each title is numbered. World Historical Fiction covers more than 6,000 works and follows the same general format, except that its primary arrangement is by areas of the world, and then by time periods within each area. This arrangement can be awkward. Three of the six titles in Dorothy Dunnett's Lymond series appear under Europe 1492–1649, while the other three appear under The British Isles 1492–1649, with no cross-references from one section to the other. Each volume has two appendixes, award-winning books and books appropriate for young adults, preceding the indexes.

What Historical Novel Do I Read Next? (Gale, 1997), listing more than 7,000 titles, has more extensive indexing, including several character indexes, and provides information on authors and on historical accuracy. It includes older titles that Adamson leaves out because they are listed in the works she is building upon. In addition, its strict by-author arrangement make it easier to identify all the titles by an author or in a series. Adamson's two volumes provide coverage of more titles, based in part on a more flexible definition of historical fiction, which allows her to include works such as Loren D. Estleman's Motown, set in 1966. Her young adult designations are a useful feature, especially for students in the upper grades. Recommended for libraries that serve avid readers of historical fiction.

American Science Fiction Television Series of the 1950s. By Patrick Luciano and Gary Colville. 1998. 261p. bibliog. illus. indexes. McFarland, $48.50 (0-7864-0434-5). DDC: 016.79145.

McFarland seems to attract writers both knowledgeable and passionate about their subjects. This is certainly true for this reference work on the early days of sci-fi TV.

The two authors share a strong historical research bent as well as philosophical respect for this then-experimental genre. They have carefully reviewed the current literature on the 1950s sf series, dug deeply into primary documents, and apparently viewed every extant episode. While they sometimes overemphasize the high quality of the programs, the authors adequately justify their belief in the significance and social relevance of this TV genre, particularly in light of contemporaneous culture. Their basic tenet, explained in a lengthy introduction, is that science fiction television series demonstrated the moral and scientific ideals of the decade.

The main body of the text describes, in alphabetical order, 20 nationally syndicated series. The greatest coverage (about 60 pages) is given to Adventures of Superman. The introduction to the Superman chapter explains the writing/production history and the leading characters, and offers a little technical and syndication information. The authors do not sugarcoat the series, asserting that episodes from seasons three through six (at that point transitioning to color) are "witless and rather simple tales of little consequence." Rather, they try hard to provide an objective view of the program—occasionally disparaging the cuts and changes that syndicators have made over the years (e.g., eliminating the ending previews of the succeeding episode, coloring B/W shows, cutting scenes in order to fit in advertising time). The production staff and casts are then enumerated as are the plots of each episode (in chronological order).

The other series' entries range in length from three to 13 pages. They too include production and plot information. In some cases, only the episode titles are offered, mainly because no copies or descriptions of the episodes exist. In most cases, a picture of the opening screen or leading actor accompanies the series entry. The episode "signature" opening narrative is usually included as well. Surprisingly, little space is dedicated to the directors or actors themselves; the producers receive the most attention.

An extensive bibliography of source material follows the A–Z entries. Two indexes conclude the volume, one listing all the episode titles, and a general index principally of names. Writing is clear and competent, if sometimes opinionated.

American Science Fiction Television Series of the 1950s offers in-depth and inside information about a specialized television age and genre. Because of the later impact of such shows as *Star Trek* and *The Twilight Zone*, information about the programs of an earlier age can be very enlightening. Thus, for academic and large public library collections with TV and sf collections, this volume makes a significant contribution.

Animated Short Films: A Critical Index to Theatrical Cartoons. By Piotr Borowiec. 1998. 240p. chronology. index. Scarecrow, $45 (0-8108-3503-7). DDC: 016.79143.

Film Cartoons: A Guide to 20th-Century American Animated Features and Shorts. By Douglas McCall. 1998. 267p. appendix. bibliog. index. McFarland, $40 (0-7864-0584-8). DDC: 016.79143.

Following a brief history of the genre, *Animated Short Films* contains an alphabetical list of approximately 1,600 films from 1906 to 1997 under 39 minutes in length, originally produced for theatrical release. Since current availability on TV or video is the defining criteria, films from Columbia/Screen Gems, such as the Krazy Kat and Barney Google series, are not included. No distributor addresses are provided for persons who might want to purchase the films. Both major studios (e.g., Warner Brothers, Disney) and independents are represented, as are all types of animation (drawings, claymation, puppets, etc.). Although most films are American or English-language, some foreign titles are listed. Each entry provides title, year, director, studio, a brief summary that may include evaluative commentary, and a star rating (from awful to excellent). Indexes by director, year (Oscar winners and nominees are noted here, rather than in entries), and four-and five-star reviews complete the volume.

Film Cartoons has a broader focus, encompassing 238 feature films (e.g., *Snow White, Who Framed Roger Rabbit*) and features with animated sequences, such as *The Pink Panther* title sequence; as well as 1,376 animated shorts. Despite the book's subtitle, some foreign shorts are included. The author notes that some selectivity according to studio, character, and series characteristics went into the compilation of entries, which is not comprehensive. Entries are listed alphabetically by title and note release date, Oscar winner/nominee, director, studio, characters, voices, production notes, and plot line. There is more information for features, including ratings, critical notes, extensive credits, honors received, and animation highlights. Concluding the volume are an appendix on animation studios and a name index.

In both titles, ratings are those of the compilers. Neither book has a character index, which would aid in finding all available Betty Boop, Mister Magoo, or Wallace and Gromit shorts. Libraries that want one catalog more representative of the genre will probably choose McCall's book, since it doesn't omit works for lack of current availability. Libraries with film collections will want both, since there are numerous listings unique to each book.

Building an ESL Collection for Young Adults: A Bibliography of Recommended Fiction and Nonfiction for Schools and Public Libraries. By Laura Hibbets McCaffery. 1998. 184p. appendixes. bibliog. indexes. Greenwood, $39.95 (0-313-29937-4). DDC: 016.4282.

Designed for librarians and educators, this annotated bibliography of more than 500 items lists fiction and nonfiction English as a second language (ESL) sources for young adults. Compiled by a librarian with extensive literacy experience, the book begins with an introduction that gives a brief history of ESL materials and usage, criteria for books selected, and an explanation of the organization of entries. The bibliography is divided into eight subject areas, such as "Adventure, Mystery and Suspense" and "Nature and Science," with nonfiction and fiction titles listed separately in each section. Each entry, listed alphabetically by author, includes complete bibliographic citations with ISBN, price, Fry Reading Level, and interest level by grade or age. The annotations are concise and end with Library of Congress Subject Headings. Two appendixes list nonprint distributors and selected publishers of print materials. Concluding the volume are author, subject, title, and ethnic group indexes.

The strengths of this bibliography are the ethnic group coverage, precise annotations, a good balance between classic and current selections, a listing of related Internet sites, and accessible indexes. An omission is the lack of a bibliography of pertinent professional resources, such as La Vergne Rosow's excellent *Light'n Lively Reads for ESL, Adult, and Teen Readers: A Thematic Bibliography* [RBB O 15 96]. Also missing are explanations of the Fry Reading Level and how the compiler arrived at the interest levels she assigns. Only four CD-ROMs are listed among the exciting array of educational ones on the market. There are no works of fiction under "Sports"; Matt Christopher's large inventory of easy-to-read sports stories would seem to be good candidates for this section. Finally, what is a 10-year-old book on AIDS doing in a current bibliography?

This book is recommended with reservations. It is suggested that school and public libraries purchasing this title also consider the previously mentioned *Light'n Lively Reads for ESL, Adult, and Teen Readers*, which provides information on theory and practice as well as a wider selection of materials.

Children's Books about Religion. By Patricia Pearl Dole. 1999. 230p. indexes. Libraries Unlimited, $32 (1-57308-515-1). DDC: 016.2.

Dole has compiled a number of other bibliographies of books for children, including several on religion. Because she has already covered older titles in previous works, she generally limits herself here to books published after 1990. More than 700 titles for preschool through middle-school level are listed, arranged in 17 chapters. The first 10 chapters cover general themes and various aspects of Christianity. Chapters 11 and 12 cover Judaism; chapters 13, 14, 15, and 16 cover Native American religions, Buddhism, Hinduism, and Islam, respectively; and the last chapter covers "other," including Maori and African religions.

Each chapter is subdivided—chapter 10, "Christian-Church History and Biography," for example, has sections on the Crusades, saints, and contemporary biography, among others. For each book, the author provides author, title, publisher, date, price, and ISBN, followed by a brief evaluative annotation. Both fiction and nonfiction are represented, although, with some exceptions, works of fiction are not identified. No age ranges are provided. Chapters end with discussions of "older and noteworthy" resources; titles cited here are accompanied only by author, publisher, and date. There are two indexes, author and title, and subject. The indexes cite entry numbers rather than page numbers, each title in the bibliography being consecutively numbered.

For libraries that need to build their collections in the area of religion, this could be a useful tool. Though many of the books are from mainstream publishers, many others come from religions publishing houses that are not as well known. *Children's Books about Religion* is recommended for religious schools or public libraries whose patrons have a strong interest in religious topics.

Children's Literature: A Guide to Information Sources. By Margaret W. Denman-West. 1998. 187p. indexes. Libraries Unlimited, $38.50 (1-56308-448-1). DDC: 016.8088.

Guides to Collection Development for Children and Young Adults. By John T. Gillespie and Ralph J. Folcarelli. 1998. 191p. indexes. Libraries Unlimited, paper, $23 (1-56308-532-1). DDC: 011.62.

As often happens in the reference-publishing world, two seemingly similar titles on children's literature have come out at the same time. What's unusual here is that they're both from the same publisher. So what's the difference?

Gillespie, author/editor of several works, including *Best Books for Children* (5th ed., Bowker, 1994), and coauthor Folcarelli have produced a bibliography intended to be used primarily for collection development in libraries serving children and young adults. Based in part upon sections of their *Guides to Library Collection Development* (Libraries Unlimited, 1994), the new work has more than 600 annotated entries for bibliographic sources, most of which were published from 1985 through the beginning of 1997. It is divided into five sections: periodicals, sources for children/young adults combined, and sources for children, for young adults, and for professionals. The chapters dealing with sources for children and young adults are further subdivided into such areas as social studies, awards and prizes, audiovisual materials, multiculturalism, genres, reference books, authors, and computer technology. Annotations are both descriptive and critical. Many titles that are not primary collection-development tools, such as Gale's biographical series Something about the Author, are noted because they contain valuable bibliographic data.

Denman-West's *Children's Literature: A Guide to Information Sources*, part of Libraries Unlimited's Reference Sources in the Humanities series, is an annotated bibliography of more than 400 bibliographies and other reference works published from 1985 to 1997. Young-adult-related resources are included despite the book's title. It is arranged in chapters on subjects such as award-winning books, multicultural literature, core periodicals, reference books, nonprint media, special collections, professional associations, and the Internet. Chapters are further subdivided into unique areas; for instance, "Recommended Reading" has categories for picture books, special needs, and read-alouds. Although there is extensive overlap with the Gillespie/Folcarelli title, the scope of this volume is much wider and includes many sources that would be used for general reference rather than collection development. *The Information Please Kids' Almanac* (Houghton, 1992), *Children's Book Illustration and Design* (v.1, PBC International, 1992; v.2, 1997), *The Children's Literature Web Guide* textbook *Children and Books* (9th ed., Harper Collins, 1997) are examples of titles unique to this bibliography. An odd omission is *International Companion Encyclopedia of Children's Literature* (Routledge, 1996). Annotations are authoritative and evaluative.

Both books have author/title and subject indexes. Public and school libraries may gravitate toward *Guides to Collection Devleopment for Children and Young Adults* as a more practical purchase, but most will also want *Children's Literature: A Guide to Information Sources* for its unique entries and different approach, which will be useful in research on children's literature.

Children's Nonfiction for Adult Information Needs: An Annotated Bibliography. By Rosemarie Riechel. 1998. 152p. indexes. Linnet Professional Pubs.; dist. by Shoe String, $30 (0-208-02447-6). DDC: 016.8088.

How do you deal with new adult readers? Sometimes information is presented in sophisticated language they can't read. Yet children's books can be condescending to the mature mind. On the other hand, some children's titles offer good information for even the most well-read adult. This annotated bibliography tries to identify those youth nonfiction titles that can provide needed material for adults.

The list contains more than 175 nonfiction books that might be found in public library children's departments. Materials are classified into 15 popular subject areas such as social sciences, sports, and technology. Materials were chosen from library and literacy program recommendations, and had to meet the following criteria: clear and easy reading, accurate and well researched, appealing illustrations, popular but complex topics, and few "childish" features. The titles also had to be reasonably available and current. The author does not intend to be exhaustive, but to include the most popular subjects and valuable titles.

Each entry is between a half to a full page long, with an extensive description and analysis in terms of adult needs. Features such as series, glossary, bibliography, and index are also noted. Examples of the selected titles include Facts On File's *How Skyscrapers Are Made*; Scholastic's *We Shall Not Be Moved: The Women's Factory Strike of 1909*; titles in the pet books series published by T.F.H.; and titles in the Eyewitness series published by Knopf. At the end of each subject section are listed between one and 15 related titles. The volume concludes with an author/title and a subject index.

This resource should prove useful for libraries serving adults that have special reading needs. Even apart from their value for the limited-proficiency adult reader, the selections are strong enough to be considered for most public libraries—and probably many high-school libraries as well. Some public libraries now interfile children's and adult titles, which makes it particularly easy to offer these kinds of books to adults. Even in libraries where the adult and children's books are separated, however, the books cited in *Children's Nonfiction for Adult Information Needs* would probably fit in well with other more "adult" offerings.

Feature Films, 1950–1959: A United States Filmography. By Alan G. Fetrow. 1999. 712p. bibliog. index. McFarland, $72.50 (0-7864-0427-2). DDC: 016.79143.

Some of the best and worst movies of all time were produced during the 1950s: lavish musicals, cheesy horror flicks, gripping dramas, and more. As television sets became a fixture in more and more homes, Hollywood feared this new invention and fought for viewers with an array of special film processes and special effects. While the small screens of 1950s television flickered black and white, the movie screens of the decade flashed Technicolor, Eastmancolor, DeLuxe color and more in wide-screen CinemaScope, Vista Vision, and Cinerama formats.

This is a simple, no-nonsense listing of all those movies—no pictures but plenty of pertinent detail. Film titles are presented alphabetically, and each entry is given a unique number that is used in the index instead of a page number. The entries are listed in double columns of text with approximately five to seven film descriptions per page. Each entry includes the year of release, name of the studio, cast (character names are provided only for Oscar nominees or winners and top-grossing films of the year; historical or nonfictional character names are also given), technical credits, running time, and availability on video or laser disc. For musicals, song titles and composers are listed. A brief synopsis of the plot is provided, and other kinds of recognition, such as appearance on "Ten Best" lists, are indicated. Alternate titles and titles used in Great Britain are mentioned, as are film formats, such as 3-D, color, or wide-screen. Subsequent remakes are noted, and in the case of original black-and-white films, computerized colorization is disclosed. Additional features include a brief bibliography and a list of award-winning and nominated films.

A solid, specialized source, this will be most appropriate for larger reference collections, particularly those already owning Fetrow's two previous works, *Sound Films, 1927–1939: A United States Filmography* (McFarland, 1992) and *Feature Films, 1940–1949: A United States Filmography* (McFarland, 1994).

Fiction Sequels for Readers 10 to 16: An Annotated Bibliography of Books in Succession. 2d ed. By Vicki Anderson. 1998. 176p. index. McFarland, paper, $29.95 (0-7864-0185-0). DDC: 016.8.
Sequels in Children's Literature: An Annotated Bibliography of Books in Succession or with Shared Themes and Characters, K–6. By Vicki Anderson. 1998. 320p. index. McFarland, paper, $35 (0-7864-0285-7). DDC: 016.8.

"I loved this book, what's the next one in the series?" Children love series, whether Clifford and Spot or the works of J. R. R. Tolkien and Laura Ingalls Wilder; so these books, one a new title and one an update of a previous title, are welcome.

The author, a practicing librarian, has accumulated titles over the years in an effort to help her patrons. The results are lists of around 7,500 titles for readers in kindergarten through grade six, and approximately 3,000 titles for children ages 10 to 16, arranged alphabetically by author. Although Anderson states that literary value was considered, readability and popularity were also factors in her selection. Books are nearly all hardcover, and all in English, although some translations are included, such as the Pippi Longstocking series. The introduction to *Fiction Sequels* indicates that 1960 was chosen as the beginning date for selection, but if some books in a series were written before that year, they are included as well. The starting date for *Sequels* appears to be the same. In-print status was not relevant. In both volumes, coverage extends into the mid-1990s. *Fiction Sequels* adds works published since the first edition appeared in 1990. A few series, such as Brian Jacques' Redwall series, appear in both volumes.

Each entry includes basic bibliographic information and usually a one-sentence plot summary. If an author has written more than one series, they are separated. General age categories are also noted only in *Sequels*. A few cross-references exist for series written by more than one author. Separate indexes by age group and by main character would have been useful.

Similar works exist, such as Susan Roman's *Sequences: An Annotated Guide to Children's Fiction in Series* (ALA, 1985). *Fantasy Literature for Children and Young Adults* (4th ed., Bowker, 1995) covers many genre sequels and series. Gale's *Something about the Author* provides information on sequence titles, including older series not covered in Anderson's books, syndicates (Nancy Drew, Hardy Boys), and popular paperback series, such as Fear Street. Anderson's volumes are not definitive or comprehensive, but are recommended as collection-development and readers' advisory tools.

The Harlem Renaissance: An Annotated Reference Guide for Student Research. By Marie E. Rodgers. 1998. 139p. illus. index. Libraries Unlimited, $28 (1-56308-580-1). DDC: 016.700.

Faint praise is all this slim volume gets. Meant for junior-and senior-high students, this bibliography describes fewer than 200 titles which shed light on people or major influences of the Harlem Renaissance. No fiction or foreign-language works are included, but, other than that, selection criteria are sketchy. The author, a school librarian, tried to include "primary" works, mostly published within the last 15 years. Books were included even if only a chapter or a few pages are relevant. Some of the sources are repeated in different categories. Nonprint materials include only six videos and two sound recordings.

Arrangement of titles is alphabetical by author within 20 chapters, organized in six parts, beginning with "Historical Overview and Biographical References" and then focusing on "Notable Contributors," "Literature and Writing," "Visual Arts," "Performing Arts," and "Sports and Entertainment." Each chapter gets a brief introduction. Well-written annotations are a paragraph or two, giving highlights and features of the titles (photos, arrangement, grade level).

The book's usefulness is hard to judge because organization seems unfocused and because so many sources have been omitted. It seems that the only periodical cited is a 1991 issue of *Cobblestone*. Not included anywhere are the well-reviewed *Emergence of the Harlem Renaissance* (Garland, 1996) and *The Oxford Companion to African American Literature* [RBB F 15 97], not to mention Jessie Carney Smith's *Notable Black American Women* (Gale, 1992). There are no listings for Web sites, such as the Library of Congress' *African American Mosaic*.

Perry's *The Harlem Renaissance* (Garland, 1982) is an annotated bibliography featuring writers of the period and meant for adults. Since there's not a comparable current title, many high-school libraries will want to add this bibliography on such a popular topic. Those that don't won't miss it.

Library Resources for Singers, Coaches, and Accompanists: An Annotated Bibliography, 1970–1997. By Ruthann Boles McTyre. 1998. 151p. index. Greenwood, $65 (0-313-30266-9). DDC: 016.783.

The head librarian at the Crouch Music and Fine Arts Library of Baylor University has compiled 471 annotated entries for print and electronic resources of interest to singers and those who train and accompany them. The number of resources listed is considerably more, however, because other works are frequently mentioned in annotations, and some entries for series consist of lists of the individual monographs. The emphasis is on opera, musical theater, and the solo voice. Only English-language works are included.

A preliminary section, "General Music Reference," was compiled by Ida Reed, coauthor with Vincent H. Duckles of *Music Reference and Research Materials: An Annotated Bibliography* [RBB F 15 98]. The body of the bibliography is arranged in 10 chapters covering various forms and approaches. "Dictionaries and Encyclopedias"; "Preparation, Accompanying, Coaching"; and "Internet and Electronic Resources" are examples of chapter headings. Most chapters have several subdivisions. Within these sections, works are arranged alphabetically by main entry heading, usually an author.

Qualitative criteria or procedures for selecting materials are not explained, other than that they should "aid and enhance the study of voice." The annotations are rarely evaluative, only a few venturing to suggest a work is "good" or "interesting" or "useful." Citations provide the standard basic information. Three indexes (author, title, and subject) make up a major portion of the volume. The subject index boasts two levels of subdivision, so that most entries are fairly specific. However, important topics are sometimes hidden under broad general topics rather than having separate headings for direct access, violating a standard practice for alphabetical subject indexes. Examples include *auditions*, *breathing exercises*, *diction*, and *vocational guidance*, all of which are hidden under the very general heading *singing*. Because the entire bibliography is about singing, this is a heading that should have been limited to very broad works about singing in general.

The essential resources are included in this bibliography. Singers and their coaches, accompanists, and librarians should find it a useful compilation.

Radio Programs, 1924–1984: A Catalog of Over 1,800 Shows. By Vincent Terrace. 1999. 399p. appendix. illus. index. McFarland, $75 (0-7864-0351-9). DDC: 016.79144.

The author is best known for his reference works on television history, facts, and trivia. This latest work updates his earlier *Radio's Golden Years: The Encyclopedia of Radio Programs, 1930–1960* (Barnes, 1981), which listed and briefly described 1,500 programs. The new work follows the same format and adds 30 years of information. Entries on 1,835 entertainment shows are alphabetically arranged and generally include a description along with names of cast members, regulars, announcers, vocalists and musicians, producers, dates, networks, running times, and miscellaneous facts. Many entries also contain a familiar opening ("It's Wednesday night so we take you now to 'Duffy's Tavern' . . .") and occasionally a closing announcement. Not included are religious, sports, and news series. An appendix lists 32 "lost" programs about which little is known.

The many reworked entries provide added value. The entry on *The Spike Jones Show*, for example, now includes more network information, a short paragraph describing the show, changed spelling for one of the characters (Fred Gass), an additional cast member, an announcer, and a typical opening announcement. Exact dates for runs are given; *Radio's Golden Years* included only the date of the first broadcast. There are fewer black and white photographs, and they are from a different source than those in the earlier work. Some entries, like that on *Ella Fitzgerald*, are short, giving only the name, type of program, network, dates, and one or two sentences of description.

John Dunning's *On The Air: The Encyclopedia of Old Time Radio* [RBB S 1 98] treats 1,500 programs from the 1930s, 1940s, and 1950s. His entry on *The Jack Benny Program* is more than seven pages, in contrast to slightly more than one page in Terrace. Dunning also includes survey articles and bibliographies, making his an important work in the field. Terrace's work spans a greater length of time but lacks the depth of Dunning's. Both reference works deserve a place in broadcast history collections and will be valuable additions to public, high-school, and academic libraries.

Science Fiction Serials: A Critical Filmography of the 31 Hard SF Cliffhangers; with an Appendix of the 37 Serials with Slight SF Content. By Roy Kinnard. 1998. 223p. appendix. bibliog. filmography. illus. index. McFarland, $39.95 (0-7864-0545-7). DDC: 016.79143.

A generation of kids with free Saturdays enjoyed movie serials, 15–20 minutes of action and cliffhanger endings. Especially with the advent of popular SF writing, science fiction serials were a big draw and presaged the science fiction craze of the 1950s. Covering all 31 SF serials, from *The Vanishing* to *Panther Girl of the Congo* this book is the result of in-depth research and commitment. Author Kinnard was able to get valuable information from Buster Crabbe and Jean Rogers (of *Flash Gordon* fame) and other actors, film curators, and librarians.

Serial entries are arranged in order of original release and include the following: production crew, cast, chapter titles, story (from one to three pages), commentary, and present-day distributor. At least one stock photo accompanies each entry; up to four black-and-white photos or posters may be included. Probably the most interesting section is the comment one in which Kinnard discusses (and sometimes editorializes about) production and studio details, actors' backgrounds and future careers, and off-shoot films and TV programs. He notes how footage and costumes were shared among series; applauds Henry MacRae, who produced the *Flash Gordon* series, for revitalizing serials for the sound stage; and derides *Superman* producer Sam Katzman, who helped push the serials toward their demise. The Board has only two complaints. The story line for each serial is presented uninterrupted, so the reader cannot tell where individual episodes begin and end. On a more minor note, Kinnard is especially generous in his appraisal of actress Linda Stirling and her beauty—but doesn't include any pictures of her.

The writing is clear and succinct, and occasional opinions are backed up with sufficient evidence. An appendix lists 37 additional serials with incidental science-fiction elements. This is followed by a brief bibliography and an index. For the academic or public library with a strong SF or serious film readership, this volume is an entertaining and useful, though not vital, addition to the field.

The Universal Silents: A Filmography of the Universal Picture Manufacturing Company, 1912–1929. By Richard E. Braff. 1999. 675p. appendix. bibliog. index. McFarland, $135 (0-7864-0287-3). DDC: 016.79143.

Although other cinema histories document a variety of artists, companies, and movies during the silent film era, this filmography focuses on the output of one company, Universal Motion Pictures. Universal, which began when several film production companies joined forces in 1912, is the oldest and still most active producer of pictures for the large screen and television. This volume provides a listing of more than 9,300 feature, split-reel, and one-, two-, and three-reel films, as well as 74 serials. Not included are documentaries, newsreels, cartoons, travelogues, and other nonfeature films.

The entries are arranged alphabetically by film title, and each entry is assigned a number. The index, which lists the performers, directors, and producers, refers to these numbers rather than page numbers to guide the reader to an entry. The format for each entry consists of the film title, release date, copyright date, producer, director, scenarist, author, length (in numbers of reels), and major cast members. There are no plot summaries. The preface provides an overview of the merger and development of several companies into Universal, and the introduction discusses some of the difficulties the author encountered in gathering information, because Universal's silent film production records are not available.

An appendix of serials and their episodes lists 74 serials alphabetically, from *Ace of Scotland Yard* to *Wolves of the North*. Episode titles are also listed alphabetically; no other information is provided. A brief bibliography and an index complete the volume.

Because of its comprehensive coverage of a single studio, this title is more specialized than Magill's *Survey of Cinema: Silent Films* (Salem, 1982) and the *Silent Film* volume of the 12-volume *Motion Picture Guide* (recently reprinted in a single volume called *The Silents: Silent Feature Films, 1910–36*, December Press, Box 302, Highland Park, IL 60035, $49.40, 0-913204-36-6). *Universal Silents* is recommended for large public libraries and academic libraries, especially those that support a film curriculum.

Internet Resources and Services for International Business: A Global Guide. By Lewis-Guodo Liu. 1998. 389p. indexes. Oryx, paper, $44.95 (1-57356-119-3). DDC: 025.04.

With the increasing globalization of business, the Internet will become of paramount importance as a resource for business, students, researchers, and reference librarians. This guide breaks new ground in seeking to bring some control to the ebb and flow of business Web sites. It covers more than 175 countries and regions and includes more than 2,500 sites. Some countries are not included, since Net access has not yet permeated certain areas of the world.

The criteria for inclusion is explicit: only those sites sponsored by business, government, or higher education were considered. The editor felt that these organizations have the necessary resources—human and technical—to sustain a commitment to long-term Internet access. Web sites created by individuals are not included. Sites were located using standard search engines, such as Alta Vista, Lycos, and Yahoo. Almost all of the sites listed have free access. However, some are free only to certain organizations, such as federal government depository libraries.

The guide is organized into seven chapters, each of which focuses on a region of the world. Within regions the countries are listed alphabetically. Each country description contains five categories: general information, economy, business and trade, business travel, and contact information. Each individual entry contains the Web page title, the URL, and a brief annotation. There are three indexes: a Web site title index, a country index, and a subject index.

Of course, the value of any printed reference source on the Internet depends on permanence of the Web sites listed. The compiler admits that this is a problem but claims that approximately 92 per cent of the sites were still valid when he checked them a year after the project began. One must still ask whether a more valuable format for this guide would be a serial with at least quarterly updates. Or perhaps a more effective way of keeping the resource up to date would be to publish it as a Web resource itself. Despite the inevitable currentness problem, however, the comprehensiveness of this source makes it a useful complement to titles such as *International Business Information: How to Find It, How to Use It* [RBB My 1 98], which is much more selective in the Web sites it includes. Recommended for business collections where there is a high level of Web-oriented international business questions.

Children's Book Awards Annual, 1998. By Matt Berman and Marigny J. Dupuy. 1998. 125p. illus. indexes. Libraries Unlimited, $18.50 (1-56308-649-2). DDC: 028.52.

This new book, aimed at librarians, educators, and parents, provides descriptive and critical reviews of 150 books given selected "major" national awards and/or appearing on notable lists for 1998. Seven awards and eight lists, among them American Library Association Notable Children's Books and *Booklist* Editors' Choice, are included. The volume was put together by two elementary-school teachers, who are also children's book reviewers, and is intended to be an annual series.

The goal is to provide reviews indicating what children like and what parents and teachers want to find in children's books. The introduction notes the awards and lists used. It also deals with how the authors assigned age levels for books, how they decided which were picture books, and how they used a PG rating for books containing "sex, drugs, rough language, or gore." Additionally, a genre and type were chosen for each book.

Books are listed alphabetically by title in four sections: picture books, chapter books, young adult books, and the authors' "personal picks." Small black-and-white photographs of book covers ornament some pages. Each entry gives the title, author, illustrator, price, publisher, ISBN, pages, ages, type, genre/subject, and awards/lists. This information is accompanied by a brief synopsis and a paragraph of evaluation. The four main sections are followed by eight indexes: Author, Illustrator, Title, Awards, Lists, Publishers, Type, and Genre. The careful indexing is a handy feature.

The most curious characteristic of this work is that the authors have left out any citations to reviews which each of these distinguished books received in journals such as *Booklist*, *Horn Book*, *School Library Journal*, and the like. This is especially unfortunate because the authors' own comments include entirely too many examples of overly general words, such as *wonderful*, *lovely*, and *terrific*. Since parents are invited to use the book, an indication of whether the selected titles are available in paperback or other formats, such as videos and sound recordings, would have been useful. Finally, the introduction needs to define terms used in the indexing such as *type* and *genre*. These are almost always difficult to explain to parents and others not acquainted with literary terms.

This having been said, the book is a useful addition to the award literature for children's books. It is unique in gathering together some of the major lists of best books which are found in the journal literature. Moreover, it is nice to see a reference book of this type with an affordable price. *Children's Books: Awards and Prizes*, published every few years by the Children's Book Council, lists more awards but does not include plot summaries or comments and, at $75, is much more expensive. *Children's Book Awards Annual* is recommended with reservations for public and school libraries, with the hope that future editions will remedy the shortcomings noted here.

The American Desk Encyclopedia. 1998. 892p. charts. illus. maps. Oxford, $21.95 (0-19-521465-X). DDC: 031.

Oxford's *American Desk Encyclopedia*, the companion volume to *The Oxford American Desk Dictionary* (1998) and *The Oxford American Desk Thesaurus* (1998), was, like these two titles, created for the home and middle-school through undergraduate markets. This compact volume contains more than 15,000 entries, 35,000 cross-references that are indicated by capital letters within entries, and 300 illustrations, as well as a 16-page color world atlas. Its format is alphabetical to allow users to locate information quickly. An international team of writers, scholars, and advisors has succeeded in their goal to include and emphasize cultures beyond the English speaking world by including a proportion of entries on international cultures, people, and religion to reflect the idea of a global society.

With an audience of secondary-school students particularly in mind, compilers give greatest emphasis to core subjects such as science and technology, history, humanities, and politics. The entries are written clearly and concisely so younger students, ages 13 or 14, for example, can easily understand concepts that are new to them. For the general or college reader, articles that discuss popular culture topics (film, sports, popular music, and so forth), current events, plants, animals, places, and important individuals are also given coverage. Articles on AIDS and nations are among those that include useful statistics. Country entries include a gray box stating geographic area, population, capital, and the population of the capital for quick reference. All measurements are given in both American and metric units. A brief history of the pertinent letter of the Roman alphabet begins each section. *The American Desk Encyclopedia* is a worthwhile and affordable purchase for home reference and for public, high-school, and undergraduate libraries needing a reliable one-volume resource for ready reference.

Dictionary of Historical Allusions and Eponyms. By Dorothy Auchter. 1998. 295p. index. ABC-CLIO, $65 (0-87436-950-9). DDC: 031.02.

Authored by a reference librarian at Ohio State University, this dictionary provides the contemporary meaning and history for approximately 550 words and phrases from all eras of history, including the twentieth century. Phrases to be included were selected from historically verifiable people and events from the Bible, ancient history, and folklore. Items originating in mythology or fictional works are excluded. The purpose is "to provide greater insight and historical background for these figures of speech than is currently available in reference literature."

Each entry includes a terse definition and a longer (approximately three paragraphs) history of the main entry. Written in a chatty, storytelling style, the longer portions are as delightful to read as they are informative. Every entry concludes with a list of sources (usually two to five) from which information was taken. A subject index groups entries under broad headings.

Obvious titles to which this volume can be compared include *Facts On File Encyclopedia of Word and Phrase Origins* [RBB D 1 97], Laurence Urdang's *Idioms and Phrases Index* (Gale, 1983), and *The American Heritage Dictionary of Idioms* [RBB D 15 97]. Although some of the content of Auchter's book is duplicated in other sources, a substantial amount is not. *Haussmanization* ("to restore and upgrade deteriorating urban areas") and *salt, not worth one's* are examples of entries that do not commonly appear in other sources. Additionally, the definitions in Auchter are often more clear than in other sources.

This dictionary will provide depth to a collection of similar sources and is recommended for larger libraries. Smaller libraries should also strongly consider purchasing the book, since it is easy to understand, attractive for browsers, and less expensive than more comprehensive titles.

DK Children's Illustrated Encyclopedia. 1998. 644p. illus. index. DK, $39.95 (0-7894-2787-7). DDC: 031.

The Kingfisher Children's Encyclopedia. 1998. 500p. illus. index. Kingfisher, $35 (0-7534-5134-4). DDC: 031.

Here are two attractive single-volume encyclopedias designed for children in grades three through eight.

DK *Children's Illustrated Encyclopedia* is a revision of *The Random House Children's Encyclopedia* [RBB Ja 1 & 15 94], which was itself a revised edition of *Dorling Kindersley Children's Illustrated Encyclopedia* (1991). Population figures, names of countries, and current events have been updated. Some main entries have been dropped, while others, such as *Gulf War* and *Lewis and Clark*, have been added. Format and illustrations are basically the same. The book is organized alphabetically, with more than 450 main entries and 1,500 subentries, beginning with *Aboriginal Australians* and ending with *Zoos*.

Each main entry covers one or two pages except for those that consider major countries, which are given four to six pages. *See also* references are boxed with the heading "Find Out More." Each entry begins with a short explanatory introduction. Under this are subentries, which are brief paragraphs providing additional information. *History of farming*, for example, includes the subentries *medieval farming* and *agricultural revolution*. Some entries include time lines. The volume opens with generally easy-to-follow instructions on how to use the book. However, some children may have difficulty locating needed items on a specific page.

Each page is lavishly illustrated (photographs, diagrams, drawings, cutaways, maps), with each illustration fully captioned. Some portions of double-spread maps and pictures are lost in the tight gutter. All the continents and major countries of the world have special map pages. These large-size maps show main regions, physical features, major cities, and some historical sites. Also on the map pages are the flag(s), a box of important statistics (e.g., population, area, currency, etc.), and small photographs of people and places. At the back of the volume is a 15-page index. A running index, arranged alphabetically, is at the top of most pages, leading to additional information. Near the end of the encyclopedia is a 22-page section entitled "Fact Finder," which provides a quick reference under these broad topics such as history and science.

Also arranged alphabetically, *The Kingfisher Children's Encyclopedia* offers more than 350 main entries with numerous subentries. The articles range from one to three pages. *See also* references appear in boxed areas. Boxes also contain key dates, essential data, and extra information. All main entries begin with a concise definition of the subject. More than 2,000 full-color illustrations (drawings, photographs, diagrams, cutaways, maps) have informative captions. The maps are smaller than those in DK.

A 12-page "Fact Finder" provides additional facts, figures, and other quick reference information via a world map, tables and charts, and time lines. There are also capsule biographies of artists, writers, composers and musicians, scientists and inventors, philosophers and reformers, and explorers. The volume closes with a one-page "Highlights of the 20th Century" and an index.

Coverage in *Kingfisher* and DK is very similar. Articles on countries are longer in DK, but *Kingfisher* covers more individual countries. For example, *Kingfisher* has separate entries for Argentina and Brazil, in addition to its four-page treatment of South America, while DK surveys all of South America in a single six-page article (up from two pages in the previous edition). DK's British origin is still apparent in the amount of space it allots to Australia (eight pages) and New Zealand (three pages). *Kingfisher* has science-related main entries (*big bang, black hole, wavelength*) not found in DK, while DK seems to have more coverage of history. As might be expected, given their reputation for high-quality visual presentations, DK's illustrations are generally more attractive. With their minimal amount of text, neither of these is an in-depth reference work, but both are visually stimulating, accurate, concise browsing encyclopedias for general library use and for families.

Kidbits. By Jenny Tesar. 1998. 320p. illus. index. Blackbirch, $29.95 (1-56711-169-6). DDC: 031.02.

The World Almanac for Kids, 1999. Ed. by Elaine Israel. 1998. 320p. illus. index. World Almanac Books, $16.95 (0-88687-827-6); paper, $9.95 (0-88687-826-8). DDC: 031.02.

Here are two titles that complement each other and will be used with enthusiasm by youngsters in school and at home. *The World Almanac for Kids* is attractive, easy to use, and well indexed, and a good introduction to more thorough almanacs like its parent, *The World Almanac*. Short facts, questions, and lists are grouped by subject in alphabetical order, beginning with *animals, art, and books* and ending with *weather, weights and measures,* and *world history*. Drawings, time lines, charts, and black-and-white photos (flags, maps, and license plates are in color) are sprinkled throughout the text. Nice features of the 1999 edition are the many Web sites listed, new words, and book awards. Reading the table in the section on countries is made easier by the fact that country names are displayed on the table's left and right sides. Indexing is adequate (*recycling* is included but not other words such as garbage, plastic, trash, or waste), and *see* references exist (Burma *see* Myanmar; symbols *see signs and symbols*). Problems for libraries may be the sections designed to encourage writing in the book, such as *puzzles* and *budgeting*. Reviews quoted on the back, "won't stay on the bookshelf" and "a must for every 8-to-12-year-old's library," are still true.

While Kidbits is attractive and fun, we can't be quite as enthusiastic about it, although it bills itself as "the first all-visual reference to present vital facts and statistics about kids." Organized in 17 sections, such as U.S. population characteristics, money, school, sports, food, and health, the book has charts, graphs, maps, and a little text. Graphics are imaginative and well done, showing the value of a college degree in mortarboards, or how math scores "stack up" in pencils. Every colorful page presents information, but its value or purpose isn't always clear. Emphasis is definitely on the popular, with separate chapters for entertainment, music, television, and movies; the chapter on food is heavy on snacks and fast foods. There's some carelessness and oversimplification (inclusion of the District of Columbia in "least populous states" and "states with the highest incomes"; motor vehicles not on the list of "products causing the most injuries"). Sources for the numerous graphs include the U.S. Bureau of the Census,

National Science Foundation, Boy Scouts of America, and dozens of commercial concerns such as Payless Shoe Source, Bausch & Lomb, and *Video Store Magazine*. *Kidbits* is a fun browsing item for ages 10 and up (though older kids may be put off by the childish-looking cover), but *The World Almanac for Kids* has more value as a reference tool.

Oxford American Children's Encyclopedia. 9v. Ed. by Ann Keene. 1998. 1,712p. charts. illus. index. maps. Oxford, $300 (0-19-511081-1). DDC: 031.

Oxford American Children's Encyclopedia is an updated, and in many ways a livelier, version of its British predecessor, the seven-volume *Oxford Children's Encyclopedia* (1994). "Created especially for American children ages 8–12," it contains 2,081 articles, including 650 revised articles, 300 new illustrations, and more than 1,000 new entries on American themes. The first seven volumes cover subjects from *aardvark* to *zoos*. The intent is not only to cover school-related topics but to grab the curious reader with articles on baseball, cartoons and comics, monsters, and MTV and rock music. Some articles (e.g., *American Revolution*) are given three pages, but many get only one-half to two-thirds of a page. This generally works for the age level intended, but the half-page article *stock market* does not enable the child to find out how to play the stock market as claimed in the introduction; it merely describes what stock markets and bull and bear markets are. The accompanying picture adds very little.

Overall, however, the illustrations, most of which are in color, are an outstanding feature of this encyclopedia. *Automobiles* features an excellent diagram of a modern American car, with its various systems color coded. There is some inconsistency in the maps. Many countries get a combination geographical-topographical map; others get only a locator map or a very sketchy map. For example, Ireland has a map showing political divisions, major cities, and some topography; while on the same page Iraq, certainly in the public eye, is only shown in its location in the Middle East. Other questions in a work directed at American children: Why are courts in the United Kingdom given two sections in the article *law and legal systems*? Why is each state identified in parentheses as "U.S.A."?

The eighth volume in this set contains biographies briefly describing the lives of nearly 600 famous men and women from the U.S. and around the world who lived between 2000 B.C. and today. The biographies are cross-referenced from the other volumes, and each biography is followed by a *see also* reference to the subject area(s) associated with that person (e.g., Anne Frank's article refers the reader to *concentration camps*, *Nazis*, and *World War II*). The article on President Clinton ends with mention of corruption and financial investigations following his 1996 election. Sketches of the presidents are done against a yellow background and are not particularly good likenesses.

The index volume, number nine in the set, may be primarily useful for its gazetteer showing countries of the world and their respective flags. Each flag is accompanied by the country's capital, population (no date given), and area. A time line of world history giving events starting before 10,000 B.C. through 1991 is included. Instructions on how to use the index itself are good. The encyclopedia is well bound with well-spaced, clear dark print. Its tight gutters will make photocopying difficult.

Some articles are simple; others, such as *Aeneid*, DNA, *economics*, and *ocean zones*, are geared to older readers. Primary use will be for class assignments, especially for projects demanding good illustrations of, for example, types of bridges, the layout of an English church, diagrams showing how electricity is distributed, or how a fax machine works. Students who just need a little information (e.g., who invented antibiotics) will find this set useful, as will younger kids seeking information on topics hard to find at their level. Not an essential purchase but useful where short, well-illustrated articles on a wide variety of subjects are in demand, whether in school or public libraries or at home. A comparable set, the 10-volume *New Grolier Children's Encyclopedia* (1998), is also nicely illustrated but has fewer main entries and briefer biographies.

Nueva Enciclopedia Cumbre. 14v. 31st ed. 1999. 4,704p. illus. maps. Grolier, $345 (0-7172-5114-4). DDC: 036.

First published in 1958 as *Enciclopedia Illustrada Cumbre*, the 31st edition of this encyclopedia has been completely revised and given a new format. Produced by a team of editors and publishers from Mexico, Puerto Rico, and the U.S., it is a Spanish-language general encyclopedia for students in middle school through high school. It will also be useful as a general reference source for adults who prefer an encyclopedia in Spanish.

This edition has 1,500 new articles, 2,000 revised and updated articles, more than 6,500 color illustrations, and approximately 300 maps. Thirty-five percent of the entries cover the arts and humanities, thirty-five percent percent deal with science and technology, fourteen percent with the social sciences, thirteen percent with geography, and two percent with sports and contemporary life. Ninety percent of the contributors are academics. They are listed at the beginning of volume one, but their affiliations are not included. The articles are not signed, and they do not have bibliographies. The editors state that they have provided balanced content covering all viewpoints. They also say that all statistics have been verified and corroborated, but they do not provide any sources for them.

The entries are arranged alphabetically. Half of them are brief, 500 words or less. Articles on broad concepts, countries, and complex subjects are longer. The set has no index, but there are ample cross-references. All maps are in the atlas section at the end of volume 14. This section has statistical and political/relief maps. The boundaries in the latter are impossible to find. The lack of individual maps in the articles about countries is a disadvantage because those in the atlas are inadequate.

The information in the entries is up-to-date. The articles on cancer and AIDS (SIDA) have current treatment information. The entry for computer (*computadora*) has a cross-section showing the major parts of the machine, and the one on compact discs (*discos compactos*) includes information on both audio and CD-ROM products and a diagram of the optical scanner. The article on Yugoslavia discusses the splitting of the country into two separate republics. The article on communications (*comunicaciones*), five pages long, covers the history of various media up to the present and has cross-references to *Internet*, *radiotelefonia*, and *telecomunicacion*. Although the briefer articles are sometimes inadequate, the long ones are very good. The entry *Pascua*, which refers to both Easter and Passover in Spanish, is a confusing mixture of the Christian and Jewish holidays and theologies, but the article on the Holocaust (*Holocausto*) covers the major points, notes the existence of denyers, and mentions the U.S. Holocaust Memorial. *Cuerpo humano* (the human body) does not explain anatomy and physiology with sufficient depth and has only one illustration that does not show the organs well, but an article on consumer education (*comprador y arte de comprar*) provides a good grasp of basic economics, advertising, and credit. There is a two-and-half page article on children's songs (*canciones infantiles*) with many lyrics, which will be useful for teachers.

The *Nueva Enciclopedia Cumbre* is more current and has a more accessible reading level than *Enciclopedia Hispanica* (Britannica, 1996). Despite some flaws, it is an excellent choice for school and public libraries in need of a general encyclopedia in Spanish.

Encyclopedia of Television News. Ed. by Michael D. Murray. 1999. 290p. bibliog. illus. index. Oryx, $69 (1-57356-108-8). DDC: 070.1.

The advent of television gave a promise that news could be disseminated quickly, with both verbal and pictorial reports. This encyclopedia covers the major individuals, programs, issues, organizations, and events involved in bringing this promise to fruition. The editor, chairman of the Department of Communications, University of Missouri–St. Louis, worked with a large number of contributors with impressive credentials.

Arranged in alphabetical order, entries vary in length based on the importance of the subject. More than 308 individuals are covered, including significant individuals such as Edward R. Murrow, Walter Cronkite, and Barbara Walters. Many of the biographical articles are accompanied by photographs. The major networks are given substantial coverage in articles providing the history and development of news programming, key people, problems, and triumphs. Traditional evening news programs, morning programs, and news magazines such as *Dateline NBC*, *20/20*, and the venerable *60 Minutes* are examined at length. Bibliographies at the end of most articles provide sources for further reading.

The great moments of television news, such as the assassination of President Kennedy and the first lunar landing, are analyzed at length. Entries on other important stories such as the Persian Gulf War tackle the issues of censorship and government/military control of the news. Concepts and issues such as tabloid television and blacklisting are discussed along with the Federal Communications Commission and Nielsen Ratings. There are also entries for coverage of sports and weather.

The high quality and thoroughness of this encyclopedia will make it valuable to browsers, students, and researchers. It will be a useful purchase for most academic and public libraries and a necessity for libraries supporting collections on broadcasting and journalism.

African American Quotations. By Richard Newman. 1998. 504p. indexes. Oryx, $49.95 (1-57356-118-5). DDC: 081.

According to Julian Bond's foreword, this is probably the largest collection of African American quotations printed. The 2,506 quotations are grouped into broad subject areas and are made accessible by three indexes—name, subject (including *see* and *see also* references), and occupation (of persons quoted)—and by the table of contents (main subject headings). The quotes are numbered, and the person's dates and occupation follow each quote.

The more than 500 individuals quoted include the famous, the infamous, and the obscure. With a few exceptions, they are African Americans. The quotations range from one-liners to short paragraphs and run the gamut from bitterness to joy. W. E. B. Du Bois, Martin Luther King Jr., and Malcolm X are among those represented most often, but there are also plenty of quotes from contemporary figures such as Tupac Shakur, Cornel West, and Oprah Winfrey. One could quibble with the inclusion of the likes of Pliny the Elder and Shakespeare in light of the title; however, their quotes on Africa are useful.

To quote George C. Wolfe: "We traded in our drums for respectability, so now it's just words." There are plenty of words to use in this attractive volume, which is a fine addition to any collection of quotations. Though not as broad in scope as Dorothy Winbush Riley's *My Soul Looks Back, 'Less I Forget: A Collection of Quotations by People of Color* [RBB N 15 93], which has more than 7,000 quotations, Newman's concentration on African Americans is useful. Recommended for high-school, public, and academic libraries.

Random House Webster's Quotationary. Ed. by Leonard Roy Frank. 1999. 1,039p. indexes. Random, $45 (0-679-44850-0). DDC: 082.

The 20,000 quotations in this volume are arranged by subject, from *ability* to *Zen*, and then alphabetically by author. The editor says he has included "the most interesting, well-phrased thoughts and observations." The quotations include factual statements, song lyrics, slogans, titles, and phrases. The time frame and authors are comprehensive, from Justinian I: "The precepts of the law are these: to live honestly, to injure no one..."; to Bill Clinton: "Character is a journey, not a destination." The great variety of other authors includes Larry Bird, George Booth, Henry Clay, James Fenimore Cooper, Olympia Dukakis, David Letterman, Madonna, Montaigne, Napoleon, Norman Rockwell, and Frances Trollope. The citations that accompany the quotations are quite complete: page number; section or line for books, plays, and poems; but unfortunately only the date for newspaper and magazine quotations.

A unique feature of the book is the extensive cross-referencing. Under the category headings are *see also* references to related categories or quotations, and under many individual quotations are *see* references to other quotations that are similar in content or form. Following the quotations are an index by author or source and an index of the subject categories.

Up to this point, *Quotationary* looks as if it could be competition for Bartlett's famous *Familiar Quotations* [RBB N 1 92], now in its sixteenth edition. However, *Quotationary* is missing a vital part—a keyword index. The importance of a keyword index is illustrated by its length in Bartlett's, which is more than 600 pages. Without this type of index it is doubtful that the quotation "The opera ain't over till the fat lady sings" would be found in *Quotationary* unless the source (sports broadcaster Dan Cook) is known, because it is under the category *optimism: examples*. Likewise, who would think to look under *voting* for the quote from an anonymous source, "When I die I want to be buried in Chicago so I can still be active in politics" (except perhaps a Chicagoan?)

Bartlett's and *The Oxford Dictionary of Quotations* [fourth ed., RBB D 1 92] are arranged by author. Because both have keyword indexes, they are better tools for finding a specific quotation. Its category arrangement makes *Quotationary* an excellent tool for browsing for quotations by subject. Recommended for high-school, public, and academic libraries as a complement to standard sources.

Philosophy, Psychology, Religion

Dictionary of Philosophy. By Mario Bunge. 1999. 316p. Prometheus, $59.95 (1-57392-257-9). DDC: 103.

Bunge is a prolific philosopher, lately concentrating on the social sciences and their relationship to philosophy. Many academic libraries hold all or part of his eight-volume *Treatise on Basic Philosophy* (Reidel/Kluwer, 1974–89). In this new dictionary of "modern philosophical concepts, problems, principles, and theories," Bunge has attempted to create a fresh entry in a crowded field. This work concentrates on Western terms and ideas, omitting concepts the author considers to be obsolete or rooted in philosophic fashion or trends. In many ways, this is a dictionary of the philosophy of science, as Bunge uses scientific examples, especially from the physical sciences, to elucidate many concepts and focuses on concepts of interest to philosophers of science.

Entries are arranged alphabetically and range in length from a few sentences to a few paragraphs. Ample cross-references are provided. The definitions are fairly clear, and the examples used to illustrate concepts are appropriate although somewhat technical. Some of the entries include declarative or judgmental conclusions without sufficient explanation (e.g., *existentialism* is described as "a hodge-podge of enigmatic utterances").

Bunge's approach is not historical. Therefore, this work cannot stand on its own for beginning students of philosophy who need to understand the historical context and evolution of philosophic thought. Entries on terms such as *form, falsifiability,* and *rationalism* make no mention of the philosophers or times of their emergence as key concepts. In fact, the uninitiated reader could easily get the sense that philosophy is not something done by people, because there is almost no reference to philosophers at all. Furthermore, there are no entries on individual philosophers or schools of philosophic thought.

The tone of the entries is decidedly unique. On the one hand, many entries read more like a logic or mathematics text than a generally philosophical one. On the other hand, many entries have a more casual, almost humorous tone (there is an entry for *hair-splitting*, described as "a favorite with theologians and with philosophers without long-term research projects"). The result can be a little unsettling, as the text suddenly shifts from readable to technical with little warning. This is compounded by a tendency to unnecessarily wander into logical notation when plain language would do and a system of cross-references that uses upward-pointing arrows.

Given the complete lack of historical context, the focus on a somewhat narrow spectrum of philosophical concepts, and the opinionated nature of many of the conclusions, this is not a first choice for a one-volume dictionary of philosophy. Better choices would be *The Cambridge Dictionary of Philosophy* (Cambridge, 1995) or *A Dictionary of Philosophy* (Blackwell, 1996). Comprehensive academic philosophy collections may want to consider this purchase. Bunge's approach will probably be best appreciated by logicians and philosophers of science.

Routledge Encyclopedia of Philosophy. 10v. Ed. by Edward Craig. 1998. 8,680p. bibliogs. index. Routledge, $2,995 (0-415-07310-3). DDC: 103.

In the more than 30 years since publication of *The Encyclopedia of Philosophy* (Macmillan and The Free Press, 1967), a whole generation of philosophers as well as new and shifting philosophical concerns have made an impact inside and outside the profession. Jean Baudrillard and Walter Benjamin, Daniel Dennett and Jacques Derrida, Julia Kristeva and Thomas Kuhn, applied ethics and African philosophy, feminism and fuzzy logic, poststructuralism and postmodernism—none of these appeared or, in most cases, should have been expected to appear in the venerable work to which the *Routledge Encyclopedia of Philosophy* is an unofficial but worthy successor. (The earlier work's editor, Paul Edwards, serves as an advisory editor here.) Also, a generation of scholarship on the perennial questions of philosophy and on the great philosophers of the past is reason enough to welcome a new encyclopedia of this magnitude. Although several recent and excellent one-volume encyclopedias of philosophy have taken up the slack, it was not their purpose to do so with anything like the thoroughness of this new set. Editor Craig has overseen 32 subject editors in providing more than 2,000 articles from more than 1,300 contributors. The result is a multivolume work packed with features that make most entries accessible and informative to academically oriented high-school students and professional philosophers alike.

Main entries cover an intriguingly broad range of philosophical concepts (*a posteriori*, *absolutism*, *alienation*, *hope*, *love*), fields of study and geographically or chronologically oriented overviews (*aesthetics, Chinese; agricultural ethics; analytical philosophy in Latin America; archaeology, philosophy of; Egyptian cosmology, ancient philosophers*) (Albert the Great, Aristotle, Ibn Bajja, Robert Nozick), and relevant nonphilosophers (Darwin, Freud, Homer, Ptolemy, Thucydides). Some of the more unexpected main entries include *engineering and ethics; photography, aesthetics of; sport, philosophy of;* and *Yoruba epistemology*. While there is still some Western and Anglo-American bias in the choice of entries (the great majority of contributors are from the English-speaking world, primarily the U.S. and the U.K.), the inclusion of "world" philosophies is admirable. As stated in the preface, "Chinese, Japanese and Korean, Indian and Tibetan, Jewish, Arabic and Islamic, Russian, Latin American and African philosophy have between them 400 entries."

Entries range in length from 500 to 19,000 words and share a uniform format designed to assist a wide range of users. Each begins with an italicized overview of the topic ranging from a paragraph for shorter entries to more than a page for the longest, such as those on *Augustine, Kant,* and *Leibniz*; these overviews provide "essential information, written where at all possible in a relatively undemanding way." An outline of topics, with numbers corresponding to the section headings to follow, precedes each main article, which is much more detailed than the overview and assumes "a somewhat more experienced reader." A list of references and sources for further reading follows each entry, and a list of primary sources follows each biographical entry. In every case these sources are annotated with at least a phrase or sentence describing the emphasis and/or importance of the work. Because many encyclopedia entries were submitted to the editors several years ago, care was taken to ensure that authors had the opportunity to update bibliographies before publication; as a result, the reader will find many titles from the mid-1990s included on the reading lists. Cross-references are found within, between, and at the end of entries. Volume 1 begins with the editor's preface and acknowledgments, short professional biographies of the editorial board members, a guide to using the encyclopedia, and a list of entries and their contributors. The guide and the list of entries (without their contributors) are repeated in each volume. Volume 5 includes a 16-page glossary of logical and mathematical terms. Volume 10 is an index of more than 78,000 entries preceded by a list of contributors with their affiliations and entries.

A few words about the pricing are in order. The 10-volume set will sell for $2,495 until the end of October, after which time it will sell for $2,995. A CD-ROM version, containing the complete text of the print version, may be used by up to 10 simultaneous users at one campus; it is available at the same cost as the print version or, if purchased with the print version, for $500 extra. Craig notes that the electronic version, "being relatively simple to update . . . could be the ancestor of a long line of subsequent editions."

As this seven-year undertaking is likely to be the definitive encyclopedia of philosophy for the next generation, it is highly recommended for academic libraries and other institutions where philosophy in any of its forms is likely to be of interest. Acquisition of this work should not be seen as an occasion for retiring the earlier *Encyclopedia of Philosophy*, which remains a reliable guide to the great philosophers and philosophies of the past.

Encyclopedia of Aesthetics. 4v. Ed. by Michael Kelly. 1998. 2,028p. bibliogs. illus. index. Oxford, $495 (0-19-511307-1). DDC: 111.86.

Encyclopedia of Aesthetics will become an immediate reference classic because of its unique scope, its level of scholarship, and the superb quality of its essays and bibliographies. Its editor and contributors have gone beyond offering factual, synthetic encyclopedia articles to provide a challenging compendium of criticism, a survey of philosophy and theory, and an examination of contemporary thought in an area of study that is comprehensive enough to include essays on topics as diverse as comics, cyberspace, food, and the theories of Pseudo-Dionysius the Areopagite.

In order to understand the importance of the encyclopedia, it is necessary to understand how its creators define aesthetics. In his preface, Kelly, managing editor of *Journal of Philosophy* and adjunct associate professor at Columbia University, notes that aesthetics is a single branch of philosophy concerned with art, but also a part of other disciplines such as history, literary theory, law, and sociology. Contemporary aestheticians believe that aesthetics is the "philosophical analysis of beliefs, concepts, and theories implicit in the creation, experience, interpretation, or critique of art," but is not particularly concerned with beauty, a quality nonspecialists are likely to associate with the word *aesthetics*. For the purpose of the encyclopedia, *aesthetics* is defined as "critical reflection on art, culture, and nature." The goal of the encyclopedia is to trace the genealogy of aesthetics in such a way as to integrate its philosophical and cultural roles. Kelly states that its purpose is not to resolve differences among various disciplines, but to "provide as much reliable information as we could assemble," and to catalog "what the differences are, how they originated, what disciplines have in common, and what is at stake in conflicting views."

Encyclopedia of Aesthetics includes more than 600 alphabetically arranged, signed essays on individuals (Eco, Umberto; Wright, Frank Lloyd), concepts (*fashion, grotesque, taste*), periods (*Roman aesthetics, Gothic aesthetics*), media (*sculpture, television*), theories (*art for art's sake, New Criticism*), issues (*forgery, sexuality*), and movements (*Outsider Art, Romanticism*), from the ancient world to the present. The 500 contributors are mostly university professors of art, philosophy, classics, literature, or other disciplines within the humanities. They include world-class scholars such as James Ackerman (Arthur Kingsley Porter professor emeritus of fine arts, Harvard) and Oleg Grabar (professor, School of Historical Studies, Institute for Advanced Study, Princeton). Topics were chosen for their philosophical or critical significance for the history of aesthetics, art, or related fields; relevance to contemporary aesthetics; or historical or contemporary importance in non-Western culture (*Chinese aesthetics, Japanese aesthetics, pre-Columbian aesthetics*). Philosophers whose work is essential to the understanding of aesthetics (for example, Michel Foucault, Immanuel Kant) are well represented, as are key figures in the history of art theory and criticism (Erwin Panofsky, Meyer Schapiro, Heinrich Wolfflin). Articles on individuals focus less on strictly biographical information, which could easily be found elsewhere, and more on the intellectual development, education, thought, teaching, writings, influence, and intellectual legacy. These articles will be invaluable to the graduate student who is trying to understand the critical and philosophical infrastructure of a particular discipline and the academic genealogies of its theorists.

Most articles are several pages in length, with longer overview essays on broad topics such as *aestheticism, metaphor,* or *perception*, or major philosophers such as Immanuel Kant, whose article is 35 pages long. Composite articles include several essays under a single headword, accompanied by the editor's explanatory note. For example, *postmodernism* includes an historical and conceptual overview plus separate essays on postmodern dance and postmodern poetry. *Fashion* includes essays on "Dress in the World," "La Haute Couture," "Fashion as Art," and "Fashion and Philosophy." Occasional black-and-white photographs illustrate selected articles. A detailed index allows the user to locate references to topics included within broader articles.

Kelly states that the encyclopedia is intended for both the general reader and the advanced scholar. Most articles examined were written to present key concepts, definitions, and origins of terms or movements in a straightforward manner at the beginning of the article, before delving into more challenging, complex issues. The essays are also valuable for their identification of key publications of particular scholars or on specific topics. For example, *aestheticism* notes that Walter Pater's conclusion to *Studies in the History of the Renaissance* became the "Bible of English Aestheticism." Bibliographies include references to carefully selected books and articles. Although many recent publications from the 1990s are included, the key sources from earlier years are well represented. Bibliographies included with articles on individuals are divided into lists of the person's work as originally published, English translations, and critical sources by other writers.

Weaknesses in the set are few. The bibliography for the article *icon* includes primarily articles in Russian. *Anthropology and aesthetics* was written by a professor of liberal arts rather than an anthropologist. It would have been more satisfying had the article on William Morris been written by someone with a greater appreciation of Morris' Arts and Crafts Movement. In their efforts to provide clear, concise introductions to their topics, contributors sometimes make authoritative pronouncements that may be, in fact, arguable. For example, the contributor of *rock music* states that "the three principal criteria by which rock is judged are authenticity of voice, rhythm, and loudness." Finally, the title of the encyclopedia may lead those unfamiliar with its content or the broader definition of aesthetics to believe that its scope is considerably narrower than it is, perhaps being concerned primarily with issues of beauty.

The occasional flaw, however, serves only to reinforce the general exceptional quality and importance of this superb set. Reference librarians and scholars will find it a fine complement to Grove's *Dictionary of Art* [RBB D 15 96], and two other sets frequently consulted for their excellent coverage of conceptual, rather than merely factual, topics: *The Dictionary of the History of Ideas* (Scribner, 1974) and Macmillan's *Encyclopedia of the Social Sciences* (and, to a lesser extent, its successor, *International Encyclopedia of the Social Sciences*). *Encyclopedia of Aesthetics* is an essential purchase for academic libraries, arts and humanities collections, and larger public libraries.

Dictionary of Theories, Laws, and Concepts in Psychology. By Jon E. Roeckelein. 1998. 516p. appendixes. bibliog. index. Greenwood, $115 (0-313-30460-2). DDC: 150.

Fully cross-referenced and source-referenced, this dictionary contains more than 1,200 entries for terms concerning laws, theories, hypotheses, doctrines, principles, and effects in the early and contemporary psychological literature. B*irth order theory, gate-control theory*, and *Freud's theory of personality* are examples of entries concerning theories. Examples of entries concerning hypotheses include *elicited observing rate hypothesis, facial feedback hypothesis, total time hypothesis/law*, and W*horf-Sapir hypothesis/theory*. Readers interested in laws and principles will find *all-or-none law/principle*, *Mendel's laws/principles*, and *Zeising's principle*. Effects, such as the Stroop effect, and doctrines, such as the doctrine of unconscious inference, are also included.

Each entry consists of the definition/description of the term with commentary, followed by a number of cross-referenced, related terms and by chronologically ordered lists of sources to indicate the evolution of the term. The first appendix, "Frequency of Usage of Concepts as Sampled in Psychology Textbooks, 1885–1996," provides supplementary material on many laws and theories not included in the dictionary itself and will be helpful to students and scholars concerned with specialty areas in psychology. There are more than 800 laws and theories in this appendix; the total time period is broken down into five separate subperiods. A second appendix lists the 136 textbooks surveyed for the collection of laws and theories listed in appendix A. A selected bibliography and index conclude the work.

Roeckelein, a professor of psychology in the Department of Psychology at Mesa Community College, Mesa, Arizona, is to be commended for his appreciation of semantic and theoretical distinctions. Although the mid-1990s have seen the publication of several dictionaries and encyclopedias in psychology, some of which are revisions of important titles, none of these titles represents serious competition for this scholarly dictionary. *The Gale Encyclopedia of Psychology* [RBB D 15 96], although full of useful information for anyone who is interested in psychology, is more appropriate to high-school students and general readers seeking an understanding of the concepts of academic psychology as employed by experts in the field. Billed as a dictionary for psychologists, Stuart Sutherland's second edition of *The International Dictionary of Psychology* [RBB Ap 1 96] attempts to include all technical terms from psychiatry, neurology, neurophysiology, neurochemistry, ethology, sociobiology, genetics, linguistics, artificial intelligence, sociology, anthropology, statistics, philosophy, and other disciplines. Benjamin B. Wolman's concise, current *Encyclopedia of Psychiatry, Psychology, and Psychoanalysis* [RBB Je 1 97] and Raymond J. Corsini's reliable four-volume *Encyclopedia of Psychology* [RBB S 15 94] also pose no competition because they differ in both scope and purpose. Written with the broadest possible audience in mind, and containing some 17,000 terms, the second edition of Arthur S. Reber's *Penguin Dictionary of Psychology* (1995) is considerably less focused and more wide-ranging than Roeckelein's work, and also more weighty and cumbersome.

This dictionary should be a valuable addition to college and university library collections, particularly those that support programs in psychology and related fields. Large public libraries may want to take a look-see to determine its potential usefulness in their settings.

Ethics and Values. 8v. 1998. bibliog. illus. index. Grolier, $265 (0-7172-9274-6). DDC: 170.3.

This set designed for upper-elementary through high-school students is a survey of the field of ethical belief and behavior, with topics that are worthy of discussion by all ages. It emphasizes making responsible choices, with a balanced approach to all topics. It includes the moral teachings of the world's major religions and points out issues that various religions approach in different ways. Political and legal systems are explored as well.

Alphabetically arranged from *abortion* to *wrong*, most of the more than 200 articles are two pages in length, with a black-and-white photo, bold topic headings, and more than six *see also* references to other articles. Sidebars give additional information on individual people or a historical issue that is significant. AIDS/HIV, for example, has a sidebar on Magic Johnson; and Buddhism has sidebars on Siddhartha Gautama and on Buddha's teachings. Entries such as *backlash, divorce, humanism, medical ethics*, and *pacifism* are handled with clarity and balance. There are also entries for topics that relate to core values, such as *courtesy, honesty*, and *responsibility*. Each volume includes a list of contents in that volume, and complete index to the set. There is a brief bibliography in volume 8.

This set is recommended for school and public libraries. Although it is designed for students through the high-school level, high-schoolers should have access to other resources, such as E*thics* (Salem, 1994), which covers many of the same topics in greater depth.

Bioethics for Students: How Do We Know What's Right? Issues in Medicine, Animal Rights, and the Environment. 4v. Ed. by Stephen G. Post. 1999. 832p. appendixes. bibliog. glossary. illus. indexes. Macmillan, $325 (0-02-864940-0). DDC: 174.

Although based on the revised edition of the *Encyclopedia of Bioethics* [RBB Ag 95], this shorter work for high schools is not as well organized or as easy to use. Instead of alphabetically arranged entries, here are 18 broader themes with lots of essaylike subdivisions. "Sex and Gender" includes articles on homosexuality, sexism, sex therapy, and women, while "Environment" includes environmental ethics, hazardous wastes, and sustainable development. Some of these issues, of course, overlap tremendously, with *confidentiality* grouped under "Ethics and Law" but also discussed under "Genetics," "Stages of Life," and "Transplants and Other Technical Devices," among other sections. *Hospice* is grouped under "Therapies" but also discussed in "Death and Dying." Fortunately, the indexing makes all of the information, even that in the many sidebars, accessible.

Page design is similar to that in other Macmillan "For Students" sets, with a minor column containing definitions, sidebars, and *see also* references. Much of the text is taken directly from the parent work, with articles shortened but not necessarily made easier. Credit is given to the original authors, and some updating has been done. Information on multiple births from 1997 and euthanasia laws and court decisions from 1998 is included, as well as completely new information on human cloning. Several appendixes list U.S. legal cases influencing medical ethics, medical codes and oaths, and a glossary is included. The selected bibliography is arranged by topic areas and lists books and articles from the 1990s. Each volume has its own index, and there is a comprehensive index in volume 4.

Unique to this work are the "Related Literature" tie-ins. As examples, Margaret Atwood's *The Handmaid's Tale* is described in the chapter on fertility and reproduction, and Edward Albee's play *The Sandbox* is suggested in the chapter on death. It's possible that these will help students explore some of the issues the articles raise. Illustrations also make this set more attractive to students.

Is this set an essential purchase? No, especially for schools and libraries that own the *Encyclopedia of Bioethics* or relevant titles in Greenhaven's Opposing Viewpoints or other similar series. However, it will be used where bioethics debates or reports are popular. Recommended for high-school and public libraries.

Encyclopedia of Animal Rights and Animal Welfare. Ed. by Marc Bekoff and Carron A. Meaney. 1998. 392p. appendix. bibliog. index. Greenwood, $59.95 (0-313-29977-3). DDC: 179.

Although this volume is not encyclopedic, as in covering all facets of animal welfare, it does have good descriptions of the animal rights movement, especially its impact on some types of medical research.

Entries were chosen "by going through numerous books and essays and listing the topics that were covered in these works." Examples include *animal boredom, genetic engineering*, Humane Slaughter Act, *hunting*, and *rodeos*. Some longer discussions, such as *animal cognition*, are divided into several subsections with different contributors. There are numerous short biographies of persons whose work influenced the animal rights movement, such as Charles Darwin and Leo Tolstoy; only deceased persons are covered. For the most part, the contributors have been careful to present differing viewpoints. Most entries have a short selective bibliography. There is a chronology at the beginning of the volume and a list of resources following the A–Z entries. These resources include an annotated directory of organizations involved in animal welfare and humane education, as well as print source material. The volume concludes with an index and a list of contributors.

A number of these contributors are professors of philosophy, and many of the entries are steeped in philosophical argument and explanation that, while important to understanding one or more views of the animal rights movement, also put up barriers to popular consideration. In addition to discussions of animal shelters, mice as laboratory animals, vegetarianism, and zoos, there are entries for *deep ethology, painism, sentientism,* and *virtue ethics*. The language and the level of discussion make the book more appropriate for academic libraries than for school and public libraries.

Encyclopedia of American Women and Religion. By June M. Benowitz. 1998. 466p. bibliogs. illus. index. ABC-CLIO, $75 (0-87436-887-1). DDC: 200.

Women have played important, though often hidden, roles in religions of the world throughout history. This title seeks to uncover the contributions of women to the American religious experience. The majority of the alphabetically arranged entries cover individual women, but organizations, denominations, and even men "who have influenced the history of American women" are included. Entries generally conclude with *see also* references and brief bibliographies. Other features include a chronology of women's participation in the American religious experience, an additional bibliography of books and articles, and an index.

While the goal of this work is unique, its execution is sometimes flawed. The contribution to the American religious experience of some women, such as Tammy Faye Bakker and Bishop Barbara Harris, is treated superficially. Better assessments of their accomplishments can be found in *Twentieth-Century Shapers of American Popular Religion* (Greenwood, 1989) and *Current Biography Yearbook* (H. W. Wilson, 1989 edition), respectively. Several concepts vis-a-vis women and religion are poorly defined. One is ecofeminism, which, while not strictly a religious or theological concept, nevertheless challenges traditional Christianity and forms the basis for some theological reflection. The entry on ecofeminism sketches its broad contours but lacks a discussion of the distinctly American responses to the idea. The entry for feminist theology is better grounded in an American context, but the thinkers mentioned in the entry as well as the supplemental bibliography represent Americans of European origin. African American and Latina women with unique definitions of feminism and unique approaches to theological reflection are not mentioned. Fine treatments of ecofeminism and feminist theology are provided in *Dictionary of Feminist Theologies* (Westminster/John Knox, 1996). Finally, though an effort has been made to include discussion of a variety of religions (including the New Age Movement and Paganism), and to have entries for women of Jewish, Native American, and other religious backgrounds, the emphasis is on Christianity. The researcher interested in a fuller treatment of women's experience outside Christianity will need to turn to other sources, such as *Jewish Women in America: An Historical Encyclopedia* [RBB Ja 1 & 15 98].

Encyclopedia of American Women and Religion is useful insofar as it pulls together information about women and the American religious experience which one would otherwise have to consult numerous sources to find. Since better treatment of many of the entries exists in other sources, convenience is not reason enough to warrant a recommendation for purchase for larger or more specialized collections, except as a supplemental title. High-school and public libraries not owning other resources on the topic should find it a worthwhile addition.

The Encyclopedia of Cults, Sects, and New Religions. By James R. Lewis. 1998. 600p. bibliog. illus. Prometheus, $149.95 (1-57392-222-6). DDC: 200.

The pages of this work contain information on approximately 1,000 religious groups, ranging from small churches with less than a hundred members (Chishti Order of America) to organizations such as the Assemblies of God that number in the millions. Most entries are relatively short. The more controversial religions, as well as religious groups that have had a high profile lately, receive more lengthy treatments. Also included are entries on broader religious movements such as the New Age and the Charismatic Movement. Some of the longer entries are signed, although no affiliations or credentials are supplied for the authors.

Lewis, chairman of the Department of Religious Studies at the World University of America, spends several paragraphs of the introduction discussing the connotations of the terms *cult, sect,* and *new religion*, explaining that they were used in his title because "they represent the most commonly used terms for non-mainstream religious groups." The introduction does not specifically address how the included groups were chosen and why others were left out, except that all are "non-mainstream." Emphasis is on the U.S., although some non-U.S. groups are included, such as Aum Shinrikyo and Wiccan Church of Canada. Starting with the *Aaronic Order*, an offshoot of the Mormon Church, and ending with *Zion's Order, Inc.* (also of Mormon derivation), the book covers a very broad range of organizations. Gnostic, Theosophist, Hindu, Moslem, Buddhist, Christian, Jewish, Native American, New Age, and occult groups are profiled. Examples of entries include *channeling movement, Druids, Hare Krishna movement, Hasidism, Heaven's Gate, Salvation Army, Satanism, Seventh-Day Adventist Church,* and *Voodoo*.

Each article outlines the history of the group, its founders and leaders, its main teachings, and an approximate number of followers or congregations. The explanations are clearly written, interesting and understandable, without too much scholarly jargon. There are a number of pictures, most provided by the religious groups. There is a table of contents, but no cross-references or index; both would have been useful. There is nothing to direct the reader searching for Nation of Islam to *American Muslims* (which the entry claims is the current name), or to link names like Jim Jones and Herbert W. Armstrong to the entries for *People's Temple* and *Worldwide Church of God*. There is a 64-page bibliography of books, pamphlets, and periodicals. A few entries included Web addresses, but none are in the bibliography.

The similarly titled *Sects, "Cults" and Alternative Religions: A World Survey and Sourcebook* [RBB Jl 97] covers only 69 groups, but the entries are longer—16 pages for *Scientology* as opposed to two pages in Lewis. In many ways, the books complement each other. Because of interest in the subject, public and academic libraries will want Lewis' book, though smaller libraries may not have the budget or patronage to justify this particular expense.

Encyclopedia of Women and World Religion. 2v. Ed. by Serinity Young. 1999. 1,152p. bibliog. illus. index. Macmillan, $225 (0-02-864608-8). DDC: 200.

Recent decades have seen a marked increase in scholarship and academic research on women and their experiences, including their participation in and treatment by world religions. As stated in the introduction, "This encyclopedia endeavors to represent this burgeoning field by serving as a culturally and historically comprehensive reference work that reflects contemporary approaches to women's history and experience in world religion from the beginning of time to the present."

Entries are arranged alphabetically, are signed by the scholars or experts who wrote them, and conclude with supplemental bibliographies, many of which are annotated. The editors have striven to include all religions of the world, but traditions such as Christianity, Judaism, Islam, and Buddhism receive more detailed coverage. In fact, the entries for these traditions are quite lengthy and are divided into sections that cover a particular chronological period or geographic area. Many specific terms and concepts are discussed within these lengthy essays instead of having entries of their own (e.g., *enlightenment*). This necessitates use of the index, and, fortunately, the index to this encyclopedia is very good. Another reason to use the index is that separate biographical entries are limited. Important women in the history of religion and important scholars of women and religion are usually mentioned within entries on larger topics.

What is particularly unique about this source is that entries strive to describe the experiences of women in particular traditions or state the relevance of a particular practice to women. The entry *monasticism* treats various types of women monastics in both Eastern and Western traditions. The entries *clothing* and *prayer* describe not only how women have used both in religious practice but also how they have been used against women by male-dominated religious traditions. The encyclopedia also includes what the editors term "transreligional terms," such as *blood*, *divine*, and *nature*, describing the significance and explaining the meaning of such terms in many traditions. Of course, all entries are not equally successful. *Critical theory* provides a good summary of that topic, but, unlike the entry for *epistemology*, it fails to provide examples how this approach has been applied in scholarship on women and religion.

Encyclopedia of Women and World Religion is an excellent resource, owing in no small measure to the fact that it is one of a kind. Two concerns limit its use for a wide audience. First, its self-admitted "feminist agenda" runs counter to the notion that reference works strive for neutrality, to the extent that this is ever possible. Second, the variety of methodological approaches represented in the entries requires a high degree of sophistication when reading them to sort out which approach is used when and how it shapes the content. The editors also concede that employing one methodological approach over another is a matter of debate. Therefore, the work is recommended primarily for academic libraries, although larger public libraries might also consider it.

The Encyclopedia of World Religions. By Robert Ellwood and Gregory Alles. 1998. 320p. bibliog. illus. index. maps. Facts On File, $29.95 (0-8160-3504-0). DDC: 200.

"*The Encyclopedia of World Religions* aims to help young people satisfy their curiosity about a very important aspect of their world: religions." So writes Associate Editor Gregory Alles in his introduction. Alles goes on to claim that most reference works are "geared to a college and postgraduate audience," whereas this work "is different in that it aims to address students directly."

Nearly 500 entries cover topics from prehistoric and ancient religions, major contemporary world religions, concepts, symbols, and personages. The entries for major religions are the longest, covering two or three pages and subdivided into sections that discuss history, beliefs, practices, organizations, and significance. The form is a traditional alphabetical arrangement of entries. As such, it's not bad, but is it the best way to introduce young readers to the variety and complexity of religions of the world? The entries for Christianity and Hinduism, among others, are extremely succinct and packed with *see* references, forcing the reader to flip from one entry to another. There are longer, more comprehensive entries available in *The World Book Encyclopedia*, to name just one example. The alphabetical arrangement, though useful from a ready-reference standpoint, does not allow for a synthesis of the history, people, and ideas of religious traditions and may not be the best format for satisfying the curiosity of young readers. Facts On File's own *Encyclopedia of World Faiths: An Illustrated Survey of the World's Living Religions* (New York, 1987) is better in this regard.

Many entries begin with a dictionary-like definition that attempts to capture the content of the entry in a single headline. *Prayer* is defined as "communication with a religious being, such as a god, spirit, ancestor, or saint." That's pretty good. But the entry for *Religion, Definition of* begins with the redundant phrase "explaining what religion is." *Judaism in America* is defined as "the practice of Judaism in the Western Hemisphere." The use of language in this work often suggests an attempt at simplification gone wrong. Although designed for young adults, the authors could have written the text in a way that would challenge readers, all the while remaining accessible to them.

In addition to form and language, the content of entries is also questionable. The entry *abortion and religion* indicates that Roman Catholicism does not permit abortion even if the life of the mother is in jeopardy. Catholic theology is very complex on this issue. The distinction between direct and indirect abortion, the precise circumstances surrounding the health of the mother, and the medical intervention necessary to save her all determine whether the death of the fetus is morally acceptable. Although all of this might well be beyond the scope of an encyclopedia for young readers, the entry as it stands is misleading.

Finally, the encyclopedia begins with a chart giving the number of adherents to religions worldwide but lacks any citation for the source of these figures. It ends with a supplemental bibliography of works geared for an undergraduate audience and beyond, including one in German. Could no books on world religions for young readers be found?

The target audience for this title is students in grades 6 through 12. Although the concept of providing an accessible reference source on religion for young adults is laudable, students at the lower end of the audience range will benefit just as much from the articles in *World Book*, and students at the higher end will be much better served by any number of one-volume encyclopedias written for adults, such as *The HarperCollins Dictionary of Religion* [RBB Ap 15 96] and *The Oxford Dictionary of World Religions* [RBB Jl 97]. Not recommended.

The Encyclopedia of Christianity. Vol. I, A–D. Ed. by Erwin Fahlbusch and others. 1999. 893p. bibliogs. tables. Eerdmans, $100 (0-8028-2413-3). DDC: 230.

Reference works on Christianity abound, but most sources are surprisingly limited in scope, treating a particular period, denomination, or geographic place. None "describes the Christian faith and community as it exists today in its myriad forms and also in its relation to the core apostolic tradition throughout the 2,000 years of Christian history." *The Encyclopedia of Christianity* (EC) attempts to do this by presenting Christianity in the following contexts: global, ecumenical, sociocultural, and historical. Volume 1 is the inaugural volume of a five-volume set that is, by and large, a translation of the third revised edition of the *Evangelisches Kirchenlexikon* (Vandenhoeck & Ruprecht, 1986–1997).

Among the 465 entries in volume I are articles on denominations, documents, doctrines, organizations, movements, terminology, practices, concepts, and cultural, social, and ethical issues. The global context is described in entries on the history and current practice of Christian faith in specific countries. One excellent feature of these country entries is the inclusion of statistical data on religious affiliation. Such data are difficult to locate in the detail presented here and were provided by David B. Barrett, whose *World Christian Encyclopedia* (Oxford, 1982) also provides country profiles with detailed data on religious affiliation. Entries such as *black theology*, which discusses differences between Africa and the U. S., demonstrate the regional diversity of Christian theology. The ecumenical context is found in articles on liturgical practice or theological concepts, which routinely give Roman Catholic, Protestant, Orthodox, and Anglican interpretations. There is also extensive coverage of international ecumenical bodies such as the World Council of Churches. EC takes into account the current sociocultural context in entries on other world religions, secular philosophies, cultural trends, and political and economic forces. For example, how is Christian missionary activity to be understood and undertaken in light of recent thinking about acculturation? Finally, the historical context is presented in various articles on books of the Bible, important biblical figures, and the life of the early church. In addition, there are biographical articles, ranging in this volume from *Athanasius* to *Bonhoeffer, Dietrich*.

Some articles not found in the German version appear in *The Encyclopedia of Christianity* (e.g., *Civil Rights Movement*), and the supplemental bibliographies have been revised to highlight English-language scholarship. Entries are alphabetically arranged, and signed by the scholars who wrote them. It's worth noting that the majority of contributors are European and that the majority of the European contributors are German. However, the articles do not betray any European or German bias, and noted American scholars of Christianity such as James Cone and Bruce Metzger are also contributors.

The only comparable work in English is the third edition of the *Oxford Dictionary of the Christian Church* (ODCC) [RBB O 1 97]. Although an excellent reference tool, it is more limited in scope than *The Encyclopedia of Christianity*. EC includes entries on conversion and church growth, not found in the ODCC. Where they do overlap, EC often provides lengthier discussions, the entry *Christology* being a good example (2 pages in ODCC, more than 15 pages in EC). The quality of scholarship combined with the unique approach of providing global, ecumenical, sociocultural, and historical context make this work an essential purchase for large public and academic libraries.

Encyclopedia of the Vatican and Papacy. Ed. by Frank J. Coppa. 1999. 484p. appendixes. bibliog. index. Greenwood, $99.50 (0-313-28917-4). DDC: 262.

The reign of Pope John Paul II has produced great interest in the papacy, owing to his travels, his prominent role in world affairs, and now his ill health and speculation about his successor. This encyclopedia is a timely and unique contribution to the reference literature about the papacy.

The volume "focuses on the historical, political, diplomatic, social, cultural, and religious role of the Vatican and the papacy in the modern world." Its unique contribution lies in the fact that it attempts to discuss these relationships in a context beyond that of an individual pope. Entries explore the relationship between the papacy and such social controversies as abortion, capital punishment, and euthanasia. Diplomatic relations between the Vatican and the Vichy government in France, Nazi Germany, NATO, and Zionism/Israel are described. There are historical entries addressing the Vatican and World War I, World War II, and one for *Holocaust and the papacy*. Earlier historical events are also treated, the Reformation in Europe being one example. Terms specific to the Vatican and papacy are also defined. For example, what is meant by *infallibility*? What is the difference between a papal bull and an encyclical? Finally, there are biographical entries for all popes and antipopes as well as descriptions of all 21 Councils of the Church.

Entries are alphabetically arranged and signed by the scholars who wrote them. Supplemental bibliographies are generally provided at the end of each entry. Three appendixes conclude the work, providing an alphabetical list of popes, antipopes, and Councils of the Church. Because the biographical entries for popes and antipopes are arranged alphabetically in the encyclopedia, the appendixes should have listed them chronologically. Fortunately, the Councils of the Church are listed chronologically.

Much of the biographical information about individual popes as well as definitions of terms can be found in any number of dictionaries and encyclopedias. Two other recent titles come closer to the content of this new work. The *Oxford Dictionary of Popes* (Oxford, 1986) contains only biographical entries for all popes and antipopes that place the lives and careers of these men in their historical contexts. Catholic scholar Richard P. McBrien's *Lives of the Popes* [BKL O 1 97] provides more information. Biographical entries, chronologically arranged, are given for popes, not antipopes. But McBrien's work also includes a glossary of terms (e.g., *curia, encyclical*), a brief description of key papal encyclicals, and appendixes on how popes are elected and removed from office, some of which is not covered in this new title.

Although there is an entry for Anglican-Vatican relations, other ecumenical dialogues are not addressed (e.g., Lutheran-Catholic). Also, the Catholic Church has not yet joined the World Council of Churches; a discussion of the reasons for this would have been useful. Nevertheless, the *Encyclopedia of the Vatican and Papacy* charts new ground in its treatment of the role of the Vatican and papacy in world and social affairs. Recommended for academic and large public libraries.

The Doubleday Christian Quotation Collection. By Hannah Ward and Jennifer Wild. 1998. 480p. indexes. Doubleday, $22 (0-385-48994-3). DDC: 270.

In a departure from many existing quotation books, two former Anglican Franciscans with feminist instincts have compiled a collection of more than 5,000 sayings from nearly 1,500 people representing all branches of the Christian community who have produced words worthy of quotation from the first through the twentieth centuries. The compilers admit that there are limitations of scope because of language and because not all great leaders have uttered memorable, pithy statements. Considering the book's emphasis on including women heretofore forgotten or neglected, and the relative paucity of quotations from the first millennium, one is not surprised to find more quotations that date from later centuries. In fact, three quarters of the volume's text deals with the sixteenth century to the present, with 42 percent devoted to the twentieth century.

Arranged broadly by century, each author entry—with vital date(s) and a brief description—has a number composed of the two digits of the century and a second number for the order within the century. Each quotation of an author is then numbered. Many authors have only one entry, but many others have a considerable number; a few, such as John Donne and Dietrich Bonhoeffer, have 20 or more. Though one needs to know the century of prominence for direct access, the 150 pages of indexes provide additional help for using the work. There is an index of sources for personal entries, an index of themes for subject approach, and an extensive keyword index. Finally, an Acknowledgments section includes nearly 200 sources from which the quotations were drawn.

Because of the somewhat random selection and the existence of other places to find such information, some will question the inclusion of poetic verses and the many first verses of hymns, frequently the only saying attributed to an author. However, this thoughtfully produced work, suitable for browsing, will be useful in some medium-to-large academic and public libraries, as well as theological and church libraries.

Encyclopedia of Hell. By Miriam Van Scott. 1998. 308p. bibliog. illus. St. Martin's, $25.95 (0-312-18574-X). DDC: 291.2.

Described as "a comprehensive survey of the underworld," this volume contains A–Z entries on topics in art, film, popular culture, television, and theater, as well as mythology and religion.

Though it describes many diverse images of hell, the volume lacks a clear focus. Many entries leave one wondering what relevance they have to hell. *Food novelties*, *greeting cards*, and *T-shirts* are among them. What does a depiction of Satan on a can of sandwich spread tell us about hell? The arrangement of the entries is odd. One can find entries for *Christian hell*, *Hindu hell*, and *Jain hell*, but should one be interested in Jewish hell, one would have to know to look under entries *Abbadon*, *Gehenna*, and *Sheol*. No index is provided, so a reader interested in the Hell's Angels, for example, would have to know to look under *Bikers*.

The *Encyclopedia of Hell* appears to be the work of someone keenly interested in the subject matter. However, the quality and relevance of the information contained in entries along with shortcomings in its construction render this work useless as a reference tool. A compilation of descriptions of beliefs about damnation or eternal punishment from the religions and mythologies of the world along with the personages who haunt these underworlds would have given this work focus, though other reference sources already exist that provide this information, the *Encyclopedia of Religion* (Macmillan, 1987) and *Mythologies* (Univ. of Chicago, 1991) being two excellent examples. A companion volume, *Encyclopedia of Heaven*, will be published this spring.

Legends of the Earth, Sea, and Sky: An Encyclopedia of Nature Myths. Ed. by Tamra Andrews. 1998. 322p. appendix. bibliog. illus. indexes. ABC-CLIO, $65 (0-87436-963-0). DDC: 291.2.

From the beginning of history, humans have given spiritual significance to natural phenomena and have told stories about why and how they exist in order to feel some sort of control over them. Many of the stories are shared across cultures. This volume is an impressive collection of information about the mythology of the natural world.

The entries are in alphabetical order and run from two paragraphs to two pages in length. There are entries for individual deities (*Benten*, the Japanese sea goddess; *Enki*, the Sumerian water god; *Ymir*, the Norse frost giant); types of deities (*nymphs*; *sun and sun gods*); ethnic groups (*Africa*; *Baltic and Slavic lands*; *Mesoamerica*); objects (*arrows*; *hammers*; *Kachinas*); and concepts (*creation myths*; *death*). Longer entries on types of deities, objects, and concepts explain cross-cultural similarities and differences. Each entry has cross-references at the end. There are a few interesting black-and-white illustrations.

The end matter includes a "Guide to Primary Sources," which identifies ancient sources for the myths of various cultural groups. Many of these sources are cited in the nine-page bibliography. There is an "Index by Culture" as well as a subject index.

This book is unique in that it takes a cross-cultural approach to one aspect of mythology. It makes fascinating reading and is recommended for public, academic, and high-school libraries as a complement to more general mythology sources.

Cassell Dictionary of Classical Mythology. By Jenny March. 1998. 416p. appendixes. bibliog. illus. Cassell; dist. by Sterling, $37.50 (0-304-34626-8). DDC: 292.1.

When the keywords *classical* and *mythology* bring up more than 500 citations in *Books in Print Plus*, do we need another dictionary of Greek and Roman mythology? With Hercules popular as both a live-action TV show and a Disney animated film, and teachers still giving out Greek and Roman mythology assignments, the answer is yes. This new one should be very helpful to both students and librarians. The author is a distinguished classicist at Oxford University, but her writing is accessible to general readers. The style is more modern than most mythology books, which enhances accessibility. Anglicisms do not interfere with an American's use of the book.

The book is in dictionary format with extensive cross-references. Roman names of gods refer the reader to the longer articles on the Greek gods. Where a Roman god was conflated with a Greek (e.g., Jupiter with Zeus or Juno with Hera), his or her distinctly Roman characteristics are described. Entries range from a couple of lines to several two-columned pages. Many of the entries have citations to Greek and Roman literary works, a number of which, such as *Iliad* and *Odyssey*, are easy to find in translation in inexpensive paperback editions. March also includes excerpts from the literature in her own translation. Her quotations from *Iliad* about the fate of Astyanax, Hector's little son, are surprisingly moving.

All of classical mythology's "usual suspects" (e.g., Apollo, Hercules, Trojan War) are included, with good, clear discussions. More obscure characters are also included, such as the men Cadmus created by sowing dragon's teeth. They are the Spartoi or Sown Men, and March has separate entries for each of them. Cross-referencing seems inconsistent. There is nothing in *Sown Men* to lead the reader to *Cadmus*, although there are links to *Pentheus*, *Teresias*, and several other entries.

At the end of the volume, March includes several appendixes: maps of the classical word, genealogies of gods and mythological families, thumbnail sketches of major classical authors, and a brief bibliography. The genealogies will be useful to students of Greek drama as well as students of mythology.

The book is suitable for large public libraries and their larger branches, academic libraries, and high-school libraries, especially those serving honors literature classes.

Encyclopedia of Greco-Roman Mythology. By Mike Dixon-Kennedy. 1998. 370p. appendixes. bibliog. index. ABC-CLIO, $65 (1-57607-094-8). DDC: 292.1.

Encyclopedia of Russian and Slavic Myth and Legend. By Mike Dixon-Kennedy. 1998. 375p. appendixes. bibliog. illus. index. ABC-CLIO, $65 (1-57607-063-8). DDC: 398.2.

These are formidable one-man compilations, with the flaws inherent in such compilations but with some genuine virtues as well. Dixon-Kennedy is the author of several other books on similar topics, including *European Myth and Legend: An A–Z of People and Places* [RBB Ja 1 & 15 98]. Both of these new volumes are in dictionary format. Mythological, legendary, and historical characters get entries ranging from a few lines to several double-columned pages. The ethnic or national origin of each entry is noted, whether Greek or Roman or Greco-Roman, Russian, Slavic, or Tatar. Entry headwords include variant spellings, and *see also* references guide the reader to related entries.

The Greco-Roman volume has more than 1,400 entries and also includes a brief essay on Greek civilization, a bibliography, a chronology, and a list of Roman emperors. It has many entries not found elsewhere (e.g., *Bellatrix*, *Vegoia*). A unique feature is its inclusion of astronomical information about constellations representing mythological figures. Appended to the 900 or so entries in the Russian and Slavic volume are a very brief glossary, a table of transliteration from Cyrillic to Latin letters, a list of Russian rulers, and a topic finder, in addition to a bibliography. The essay on Baba Yaga is longer and more informative than any of those in general folklore dictionaries. There are some omissions, such as a lack of an entry in the Russian and Slavic volume for Alexander Nevsky, who is both a legend and a real man and is discussed within other entries. In both volumes, birth and death dates are provided inconsistently for historical figures. The Greco-Roman volume could have used a map of the Greco-Roman world.

Although it may not be a first choice for smaller libraries because of its lack of illustrations, maps, and genealogical charts, the Greco-Roman volume will complement the numerous similar works found in larger public and academic library reference collection. The Russian and Slavic volume should find a wider audience, since there is no comparable reference work.

Historical Dictionary of Judaism. By Norman Solomon. 1998. 521p. appendixes. bibliog. tables. Scarecrow, $60 (0-8108-3497-9). DDC: 296.

The remarkable popularity of Thomas Cahill's best-seller, *The Gifts of the Jews* (Talese, 1998), demonstrates the continuing interest among both non-Jews and Jews in the world's oldest monotheistic faith. Authored by a distinguished British scholar, this dictionary primarily covers the Jewish religion; it is not a history of the Jewish people nor a history of the Bible. The introductory essay clearly distinguishes this work from other dictionaries of Judaism, especially noting its usefulness to "libraries and librarians." Most of the text is made up of alphabetically arranged entries generally ranging in length from a few sentences to three pages and citing reference works, bibliographies, and primary texts as sources. Examples of entries include *Buber, Martin; death and mourning; Elijah; Holocaust; kasher; sanhedrin;* and *seder*. Borrowing from the "hypertextuality" of electronic media, the volume uses an "open file" icon as well as capitalization to indicate cross-references. Supplementary material—including a complete list of the 613 Commandments, or mitzvot—enhances the reference value of this work.

Although almost six-dozen dictionaries of Judaism have been published in English alone (and many more in languages from Czech to Spanish), ranging from very brief entries in nonacademic works such as *Popular Dictionary of Judaism* (Curzon, 1995) to the more scholarly *Oxford Dictionary of the Jewish Religion* [RBB Jl 97], *Historical Dictionary of Judaism* secures an important place in this vast literature by providing informative and reliable information. Recommended for academic and public libraries.

The Shengold Jewish Encyclopedia. Ed. by Leon Klenicki and others. 1998. 305p. illus. maps. Shengold, P.O. Box 4193, Rockville, MD 20849, $36 (1-887563-43-1). DDC: 296.

First published nearly half a century ago as *Junior Jewish Encyclopedia*, this source has been revised and rewritten as a tool for all age groups. It is a ready-reference source with brief entries on a wide variety of Judaica-related subjects. Users are encouraged to consult other sources for more comprehensive, in-depth information.

The layout is attractive, with double columns and ample margins. The alphabetical entries range in length from a few sentences to four pages. They cover people (*Abraham; Buber, Martin; Jeremiah*), places (*Iowa, Poland, Uruguay*), religious concepts (*heaven and hell, Kabbalah, Teshuvah*), holidays (*Passover, Sukkot*), historical events (*Holocaust, Yom Kippur War*), and arts and letters (*Hebrew literature; music, Jews in; stage and screen*). There are also articles on exotic groups such as the Karaites and the Khazars, as well as diverse subjects such as stamps, sports, and education. Maps, charts, tables, and illustrations augment the text. Cross-references appear in bold type within the entries. *See* references direct users to the proper entry when necessary. The volume concludes with a list of some of the books that have shaped Jewish history, a list of important Jewish women, and a few maps.

As in any general work, there are some inconsistencies. Well-known musicians Jan Peerce, Andre Previn, and Isaac Stern are in the article on Jews in music, while Itzhak Perlman, Artur Rubenstein, and Pinchas Zuckerman have their own entries. Reconstructionism has an article, but the Orthodox, Conservative, and Reform denominations are covered in *Judaism*. There is no entry for the term *kosher*, but if one looks up *kashrut*, there is a *see* reference to *dietary laws*.

Although less comprehensive than *The New Standard Jewish Encyclopedia* [RBB Ja 1 93] or *The Encyclopedia of Judaism* (Macmillan, 1989), this is an excellent, inexpensive ready-reference source. It is a good choice for school, synagogue, and small public libraries.

Dictionary of Celtic Mythology. By James MacKillop. 1998. 402p. bibliog. index. Oxford, $45 (0-19-869157-2). DDC: 299.

With the possible exceptions of the Arthurian legend and the saga of Tristan and Iseult, both of which can be traced to Celtic sources, the mythological world of the ancient Celts is not as familiar to most Americans as are the classical myths of Greece and Rome. This gap in our cultural literacy is unfortunate, for, as this dictionary reveals, the Celtic peoples developed a rich and fascinating tradition of legends and myths.

In compiling this volume, MacKillop, an English professor who specializes in Celtic studies, drew not only upon texts written in Irish and Welsh but also on Breton, Cornish, Manx, and Scottish Gaelic sources and traditions. In addition to gods and goddesses, heroes and heroines, creatures, and other mythological figures, the approximately 4,000 entries cover real and imaginary places, archaeological sites, animals and plants, narrative cycles, and ideas. Entries, which frequently include variant spellings and etymologies, vary in length from a single identifying phrase to more than four pages, but the majority are one or two paragraphs. Asterisks within the text of an article indicate those terms that are treated further in separate entries, and numerous cross-references guide the user from alternate titles, names, and spellings to the forms used by MacKillop. Supplementing the dictionary portion of the work are a general guide to pronunciation of the various Celtic languages and a 13-page bibliography of selected sources pertaining to Celtic literature and culture. Especially helpful is a topical index that classifies entries under 36 broad categories, such as concepts, games, literary forms, monsters, rituals and curses, and saints.

Although a number of dictionaries pertaining to Celtic myth have appeared in the last decade, none are as extensive as this work. For example, Peter Ellis' *Dictionary of Celtic Mythology* [RBB Ag 92] and its companion volume, *Dictionary of Irish Mythology* [RBB N 1 89], were designed for lay readers and therefore have far fewer, and generally less-detailed, entries. With only about one-tenth the number of entries, Miranda Green's *Dictionary of Celtic Myth and Legend* [RBB Ap 15 92] lacks the breadth of coverage of this work, but it is important for its illustrations and its links to archaeological evidence and to literary sources. Since each of these earlier works has unique entries or features, this new compendium does not supersede them but rather complements them by offering a more comprehensive approach. Supplementing the coverage of both *The Oxford Companion to Irish Literature* [RBB Ap 15 96] and *The Oxford Companion to the Literature of Wales* (Oxford, 1990), this scholarly dictionary should be a valuable addition to academic and large public libraries.

Historical Dictionary of Taoism. By Julian F. Pas. 1998. 415p. appendix. bibliog. chronology. illus. Scarecrow, $64 (0-8108-3369-7). DDC: 299.

Over the past five years, Scarecrow Press has published nearly 20 titles in its Religions, Philosophies, and Movements series. *Historical Dictionary of Taoism*, like its predecessors in the series for Buddhism, Sikhism, Hinduism, and Bahaism, is a welcome addition to the reference literature for Asian and other non-Judeo/Christian religions, given the paucity of English-language sources devoted exclusively to a particular tradition.

The volume consists of nearly 275 alphabetically arranged entries covering persons, practices, and concepts, although structural flaws detract from its usefulness. First, this work needs an index. Writing for nonspecialists, Pas has "tried as much as possible to provide names and titles in English, rather than in Chinese." *See* references are provided from transliterated Chinese to English, but, in some cases, vice-versa. An index would have minimized the use of *see* references and allowed for the inclusion of variant forms of transliteration, names/terms included within an entry but for which no separate entry exists, and a grouping of related entries by subject. Second, entries occasionally give citations to supplemental works, but the references are abbreviated, forcing the user to turn to a bibliography at the end of the dictionary for the complete bibliographic citation. This is especially annoying when one finds that the bibliography is divided into subjects, with citations arranged alphabetically by author under each subject heading. Consequently, the user must search for a citation under every subject heading.

Other features of this dictionary include a 20-page chronology, consisting of three columns which juxtapose Chinese dynasties, events in Taoist history, and events in Buddhism and other schools in China. This is followed by a 50-page introduction to Taoism. But the reader would do better by first consulting the entry for Tao (The Way) or by reading the last section of the introduction which addresses the nature of Taoism. Otherwise, the reader will end up with historical information about a concept that is never defined.

Historical Dictionary of Taoism has advantages over the existing reference literature in English. *The Shambhala Dictionary of Taoism* (Shambhala, 1996) is shorter, contains fewer entries, and is less academic in tone and presentation than Pas' work. *The Shambhala Guide to Taoism* (Shambhala, 1997) provides some historical overview and much information on Taoist ritual practice. The overview articles on Taoism in *Encyclopedia of Religion* [RBB O 1 87] are excellent, but this source is perhaps not the best for a quick lookup of terms or individuals. Finally, *Companion Encyclopedia of Asian Philosophy* (Routledge, 1997) includes a chapter on Taoism in Chinese philosophy, though the concern of this work is philosophy and not religion.

In his preface, Pas recognizes that his work is quite modest when compared to reference sources in Japanese and Chinese, and hopes that readers will forward suggestions to him for a future improved second edition. In addition to the aforementioned structural issues, expanded content will be necessary. For example, some regard Tsao-chun as an important deity in Taoism, but Pas' work has no separate entry for him, nor is he mentioned in the entry *Gold Cinnabar Taoism*. Libraries, however, needn't wait for that new and expanded edition but would do well to purchase the present volume, since it is the most comprehensive English-language guide to Taoism to date.

Social Sciences

CensusCD+Maps. Version 2.0. CD-ROM. 1998. GeoLytics, $249.50.
System requirements: Windows 98, 95, NT, *or* 3.1; 8MB RAM.

Demographic information is essential for planning everything from business and government to educational and social-service programs. Obtaining the data from the decennial census can be a formidable task. A CD-ROM that contains the complete information from the 1990 census STF 3 A–D files along with area maps makes it quite simple for users to create customized demographic profiles for more than 375,000 geographic areas in the U.S. A previous version of *CensusCD* contained census data but no maps.

The manual and the Five Minute User Guide found in the Help menu provide instructions that are easy to understand. The toolbar provides both icons and commands for navigating the system. To create a report, users must select an area. This can be as large as Nation or as small as Block Group. By combining block groups or using zip codes, one can create neighborhood profiles. To do this, one selects larger areas such as State and then a subarea for the block group or zip code. Once the area is defined, one can select the necessary statistics from the Counts menu. This can be a standard profile of 37 categories (income, housing, race, 1997 estimate/2002 projection, etc.), or a list of specific items such as income/poverty, housing characteristics, or ethnicity. When all the data are compiled, the Run command will produce a report with a color map and statistical tables. The software allows customization of the maps and tables; sorting counts in ascending and descending order; and exporting, printing, and copying to a clipboard. Some of the same data are also available free at the Census Bureau's Internet site busy site. It works best with a fast modem and processor, since downloading graphics can take a long time.

CensusCD+Maps menus are easy for unsophisticated patrons to use. In a few minutes, it is possible to create a basic neighborhood demographic profile. This CD-ROM will be very useful for business and social-sciences collections that are not federal depositories and/or do not want the frustration of the "world wide wait."

History of the Mass Media in the United States: An Encyclopedia. Ed. by Margaret A. Blanchard. 1998. 752p. bibliogs. illus. index. Fitzroy Dearborn, $125 (1-57958-012-2). DDC: 302.23.

Alphabetically arranged by subject, this volume covers the mass media, beginning with the first newspaper founded in Boston in 1690 and ending in 1990. The editor is a professor of journalism and mass communications at the University of North Carolina, Chapel Hill, and the numerous contributors have similar credentials.

The entries range in length from a few paragraphs to several pages. They cover advertising (*advertising in the nineteenth century*, *retail advertising*); books (*best-sellers*, *textbook publishing*); broadcasting (*docudramas*, *Federal Communications Commission*); magazines (*magazines for women*, *muckraking*); motion pictures (*Hollywood in World War II*, *motion picture ratings*); newspapers (*newspaper columnists*, *New York Times*); radio (*payola*, "*War of the Worlds*"); and television (*Army-McCarthy hearings*, *television violence*). Other entries cover alternative media, legal issues, photography, public relations, technology, and such general topics as codes of ethics, comics, and propaganda. A number of entries treat the relationship between mass media and war, from the French and Indian War to Vietnam. Although some entries cover specific, representative manifestations or events (*Huntley-Brinkley Report*, *quiz show scandals*, *Radio Act of 1927*), most entries are quite broad. Major people and institutions have been largely omitted because information is readily available elsewhere. Among the exceptions are Matthew Brady, William Randolph Hearst, and Time Warner.

Beautifully designed, with a nice clear typeface, this work is also enhanced by superb illustrations and well-chosen photographs. Probably the most salient reference features are the bibliographic references at the conclusion of each entry. Most entries contain useful cross-references and the concluding index, as well as alphabetical and topical lists of entries, which provide easy access.

Obviously, a work covering such a prodigious amount of information

Social Sciences

cannot be comprehensive. Nevertheless, some omissions are unfortunate e.g., the Jewish American media, which is the largest ethnic press, and the lack of entries for other media watchdog groups besides Accuracy in Media. Still, this volume is outstanding. Recommended for larger public and academic libraries.

American Immigration. 10v. Ed by Dorothy Anderson and others. 1999. 1,080p. bibliog. charts. illus. indexes. Grolier, $325 (0-7172-9283-5). DDC: 304.8.

Grolier has published a multivolume set on American immigration for school and public libraries, describing the journey to American shores that began more than 400 years ago. The first two volumes of the set introduce the topic and tell the story of Ellis Island during the nineteenth and twentieth centuries. The remaining eight volumes of the set contain more than 100 A–Z entries, from *Afghans* to *West Indian immigrants*. The set is extensively cross-referenced. *See* references refer the reader to appropriate headings (*anti-Semitism* SEE *prejudice and discrimination*). At the end of most entries, a *see also* box (denoted by a Statue of Liberty icon) refers the reader to related topics within the set. For example, *forced immigration* has *see also* references to *Africans, economic effects,* and *immigration law and policy.* These cross-references are important because some entries appear under headings that would not be obvious choices for the reader—*literature, the media,* and *ethnicity; relations and conflicts within ethnic groups.*

More than half of the entries cover immigrant groups and discuss the history of their native country, the history of immigration, and their life in the U.S. Mention is made of each group's contributions to U.S. culture and efforts to retain their own heritage. Locator maps show places of origin. Smaller groups, such as Bulgarians and Romanians, are covered in 2 or 3 pages; 20 pages are devoted to the Irish. In some cases, several groups are treated in a single entry, such as *Central and South Americans* and *Southeast Asians.* Entries such as *assimilation, prejudice and discrimination,* and *quotas* treat some of the struggles and controversies related to immigration. Other issues are discussed in entries such as *baggage, immigrant aid societies, occupations, passports and visas,* and *schools.* Throughout the set, sidebars add additional facts and stories relating to the immigrant experience. A personal touch is provided by the inclusion of numerous transcripts from the Ellis Island Museum Oral History Project, denoted by a ship icon. A brief bibliography is repeated at the end of each volume, as is a set index. A table of contents would be helpful. The text reads easily and the pages are attractively designed, enhanced with historical photographs.

For the middle-school student, this set does a nice job of bringing to life the experiences of different immigrant groups and providing balanced coverage of various issues related to immigration. Older students in search of statistical tables, distribution maps, and more in-depth discussions of a greater number of ethnic groups will need to turn to other sources such as *Gale Encyclopedia of Multicultural America* [RBB D 1 95] and *We the People: An Atlas of America's Ethnic Diversity* (Macmillan, 1988). *American Immigration* is recommended for young adult (grades 6–9) collections in school and public libraries. There is a companion Web site at http://immigration.grolier.com.

Atlas of American Migration. By Stephen A. Flanders. 1998. 214p. bibliog. charts. illus. index. maps. tables. Facts On File, $85 (0-8160-3158-4). DDC: 304.8.

This source, rather than having an alphabetical or chronological arrangement, is divided into 10 thematic chapters, from "A Shifting Mosaic: America and Migration," to "The Suburban Frontier: Migration Since 1945." Intervening chapters cover such topics as slavery, Native American migration, the settlement of the West, and the move to the cities after 1890. Each chapter is an extended essay that is broken into various headings and subheadings. The most important features of the atlas are the many tables, graphs, and maps. For example, chapter two, "The Earliest Americans: Pre-Columbian Migration," has a time line as well as maps showing, among other things, settlement in the Pre-Columbian Southwest, distribution of the Mississippi Temple Mound culture, Norse exploration, and Native American language families. The chapter on American slavery, entitled "Migration in Chains," includes the maps "Underground Railroad," "Slave Revolt and Flight," and "Slavery's Westward Migration after 1820," among others. All maps were created especially for this volume. Data in charts and tables were drawn primarily from sources such as the U.S. Bureau of the Census and the U.S. Immigration and Naturalization Service. The volume concludes with a selected bibliography, mostly of secondary sources, and an index. The index would be improved if it identified the illustrations, maps, and other graphics that are listed.

We the People: An Atlas of America's Diversity (Macmillan, 1988) also looks at migration patterns in the U.S. A more scholarly source, it is now somewhat out-of-date. *Atlas of American Migration* contains information up to the mid-1990s. Because of its arrangement, libraries may be tempted to put it in the circulating collection. However, it contains many valuable maps and statistics for reference use in high-school, public, and academic libraries.

Encyclopedia of Global Population and Demographics. 2v. By Immanuel Ness and James Ciment. 1999. 967p. bibliog. charts. index. tables. M. E. Sharpe, $185 (1-56321-710-0). DDC: 304.6.

According to the authors, "the population of planet Earth is increasing at an awesome and, perhaps, even unsustainable pace." This reference source on the population of the world begins with 10 well-written overview essays dealing with a multiplicity of demographic topics (vital statistics, cultural identity, migration, families, etc.). The essays analyze history, trends, and concepts dealing with each topic. Following the essays, there is a section of tables, graphs, and other data dealing with world regions (continents and subcontinents) containing statistical information related to geography, population, and birth and death rates.

The main body of the book consists of three-to-five-page statistical profiles, arranged alphabetically under 194 countries, each including a wide variety of data dealing with geography, population, households, education, health, transportation, media, economics, religion, race, and birth/death and marriages. The statistics in each profile are identified for 1965, 1980, and 1995—this allows readers to detect statistical patterns and trends in each country. The statistics in almost every profile are taken from authoritative resources such as the CIA's *World Factbook,* the International Labor Organization's *World Labour Report,* the United Nation's *Demographic Yearbook* and *Statistical Yearbook,* and the World Bank's *World Development Indicators.*

The encyclopedia's index is primarily valuable for its subject access to the essays beginning the book.

Although the statistical information is available in other resources, the introductory essays provide a very useful context in which to interpret the statistics. This set is recommended as a well-designed, easily understood summary source for important world demographic information, especially for academic and public libraries that do not have the UN's *Demographic Yearbook.*

People and the Earth: An Environmental Atlas. 6v. Ed. by Andrea Due. 1999. 276p. charts. illus. indexes. maps. Grolier, $225 (0-7172-9204-5). DDC: 304.2.

This ambitious work attempts to examine the history and development of human beings and their impact on the environment. Because there is no introduction or preface, it is difficult to discern the intended audience or purpose of the work, although it seems to be designed for the upper-elementary level and above. The individual volumes concentrate on broad time periods—"Prehistoric Times," "Ancient Times," "Medieval Times," "Age of Expansion," "Age of Revolutions," and "The Modern World." Each contains 17 double-page spreads on specific topics like the Benedictines (volume 3), the Renaissance (volume 4), and World War II (volume 5). The broadness of these double-page spreads precludes any in-depth treatment of the topics, and no bibliographies are included for further reading. The spread on World War II covers the entire conflict in just four brief paragraphs, along with another paragraph on U.S. aid to Germany and Japan after the war. The impact of the war on the environment is never made clear.

The usefulness of the set is further hampered by the fact that each volume is self-contained. The index and glossary refer only to the particular volume; there is no overall index. The only aid for the user who is motivated to seek additional information is a page at the back of each volume listing the contents of all the volumes in the set.

On the plus side, the color illustrations and maps (although they have no scale) are attractive. Most of the illustrations are original renderings. The time lines in the first volume are useful and serve to orient the user to the time period under consideration. Some of the graphics are overwhelming for the text. For example, the double-page spread on "The First Americans," which briefly covers slavery and Dred Scott, the Cherokee Nation, life on reservations, and treaties with Native Americans, contains several large-scale illustrations, including a family of slaves; an incomplete map of Native American reservations (with only six groups named), which also includes the percentage of black population around 1930; and a color illustration of life on the Plains. It is difficult from the illustration to tell exactly which nation is depicted—the teepees might be Gros Ventre or Blackfeet, but the dress is generic. In most of the entries, the illustrations fill at least one page—the spread on railroads in volume 5 is nearly three-quarters illustration.

There are so many difficulties and shortcomings in this set that the Board cannot recommend it. Perhaps it is more appropriate for the home user who would sit down and read the entries in sequential order. It would not be useful in a reference collection.

Gay & Lesbian Almanac. Ed. by Neil Schlager. 1998. 680p. bibliog. illus. index. St. James, $100 (1-55862-358-2). DDC: 305.9.

"But suddenly, our movement was transformed. . . . Where we had quietly discussed 'the problem' we began to confront the world. Where we'd begged for understanding, we demanded equality." Activist Jim Kepner's words, quoted in the chapter on politics in this volume, characterize the post-Stonewall shift. Certainly those same words characterize the book; the thought of a work such as the *Almanac* being produced at any time in history prior to the 1969 Stonewall Rebellion is unimaginable. Offering much more than fast-attack fact searching, the book very capably facilitates in-depth study of twentieth-century American lesbian and gay experience and culture. At nearly 700 pages, weighing in at just under five pounds, pricey, and wonderfully designed and illustrated, this is a work to be reckoned with.

The *Almanac* is divided into 23 chapters covering such topics as family, health, law, employment, and religion. Most chapters include profiles of prominent people. Each chapter ends with a truly extensive bibliography listing books, parts of books, periodical articles, master's theses, videos, and also, when appropriate, references to both organizations and Internet sites. An annotated general bibliography is also provided.

Of particular note is chapter 3, "Significant Documents." Here may be found complete papers such as Carl Wittman's "Gay Manifesto," written in 1969; Audre Lorde's "I Am Your Sister: Black Women Organizing across Sexualities"; Harvey Milk's "That's What America Is" speech from 1978; and EDNA, the still nonexistent Employment Non-Discrimination Act. Also noteworthy is chapter 20, "Travel and Leisure." Here the reader will discover a discussion of the powerful roles that women's independently owned bookstores have played in the lesbian community, as well as an overview of the evolution of the International Gay Rodeo Association. Chapter 23, "Local and Regional Views," offers a look at the quality and substance of gay and lesbian life in the U.S. The East, South, Midwest and Great Plains, Intermountain and Southwest, and the Pacific states regions are considered through such perspectives as demography, jurisprudence, and local or regional events important to the lesbian and gay movement.

Regarding the question of balance, which will surely be raised, the chapter authors seem fairly evenly split by gender. The content also *feels* as if every attempt was made to achieve balance between females, males, and shared issues and interests. A weakness lies in the book's index. The *Almanac* deserves a strong, carefully authored index, with many more *see* and *see also* references. Such an index greatly enhances a sense of unity, especially important when a work is multiauthored and contains overlapping information. For example, no index reference could be found to the Kepner statement used to open this review.

The *Almanac* is highly recommended for both the public library and the academic library setting, from the very smallest to the largest. This recommendation also stands without reservation for those libraries that have acquired *Completely Queer: The Gay and Lesbian Encyclopedia* [RBB Je 1 & 15 98]. Although certainly some of the content of the two is duplicated, the tone, context, and bibliographic support supplied by the *Almanac* is very different and will prove over time to be an invaluable resource to library users, researchers, and "invisible" members of the lesbian and gay community alike.

The Girl Pages: A Handbook of the Best Resources for Strong, Confident, Creative Girls. By Charlotte Milholland. 1999. 428p. Hyperion, paper $14.95 (0-7876-8109-7). DDC: 305.23.

Society's growing awareness of the special needs of young teenage girls is reflected in the greater availability of resources for these young people. This reference book offers an overview of information and opportunities and is written for girls and their parents. The author is a freelance writer and a volunteer at the Lower East Side Girls Club in New York.

There are six sections for girls: "Outdoor Adventures," "Sports," "Science and Technology," "Writing and the Arts," "Leadership and Activism," and "School and Work." The emphasis is on preparing for profitable careers. Each section includes statements from women in the field, development and educational opportunities (including contests, summer programs, scholarships, volunteer programs, and Web sites), book lists (often annotated), and career options. Sidebars include reinforcing quotations, and movies related to the topic are noted. A seventh section focuses on resources for parents.

This is a good browsing reference. It gives much useful information, though not in the most effective way. Coverage seems somewhat arbitrary (well-established girls' youth groups, such as the Girl Scouts, get relatively short shrift). Traditional women's fields, such as nursing and education—and librarianship—are not mentioned. This handbook has a profeminist perspective. It is interesting as such but should not be construed as a definitive source for girls. Most appropriate for circulating collections in school and public libraries.

Significant Contemporary American Feminists: A Biographical Sourcebook. Ed. by Jennifer Scanlon. 1999. 361p. bibliogs. index. Greenwood, $75 (0-313-30125-5). DDC: 305.42.

U.S. feminists whose activism and scholarship helped shape the second wave of feminism in this country are profiled here, along with some of the next generation of leaders. The signed essays, four to seven pages each, are biographical and analytical with accompanying bibliographies of works by and about the subjects. Fifty theorists, writers, activists, artists, and politicians are treated. The time span is generally from the late 1960s into the 1990s, covering three decades of social change. Included are pioneers from the beginning of the modern feminist movement such as Bella Abzug, Betty Friedan, and Robin Morgan; well-known political figures such as June Jordan and Patricia Schroeder; and activists from minority communities such as United Farm Workers cofounder Dolores Huerta and Cherokee Chief Wilma Mankiller. Very contemporary figures—Susan Faludi and Anna Quindlen, for example—are also included, with other representatives of the young "third wave" of feminism.

In addition to giving the basic biographical information about education and family, the entries document each woman's engagement with feminism and significance in the movement, highlighting contributions and accomplishments. Many of the names (Gloria Steinem, Shirley Chisholm) are very well known; others are not so immediately identifiable outside of feminist circles. Picking only 50 women of course leads to questions about who should have been included—Catherine Mackinnon is but Andrea Dworkin is not, for example—and the editor acknowledges that the work is highly selective.

Reading through the entries, one is impressed with the variety of identities and affiliations that comprise the group "feminists" and the different paths that led these women to feminism. Some are liberal feminists; some, academic theorists; some come out of labor struggles; others, from gay and lesbian activism. Many of the women are very concerned with issues of race and class as well as gender.

Most of the women are included in other biographical works such as Gale's *Contemporary Authors*, but the analysis presented in this volume of the work and the influence of these women is unique. Although the index occasionally lists women under areas of professional activity (*academics, journalists, lawyers, writers*), it would have been useful to provide more links to assist in making comparisons. An extensive bibliography of readings about second-and third-wave feminism is appended.

The editor and most of the contributors are academics, either professors or graduate students. The quality of the writing varies in the individual entries. Most academic libraries, and any library with a women's studies collection will probably want to acquire this reference work.

Susan B. Anthony: A Biographical Companion. Ed. by Judith E. Harper. 1998. 335p. bibliog. illus. index. ABC-CLIO, $45 (0-87436-948-7). DDC: 305.42.

This new addition to the publisher's Biographical Companion series is a thoroughly researched volume that will enhance any women's history collection. Alphabetically arranged from *abolitionist movement* to *Wright, Martha Coffin* (one of Anthony's closest friends), the book has 120 entries on Anthony's family life, colleagues, and social and political influences. Separate entries exist for family members and many individuals in her circle, including suffragist Carrie Chapman Catt, authorized biographer Ida Husted Harper, and temperance leader Frances Willard. Controversies such as the split between the American Woman Suffrage Association and the National Woman Suffrage Association are objectively described. Each entry, usually two to three pages, includes suggestions for further reading, many of which are listed again in the extensive bibliography cited at the volume's end. Indexing and cross-references are adequate. There no index entry for the League of Women Voters, although it is mentioned several times in the text.

One of the most useful (but not indexed) sections is the 40-page collection of documents. These range from Anthony's first speech (to the Daughters of Temperance in 1849) to articles she wrote for the *San Francisco Examiner* in 1896. The introduction to the volume is a fine summary of Anthony's reform work as suffragist, abolitionist, and scholar of constitutional law. Also included is a separate chronology of events in Anthony's life.

This accessible work will be tremendously useful, both for casual browsing and for serious researchers. Much more than a biographical work on Susan B. Anthony, it is a worthwhile introduction to the temperance, abolitionist, and women's suffrage movements. Recommended for high-school, public, and academic libraries.

Encyclopedia of Family Life. 5v. Ed. by Carl L. Bankston III. 1999. 1,498p. bibliog. charts. glossary. illus. index. tables. Salem, $380 (0-89356-940-2). DDC: 306.85.

This work serves as a reference for high-school and college students, professionals, parents and spouses, and general readers on the different aspects of the central and rapidly changing institution of the family. Bringing together up-to-date discussions of the full range of family issues that confront modern society in Canada and the U.S., the set offers 452 signed, alphabetically arranged essays ranging in length from 250 to 4,000 words. These essays are the work of more than 240 contributors, most of whom have academic affiliations.

Articles define terms, discuss controversies, and cover historical trends and events, health concerns, laws, court cases, people, organizations, and much more. Examples of entries include *adultery, attention-deficit hyperactivity disorder, birth order, displaced homemakers, foster homes,* Head Start, Hull House, *interracial families,* Korean Americans, *latchkey children, mother-daughter relationships,* Planned Parenthood Federation of America, *prenuptial agreements,* and *sandwich generation.* More than half of all articles are 1,500 or more words in length; these end with specialized bibliographies collectively listing nearly 3,000 relevant books and articles. Bibliographical entries in articles of 2,500 to 4,000 words are annotated, as are the entries in the general bibliography that can be found at the end of volume 5. That volume's appendix section contains an annotated listing of support organizations, as well as a lengthy chronology of legislation and court decisions, a general time line, and an extensive glossary. A variety of features serve to help readers find the information they seek quickly, including the encyclopedia's alphabetical arrangement, cross-references at the end of every essay, "List of Subjects by Category" located at the end of volume 5, and a comprehensive index.

This ambitious set is not without its shortcomings, many of which surface only upon closer examination. Alcoholism and drug abuse are treated in the same article. The article *alternative family types* consists of two skimpy paragraphs, despite evidence that alternative familial structures may become the social equals of the traditional nuclear family. W*eddings* includes no mention of the rise in gay and lesbian weddings, although same-sex marriages are discussed in the article *domestic partners.* There are no index entries or article headings for nature versus nurture, parent education, psychological development of boys and girls, runaway children, or sex therapy.

Public, high-school, and college libraries will want to own this new set. It is more comprehensive than Macmillan's two-volume E*ncyclopedia of Marriage and the Family* [RBB F 1 96]. A useful complement is Oryx's *Statistical Handbook on the American Family* (2d ed., 1999).

Junior Worldmark Encyclopedia of World Cultures. 9v. Ed. by Timothy L. Gall and Susan Bevan Gall. 1999. 2,078p. bibliog. glossary. illus. indexes. maps. UXL, $225 (0-7876-1756-3). DDC: 306.

There have been a number of encyclopedias of ethnology published in the last few years. This trend is probably due at least in part to the refocusing of educational curriculum from a geopolitical approach to an emphasis on multicultural awareness. This latest offering is from UXL, the Gale Group imprint that publishes resources aimed specifically at middle-school students. Based on Gale's *Worldmark Encyclopedia of Cultures and Daily Life* [RBB My 1 98], this set features rewritten articles that consider the traditions, living conditions, and other characteristics of more than 290 culture groups.

This set's organization parallels that of its sister publication, *Junior Worldmark Encyclopedia of the Nations* [RBB My 1 96]. The nine individually numbered volumes feature a straight alphabetical listing of 71 countries, Afghanistan through Zimbabwe. Each country entry begins with a one-paragraph overview of its population composition, followed by individual culture group entries, ranging from coverage of one or two groups (Liechtensteiners, Seychellois, Trinidadians and Tobagonians) through multiple listings for more populous nations (six for both Russia and Spain, seven for India, eight for China), in order according to population size. Culture group entries are organized according to a standardized 20-heading outline. This includes a fact summary (pronunciation, alternate names, population size, etc.), and brief descriptions of location, language, folklore (with some excerpts from traditional stories), religion, rites of passage, family life, clothing, food, education, cultural heritage, recreation, social problems, and more. Bibliographies list age-appropriate articles, benchmark publications, standard reference works, and Web sites. Sprinkled throughout the text are maps, black-and-white captioned photos, vocabulary lists of foreign terms and phrases, and typical recipes that have been Americanized and that call for ingredients readily available in most supermarkets.

An identical glossary of more than 150 terms appears in each volume, as does an index covering all nine volumes. Index terms are limited to culture groups, countries, and regions. Numerous cross-references are provided throughout the set. Text is laid out in a double-column format and features a crisp font on bright white paper. Information is presented in manageable paragraphs with bulleted, numbered outline headings. The lack of color illustrations in no way diminishes the set's visual appeal.

Representative as opposed to comprehensive (there is no entry for the U.S., for example), and concerned with present-day status versus historical development, this set will be useful as introductory material and should be considered as an enhancement to standard titles. Used in conjunction with the aforementioned *Junior Worldmark Encyclopedia of the Nations,* or a comparable set, such as *Lands and Peoples* [RBB Jl 97], this resource is most appropriate for elementary-and middle-school collections or those serving ESL/LEP populations. Libraries desiring more complete coverage or serving a more sophisticated clientele might be better served by the parent set, *Worldmark Encyclopedia of Cultures and Daily Life,* which covers more than 500 culture groups. Public, middle, and high-school libraries should also consider Marshall Cavendish's *Peoples of the Americas* [RBB Ap 1 99], more suited to student research projects but limited to North and South America.

Macmillan Encyclopedia of World Slavery. 2v. Ed. by Paul Finkelman and Joseph C. Miller. 1998. 1,065p. bibliog. illus. index. maps. tables. Macmillan, $195 (0-02-864607-X). DDC: 306.3.

Designed for a wide audience, from high-schoolers and general readers to students at the undergraduate and graduate level to professional historians, this work strives to cover "all aspects of the history of human slavery." Its 550 alphabetically arranged entries provide geographical, historical, legal, biographical, cultural, social, and religious perspective. Examples of entries include *abolition and antislavery movements; ancient Rome; concubinage;* Equiano, Olaudah; *Japan; literature of slavery; Louisiana; plantations; Quakers;* Thomas Aquinas; *utopias and slavery;* Vesey Rebellion (1822); and *wet nurses.*

Numerous contributors, all with academic affiliations, wrote the entries, which vary in length from a few paragraphs to more than 40 pages. Longer entries are generally divided into sections. *Law,* for example, is divided into articles on law and slavery in different societies, from the Ancient Middle East to the U.S. Entries conclude with a list of mostly scholarly titles, many of which are also cited in the general bibliography. Preceding the A–Z section are 25 maps, and black-and-white photographs and illustrations supplement the text. An alphabetical list of entries appears at the beginning of volume 1, and a topical list of entries appears in an appendix, along with a time line. Navigation is further aided by an index and cross-references. At least one cross-reference is inaccurate. There is a *see* reference from *branding and branding irons* to the entry *badges of slavery*, but *badges of slavery* never mentions branding. Rather, it discusses the ratification of the Thirteenth Amendment, which not only outlawed slavery but also gave Congress the power via legislation to eliminate civil constraints or "badges of slavery" for freed slaves. Branding is discussed, however, in the entry *discipline and punishment*.

This resource has the decided disadvantage of appearing on the heels of another reference work on slavery, ABC-CLIO's *Historical Guide to World Slavery* [RBB My 1 98]. Both have similar titles, both appear in two volumes, and both treat slavery in its global and historical context. Entries in both titles are arranged alphabetically, signed by the scholars who wrote them, and conclude with supplemental bibliographies. Although coverage in both is quite similar, there are important differences. ABC-CLIO, with approximately 100 more entries, tends to cover more specific topics in shorter articles. A good example is its discussion of abolition, which is spread across a number of separate entries; Macmillan has one long article, *abolition and anti-slavery movements*. Macmillan takes the in-depth approach with other topics as well. The entry *Africa* is 25 pages; ABC-CLIO covers it in two. Both sets have entries not found in the other. In ABC-CLIO one finds *enconmiendo, Gullah, Harpers Ferry raid, Hittite code, Juneteenth, Nashoba Plantation, occupations, serfdom in medieval Europe,* and *Peru*. In Macmillan, one finds *gladiators, Hinduism, Maori, overseers, Philippines, reparations,* and *spirituals*. ABC CLIO has entries for many more people than Macmillan; Macmillan has entries for almost 40 U.S. states. Macmillan generally has more coverage of cultural topics, in entries such as *film and television, slavery in; music by slaves;* and the 12-page *literature of slavery*, a topic to which ABC-CLIO devotes two pages. The Macmillan article on slavery and Nazism is longer than that in ABC-CLIO, and includes a more scholarly list of references.

As stated in the preface, "For most Americans, 'slavery' evokes an image of black bondsmen, white masters, and cotton fields." Both of these encyclopedias demonstrate that slavery extends far beyond the North American experience. Because each set covers many topics not found in the other, larger libraries should have both. With its generally shorter articles and many biographical entries, the ABC-CLIO set might be a better choice for high-school libraries. The more scholarly Macmillan encyclopedia is recommended for public and academic libraries.

Peoples of the World: Customs and Cultures. 10v. 1998. 1,280p. illus. index. maps. Grolier, $289 (0-7172-9236-3). DDC: 306.

This encyclopedia is a guide to more than 1,200 ethnic groups that inhabit the earth. According to the foreword, several criteria determined inclusion: a common history; a unique language; shared traditions, religion, or folklore; a sense of common identity in the face of strong pressure to be absorbed by others; people defining themselves as a group; or those living together in the same geographic area. Limited to groups that are still in existence today, even if they are in the process of being absorbed, coverage ranges from those that include fewer than a hundred members (Brazil's Uru-Eu-Wau-Wau) to those that number in the millions.

Arranged alphabetically, entries can consist of one sentence (*Dyawara*" An ethnic group that lives in Mali") or run to several pages (*Americans, Chinese, Russians,* etc.). Most one-line entries refer readers to at least one related article. Individual articles are not signed, but a list of editors and contributors and their geographic areas of expertise are listed at the beginning of the first volume. Common English names and spellings have been used, with alternatives appearing in parentheses. Numerous *see* references guide users from variant spellings and colloquial names to actual articles (Asante—*see* Ashanti). Words that appear in boldface are defined in a glossary that is repeated in each volume. Definitions are provided for terms such as *tribe, clan, cannibal, shrine,* and so on.

Most extended entries include the various names of a group, the population size, where it lives, the language, religion, main economic occupations, and some history. Cross-referencing is frequent. The writing style tends to be dry, and presentations range from short, simple sentences to lengthy, dense passages. Numerous full-color photos with captions, sometimes several to a page, and 280 maps accompany the text. An index to the entire set appears in each volume.

This is an attractive resource, but there is some concern about how much actual usage it will receive. The curricula and type of assignments generally associated with the publisher's intended audience, students in middle through high school, will be better served by established reference works. For example, a middle-school student looking for basic data about a Native American Indian tribe should be able to find all the required information (locale, history, socialization, language, etc.) in any standard encyclopedia. In this set, the entry on the Seminole runs eight sentences; the Apache receive twelve sentences; the Ottawa, seven. Little cultural information is provided. Instead, the focus is on the geopolitical history of the tribe, and its efforts to survive (this emphasis is seen in other entries: *Ponti, Waorani,* etc.). When faced with another typical assignment, *Cossacks,* the researcher is referred to *Ukrainians* and *Kazakh*. The four-page entry on the Ukrainians does include three pertinent paragraphs, buried in the middle of the third page. The three-column Kazakh article yields a one-sentence contribution that misspells the term as *Cossaks*.

Of additional concern is that some entries reinforce negative ethnic stereotypes. One example: "The Corsicans are famous for certain cultural traits: they have large extended families and are known for the violent way they 'solve' arguments." Another problematic area is picture captions. Subjects are always identified ("A Singaporian bride," "A band of Jewish musicians in Lima, Peru"), but no accompanying information explains their significance or provides any correlation to the text.

There is additional evidence of uneven editing that goes beyond the occasional misspelled word. There are grammatical errors. Even the 22-page index is of limited usefulness in that it simply mirrors the entry headwords and cross-references instead of providing ways to pull scattered information together. There is no index term *Native Americans,* for example, because there is no article on Native Americans, just articles on individual tribes. Continents and regions are not indexed. Occasional two-page spreads highlight a single aspect of an ethnic group (*Japanese mythology, Melanesian secret societies,* etc.), but these special features are not listed anywhere nor is their existence indicated in the index.

Despite the book's vivid artwork and extensive coverage, it is difficult to recommend it. School and public libraries should continue to rely on standard sources that better support the curriculum—*Lands and Peoples* [RBB Jl 1 97] and *The World Book Encyclopedia of People and Places* [RBB Je 1 & 15 98] among others. Gale's upcoming *Junior Worldmark Encyclopedia of World Cultures* should be another valuable resource.

Encyclopedia of Urban America: The Cities and Suburbs. 2v. By Neil Larry Shumsky. 1998. 974p. bibliogs. illus. index. ABC-CLIO, $175 (0-87436-846-4). DDC: 307.76.

This companion to last year's well-received *Encyclopedia of Rural America* [RBB Ap 1 98] is a unique undertaking. Shumsky surveyed major works that treat the evolution and condition of life in the cities on this continent and solicited 547 signed articles that treat every subject that appeared in the indexes of those works more than twice. The list of nearly 400 contributors includes only 21 not identified with some institution of higher education. The academics come from many fields, including archaeology, electrical engineering, and forestry, in addition to criminal justice, history, sociology, and public administration.

With such broad coverage, it's too bad that there is almost nothing about libraries or their impact on the lives of immigrants and their descendants, much less any acknowledgment of their role in supplying information to the information have-nots of contemporary society. There are occasional allusions to libraries in some of the entries, including *Chicago,* charity (as in Andrew Carnegie), *commercial strips,* and *resort towns*. By comparison, there are lengthy articles devoted to public baths, public disorderliness, public health, public housing, and public works—just nothing about public (or other) libraries.

That quibble aside, this is a resource that should prove useful in academic and large public libraries. The articles are arranged alphabetically and include *see also* references and brief bibliographies; length ranges from approximately half a page to eight pages. Some longer entries, such as *Asian Americans in cities* (although not *African Americans in cities*) are subdivided. The list of entries at the beginning of volume 1 helps the user comprehend the scope of the work and find articles that might not occur to someone using only the index, which is extensive but not totally satisfactory. For example, while there are a few references under *new towns* and the book indexes articles that mention Reston, Virginia, and Columbia, Maryland, they do not distinguish between passing references and substantive articles or direct the researcher to the article on Columbia's planner, James Rouse. There is a good article on John Nolen, who planned more than 400 towns and authored *New Towns for Old* but this article is not referenced in the index under *new towns*.

A seven-page list of entries by subject helps identify articles that address topics such as building types, law enforcement, politics, race, recreation, and transportation. A selected nine-page bibliography directs the reader to other sources, grouped by topics such as urban government and urban economics.

Academics interested in urban evolution will find this tool useful for ready reference and for planning courses and assigned readings for advanced students. Large public libraries will use it for ready reference and to help interested researchers identify scholarly sources for interlibrary loan. This resource is recommended in particular to libraries that have already acquired *Encyclopedia of Rural America*.

Encyclopedia of World Cities. 2v. By Immanuel Ness. 1999. 740p. appendixes. bibliog. index. maps. Sharpe, $179 (0-7656-8017-3). DDC: 307.76.

This new reference set is a compilation of information on 132 of the world's leading cities. According to the editor, "50% of people live in urban areas currently, and by the year 2025, about 2/3 of the world's population will be city dwellers."

Cities were selected based on size, location (an effort was made to include all the major cities of each continent), and historical and cultural importance. Arrangement is alphabetical by city, from *A*bidjan to *Z*urich. Among the other cities covered are Maputo (Mozambique), Montreal, Prague, Taipei (Taiwan), and Nairobi. There are 24 U.S. cities, including Anchorage, Chicago, Cleveland, Denver, and San Diego. It would be helpful to have a list of the cities grouped by country, either in the index or in an appendix.

Each entry is five to six pages long and examines 10 "key areas of life in the urban areas of the contemporary world": location, population/demography, history, government and politics, economy, transportation, health care, education, housing, and culture/arts/entertainment. In addition, each entry has a very clear full-page map and a table displaying such data as annual precipitation, population, and vital statistics, most taken from various United Nations and U.S. government documents. Some of these data are fairly current, but some are quite old; the introduction states that "the data presented reflect the data available." The maps are not of the cities, as one might expect. Instead, they show where each city is located within the country. A series of icons appears at the beginning of each entry (e.g., a piano means "cultural," a soccer ball means "sports"), but the relevance of these icons is not clear, nor is it ever explained. There are no cross-references, so one would not know, without consulting the index, that Bombay appears under Mumbai. Appendixes include five comparative tables of information concerning population increases and rank. There is also a general index and bibliography.

Far superior treatment of larger cities, such as London and New York, is readily available in any standard encyclopedia—*World Book*, for example. Gale's *World Encyclopedia of Cities* [RBB My 1 94] has in-depth coverage of many more U.S and Canadian cities. *Encyclopedia of World Cities* has more information on smaller, non-U.S. and Canadian cities, such as Bucharest, Kinshasa, and Montevideo; and having so many cities in a single source facilitates comparisons. Public and academic libraries that need this type of coverage might consider adding this set to their collections.

A Statistical Portrait of the United States: Social Conditions and Trends. Ed. by Mark S. Littman. 1998. 476p. appendixes. Bernan, $79 (0-89059-076-1). DDC: 317.3.

Compiled from a large number of government and private sources, this volume has 12 chapters covering a wide variety of topics, including population growth, income and wealth, housing, voting, and environmental trends. Each chapter provides a summary of significant changes over the past 25 years, with emphasis on the 1990s. The book's aim is to fill a gap in the reporting of trends since the cessation of *Social Indicators*, published by the U.S. government in 1974, 1977, and 1980. Some international comparative data are also presented.

A statistical summary and a brief introduction begin each chapter, followed by a series of figures and tables, accompanied by text. Among the figures in the chapter on population characteristics are teen births as a percent of all births in the U.S., 1970–1993; and proportion of immigration to the U.S. by world region, 1955–1995. The chapter on crime and criminal justice includes a map showing violent crime rates in the U.S. by county in 1996, and a graph that displays arrest rates in the U.S. by type of offense, 1971–1995. An appendix provides more detailed tables for each of the 12 broad subject categories.

The reference value of the book is enhanced by citations of sources listed at the bottom of each table and chart, and also by the bibliography of print publications and Web sites included at the end of each chapter. Lucidly written, with an easy-to-read typeface and colorfully presented charts and tables, this volume is an excellent synthesis of statistics on American social conditions. It is recommended for academic and public libraries that need this type of information.

Encyclopedia of American Government. 4v. Ed. by Joseph M. Bessette and R. Kent Rasmussen. 1998. 815p. bibliogs. glossary. illus. index. maps. Salem, $210 (0-89356-117-7). DDC: 320.473.

This overview of American government is designed to assist everyone from middle-school age up in understanding how government and politics work at local, state, and national levels. It covers the structures, functions, and processes of government and related issues, such as economics and the military.

The 200 entries are alphabetically arranged, from *accountability in government* to *women in politics*. They range in length from 500 to 2,500 words and address the expected basic subjects, such as the Bill of Rights; contemporary topics that affect government (*gay rights*, *gender politics*); and many aspects of justice, including criminal procedure. Entries such as *Civil War amendments* and *Watergate* lend historical perspective, and those on political philosophy (*citizenship*, *separation of powers*) and on international politics give an even broader view. President Clinton's impeachment and trial occurred too late to make it into the article on impeachment.

Most of the articles are signed; the authors are identified by academic affiliation or are listed as "independent scholars" (except for one lawyer). The articles are enhanced by photos, maps, charts, and tables. Some essays are supplemented by sidebars. For example, the entry *veto power* contains two sidebars, one showing the meaning and derivation of the word *veto* and the other showing how some presidents exercised the power. Each article ends with a brief bibliography, and there is a 21-page general bibliography in volume four. Nearly all the bibliography items are from the 1990s.

The final volume includes the text of the Constitution and its amendments. There are also an extensive (20 pages) glossary and a list of the essay topics, arranged by category, which would make this set useful for teachers planning assigned readings. The index is comprehensive and indicates in boldface the topics that are addressed in full articles. This set will be a valuable addition to school and public libraries.

Encyclopedia of Political Anarchy. By Kathlyn Gay and Martin K. Gay. 1999. 242p. appendix. bibliog. index. ABC-CLIO, $75 (0-87436-982-7). DDC: 320.5.

The preface to this volume opens with a description of anarchy as "history's most misunderstood social movement," and the balance of the text is devoted to correcting such misunderstandings with clearly written, well-researched, readable, browseable material.

The goal is "to provide a reference source for others who are fascinated by the possibilities manifested in the actions, the dreams, the writings, and the people who influenced anarchism." This work appears to have found a niche; certainly there does not appear to be an abundance of ready-reference resources that cover the subject of anarchy. Among the 170 entries are *Alien and Sedition Acts of 1798*; *anarchist songs*; *Black Panthers*; *Chomsky, Noam*; *Earth First!*; *French anarchism*; *Goldman, Emma*; *modern school movement*; *New Left*; *Wollstonecraft, Mary*; and *Zapatista National Liberation Army*. Coverage is international in scope and ranges through time from Zeno of Citium (342 B.C.–ca. 267 B.C.) to *Internet anarchism*, which is discussed in an appendix

Entries are arranged alphabetically, and each provides *see* references and brief bibliographies (including numerous Web sites) that encourage and support the targeted readers, defined as "the curious student and the interested scholar." A general bibliography is offered, as is a well-developed index.

The entries range in length from the single paragraph used to describe the *A*narchist *Cookbook* as a book "filled with 1960s rhetoric and a great deal of incomplete or dangerously incorrect information" to the nearly two full pages allotted to Lucy Parsons: "History has often ignored [her], primarily because she was thought to have devoted her life to her husband, Albert, one of the eight Haymarket martyrs . . . but Lucy was a strong revolutionary activist and spent nearly 70 years fighting for the oppressed and the rights of women, workers, people of color, and political prisoners."

This title is recommended for public, college, and high-school library users. In addition, it should also prove to be a very useful curriculum-support tool for high-school social studies, current events, and history teachers.

Global Links: A Guide to People and Institutions Worldwide. By Cynthia J. Levy and Jeffrey D. Schultz. 1998. 177p. indexes. Oryx, paper, $59.95 (1-57356-224-6). DDC: 320.

Professor Cynthia J. Levy began compiling lists of U.S. government information sources as a way to help students gather information for research. *Global Links* expands the scope to include contact information for countries and territories around the world. Arranged alphabetically by country, each entry includes the names of the heads of state, cabinet ministers, legislative leaders, major political parties, Central Bank directors and television/radio commissioners, along with their phone numbers and/or fax numbers and e-mail addresses. This work contains two indexes: heads of state and country and ministry Web sites, when available.

The compilers claim the information is accurate as of April 1998, including some entries updated in June 1998. *Worldwide Government Directory with International Organizations* (Keesing's Worldwide, annual), an almost 1,000-page hardcover volume, is the most authoritative and comprehensive directory for government information, including, among other items in each entry, subcabinet ministers, foreign diplomatic missions, and international and regional memberships. However, *Global Links*, which is a far less expensive paperback, is a useful ready-reference source suitable for many public libraries and smaller academic libraries needing basic government contact information.

Government on File. By Valerie Tomaselli-Moschovitis. 1998. illus. index. loose-leaf binder. Facts On File, $165 (0-8160-3560-1). DDC: 320.973.

Government on File will be useful to history and government students and teachers, immigration/citizenship classes, and anyone who wants simple, graphic explanations of how U.S. government is structured and operates. Based on the National Standards for Civics and Government and major state curricula, it presents information in the familiar On File format.

The first section includes background information on the foundations of government and the foundations of U.S. democracy. Subsequent sections covering the structure and function of the legislative branch, the executive branch, and the judicial branch include rules and procedures, how a bill becomes a law, the jobs of cabinet members, the history of the Supreme Court, and the organization of the Justice Department. Other sections address citizenship, policymaking, state and local government, international issues, and the Constitution. The bibliography suggests print and Internet sources for additional research. The index is comprehensive and directs users to maps and illustrations as well as text.

Most topics are covered in one or two pages. Information is clearly presented. Among the topics are how a bill becomes a law, the electoral college, the organization of the federal court system, the history of immigration and immigration policy, and foreign exchange and balance of trade.

Middle-and high-school, public, and undergraduate libraries should find this resource useful.

ResourceLink: American Government. CD-ROM. 1998. ABC-CLIO, $79 (1-57607-012-3). Networking available. DDC: 320.473.
ResourceLink: Twentieth-Century American History. CD-ROM. 1998. ABC-CLIO, $79 (1-57607-013-1). Networking available. DDC: 973.9.
System requirememts: PC: Windows 95/98/NT 4.0; Pentium-capable processor; 16 MB RAM (32 MB *recommended*); 30 MB *free hard disk space*. Macintosh: System 7.5.3 or later; 68040 or faster processor, including Power Macintosh; 16 MB (32 MB *recommended*) 30 MB *free hard disk space*.

These two CD-ROMs offer primary sources and reference information on the U.S. Each disc contains more than 1,500 resources. Textual resources include biographies, documents, glossary terms, organization profiles, quotations, and tables. Audiovisual resources include animations, audio clips, flags, illustrations, maps, photographs, and video clips. Videos are launched with QuickTime (for Mac version) or Direct X 5 and DirectShow 2, and tables use Adobe Acrobat 3.0 for viewing; all are included on the CDs and automatically installed.

The strength of this series is the search-and-display process. The user can locate sources by topic, type of source (audio clip, biography, etc.), or keyword. The American history disc includes the topics Culture, Economics, History, Government, Law, Population, and Society. The government disc's topics are more specific and include Civil Rights and Liberties, Congress, Constitution, Domestic Policy, Economic Policy, Foreign Policy, Judiciary, Political Parties, Presidency, and Voting and Elections. The user sees a preview of each item and then chooses it to add to a resource file. Resources can be used in many ways—added to a custom notebook, enhanced with added text or drawings, prepared for onscreen presentations, printed onto tranparencies, or exported and used with another program.

A broad range of resources is included—biographies of Susan B. Anthony and James Dean, pictures of the Dust Bowl and the Berlin Wall, animations on how a bill becomes a law and a table showing U.S. immigration and emigration by decade, video clips of Richard Nixon's April 15, 1973, Watergate speech and Bill Clinton's 1994 State of the Union message. It should be noted that many of the items can be found on both discs. Tables are short but useful. Pictures and videos are often in color. Sound quality is fine. In general, the selection and reproduction are high quality, and the quotations are of particular interest. Sources of information are not always identified, and those that are vary in terms of currency. The bibliography for the article on Amelia Earhart includes a title from 1997, but the article on the Central Intelligence Agency cites references only from the 1980s.

More than archives of text and images, these CD-ROMs offer options for viewing, organizing, and editing the content that make them useful for creating presentations. Recommended in particular for high-school libraries.

Encyclopedia of Religion in American Politics. Ed. by Jeffrey D. Schultz and others. 1998. 424p. appendixes. bibliogs. illus. index. Oryx, $99 (1-57356-130-4). DDC: 322.
Encyclopedia of Women in American Politics. Ed. by Jeffrey D. Schultz and Laura van Assendelft. 1998. 354p. appendixes. bibliogs. illus. index. Oryx, $99 (1-57356-131-2). DDC: 320.

These titles from the publisher's American Political Landscape series trace the interface between religion and politics and women and politics in U.S. history from the colonial period through the 1990s.

Each volume contains more than 700 alphabetically arranged entries on individuals, events, court cases, and movements, ranging from a paragraph to a few pages, written by a variety of contributors. Entries are concise, readable, and balanced. Cross-references in the text and *see also* references and bibliographic references at the end of each entry lead the reader further. Nearly all entries are signed. Extended introductions provide the context for the entries.

Entry headings include years of birth and death for individuals (if the dates given for Sarah G. Bagely in the *Women* volume are correct, she founded the Lowell Female Labor Reform Association when she was nine and lived to be 112; Frances Cleveland's year of birth is given as 1846 instead of 1864) and, when appropriate, location and date for events. Captioned photos illustrate many articles. Longer entries, such as *abortion and birth control* in the *Religion* volume, provide the history, twentieth-century background, complexity of ethical questions, and arguments. There is also a lengthy entry on abortion in the *Women* volume, but this one examines abortion more as a gender issue than as an ethical issue. Birth control is covered in a separate entry, *reproductive and contraceptive technologies for women*. Some other topics that are covered in both volumes, but from different perspectives, are Dorothy Day, Operation Rescue, pornography, Elizabeth Cady Stanton, and welfare.

Bibliographies list scholarly and trade publications as well as newspaper and journal articles. Besides an index, each volume concludes with several extensive appendixes: "Speeches and Documents" (25 in *Religion*, 14 in *Women*), "Organizations," and "Timeline." *Women* also has a list of tables, including women elected to Congress or state governorships, women Cabinet members, and First Ladies.

Coverage ranges from Pilgrims to Promise Keepers, from plantation-owner Margaret Brent (b. 1601) to Mary Bono. Although much of the information can be found in other works, both these titles tie it together in balanced, current, convenient volumes that will prove useful to many high-school, public, and academic libraries. Forthcoming titles in the American Political Landscape series include *Encyclopedia of Minorities in American Politics, Encyclopedia of Media in American Politics,* and *Encyclopedia of Corruption in American Politics.*

Civil Rights in America: 1500 to the Present. By Jay A. Sigler. 1998. 710p. bibliogs. glossary. illus. index. Gale, $95 (0-7876-0612-X). DDC: 323.

It could be said that the history of the U.S. is the history of civil rights. From the onset, our government was based on the assumption that all men were entitled to the basic civil rights that had developed over centuries to become English Common Law. In the newly formed United States of America, those rights were restricted to a small group of white, male property owners. In the more than 200 years since, those rights and more have been extended to include women, minorities, children, and the disabled.

This impressive book explains how this came to be in four clearly delineated sections: the history of American rights; a survey of the historical experiences of nonwhite groups who have come to America; an explanation of the general rights that all Americans share; and the significant documents and major civil rights cases that have shaped and defined our current civil rights. A chronology, beginning in 5000–8000 B.C. with the migration of native peoples from Asia, begins the book. It concludes with selected documents, such as the Magna Carta; important court cases, such as *Dred Scott v. Sanford;* a short but useful glossary; and a general bibliography that includes books, selected videotapes, Internet resources, and a list of prominent rights interest groups. The two indexes, one arranged by case name and one by subject, make topics easy to locate.

The signed chapters within the book explain the history of each rights issue, liberally using official documents as a springboard. Contributors offer well-reasoned clarifications of difficult concepts and Supreme Court decisions. Black-and-white photographs, drawings, charts, and graphs further the understanding of the issues discussed in the text. There are sidebars that profile major civil rights individuals, such as Martin Luther King Jr. and Dorothea Dix, and major case problems. The format is crisp and easy to read, and subdivisions within each chapter are clearly marked by bold subheadings.

The Encyclopedia of Civil Rights in America [RBB F 15 98] takes an A–Z approach to the topic that is more useful for ready-reference, but the Gale volume's thematic approach helps put issues in context. Geared toward college students, the book will also be useful to upper-level-high-school students seeking to understand the background and complexity of the civil rights issues facing America, or to any American wishing to grasp the rich history of our evolving civil rights.

Encyclopedia of American Activism: 1960 to the Present. By Margaret B. DiCanio. 1998. 336p. bibliogs. illus. index. ABC-CLIO, $65 (0-87436-899-5). DDC: 323.

The years since 1960 have seen many changes in the U.S. From the civil rights and antiwar movements of the 1960s to the environmental and right-wing militia movements of the 1990s, this volume chronicles "the people, events, movements, organizations, and issues associated with activist movements in late twentieth-century America." In more than 190 entries, it covers issues such as homelessness and urban renewal; people such as Joan Baez, Martin Luther King Jr., and Ralph Nader; events such as the occupation of Alcatraz and the Million Man March; and organizations such as Greenpeace and the Symbionese Liberation Army.

Entries are arranged alphabetically and vary in length from three or four paragraphs to more than five pages for *Chavez, Cesar.* Each entry cites one or two sources, many of which are cited again in the general bibliography. Cross-references and an index facilitate access.

Because topics on counterculture and activism often overlap, this volume and the ABC-CLIO *Companion to the 1960s Counterculture in America* [RBB Mr 15 98] have some similar information. Because the *Encyclopedia of American Activism's* chronological coverage extends to the present, there is more information on subjects like Tom Hayden and the sexual revolution. The *Encyclopedia* also has a broader scope, treating topics such as neo-Nazis and the 1988 protest at Gallaudet University as well as hippies and Black Panthers.

This book will fill a need in high-school, college, and public libraries for an unbiased information source on various forms of activism over the past 40 years.

Political Market Place USA. By George Thomas Kurian and Jeffrey D. Schultz. 1999. 345p. indexes. Oryx, $65 (1-57356-226-2). DDC: 323.

This new annual publication, compiled by an experienced reference book editor (Kurian) and a political scientist–historian–editor, is a potpourri of information and contact data about the politics industry in the U.S. According to the introduction, it is intended to be "an educative and empowering tool, providing information on resources available to citizens to help them make informed political decisions"; and "an inventory of resources available to political professionals, legislators, public officials and journalists." Most of the 24 sections are directories of particular types of groups or organizations related to the political enterprise, including political parties, political associations, political actions committees, research institutes and think tanks, national and state organizations, and consultants. Several sections deal with various information sources—political journals and newsletters, books, publishers, commentators, Internet resources, and so on. There is also a section on awards and prizes.

Interspersed among the directory sections are three overview essays on political associations, elections, and the media. The volume concludes with tables of recent political data for the states (initiative, referendum, and recall provisions; terms, limits, and powers; party gains, losses, and current positions; plus national major party expenditures); and the 1998 State of the Union address, plus Republican response. There are three indexes: name/organization, geographic, and key subject.

In most of the sections, directory listings are arranged alphabetically by name of the entity and provide contact information: names, personnel and position titles, addresses, phone and fax numbers, and Internet and Web addresses, without any commentary. Additional information is provided in some sections. For example, third parties (of which there are many), political associations, and think tanks each get a brief summary of history, purpose, and publications. Political action committee entries include "total disbursements." Information-resource entries include basic citations and ordering information. Journals, newsletters, reference books, and nongovernmental Web sites get brief descriptions of content.

Unfortunately, the indexes lead to pages rather than individual entries, as in many directories. This is not so serious in the name/organization index when the name corresponds to the leading element in an entry, but for names of persons who are buried within an entry, such as an officer of an organization, the user must read through a whole page of entries to find the right one. The geographic index has entries only for states, each subdivided by a standard list of subheadings that correspond to the directory sections. If the directory sections are not arranged by state (and only the sections for major parties, election bodies, and League of Woman Voters are), then here too one must wade through many entries to find the one relevant to a particular state. The very brief key-subject index is limited to only 43 subjects. If one were interested in the growing political controversy over same-gender marriage and civil rights for lesbian, gay, bisexual, and transgender persons, the subject heading is *sexuality,* which includes the enormous spectrum of women's issues as well.

Any public or academic library focusing on politics will want this directory. Future editions should number entries in such a way that index entries can lead the user directly to the relevant directory entry, and the subject index should be expanded to cover all relevant specific subjects.

Shapers of the Great Debate on Immigration: A Biographical Dictionary. By Mary Elizabeth Brown. 1999. 322p. appendix. bibliogs. illus. index. Greenwood, $59.95 (0-313-30339-8). DDC: 325.73.

This first volume of a new series called Shapers of Great American Debates focuses on one of the most controversial issues in American history, immigration. Although everyone who has ever set foot in North America is, in one sense, an immigrant, this topic has been a thorny one since the American Revolution, when the new republic had to decide whom it would let in and whom it would keep out.

What makes this volume's approach unique is the concentration on the people who shaped the issues—those who took sides or whose lives illustrate one point or another. Following an overview on immigration history and law, the book contains 20 biographical profiles of individuals who wrote about immigration, framed laws, or made other significant contributions. Arrangement is chronological by date of birth. The earliest individual treated is Thomas Jefferson, and the most contemporary is John Tanton, founder of the Federation for American Immigration Reform (FAIR). Essays on these and the other men and women covered, among them Jane Addams, Cesar Chavez, Henry Ford, Jacob Riis, and Booker T. Washington, demonstrate changes in thinking, development of laws, and controversial aspects of the issue. Each 10-to-20-page profile contains a picture of the person covered, an overview of the person's life and contributions to the immigration debate, and a fairly extensive bibliography that describes primary and secondary sources. Following the profiles is an appendix with brief biographies of other key figures, from reformer Grace Abbott to writer Israel Zangwill. A selected bibliography in essay form and an index conclude the volume.

Although information on most of these individuals is readily available elsewhere, this is an interesting work with a unique approach. It is recommended for high-school, public, and college libraries.

ABC-CLIO World History Companion to Capitalism. By Larry Allen. 1998. 404p. bibliog. illus. index. ABC-CLIO, $60 (0-87436-944-4). DDC: 330.12.

ABC-CLIO World History Companion to Utopian Movements. By Daniel W. Hollis III. 1998. 303p. bibliog. illus. index. ABC-CLIO, $60 (0-87436-882-0). DDC: 335.

These new works in the ABC-CLIO World History Companion series intend, through a compendium of articles, to pull "various threads of . . . development together into a unified perspective." Both cover the period from 1450 to the present.

Primarily directed at high-school and college researchers, the books both have a well-balanced selection of topics, with larger areas (*labor unions*, *utopian socialism*) receiving lengthier treatments. *Capitalism* has more than 300 entries, from *Age of Steel* (1854–present) to *Zollverein* (Germany). *Utopian Movements* has more than 100 entries covering movements and theories, including *Amana Society*, *Bolshevism*, *Brave New World*, *Jonestown*, and *Welfare state*. Coverage is clear and detailed for all aspects of these topics, domestic and foreign. Opposing views, such as the strong anticapitalist views of Karl Marx or the dystopias of many twentieth-century authors, are presented and discussed. Balanced, straightforward presentations cover events and people current to 1997. The entries in *Capitalism* are shorter, in general, than the ones in *Utopian Movements*, though both tend toward brief, information-dense articles.

Entered alphabetically by topic or last name, each entry is thoroughly cross-referenced at its end so that users of the works are aided in making connections that might not otherwise be apparent. Lists of further reading and/or source references are appended as well. The thorough indexes are consistent and correct, with main entries in *Capitalism* being noted in bold, though this convention is not followed in *Utopian Movements*. The dry writing style is clear enough, with information easily garnered. Lengthy bibliographies employing standard citation formats are provided, though the arrangement varies between volumes. The bibliography in *Utopian Movements* is divided into Anthologies, Bibliographies, and Secondary Sources, while the one in *Capitalism* is in straight alphabetical order. Both books are enhanced by the use of clear black-and-white photographs and reproductions, around 40 per volume. Comprehensive chronologies listing events and publications that influenced the course of either movement precede the bibliographies.

Each volume provides a good starting point and/or augmentation for research in either area, in a single-volume format and with a specificity of purpose and clarity not available elsewhere. Recommended for high-school, public, and academic libraries.

The Lexicon of Labor. By R. Emmett Murray. 1998. 208p. appendixes. illus. New Press, paper, $13.95 (1-56584-456-4). DDC: 331.03.

Here is a handy, lively encyclopedia of 500 entries for terms, concepts, people, legislation, places, and events in U.S. labor history. The author, a Washington state newspaper labor leader, is clearly pro-union in his focus. At the same time, he admits that trade unions have not always been realistic, have sometimes used violent tactics, or have not consistently been in the vanguard for social justice. He sees the movement as "both bane and blessing" for African American workers.

Many entries are for lesser-known organizations, people, or events, such as the progressive Knights of St. Crispin and the African American labor leader Isaac Myers, both from the nineteenth century. Entries are generally brief, but *working women's movement* is almost four pages.

As the book's focus is on organized labor, there are no entries for migrant farmers, sharecroppers, or tenant farmers. The Women's Trade Union League is entered incorrectly as *Working Trade Union League*. Cross-references are noted in bold type. Appendixes list affiliate and independent unions and print resources which the author used.

A wide range of users in high-school, public, and academic libraries will find the work valuable for quick access to terms such as *company store*, *exempt employee*, and *sweetheart contract*, and biographies of past and current national leaders. It is accurate in describing such historic strikes as "Little Steel" in 1937, balanced in assessing the Industrial Workers of the World, and current in explaining NAFTA and changes in the national AFL-CIO. No comparable work is available.

Endangered Species. 3v. By Rob Nagel. 1999. 570p. bibliog. glossary. illus. index. maps. UXL, $84 (0-7876-1875-6). DDC: 333.95.

For middle-school students, UXL has published an impressive set describing 200 endangered species. Volume 1 covers mammals; volume 2 covers arachnids, birds, crustaceans, insects, and mollusks; and volume 3 covers amphibians, fish, plants, and reptiles. The animals and plants "were chosen to give a glimpse of the broad range of species currently facing endangerment."

Entries for individual species are arranged alphabetically within each class and cover two to four pages. The most helpful feature of each entry is the fact box, which provides scientific phylum, class, order, family, status (according to the World Conservation Union [IUCN] and the U.S. Fish and Wildlife Service), and geographic range, along with a locator map. Essays cover biology, habitat, history, and conservation measures.

Each volume contains a table of contents for the entire set, an overview of endangerment, an explanation of the classification system outlined in the fact boxes, information about IUCN, the text of the Endangered Species Act, a glossary, a list of materials for further research, and a cumulative index. The "Further Research" section is well annotated and includes a number of Web sites and organizations as well as books and will be useful for teachers. Throughout the set, large type and ample spacing give the impression of readability to a reluctant student. Although illustrations are smaller than those found in other sets, students will like the fact that many are in color.

For students at the upper range of the target audience, the 10-volume *Grolier World Encyclopedia of Endangered Species* [RBB S 1 93] and Marshall Cavendish's 11-volume *Endangered Wildlife of the World* [RBB My 1 93] are the closest competitors. Neither includes plants, but both cover many more animals, in entries that are often more in-depth and detailed. Arrangement in the Grolier set is geographical, demonstrating that the forces that threaten the world's wildlife are usually regional in scope. Many illustrations are full page and all are in color. The Marshall Cavendish set is arranged alphabetically by animal and is also lavishly illustrated. Because these sets were published several years ago, some of the information regarding status is now out of date. UXL's *Endangered Species* will be accessible to students in grades five and up and is recommended for school and public libraries.

Natural Resources. 3v. Ed. by Mark S. Coyne and Craig W. Allin. 1998. 976p. appendixes. bibliog. glossary. illus. index. Salem, $290 (0-89356-912-7). DDC: 333.7.

Along with 125 scholars from throughout the U.S., professors Coyne and Allin, affiliated with the University of Kentucky and Cornell College, respectively, have put together an interesting new reference work on natural resources. The editors have interpreted natural resources in the most comprehensive manner to include resource exploitation, environmentalism, geology, and biology. The work consists of 438 alphabetically arranged articles that range from 250 to 4,000 words in length. There are 84 core articles on minerals. Other areas of interest are energy resources including nuclear, solar, and wind; and plant-and animal-related topics like crops and animal breeding. In addition, there are articles on ecological resources such as forests, grasslands, lakes, and wetlands. There are also articles on secondary resources, such as cement, paper, and steel. There are brief articles on 28 organizations and 15 historical events, and 22 biographies of people like Barry Commoner and Stewart Udall.

All articles are signed; a list in the front of volume 1 gives the authors' affiliations. Appropriately placed throughout the text are 200 black-and-white photographs and 135 charts and tables. Articles at least 1,000 words in length have internal subheadings and annotated bibliographies of further readings at the end. Also at the end of articles are cross-references to other entries. A table of contents in the front of each volume directs users to articles only in that volume. Volume 3 contains many useful aids—an alphabetical table of elements, a periodic table of the elements, lists of major resources arranged by states and countries, a time line from 10,000 B.C. to 1997, and a glossary. A bibliography lists approximately 242 books grouped under broad subject headings. Rounding out the third volume are a list of entries by category and a comprehensive index.

There are numerous reference works dealing with specific natural resource topics like energy, pollution, agriculture, and minerals, but there are few if any surveys like *Natural Resources*. The broad nature of this set makes it unique and it should prove to be popular with students doing term papers and the general public seeking information. Recommended for high-school, public, and academic libraries.

Encyclopedia of American Communes, 1663–1963. By Foster Stockwell. 1998. 268p. appendixes. bibliog. illus. index. McFarland, $55 (0-7864-0455-8). DDC: 335.

Communes refers to the utopian communities that were a part of America's idealistic past. Cooperative, collective, experimental, socialistic, and sometimes religious, these communities aspired to reshape the future and form a new and better society. This volume covers 516 such communities. The ending date mostly eliminates the "hippie" communes that sprang up in the 1960s.

After an introduction, communes are listed alphabetically. Their dates of operation and descriptions of their location, organizers, affiliations, beliefs, activities, and final disposition are given. Entries are lively, with many interesting details. Cross-references refer readers to related entries, and relevant source materials are mentioned. Familiar names include Amana, Brook Farm, Ephrata, Nauvoo, New Harmony, and Oneida. When available, drawings and photographs are included.

An appendix lists communes chronologically by date founded; another lists government-formed cooperative farms and communities begun during the Depression (1933–43). An extensive bibliography and a good index complete the book. The latter includes individuals' names (*Owen, Robert; Sinclair, Upton*) and types of communities (*Catholic Worker communes; Jewish settlements; vegetarian communes*).

A number of the same communes are also discussed in ABC-CLIO *World Companion to Utopian Movements*, reviewed on p.49. However, the McFarland title provides more comprehensive coverage of communes in the U.S. This useful reference book gives a thorough treatment of its subject. It is appropriate for academic and large public libraries.

Business Leader Profiles for Students. Ed. by Sheila M. Dow. 1999. 914p. bibliogs. illus. index. Gale, $95 (0-7876-2935-9). DDC: 338.7.
Company Profiles for Students. 2v. Ed. by Donna Craft. 1999. 1,585p. bibliogs. illus. index. Gale, $150 (0-7876-2936-7). DDC: 338.7.
Federal Agency Profiles for Students. Ed. by Kelle S. Sisung. 1999. 1,070p. appendixes. bibliogs. glossary. illus. index. Gale, $85 (0-7876-2795-X). DDC: 351.73.

Q: When might you purchase costly reference volumes when similar information can be found on the Internet?

A: When the material is clearly presented, easy to locate, and well documented. These three new tools are designed "for high-school students and their teachers and up" and should become standards in technical, community-college, and public libraries with business collections. *Business Leader Profiles* includes 250 prominent figures of industry (mostly white American men), alphabetically from *Dilbert* creator Scott Adams through Darryl Zanuck, and chronologically from Benjamin Franklin to Michael Dell. Each entry of two to three pages includes an overview of the individual's career, plus information on personal life, management style, social and economic impact, photo, and a bibliography of related business articles. Web sites are almost always noted, and information seems unbiased and current through 1998. As usual with a work like this, one notices who is not included—Julius Erving, R. H. Macy, and Paul Newman, to name three possible candidates. Layout, readability, and consistently good indexing make this a quality purchase.

Even more useful for most libraries is *Federal Agency Profiles*, despite the "for students" in the title. More than 175 agencies (departments, government corporations, commissions, etc.) are alphabetically listed, with entries including parent organization, history and date established, number of employees, mission, agency head, structure, budget, controversies, successes and failures, future direction, publications, and bibliography. Entries may also include "Fast Facts," how to get involved, biographical sidebars on important individuals (though the only Supreme Court justice profiled is John Jay), chronology, illustrations, and glossary. Some of this, of course, is available elsewhere, especially in the *United States Government Manual*, but here there is far more history and context. A chronology, glossary, and appendixes showing, for example, a breakdown of federal government expenditures and how a bill becomes a law add to the work's usefulness. This is the first volume in a series that will also include *Special Interest Profiles for Students* and *Presidential Administration Profiles for Students*.

Though "designed specifically to meet the curricular needs of high school and undergraduate college students taking courses in economics, business, and history," the two-volume *Company Profiles* is a must for most libraries. Although it features only 280 companies, this volume compares favorably with the much more comprehensive *Hoover's Handbook of American Business*. Alphabetically arranged by company, articles run from four to seven pages and may discuss finances, analysts' opinions, history, strategy, current trends, products, corporate citizenship, global presence, and corporate culture. Entry headings include a summary of contact information and other basic facts. Sidebars highlight various topics such as airline food and the Budweiser Clydesdales. There may also be a company chronology. The companies are those that "are typically studied in high school" and range from General Motors and IBM to MTV Network, Snapple Beverage, and Victoria's Secret. Although there are no five-year financials here (as in *Hoover's*), annual reports and other information are often available on Web sites, for which URLs are given. Bibliographies citing journals from 1995 and later show how up-to-date the profiles are. Users are also provided with the company's SIC (Standard Industrial Classification) Code, in case they want to investigate similar companies. A "Directory of Specialized Business Web Sites" follows the profiles.

These volumes are attractive, easy to use, clearly written, and even inviting for browsing. Yes, this line is designed for students; but with the layout, quality of information, and detailed indexing, they will quickly find fans everywhere. Recommended for high-school, public, and undergraduate libraries.

Business, Economics

Dun and Bradstreet/Gale Industry Reference Handbooks: Computers and Software. Ed. by Stacy A. McConnell and Linda D. Hall. 1998. 1,071p. appendix. index. Gale, $99 (0-7876-3002-0). DDC: 004.
Dun and Bradstreet/Gale Industry Reference Handbooks: Pharmaceuticals. Ed. by Stacy A. McConnell and Linda D. Hall. 1998. 406p. appendix. index. Gale, $99 (0-7876-3004-7). DDC: 615.1.
Dun and Bradstreet/Gale Industry Reference Handbooks: Telecommunications. Ed. by Stacy A. McConnell and Linda D. Hall. 1998. 893p. appendix. index. Gale, $99 (0-7876-3005-5). DDC: 384.

If these industry handbooks are indicative of a trend in business information publishing, libraries trying to squeeze more data from each dollar have a reason to smile. Pulling together material from some of their top-of-the-line (i.e., expensive) sources, Gale and Dun and Bradstreet (D&B) focus on three of the hottest areas of American industry: computers and software, pharmaceuticals, and telecommunications.

Each stand-alone title covers its segment of industry as defined by the Standard Industrial Classification (SIC) system. For example, the pharmaceutical industry, with SIC code 283, encompasses 2833: Medicinal and Botanicals; 2834: Pharmaceutical Preparations; 2835: In Vivo and in Vitro Diagnostic Substances; and 2836: Biological Products. The editors acknowledge that the SIC system is in the process of being replaced by the new North American Industry Classification System (NAICS) but explain that most data providers still use the older system. Conveniently, SIC/NAICS and NAICS/SIC conversion tables are appended to each volume.

These handbooks all follow a uniform arrangement of 10 chapters: industry overview, statistics and performance indicators, financial norms and ratios, company directory, rankings, mergers and acquisitions, associations, consultants, trade information sources, and trade shows. The first chapter, "Industry Overview," includes an industry snapshot, background and development information, industry newsmakers, projections, and research. Following this, the "Statistics and Performance Indicators" chapter gives federal statistics covering employment, production, compensation, and revenues. Data are drawn from such Gale titles as *Manufacturing USA* and *Service Industries USA*. In the third chapter, "Financial Norms and Ratios," we get proprietary data from D&B, including cash, assets, liabilities, solvency, efficiency, and profitability. The company directory chapter is where location, phone number, sales figure, SIC code, number of employees, and parent company are given. Each company listed here is ranked in the next chapter based on sales and employment. These entries have the D&B rank, location, type (i.e., public, private, or public family member), sales, employees, and primary SIC code. Chapter 6 lists recent merger-and-acquisition activity. The remaining four chapters pull material from standard Gale sources such as *Consultants and Consulting Organizations Directory*, *Encyclopedia of Associations*, *Encyclopedia of Business Information Sources*, and *Trade Shows Worldwide*. Also provided in each volume is an index of companies, organizations, SIC industry names, and terms.

Gale and D&B provide some of the best business information available. However, their titles are not inexpensive. *Dun and Bradstreet/Gale Industry Reference Handbooks* are unique in that they offer, for a modest price, a tremendous amount of proprietary information from the files of these two business information powerhouses. They are very suitable for academic and public libraries with a need to provide quality data on the computer and software, pharmaceutical, and telecommunication industries without spending a fortune on all the separate titles from which they are compiled.

The Encyclopedia of Native American Economic History. Ed. by Bruce E. Johansen. 1999. 301p. bibliogs. index. Greenwood, $85 (0-313-30623-0). DDC: 330.973.

This work covers fundamentals of traditional Native American economies throughout North America (considered to be Canada, the U.S., Mexico, and Guatemala); changes in economies brought about by European contact; current economies on reservations and controversies surrounding them (e.g., debates on gambling); and environmental issues as they impact Native American economic systems. Approximately 150 unattributed, alphabetically ordered articles written by subject area experts, most of whom hold college or university posts in Native American studies, political science, or history, present these topics at lengths varying from a single sentence to 14 pages for *Haudenosaunee (Iroquois) economy*, with most being one or two pages. Written in a clear, crisp style, articles are slightly dry, but certainly informative, and are current for events through the mid-1990s.

Examples of entries include *Cahokia, Cheyenne economy, corn, fishing rights, James Bay hydroelectric project, termination policy (1950s)*, and *trade*. Articles dealing with the exploitation of the environment are included because "the Native American point of view often considers environmental and economic themes as part of the same process." The apparent goal of creating an in-depth consideration of Native American economies as a field is more or less achieved. Aimed at college and university audiences, the information is also accessible to high-school students. All the articles are followed by short bibliographies of works related to the topic. An up-to-date bibliography and an index are located at the volume's end. The index is not always complete. The single index citation for *Tenochtitlan* leads to the article *slavery and Native Americans*, but *Tenochtitlan* appears elsewhere in the volume, especially in the article *Aztec economy*.

Though much of the cultural information given here can also be found in such works as *The Encyclopedia of North American Indians* [RBB D 15 96], the focus on economics gives this a unique place on the shelf. Recommended for academic and large public libraries.

Plunkett's Employers' Internet Sites with Careers Information. Ed. by Jack W. Plunkett and others. 1999. 701p. indexes. Plunkett Research, $149.99 (1-891775-01-4). DDC: 331.7.

This new publication provides comparisons of online data posted by the U.S.'s largest companies. Plunkett's On-line Employers 500, arranged alphabetically, were chosen because they provide jobs to the greatest number of employees. They also meet the following four criteria: they are U.S.-based, nongovernmental employers; stocks or bonds are publicly traded; the company has a user-friendly careers Web site; and they are midsize to larger. The companies are indexed by the new North American Industry Classification System (NAICS) and by three geographic indexes: company headquarters locations by state; plants, offices, and subsidiaries by regions of the U.S.; and firms with international operations. These indexes alone make purchase of this title worthwhile for job seekers.

The profile for each company is formatted identically to make comparisons of employers easy. Profiles are very similar to those in other Plunkett directories, such as *Plunkett's Entertainment and Movie Industry Almanac* [RBB O 15 98], with the addition of Web site information. Main areas answer questions on specific job openings listed, whether the Web sites are searchable by job type and/or location, whether internships are available, whether one can apply for jobs online, employment contact and college recruiter names, annual report, standard benefits, recommendations for specific career areas (management, sales/marketing, liberal arts, information systems professionals, and technical/scientific personnel), and the number of women and minority officers or directors. Some companies are identified as a "hot spot for advancement for women/minorities." There are comments about specific Web site features and tips on accessing corporation profiles, press releases, and financial information.

Three final indexes pull out firms noted as "hot spots," list brands or subsidiaries followed by related corporation, and list companies for specific types of job seekers. More than just listing Web sites, Plunkett has added value by the formatting and indexing of this data. Placement offices and libraries will want to purchase this latest Plunkett title for job seekers, career changers, and new college graduates.

International Encyclopedia of the Stock Market. 2v. Ed. by Michael Sheimo and others. 1999. 1,320p. appendixes. bibliog. illus. index. Fitzroy Dearborn, $275 (1-884964-35-4). DDC: 332.64.

The development of this specialized encyclopedia was propelled by the observation that "the stock market, whatever its residual regional variations" is now "a worldwide institution, its constituent parts having more in common with each other, country by country, than at any time in the past." It no longer makes sense to produce a reference source that focuses solely on the British, Japanese, American, or any other country's individual stock exchange.

Sheimo has written several other books on the stock market. *International Encyclopedia of the Stock Market* (IESM) defines more than 2,000 terms that relate to regional and world stock market practice. It describes the economies of both economically advanced and developing countries and contains entries on individuals like Adam Smith and Michael Milken, institutions such as the Deutsche Bundesbank and the Federal Reserve System, and stock market lingo (*Acapulco spread, greenmail, haircut*). The scope is historical as well as international, with entries on such topics as banking in ancient Egypt and Greece. Specific stock exchanges appear under the country in which they are located. Entries are presented in one alphabetic sequence, with *see* and *see also* references used to tie together related topics.

As would be expected, entry length varies widely. For example, *stockholder* is defined simply as "any person or group of persons owning shares of a company." At the other end of the extreme is the entry for the U.S., running for almost 40 pages. It offers a full-page, black-and-white photo of the modern N.Y. Stock Exchange, a similar photo of the nineteenth-century Philadelphia exchange, share prices (1997) for hundreds of specific companies, specific listing requirements for each exchange, and more. Entries for other countries are similarly detailed, if not as long. Many entries include valuable directory information—trading hours for each exchange; names, addresses, and phone numbers for brokerage firms in each county, for example. The volume concludes with a discussion of emerging markets, a list of world currency, a list of organizations, an annotated bibliography, and an index. The bibliography lists only a handful of titles, but these are annotated in considerable detail. Rather than indexing terms, the index groups entries under selected topics.

IESM is geared to investment advisors, professional and private investors, and to researchers and libraries that serve them. Intelligibly written, it manages to explain complicated ideas in straightforward language. Because of its currency and global treatment of the stock market, it is a unique source and is recommended for medium to large public and academic libraries and all specialized business libraries.

Weiss Ratings' Guide to Mutual Funds: A Quarterly Compilation of Mutual Fund Ratings and Analysis Covering Equity and Balanced Funds. 1998. 320p. indexes. Weiss Ratings, $219. DDC: 332.63.

Weiss Ratings' guides are written for amateur investors, not for professionals. Weiss aims to be the information provider for consumer-level investors, those individuals who invest their own money and who do not have formal training in financial analysis. With this goal in mind, their various guides cover a wide range of financial topics, including insurance, banks, brokerage houses, annuities, HMOs, and mutual funds. As an independent rater, Weiss never takes "a penny from rated companies" and publishes their ratings "without regard for the companies' preferences."

Weiss Ratings' Guide to Mutual Funds (WRGMF) condenses "all of the available mutual fund data into a single composite opinion." This allows the investor to "instantly identify those funds that have historically done well and those that have underperformed the market," providing a "solid framework for making informed investment decisions." The A through E ratings (excellent to very weak) indicate the Weiss opinion regarding a fund's "past risk-adjusted performance." This guide covers growth funds, index funds, balanced funds, and international (sector) funds. Pure bond funds and money market funds are excluded.

Section I of WRGMF is a 200-page chart listing more than 5,000 funds in alphabetical order by name. Following the name of the fund, and arranged on one line running across two facing pages, the investor will find 37 columns of information. These include fund type, Weiss overall rating, rating percentile, performance rating, return (three month, six month, one year, three year, five year), risk rating, net asset, average earnings, manager quality, manager tenure, initial purchase minimum, front-end load, and back-end load. Each of these indicators is briefly explained in a simple, clearly written six-page guide.

Following Section I, Weiss provides a number of short specialized sections that group the top and bottom mutual funds by performance and risk, by risk category, and by fund type, such as aggressive growth, global, and small company. WRGMF ends with a four-page "Investor Profile Quiz." This quiz asks questions about age, cash reserve, experience, investment attitude, and so forth; and, using a point value system, rates the individual investor from "very conservative" to "very aggressive" and gives brief advice on appropriate investment strategy.

A comparable source is Morningstar Mutual Funds. Published twice monthly, Morningstar ranks 1,700 funds on the basis of performance, risk, and return, and also provides fund profiles. Since Morningstar is so well known for its mutual fund ratings, it is probably the first choice for smaller collections. WRGMF is recommended for larger public and academic libraries needing to fill in another piece of the mutual fund puzzle. It is clearly written, reader friendly, and nicely designed. It is also a serious investment guide that assumes some basic knowledge of finance.

Hoover's MasterList of Major International Companies, 1998–1999. 1998. 317p. indexes. Hoover's, $89.95 (1-57311-043-4). DDC: 338.7.

Hoover's publishes two types of print directories: handbooks and MasterLists. The handbooks, such as Hoover's Handbook of American Business and Hoover's Handbook of World Business, are relatively selective, usually covering several hundred companies. They offer the business researcher a one-or two-page profile of a company, including an overview of activity, a company history, the names of chief officers, a financial statement, and a list of competitors. In contrast, the MasterLists cover many thousands of companies and provide succinct, directory-type information for each.

The first edition of Hoover's MasterList of Major International Companies (HMMIC) is similar to Hoover's MasterList of European Companies and Hoover's MasterList of Major Latin American Companies, but with expanded capsule summaries and sales information. Data on 1,658 public and private companies, which are listed alphabetically, were pulled from Hoover's database. The volume aims to cover "all non-U.S. business enterprises with sales greater than $5 billion, as well as all companies that make up the major non-U.S. stock indices." The brief entries (six to a page) provide contact information, Web-site addresses, names of chief officers, ownership (e.g., government owned, public, privately held), stock exchange and ticker symbol, an activity description, plus five years of figures for sales, net income, and number of employees. Also included in HMMIC are rankings tables for the top 500 companies by sales and by number of employees, plus indexes by industry and by headquarters location. The activity descriptions are written in a refreshing and often-whimsical style that is definitely not characteristic of business-reference sources

Like other Hoover's sources, HMMIC offers basic information on selected companies in a user-friendly style and at a user-friendly price. It is recommended for academic and public libraries as a supplement to standard sources such as Dun & Bradstreet's Principal International Businesses and Gale's World Business Directory, both of which list many more enterprises. HMMIC is also a good choice for libraries that want to provide some information on international companies, but do not need comprehensive coverage.

The New Palgrave Dictionary of Economics and the Law. 3v. Ed. by Peter Newman. 1998. 2,550p. bibliogs. Grove's Dictionaries, $550 (1-56159-213-5). DDC: 343.

The "New Palgrave" name is associated with two of the most respected scholarly reference sources in economics: The New Palgrave: A Dictionary of Economics (1987) and The New Palgrave Dictionary of Money and Finance [RBB F 15 93]. Grove's and editor Newman (who was a co-editor of the other titles) have hit another home run with The New Palgrave Dictionary of Economics and the Law. Like the other titles, this one provides encyclopedic academic coverage of its subject matter—here, the legal subjects "on which economic analysis has had something of interest and importance to say; and similarly for entries on economic subjects, vis-a-vis the law." It often goes beyond the intersection of law and economics to include coverage of relevant subject matter in the realms of ethics, philosophy, political science, and public administration, thus responding to the call made in the 1998 report "Reinventing Undergraduate Education: A Blueprint for America's Research Universities," by the Carnegie Foundation for the Advancement of Teaching, to emphasize interdisciplinary learning at the college level.

Most of the dictionary's 399 signed essays were written by economics and law-school faculty from well-respected institutions, with a few contributions from practitioners. The essays average close to 5,000 words, with a range from 2,000 to 15,000 words. Underlying the single alphabetical presentation of the material is a subject classification (detailed in volume 1) that groups articles into broad subject areas (society, economy, polity, law in general, common-law systems, regulation, and biographies), each of which is divided into headings and subheadings. Each entry is assigned to one or more of the headings or subheadings, making it fairly simple for a researcher to locate relevant essays on a topic, although an index would have been useful. Entries also include cross-references to related entries, lists of relevant cases and statutes, and bibliographies. The book concludes with two lists: one covers cited statutes, treaties, and directives; the other lists cited cases.

The dictionary will help students, academics, and professionals make connections between the various disciplines and understand the effect one has on the others. Issues of topical importance such as airline deregulation, the future of the European Union, and sexual harassment are addressed, as well as more general questions like social justice, property rights, and the evolution of common law. Researchers accustomed to viewing a topic within the confines of one discipline will be enriched and perhaps challenged by the perspective offered in the essays. Adoption, for example, reviews the variables affecting the changing supply of and demand for adoptable children during the twentieth century, explains the reasons for state intervention in the adoption market, critiques the current method of agency adoptions as creating a lost consumer surplus, and postulates how market allocation would work. Public policy decisions such as offering tax credits for adoptive parents and limiting the time in which biological parents can contest adoptions are analyzed within the context of their effect on the adoption market.

The New Palgrave Dictionary of Economics and the Law is a welcome addition to the scholarly reference literature and should join its companion titles on the shelves at most academic, law, larger public, and relevant special libraries.

China Marketing Data and Statistics 1998. Ed. by Yutaka Oka. 1998. 643p. appendixes. charts. maps. Euromonitor; dist. by Gale, $390 (0-86338-780-2). DDC: 380.10951.

Printed in both Chinese and English, this marketing source was produced by the State Statistical Bureau of the People's Republic of China in response to China's rapidly expanding importance to the global economy. The volume was designed to serve the needs of both scholars studying China's economy and entrepreneurs wanting to do business and invest in China. It provides descriptive and statistical information for provinces, autonomous regions, municipalities, and prefectures; and, because of their large amount of economic activity, gives special attention to Beijing, Shanghai, and Tianjin.

First, a 10-page overview summarizes China's economic resources and physical characteristics, and comments on China's place in the world. Following is a collection of ranked lists such as "Top 100 Industrial Enterprises Based on Sales Income" and "Top 20 Corporations Based on Import and Export Value." Next, each province, autonomous region, and municipality is profiled in a three-to five-page chapter. Following a simple political map are sections covering topics such as geography, natural resources, tourism, industry, infrastructure, and standard of living. The last section presents several hundred well-designed statistical tables, which cover a wide range of concerns including average rainfall, forest areas, livestock, marriage, divorce, education, savings deposits, wages, cultural institutions (e.g., number of theaters, libraries, performance troupes), and industry. There is no index.

Specialized business libraries and academic libraries supporting upper-level marketing research will want to take a serious look at this first edition of what is planned as an annual publication. Undoubtedly some of the information it presents may be gleaned from other sources. However, there really is no comparable, up-to-date, comprehensive marketing source for the People's Republic of China.

Law, Public Administration, Social Problems and Services

The Constitution and Its Amendments. 4v. Ed. by Roger K. Newman. 1999. 576p. glossary. illus. indexes. Macmillan, $225 (0-02-864858-7). DDC: 342.73.

Although the introduction indicates that this resource is designed as a "primer for students," there are few adults who will fail to learn something new about the Constitution on almost every page. In volume 1, for example, the section "The Impeachment Power" offers the reader Alexander Hamilton's definition of impeachment: "a method of national inquest into the conduct of public men." This section also compares and explains differences between nineteenth-and twentieth-century impeachment practices, defines "high crimes and misdemeanors," and pictures the ticket issued for President Andrew Johnson's impeachment trial.

The set contains 160 articles organized generally by constitutional clauses. They provide the text and discuss each of the parts of the Constitution and its amendments. The articles range in length from more than 100 pages for "Article I: The Legislative Branch" to two pages for "Twenty-Fourth Amendment." Longer articles, such as the one on the Fourteenth Amendment, are divided into sections that discuss the history of the amendment along with various concepts (*affirmative action*, *the right to die*), subjects (*abortion*, *sexual orientation*), and important cases (*Brown v. Board of Education*) that relate to constitutional history and law. Highlighted terms are defined in the margins. Black-and-white illustrations lend interest and information, as do the many sidebars, such as the one that quotes Thurgood Marshall just after he won *Brown v. Board of Education*: "There is only but so much lawyers can do."

The list of 121 contributors includes their institutional affiliations and identifies which articles they wrote. Each volume has a table of contents for the entire set, and volumes 1–3 have their own indexes. Volume 4 has a cumulative index and a glossary. There are cross-references but, unlike most resources of this type aimed at students, there are no suggested further readings or bibliographies. That, and the lack of footnotes, makes it difficult to verify the contents or to direct those readers who like to see additional sources.

Nevertheless, this will be a useful addition to school and public libraries serving students at the middle-school level and up, and will help those who want to expand their knowledge of the basis for our legal and political actions.

State Constitutions of the United States. By Robert L. Maddex. 1998. 518p. appendixes. bibliog. glossary. index. Congressional Quarterly, $115 (1-56802-373-1). DDC: 342.

The author of *Constitutions of the World* [RBB O 15 95] and *The Illustrated Dictionary of Constitutional Concepts* [RBB Ap 15 97] has provided a valuable resource on the constitutions of each state and three U.S. territories. Introductory material provides perspective on the significant role of the state documents in the nation's history and in recent years. Charts convey the structure of the three branches of government in each state (e.g., number of statewide elected officers, appointment or election of Supreme Court members, and the legislative vote needed for amendments). Special provisions, such as a balanced-budget requirement, home rule, and abortion rights, are also shown in comparative charts.

The bulk of the resource is an alphabetically arranged seven-to nine-page profile on the constitution of each state or territory. Basic data on the state and the origin and historical highlights of the document appear at the beginning. A readable summary of each article or section follows, with the actual words from the document excerpted or summarized. The full text of the constitutions is not provided. The years the sections were added or amended and pertinent court decisions are noted. The format allows for easy comparisons on how states have arranged their governance.

After the profiles, the text of the U.S. Constitution, table of pertinent state cases, glossary, sources used, and an index complete the work. The index is accurate in page numbers, but space considerations may have made the state summaries especially selective. Is Rhode Island the only state where libraries are mentioned in its constitution?

The work succeeds in making the state documents understandable and accessible to the average citizen. As a reference resource, it will be valuable for high-school and college students as well as researchers seeking to learn how other states handle societal issues.

FedLaw EasySearch: U.S. Code and Statutes at Large. CD-ROM. 1998. Oryx, $195 (1-57356-145-2). Networking available. DDC: 349.73.

System requirements: Windows 3.1/95/NT, 4 MB RAM, 1 MB *available hard drive space.*

Refreshingly, this product offers exactly what its title advertises, every Federal Title and Statute of the U.S. Code plus the Statutes at Large, through a simple, friendly interface. Reviewed on a Pentium-level PC running Windows 95, it was up and running within five minutes. An experienced database searcher can master the interface in 10 minutes and teach the search basics to the uninitiated in another five minutes.

The screen design is clean and clear with eight buttons across the top: home, search, help, back, trail, print, copy, exit. The help screens offer basic, focused, practical help. A searcher does not have to contend with pages of documentation just to figure out, for example, how to search by public law number. More sophisticated and detailed help is also available if desired.

The search button allows the researcher to do keyword searches, and limit searches to contents pages, public laws, tables, or specific U.S. Code title. It accommodates phrase or single-term searching, use of logical operators (AND, OR, NOT), nesting, and truncation. The trail button lets the researcher view a list of up to 100 previously searched topics and link directly to them. Downloading to a file is done by clicking on the copy button. This automatically takes the document and saves it to the Windows clipboard.

Perhaps because it is designed for researchers who are not legal professionals, the search interface is very lean. To locate a particular statute, there are only two quick steps—first, clicking on the statutes link that appears at the bottom of the screen (along with a link for U.S. Code and for tables); and second, clicking on the appropriate public law from the presented list. This brings up the full text of the law and a minimal legislative history.

The same material is available from a number of electronic alternatives: Web-site access from Lexis-Nexis or LOIS (Law Office Information System), and compact disc format from West Publishing. *FedLaw* may be the best alternative if users prefer the reliability of a locally mounted CD platform to the vagaries of Internet access. As compared to the CD-ROMs from West, *FedLaw* offers the simplicity of a well-designed though less sophisticated search engine. *FedLaw* is not recommended for law libraries but is a good choice for academic and public libraries that provide basic legal material to general researchers. It is simple enough to be offered as an end-user service.

Historical Dictionary of the Green Movement. By Elim Papadakis. 1998. 223p. bibliog. chronology. Scarecrow, $62 (0-8108-3502-9). DDC: 353.7.

Many definitions of "green" within green movements are introduced in the 31-page essay setting the scene for an extensive, useful, and very interesting, though not exhaustive, set of entries. The essay and entries describe many types of green movements, their complex relationships, contributing events, and influential persons. Examples of the alphabetically arranged entries include *animal rights*; *Chernobyl*; *Earth First!*; *Muir, John*; *Nature Conservancy*; and *think globally, act locally*. Some of the longest entries (three to four pages) are devoted to specific countries (*green parties, Austria*; *United Kingdom*). The international scope means that some local or regional concepts and activities, though relevant, are missing or appear tangentially.

The 200-year chronology section illustrates the steady march of significant "green" events that have occurred. The author's careful scholarship is demonstrated in the 40-page bibliography, which is arranged by topic and augmented by its own table of contents. The entries are densely packed with information and have appropriate *see also* links throughout. While individual readers may take exception to the impact and interpretation of some events, the collection of so many names, ideas, concepts, and keywords in one volume offers a useful stepping stone to broadening and sharpening understanding of this extremely important movement. Recommended for large public and academic libraries, especially those needing an international perspective.

Outlaws, Mobsters and Crooks: From the Old West to the Internet. 3v. By Marie J. MacNee. 1998. 500p. bibliogs. illus. index. UXL, $84 (0-7876-2803-4). DDC: 354.1.

MacNee presents the lives of 75 North American criminals, from Blackbeard to 1997's computer criminal, Kevin Mitnick. The criminals have been grouped into ten categories. Volume 1 covers mobsters, racketeers and gamblers, and robbers. Volume 2 covers computer criminals, spies, swindlers, and terrorists. Volume 3 covers bandits and gunslingers, bootleggers, and pirates. A time line is provided at the beginning of each volume, listing outlaw landmarks and other important international events that coincided with criminal activity at a particular time.

Within each criminal category, entries are arranged alphabetically by the outlaw's last name and vary in length from three to 11 pages. Exceptions to the arrangement relate to those outlaws who are known by their common names, such as Bonnie and Clyde, who are listed under B for *Bonnie*. Each entry provides personal background of the person/s, the crimes committed, the legal aftermath, and the law as it relates to the crimes. A bibliography for additional reading, including both books and popular periodicals, concludes each entry. A comprehensive index found at the end of each of the three volumes provides a listing of all the criminals and their common names, with reference to the appropriate volumes and page numbers. Access is further aided by a volume-by-volume list of contents, which is repeated in all three volumes. Illustrations, both black-and-white photographs and drawings, enhance the volumes' appeal. Sidebars provide additional information. Unfamiliar vocabulary is defined within the text, enabling students to learn terms without having to refer to outside sources.

This set, although lacking in detail, does offer a wealth of information on North American criminals and is a good beginning resource for students studying crime. Highly recommended for public libraries and school libraries serving students in grades six through ten.

Encyclopedia of Guerrilla Warfare. By Ian F. W. Beckett. 1999. 303p. bibliog. chronology. illus. index. ABC-CLIO, $75 (0-87436-929-0). DDC: 355.4.

Written by a British military historian, this comprehensive work begins with a table of contents and a clearly written introduction on how indigenous peoples have fought against occupiers or oppressors throughout history. The alphabetically arranged entries average one-half page although they are longer when necessary, such as nearly three pages for Northern Ireland. Although the introduction refers to guerrilla fighting in ancient history, the entries focus on the past few centuries, beginning in the American colonies.

The coverage is truly all-encompassing, from the Peninsular War against Napoleon (where the term *guerrilla* originated) to the Maori wars in New Zealand in the nineteenth century and from an uprising in Soviet Central Asia after the 1918 revolution to Cyprus after World War II. In addition to individual wars and campaigns, entries include individuals (George Armstrong Custer, Ernesto Che Guevara), groups (*Italian army*, *Kuomintang*, *Tamils*), locations (*Ho Chi Minh Trail*, *Nicaragua*), and terms (*foco*, the strategy that brought Fidel Castro to power in Cuba). Biographical entries include known theorists and leaders and the lesser known, for example, the developer of Soviet counterinsurgency (Mikhail Nikolaievich Tukhachevsky) and the leader of the Angolan independence movement (Dr. Agostinho Antonio Neto).

Entries are well written and current (the death of Pol Pot in April 1998 is included) and are followed by helpful *see also* references and suggestions for further reading. An extensive bibliography includes many recent titles, and an accurate index completes the work. Black-and-white photos are scattered throughout.

Although elements of guerrilla warfare can be located in other works, the thoroughness and comprehensiveness of this unique volume make it a useful title for many high-school, public, and academic libraries.

Encyclopedia of Warrior Peoples and Fighting Groups. Ed. by P. Davis and A. Hamilton. 1998. 294p. bibliog. illus. index. ABC-CLIO, $65 (0-87436-961-4). DDC: 355.

The preface of this work, compiled by two history professors, lists the criteria for inclusion: populations that used a military structure to maintain societal discipline or dominate neighbors, soldiers whose specialized training or fighting styles dominated action during their time, units that rose through leadership or circumstance to military fame, and units that seek high-quality fighters to become an elite force. The 100 two-to four-page entries are arranged alphabetically in a double-column format, with references to two or three books or articles from which the information was drawn.

The peoples and groups represented range widely from around the globe and throughout history—warrior priests who developed kung fu in sixth-century China; the Ashanti of nineteenth-century West Africa; Russian Cossacks; Viking berserkers; the nineteenth-century African American troops known as Buffalo Soldiers; the ANZACs of Australia and New Zealand; the Sikhs of India. The writing is objective and provides sufficient historical and contemporary background for a clear understanding of questions, such as why the British and later the Russians lost wars in Afghanistan. Illustrations depict many of the groups. The bibliography brings together the sources listed after each entry, and the index is accurate.

As with many reference works, much of this information is available in existing resources. However, this volume brings together a wide range of fighting peoples and groups. High-school, public, and academic libraries that have a need for such a compilation will find it useful.

The Hutchinson Dictionary of Ancient & Medieval Warfare. Ed. by Matthew Bennett. 1998. 365p. bibliog. Fitzroy Dearborn, $75 (1-57958-116-1). DDC: 355.

Assisted by three consultants and 16 contributors, all of whom are distinguished scholars of ancient and medieval history and warfare, editor Bennett has compiled an interesting new reference work that is very extensive in scope. It encompasses 3,500 years of military events from earliest recorded times to 1500 A.D. That cutoff point was selected because of the invention of gunpowder and new advances in military and naval warfare. Coverage is universal with entries on Europe, Egypt, Greece, China, Japan, Persia, and Central and South Asia.

Arranged alphabetically, the book contains 2,500 entries, which cover battles, wars, heroes, commanders, places, and terminology. There are also entries for types of warriors (*candidati*, *franc-archer*, *samurai*) and equipment (*arquebus*, *harness*, *lambrequin*). A random sampling determined there are approximately seven entries per page, which vary in length from a few sentences to half a page. Entries provide dates when appropriate, and measurement is given in both metric and English units. Small arrows designate cross-references within an entry. Some important topics are given extended treatment in sidebars; examples include *Constantinople, siege of* (1203–04); *Hindu armies*; *military orders*; and *Peloponnesian War*. Reference value would have been enhanced by the addition of maps, diagrams, and other illustrations. Rounding out the volume is a briefly annotated bibliography of 97 titles, arranged by subject.

There are other reference works on the history of warfare, most notably Dupuy's classic *Harper Encyclopedia of Military History: From 3500 B.C. to the Present* [RBB N 1 93], which includes line drawings of weapons and battle formations and numerous maps. However, the Hutchinson title is unique in its concentration on ancient and medieval warfare, and will be useful in large public and academic libraries with specialized military-history collections.

Wars of the Americas: A Chronology of Armed Conflict in the New World, 1492 to the Present. By David F. Marley. 1998. 722p. bibliog. illus. index. ABC-CLIO, $99 (0-87436-837-5). DDC: 355.

Wars of the Americas is the most recent entry in the crowded field of chronologies. Seeking to fill a gap, Canadian writer-historian Marley has created a work that fleshes out a military chronology of the Americas. He warns at the outset, "inevitably, any attempt to compress 500 years of warfare into a single volume must entail certain compromises." These compromises turn out to be what the author considers underreported or ignored minor confrontations, and they do seem to be minor, indeed.

The volume is divided into eight sections, each of which takes on 50 to 100 years of history and is subdivided into important military themes. For example, the beginning section, "Discovery and Conquest (1492–1572)," is divided into smaller chronologies such as "Initial Contacts (1492–1498)"; "Conquest of Mexico (1517–1521)"; and "Conquest of Peru (1524–1539)." Each subsection is introduced by a brief overview. Each of the events in the chronology that follows includes a paragraph or two of narrative explaining its historical significance. The last section, "Pax Americana (1898–Present)", ends with such recent events as the occupation of the Japanese embassy in Lima by Tupac Amaru guerrillas and the retirement of Chile's General Augusto Pinochet in March 1998.

The volume includes many illustrations from famous works of art or historical photographs—many from the author's own private collection—as well as line drawings of military maps. A 12-page, topically arranged bibliography lists a selection of the works that were consulted by the author. An index provides access by major event or personal name, enhancing the usefulness of the resource.

With so many chronologies available, reference librarians must choose carefully. The well-reviewed Harper's Encyclopedia of Military History: From 3500 B.C. to the Present [RBB N 1 93], also arranged chronologically, may satisfy many smaller libraries' needs in this area. But if more comprehensive American coverage is needed, one could not go wrong with the purchase of Wars of the Americas. Recommended for academic, public, and high-school libraries.

The Encyclopedia of Housing. Ed. by Willem van Vliet. 1998. 712p. appendixes. bibliogs. illus. indexes. Sage, $169.95 (0-7619-1332-7). DDC: 363.5.

Literature on housing covers a vast array of disciplines, including urban studies, sociology, architecture, law, and real estate, to name a few. In the last decade or so, a number of reference works have been published on the topic, including Housing: A Multidisciplinary Approach, edited by Kamal S. Sayegh (Academy, 1987), and Dictionary of Housing, by Jack Rostron (Ashgate, 1997). Unlike those works, this volume generally contains longer entries and many specialized essays on topics about which information is not readily accessible. It includes, for instance, essays on children, adolescents and the elderly, providing a fascinating age-related approach to housing issues.

Containing more than 500 entries written by almost 250 scholars, government officials, and housing professionals, this work is aimed at the lay public, students, and professionals. Entries cover federal legislation, policy, and programs (Home Mortgage Disclosure Act, Model Cities Program); types of housing (congregate housing; pueblos; slaves, housing of); social and health issues (acquired immune deficiency syndrome, dementia); and a host of other related topics: commuting, eviction, fixed-rate mortgage loan, housing starts, redlining, sweat equity. Especially noteworthy are the individual entries for journals, such as the Journal of Real Estate Research, which provide the publishing history, address, cost, circulation, and even editorial submission requirements.

Appendixes cover major federal legislation and list major organizations and journals. In addition, there are subject, author, and contributor indexes. Extensive cross-references at the end of the entries offer easy access to further related information. Almost all the entries include a brief bibliography listing classic works and recent studies.

The editor's introductory essay offers an excellent overview of the book, noting both its strengths while acknowledging its limitations. Printed in a durable binding with easy-to-read type and a clear layout, this unique source superbly exemplifies some of the major qualities of an outstanding reference work—authority, accessibility, and a clearly defined objective. While the volume's price might limit the purchase to larger libraries, it is an important and useful work for both public and academic libraries. Highly recommended.

Environmental Disasters: A Chronicle of Individual, Industrial, and Governmental Carelessness. By Lee Davis. 1998. 246p. bibliog. illus. index. Facts On File, $45 (0-8160-3265-3). DDC: 363.73.

Events such as the Exxon oil spill in Valdez, Alaska, the Union Carbide explosion in Bhopal, India, and the nuclear disaster at Chernobyl get big headlines and stay in the memory of those who lived through them. However, there are many more stories of environmental damage resulting from human carelessness, hubris, or negligence. This volume chronicles nearly 100 different environmental tragedies. Although the concentration is on the twentieth century, Davis has also included some events, such as deforestation, that began earlier. The author has written on a wide variety of subjects, including two previous works on related topics for Facts On File.

The content is divided into five sections, each beginning with a listing of the events within the category, first by country, then chronologically. This is followed by a short introduction to the type of event treated in the section. Within each section, the events are presented chronologically by country. An adequate selected bibliography is followed by a very complete index. The 72 black-and-white photographs are clearly chosen for their dramatic impact.

In the first section, "Collective and Individual Assaults Against the Environment," Davis documents disasters that are the product of mostly unintentional and accidental events. These include fires, deforestation, and floods. The second section, "Industrial and Governmental Disasters," chronicles events that occurred as the result of governmental or corporate operations. These include factory explosions, toxic leaks, and industrial pollution of land, water, and air. The third section covers oil spills from 1967 through 1996. The fourth treats nuclear disasters, including Chernobyl and Three Mile Island. The final section, "War Crimes Against the Environment," chronicles what Davis characterizes as intentional, nationalistic attacks on the environment. These include atomic tests, defoliation with Agent Orange in Vietnam, and the fires set in the oil fields of Kuwait during and after the Gulf War in 1991.

The strength of this work is in its coverage of events that did not have the international impact of Chernobyl or Bhopal. Davis makes a strong effort to include the underlying causes of these disasters, whether they be agricultural, industrial, or governmental. The tone can be somewhat polemical, as the author seems to want to sound an alarm about humanity's lack of care for the environment. The treatment is more newsy than scholarly, and lacks specific references for the information within specific entries. The work would also have benefited from cross-references between entries.

This volume is highly recommended for school and public libraries as well as undergraduate-level academic institutions. Students in search of a topic for a term paper will find much that is helpful here. Since it lacks any substantial treatment of the environmental movement in general, and has a pronounced environmentalist bias, the book should not stand alone. A nice companion would be Conservation and Environmentalism: An Encyclopedia [RBB F 15 96]. For more complete chronological coverage of environmental events in the twentieth century, a much more comprehensive and scholarly work is Magill's five-volume Great Events from History II: Ecology and the Environment Series [RBB Ag 96], offering extensive bibliographies after each entry as well as a more neutral tone.

The FBI: A Comprehensive Reference Guide. Ed. by Athan G. Theoharis. 1998. 464p. bibliog. illus. index. tables. Oryx, $85 (0-89774-991-X). DDC: 363.25.

Here is an in-depth look at the history, people, controversies, and cases of the Federal Bureau of Investigation. Editor Theoharis and several contributors provide a balanced look at this sometimes secretive agency.

The work is divided into 10 chapters, each covering one broad topic, beginning with "A Brief History of the FBI's Role and Powers" and ending with "Chronology of Key Events." In between are chapters detailing famous cases, traditions, and culture of the FBI; the organizational structure and day-to-day operations; the facilities; the impact of the Bureau on American popular culture; and biographies of key agents and figures in the FBI's history. Illustrations, photographs, tables, and graphs support the text.

Each chapter is signed by the contributing editor and opens with an outline of the material to be presented. Headings guide the user to the correct section of the chapter. As an example, Chapter 2, "Notable Cases," is divided into five subsections: "Introduction," "The Early Years (1908–24)," "The Hoover Years (1924–72)," "The Modern Era (1972 to the Present)," and "Summary." "The Hoover Years" includes subsections on "Gangster Cases of the 1930s," "Organized Crime," and "Civil Rights Cases of the 1960s," among others; with discussion of particular cases (Bonnie and Clyde, La Cosa Nostra, the Medgar Evers murder) within each of these categories. Chapter 8, "The FBI in Popular American Culture," includes a filmography of movies and television shows which deal exclusively or peripherally with the agency, listing for each the director, cast, and a brief synopsis of the plot. More than 100 FBI personnel, including top level executives, employees associated with FBI firsts (a table of firsts is provided), and other notables, are profiled in Chapter 9. See references throughout the work guide the reader to the correct entries. An annotated bibliography and index complete the volume. Given the book's arrangement, the index is essential.

There is no other reference book that covers the FBI in such detail. This would be an extremely useful volume for high-school, public, and academic libraries.

Education, Communication, Customs

Education Statistics on the United States. Ed. by Mark S. Littman and Deirdre A. Gaquin. 1999. 643p. tables. index. Bernan, $65 (0-89059-066-4). DDC: 370.973.

Compiled from U.S. Bureau of the Census school enrollment data as of October 1996; the March 1997 Current Population Survey; the National Center for Education Statistics' *Digest of Education Statistics*, 1997; and the Common Core of Data (CCD) computer file for 1995–1996 collected by the National Center for Education Statistics. This new compendium provides a wide range of statistical information in four sections: "School Enrollment," "Educational Attainment," "Education Characteristics by State," and "State and County-Level Education Statistics." Each of the four sections contains a notes and definitions section describing the data sources. Within each section, tables display such information as preprimary school enrollment by family income and race; annual average secondary school teachers' salaries by state; and average eighth-grade science scores by county. The volume concludes with a general subject index, citing page numbers, not table numbers like the original government publications.

This reference source is not as graphically pleasing as *The Condition of Education*: 1998, NCES-013 (National Center for Education Statistics), which includes multicolored tables. Although its larger type font makes it easier to read than the *Digest of Education Statistics*, the *Digest* is a better source, containing many important statistical tables omitted in *Education Statistics*, such as enrollment in historically black colleges and universities, public school libraries, and public opinion on education. A serious shortcoming of *Education Statistics* is the broad and general index subject headings, which omit, for example, specific table references for statistics on Asian-Americans and Hispanics. Although this work does contain some updated and aggregated statistical information not found in the other government-published sources, *Education Statistics* is significantly more expensive; and the selective nature of the data does not favorably compare with the *Digest of Education Statistics*. Recommended for education libraries needing comprehensive statistics. Otherwise, most libraries should find the *Digest of Education Statistics* sufficient.

The Comparative Guide to American Elementary and Secondary Schools. 1998. 774p. index. Toucan Valley, paper, $85 (1-884925-63-4). DDC: 371.00973.

This work provides selected statistics for all public school districts serving 2,500 or more students. Besides address and telephone number of the main district headquarters, the information for each of the approximately 3,900 entries includes grade span, school types (regular, special education, and alternative or vocational), numbers of students and teachers, student/teacher ratio, expenditures per student, numbers of librarians and guidance counselors, ethnic composition, and a national socioeconomic status indication (derived from the count of students eligible for the Free Lunch Program under the National School Lunch Act). For the most part, data are taken from the National Center for Education Statistics, in the *Common Core of Data Public School Universe* and the *Common Core of Data Agency Universe* files, of which the most current available are from the 1995–96 school year. Web addresses were researched independently.

Organized alphabetically by state and then by county, the information for each district is formatted in charts, with about six entries per page. The city index which follows the entries is essential, as district names often differ from the city names. Under each city, the index lists each district operating schools within that city, and the number of schools operated by that district, as well as the page number on which information on the district can be found.

Most New York City school districts have, unaccountably, been omitted. The only New York City school district included, as far as the Board can determine, is the Kings County or Brooklyn school district. Additionally, there are flaws in the indexing which do not inspire confidence. Flushing, NY, is not a city, but rather part of the Borough of Queens, which in turn is part of New York City. Staten Island, Bronx, and Flushing are listed in the index as having entries on page 382, but there are no such entries on that page. An entry in the index for Queens is missing altogether. A relatively expensive book such as this should have handled a large geographical and population-dense area such as New York City better.

It is not quite clear who the intended audience is for this book. Other sources with school district information, such as Educational Directories' *Patterson's American Education* and *Patterson's Elementary Education* (both annuals), are more useful for parents; they cover more districts and also provide information on individual schools. *The Comparative Guide to American Elementary and Secondary Schools* might be considered by libraries that want to supplement the *Patterson's* guides with additional statistical data and a format that facilitates comparisons across districts. Another source for information on public schools is *SchoolMatch* at schoolmatch.com, a school research and database firm specializing in rating schools.

Encyclopedia of Bilingualism and Bilingual Education. 2v. By Colin Baker and Sylvia Prys Jones. 1998. 758p. bibliog. illus. index. Taylor & Francis, $99 (1-85359-362-1). DDC: 371.97.

Language is more than a means of communication. It is tightly bound to culture, politics, and ethnic identity. With increasing migration and globalization, the need to function in more than one language is becoming more important. Bilingual education, the topic of many heated discussions in political and educational circles, is not easy to understand. The authors, bilingual scholars at the School of Education, University of Wales, Bangor, want to "promote the subject of bilingualism in an attractive, comprehensible and comprehensive manner . . . to be academically sound while being accessible to as wide an audience as possible."

This encyclopedia has four major sections: "Individual Bilingualism," "Languages in Society," "Languages in Contact in the World," and "Bilingual Education". Each section contains broad topical articles on subjects such as "Who Is Bilingual?" "Aims of Bilingual Education," and "Multiculturalism in Education." These articles are broken down into shorter sections that cover individual aspects of the subjects, such as immersion in bilingual education, bilingual education for deaf students, and second-language acquisition. Section 3, "Languages in Contact in the World," discusses bilingualism in specific countries. Most articles have short lists of sources for further reading. Graphs, maps, charts, and photographs accompany the articles. Sidebars present extra material such as brief biographies of scholars working in the field, portraits of bilingual families, current educational and linguistic theories, and contemporary events such as the controversy about Ebonics in the Oakland, California, public schools. Cross-references direct users to related articles. A bibliography of more than 2,000 sources and author and subject indexes complete the work.

Although much of the material presented here deals with complex theories in the areas of linguistics, psychology, sociology, and education, the authors discuss things like language acquisition, cognition, and social and ethnic identity in terms that are easy for all readers to understand. They also offer a great deal of practical information about the implementation of bilingual and multicultural education. This is an interesting and useful source for academic and large public libraries.

Encyclopedia of Student and Youth Movements. By David. F. Burg. 1998. 320p. bibliog. illus. index. Facts On File, $50 (0-8160-3375-7). DDC: 371.8.

The most significant events, organizations, and people among student and youth movements, which had either a large impact during their time or influence afterwards, are the focus of this work. It covers groups and activities, across the globe and through the centuries, which have sought personal improvement, social progress, or political change. The author, a freelance writer and editor with a background in history and humanities, has written previous reference books.

The alphabetically arranged entries are all-encompassing, from early dissent in European universities to political upheaval in China and India in the nineteenth and twentieth centuries; from self-improvement clubs in England over the past century to revolts in Africa in the last half-century. As Burg states in his introduction, youth movements have had a variety of aims; among the entries to be found here are *Black Panthers*, *Boy Scouts of America*, *Children's Crusade*, *Hare Krishna*, *Hell's Angels*, and *Red Guards*.

Most entries are a paragraph long, which is sufficient; but greater detail is given when needed, such as two pages for the Hungarian Revolution of 1956. The information is accurate and the writing is lively, but it is not always clear if an earlier group is still active today. Cross-references are provided in capital letters. Each entry notes the nation immediately after the title, thus *Gaulledet University Revolution* (*United States*).

The four-page bibliography is wide-ranging, including items such as an article in an educational journal on student power in medieval universities and books on Puritanism and Arabic social movements. In a few instances, a source is cited at the end of an entry. The index is accurate, containing individuals, organizations, and events, but does not group all of the movements for a nation under the heading of the country. A user seeking all Japanese organizations or events would need to scan the entire work.

This is a wonderful resource for seeking specific information and browsing. While the author does not claim that it is exhaustive, but rather a beginning, many small groups are included. Most libraries should consider adding this moderately priced resource.

Historical Dictionary of Women's Education in the United States. Ed. by Linda Eisenmann. 1998. 584p. appendix. bibliogs. index. Greenwood, $95 (0-313-29323-6). DDC: 371.822.

This work is an encyclopedic dictionary of significant events, ideas, movements, institutions, and people related to the history of women's education in the U.S. One hundred and four scholars contributed entries within their fields of expertise. Each of the 245 entries defines a subject and describes its significance to women's educational history. Topics covered were selected according to the following criteria: equal representation of geographic, racial, and socioeconomic diversity of schooling for girls and women throughout U.S. history; and inclusion of both formal and informal educational settings. In addition to entries for important institutions, there is coverage of suffrage organizations, women's clubs, advocacy groups, and popular writers. Biographical entries were limited to allow for broader treatment of issues, events, and themes.

Length of entries ranges from a few sentences to more than three pages for broad topics such as *Asian American women's education*, *colonial schooling*, and *graduate education*. Cross-references are indicated in bold type with an asterisk, providing the reader with an easy mechanism for expansion of a topic. Each entry is followed by a short bibliography directing the user to further reading on the topic and related issues. A selected bibliography at the end of the volume provides a reading list of additional sources.

Entries cover a wide range of topics. Examples include *affirmative action*, *Barnard College*, *Catholic teaching orders*, *Immigrant Protective League*, *normal schools*, *Lowell mills*, and *temperance movement*. Among the individuals who are profiled are Abigail Adams, Mary McLeod Bethune, and Emma Willard. An introduction provides background on the various eras of the history of women's education in the U.S. from the 1600s to the 1900s. An appendix contains a chronology, 1675–1996.

This volume is a valuable resource for learning about the educational history of women in the U.S. It would be a useful reference tool in academic and large public libraries.

Historical Dictionary of School Segregation and Desegregation: The American Experience. By Jeffrey A. Raffel. 1998. 316p. bibliogs. index. Greenwood, $75 (0-313-29502-6). DDC: 379.2.

Tracing the topic of school segregation and desegregation in the U.S. from the eighteenth century to the present, this work presents a comprehensive review of the forces and events that have driven and shaped this controversial issue. Essays ranging from several paragraphs to several pages in length describe the more than 260 alphabetically arranged topics, including significant court cases, legislation, persons, organizations, types of school desegregation plans, and concepts and terms. The introduction provides valuable analysis, including discussion on the stages of school desegregation, evaluations of the topic from the research literature, today's issues, and thoughts on possible future developments. Each entry includes a factual description, a summary of different viewpoints, and a brief bibliography. Within the essays, asterisks mark terms and names that have their own entry, in order to alert readers to related information. A chronology of key dates and events covers September 17, 1787, when the U.S. Constitution was adopted, to November 5, 1996, when California voters adopted Proposition 209, limiting affirmative action. The main focus, however, is on the last 50 years in elementary, secondary, and post-secondary education.

Author Raffel points out that selectivity was required, and thus not all segregation-related court cases and people are included. Likewise, this book is not intended to be a historical dictionary of civil rights or African American education. The volume does, however, cover expected topics plus major related ones. For example, *ability grouping*, *affirmative action*, *busing*, *magnet schools*, and *racism* are here, along with entries for Linda Carol Brown, daughter of the first plaintiff in the landmark 1954 *Brown v. Board of Education* decision, and Supreme Court Justice John Marshall Harlan, the lone dissenter in the *Plessy v. Ferguson* case. The general bibliography at the end of the volume provides a wealth of additional sources for further exploration, and a separate geographical bibliography will help users interested in locating particular cases by city or school district.

Essays are written in a nonjudgmental style, giving the arguments and reasoning of those with different opinions on both sides of the issues. This is a thorough and objective work for study of the issues of race and equity in education. Academic and large public libraries will want to acquire it for their students, teachers, scholars, practitioners, and interested public.

McGraw-Hill Illustrated Telecom Dictionary. By Jade Clayton. 1998. 501p. appendixes. illus. index. McGraw-Hill, paper $29.95 (0-07-012063-3). DDC: 384.

Many of the most significant technological advancements of the 1990s have come as a direct result of the changing telecommunications environment. Cell phones, voice mail, modems, and the Internet are all possible due to improvements and innovations in telecommunications. The field has also developed a highly specialized and technical vocabulary, which this dictionary helps to explain.

The work contains over 2,000 entries for terms used in the industry, arranged alphabetically from A (*amp*, *ampere*) to *Zulu time*. A section on numbers from 0 to 965TD precedes the A–Z entries. Although aimed primarily at professionals in the telephone industry, the book will also be valuable for anyone interested in computing and electronics. Entries are short and easily understandable to the lay reader. Six appendixes supply additional information, such as international calling codes and twisted-pair cable color codes (used in communications wiring).

The work is especially strong in covering hardware, although the accompanying photographs are often of poor quality. Despite this minor problem, McGraw-Hill has done a fine job of producing a reference tool to cover this complex field. Telecommunications will continue to change at a rapid pace, but for now this dictionary is the best reference work in the field.

Weddings: Dating & Love Customs of Cultures Worldwide, Including Royalty. By Carolyn Mordechai. 1999. 274p. bibliog. illus. index. Nittany, P.O. Box 80362, Phoenix, AZ 85060, $28 (0-9613823-2-5). DDC: 392.

Any librarian who has to find information about wedding customs around the world will welcome this volume. It begins with a chapter on religious weddings and includes information on ceremonies from the Baha'i, Zen Buddhist, Eastern Orthodox, Hindu, and Jewish traditions, among others. Following the section on religious weddings are chapters on Africa, North America, Central America, South America, Asia, Europe, the Middle East, and Oceania. These chapters are subdivided by country, an approach that allows the reader to find information on weddings in Greece, Sri Lanka, or Zambia, to name a few examples. The length of entries of each country ranges from a few paragraphs to two or three pages and seems to depend on how much information the author was able to find. Some entries include illustrations and sidebars that describe typical customs and ceremonies. All entries cite the source or sources for the information. These citations are sometimes insufficient. Only author and title are given, a problem since many of the sources do not seem to be included in the bibliography at the end of the volume.

The chapter on royalty provides descriptions of modern royal weddings, such as the marriage of Grace Kelly and Prince (called *Princess* here) Rainier III of Monaco; also included here is the John F. Kennedy–Jacqueline Bouvier wedding. A glossary, a bibliography, and an index complete the volume. The Board noted some errors in the bibliography, and works are not cited in a consistent style. A few Web sites are listed, but no URLs are provided.

Mordechai gathered her information from many different sources, including anthropological journals, clergy, embassies, wedding magazines and guides, libraries, and interviews. In her introductory note, she states that she could not cover all variations in wedding customs and welcomes information to consider for a second edition. Although not a source to be used for serious research, this book should prove very useful in public libraries.

Clowns and Tricksters: An Encyclopedia of Tradition and Culture. By Kimberly A. Christen. 1998. 271p. bibliog. illus. index. ABC-CLIO, $65 (0-87436-936-3). DDC: 398.2.

Although they are archetypical figures and appear in nearly every culture, there are few reference works that attempt to give a broad overview of clowns and tricksters. The author, an adjunct instructor in the Religious Studies Department at Arizona State University, has produced a one-volume encyclopedia on these characters. Her introduction outlines the figure types and discusses how they vary from culture to culture. Also presented is a broad overview of scholarship in the field, ranging from the reports of seventeenth-century missionaries to the classic work of Franz Boas and Paul Radin, among others, and the work of such contemporary researchers as Barbara Babcock-Abrahams.

The body of the encyclopedia consists of more than 150 lengthy A–Z entries on multicultural tricksters and clowns from antiquity to the present. There are articles on Hermes and Isaahkawuattee (Crow Indian creation figure), Bugs Bunny and Ken Kesey. Each entry begins by noting the cultural origin of the character, as well as the geographic location. The entry then describes the character, details how the traits are displayed or manifested, and generally contains one or two stories demonstrating the character's personality. Important entries contain *see also* references to other entries on related topics, and each entry has one or more references that refer the reader to the detailed "References and Further Reading" list at the back of the book. In addition to entries on characters, there are also some entries on concepts, such as *healing* and *ritual performance*.

An important feature of this volume is the "Cultural Topic Finder," which permits users to locate clowns or tricksters of different cultures by geographic region (Africa, Asia, Europe, Arabic countries, etc.) and then by individual country and cultural group. The extensive 17-page bibliography contains articles, books, and chapters and could serve as a selection guide for further materials on the topic. The index helps to link entries on character types. For example, a reader who wants all the information on spider tales would find the relevant entries listed under *spider* in the index.

With every undertaking of this scope there will be omissions. There is no entry for the raven figure; only by looking under *raven* in the index can the reader find references to the raven in Northwest Coast Indian cultures. The index listing for *spider* does not include a citation to the entry *Brer Anancy*. The cross-referencing needs to be more consistent. The entry *rabbit* guides the reader to several examples, such as *Palu* and *Zomo*, but not to *Brer Rabbit* or *Bugs Bunny*, although these are listed under *rabbit* in the index.

These shortcomings notwithstanding, the entries are readable, enjoyable, and informative; the bibliography is helpful; and the arrangement is logical. High-school libraries, public libraries, and academic libraries where there is interest in the topic will want to have this title in their collections.

Encyclopedia of Fable. By Mary Ellen Snodgrass. 1998. 451p. bibliog. chronology. illus. index. ABC-CLIO, $75 (1-57607-026-3). DDC: 398.2.

For centuries children and adults have been entertained, enlightened, and instructed by fables and their underlying moral messages. In her fifth contribution to the ABC-CLIO Literary Companion series, Snodgrass explores not just the traditional realm of fable but the "wealth of world literature that belongs in the domain of illustrative wisdom lore." Thus, she also encompasses such areas as cruelty jokes, exemplary tales, pourquoi stories, and storytelling, and she includes animal stories that are not generally considered fables.

Of the 68 entries, 33 are biographical treatments of principal fabulists, among them Aesop, Geoffrey Chaucer, Marie de France, and James Thurber. Prominent illustrators of fables are treated in a single article. Offering broader perspective on the history and development of fable and briefer sketches of additional writers, translators, and collectors of fables are a variety of more general articles that focus on fable as a genre and its related forms, historic periods, and the fable heritage of specific civilizations, nationalities, or religious and ethnic groups (e.g., African American, Celtic, Greek, and Oriental). Only a small number of entries treat specific fables or fable collections (for instance, A*nimal Farm*, P*anchatantra*, and *A Thousand and One Nights*) and characters or character types (such as Brer Rabbit, Reynard the Fox, and Trickster). Ranging in length from two to thirteen pages, entries are often accompanied by black-and-white illustrations and frequently provide *see also* references to related articles. All articles conclude with abbreviated citations to sources consulted. Additional features include chronological, author, and title lists of major fables and fable collections and a brief list of films based on fables. Bibliographies of primary and secondary sources cite selected print, audiovisual, and Internet materials.

Although the index covers authors, titles, and topics, it unfortunately includes only a small number of the titles of individual fables that are discussed or mentioned in the entries. Thus, such popular fables as "The Hare and the Tortoise" and "The Fox and the Grapes" do not appear in the index, even though these titles are mentioned in various entries, and the former is the subject of a full-page illustration. Like the aforementioned title list, the index follows the questionable practice of alphabetizing foreign-language titles under their initial articles. Of even greater concern are the numerous careless errors, including incorrect page references in the index, misspelled and misused words, inconsistent and incorrect citation of certain titles, and nonsensical statements, that mar this work. Its most serious limitation, however, is its paucity of entries, which results in an overemphasis on biographical and historical material and a deemphasis on individual fables and fable motifs. In a truly encyclopedic work, one would expect to find articles on specific animals in fables (such as the crow, lion, and wolf), on plant fables, and on common fable motifs (such as vanity, greed, social status), as well as entries providing synopses of and commentary on many of the most well known and best-beloved fables.

A number of dictionaries of folklore, mythology, and legend cover fable, but this is the first encyclopedia devoted exclusively to the genre. Although it is far from the definitive reference work on fable and suffers from serious flaws, its lengthy articles provide overviews that could be used to supplement the more specific entries pertaining to fable in such standard compilations as *Funk & Wagnalls Standard Dictionary of Folklore, Mythology, and Legend* (Harper, 1972) and the *Facts On File Encyclopedia of World Mythology and Legend* (1988).

Storytellers: A Biographical Directory of 120 English-Speaking Performers Worldwide. By Corki Miller and Mary Ellen Snodgrass. 1998. 360p. appendix. bibliog. illus. index. McFarland, $55 (0-7864-0470-1). DDC: 398.2.

Storytelling is on the upswing, so a directory of contemporary English-speaking performers is very helpful. The authors interviewed and contacted numerous professionals to create this book of 120 storytellers. The criteria for inclusion are not provided, but it seems the storytellers had to agree to participate and had to be presently performing. Their styles range from traditional to contemporary urban fables, from imaginative telling to music and dance. A few use sign language. Most are active in storytelling festivals or organizations.

Each entry includes address, focus (e.g., types of tales), audience (all ages are represented), style, and instruments/props. Most include a photo of the subject. The main part of the entry, usually about a page, covers the storyteller's personal life and achievements. Many entries also include a section that may list articles, audiography, videography, bibliography of main story sources, awards, and additional sources of information, both print and electronic. The Board found some errors. Dominican University, which until recently was called Rosary College, is referred to both as Rosary College and Dominican College in the entry on Janice Del Negro. That entry also describes Del Negro as "currently an adjunct faculty member of the Graduate School of Library and Information Science at Rosary College," but she has not taught there in several years.

One appendix lists storytellers by state (largely New York, California, Illinois, Texas, and North Carolina) and country; 14 of the storytellers are from outside the U.S. A glossary defines common storytelling terms. The bibliography contains titles on techniques and sources. The index is quite thorough.

While this book is not definitive, there is nothing else quite like it, and it does give a representative picture of current storytelling practices. It would probably be best purchased for large collections with a strong emphasis on the topic.

Language

Dictionary of Languages: The Definitive Reference to More Than 400 Languages. By Andrew Dalby. 1998. 734p. charts. glossary. index. maps. Columbia, $50 (0-231-11568-7). DDC: 403.

Language is both a means of communication and a source of insight into culture. Because languages are linked to political, social, and technological events, they evolve with the changes that occur in society. A basic knowledge of the languages used in an area will enrich understanding of its life and culture. This dictionary, written by a linguist, provides an introduction to the world's languages.

The subtitle of the book demonstrates its scope. The alphabetical entries cover all languages with official status as well as those with a written literature and 175 minor languages with significant historical and/or anthropological interest. A preface explains the author's pronunciation scheme. He does not use the International Phonetic Alphabet, but he does use pinyin transliterations for Chinese. An introduction offers a basic overview of linguistics and the study of languages.

The entries themselves are from two to four pages long. Each one discusses a specific language (*Diola, Chinese, Zapotec*) or language family (*Afroasiatic languages, Indo-Aryan languages, Niger-Congo languages*). Entries for individual languages include the language name, estimated number of speakers, the country or countries in which it is spoken, an essay on the origin of the language, its characteristics and cultural links, a map, a list of dialects and related languages, and an example of the script and/or alphabet. Some entries also have quotations of proverbs or poetry. The entries for historical languages that are no longer spoken (*Gothic, Old Slavonic, Sumerian*) are briefer and do not have maps.

The extensive range of languages covered makes this an extremely useful source. The alphabetical arrangement is, for the most part, a good feature, but some languages are hard to find. There is no entry for Farsi within the text or the index. The article *Persian, Dari, and Tajik* explains that Farsi is the name of the Persian language, but the lack of cross-references may be frustrating for users. The use of variant spelling (e.g., *Panjabi* for *Punjabi, Pashto* for *Pushtu*) with no cross-referencing in the text and very few cross-references in the index may be confusing. Perseverance will bring success.

The Atlas of Languages (Facts On File, 1996) covers similar material but discusses only 200 languages. It has color illustrations and maps, but *Dictionary of Languages* has more-detailed articles on a greater number of languages as well as a glossary of linguistic terms. The two works complement each other. With coverage of languages from Abkhaz to Zulu, explanations of Egyptian hieroglyphics and Sumerian script, and a discussion of Chinese dialects and characters, *Dictionary of Languages* is a welcome addition to public and academic library collections.

Key Concepts in Language and Linguistics. By R. L. Trask. 1999. 378p. bibliog. index. Routledge, $75 (0-415-15741-2). DDC: 410.

Neither a dictionary nor an encyclopedia, Trask's latest entry in the field of linguistics and phonetics deals with important key concepts that every beginning student is likely to encounter from every area of language study. Besides Trask's own previous works, the volume depends heavily on the work of David Crystal, whose encyclopedias and dictionaries of language and linguistics are well respected; the essay on the IndoEuropean language family is an example. There are essays, however, on topics not found in Crystal's *Dictionary of Linguistics and Phonetics* (Blackwell, 4th ed., 1997), one being *animal communication*. *Key Concepts* offers terms related to grammatical analysis, branches of linguistics, discourse analysis, varieties of language, related phenomena, and simple grammatical concepts such as *adverb* and *noun*. Students will be pleased to find topics like *Black English, nonverbal communication*, and *sex differences in language*. For more serious scholars, terms like *deitic category, onomastics*, and *syntagmatic relation* abound.

Most entries run three or four short paragraphs, and many are valuable browse material. Each entry begins with a brief definition followed by an indepth discussion of the concept. Historical origins are given where possible. The author admits he has tried to provide the "kind of explanation not readily available elsewhere for concepts not found in textbooks." There are no separate entries for key individuals. Related concepts are adequately crossreferenced not only in the text but also at the ends of entries. Each entry concludes with further reading that identifies the author's sources, and there is a lengthy bibliography at the end of the work. The index is important because there are no *see* references to guide the reader who may be looking for *Ebonics*, for example, to the article *Black English*.

Middle-and high-school students may enjoy the much briefer definitions of many of these concepts in Trask's *Student's Dictionary of Language and Linguistics* (Arnold, 1997). A work for more advanced scholars is Hadumod Bussmann's *Routledge Dictionary of Language and Linguistics* (1996), which defines most of Trask's concepts, with lengthier bibliographies and brief etymologies. *Key Concepts in Language and Linguistics* would be a worthwhile addition to language and linguistics collections in academic and large public libraries.

Language and Communication: A Cross-Cultural Encyclopedia. By Michael Shaw Findlay. 1998. 229p. appendix. bibliogs. illus. index. maps. ABC-CLIO, $55 (0-87436-946-0). DDC: 410

The purpose of this volume in ABC-CLIO's Encyclopedias of the Human Experience series is to explore Western and non-Western traditions and sociocultural language conventions in an effort to deemphasize the Indo-European approach often used in the past. Findlay, a social scientist, defines 151 terms from an anthropological, ethnographic, and sociolinguistic point of view. Entries range from one or two paragraphs to several pages depending upon the topic. *Discourse analysis* and *gender differences*, for example, are among the longest. The author presents complex concepts in cross-cultural communication in thoughtful, clear terms.

Some entries feature brief bibliographies. There is a lengthy bibliography in an appendix. Cross-referencing is adequate, and there are simple line-drawn maps in the front matter showing location of language groups mentioned in the text. The index leads the reader to individual ethnic groups (*Apache, Hmong, Yanomamo*), to individuals (*Chomsky, Noam*), and to topics (*Black English, ethnographic methods*, etc.)

This is a compact volume that is easily held in the hand for quick referral and is a reliable source of information. It complements, but does not replace, David Crystal's *Cambridge Encyclopedia of Language* (2d ed., Cambridge, 1997), which is still the leader in the field of linguistics for the lay reader. Rather than using the alphabetical arrangement of Findlay's book, Crystal's work is divided into 11 thematic sections, allowing the author to explore topics more fully. One of these sections deals with language and communication. Another, which deals in depth with the origin of language, includes the following theories: *Bow wow, Pooh-pooh, Ding-dong, Yo-he-ho,* and *La-La*; Findlay discusses only the last three. In the Cambridge volume, the maps accompany the text along with photos and illustrations and are, therefore, easier to follow. Many topics, such as pidgins and Creole, are treated more fully.

Nonetheless, Findlay's work is valuable, informative, and very browsable, offering a concise approach for undergraduate, high-school, and popular linguistics collections.

Language

A Dictionary of Modern American Usage. By Bryan A. Garner. 1998. 752p. appendix. bibliog. Oxford, $30 (0-19-507853-5). DDC: 423.

The purpose of this dictionary is to help writers "use language deftly so that it's fit for their purposes." Garner is a lawyer and lexicographer, has written books on legal usage and style, and is the editor-in-chief of Black's Law Dictionary. His overriding criterion for correct usage is the "actual usage of educated speakers and writers." He has compiled more than 5,000 illustrative quotations and examples from a variety of sources, including the New York Times, the NEXIS and WESTLAW databases, local newspapers, books, and scholarly journals.

Unlike other usage dictionaries, this volume relies on linguistic evidence from modern sources rather than conservative historical precedent to determine correctness. For example, instead of ethician, Garner identifies ethicist as correct because it is used 400 times more than ethician in the NEXIS and WESTLAW databases. Similarly, Garner indicates the traditionally correct usage of transpire ("to pass through a surface; come to light; become known by degrees"), traditionally incorrect usage ("to happen, occur, or take place"), and concludes by advising writers to "avoid it altogether simply to avoid distracting readers, whether traditionalists or revolutionaries."

The dictionary provides two types of main entries. Approximately 170 essay entries provide lengthy discussions of usage and style (e.g., -able, computerese, gerunds, needless variants, sexism, titular Tomfoolery), and approximately 7,000 word entries discuss a particular word or set of words. Entries are written in narrative fashion, and provide definitions, discussions of usage and alternative senses, illustrative quotations, and citations to references from which quotations or senses of words have been taken. Traditional sources including Webster's Third New International Dictionary of the English Language (1961), Evans and Evans' Dictionary of Contemporary American Usage (Random, 1957), Follett's Modern American Usage (Hill & Wang, 1966), and The Oxford English Dictionary (2d ed., Oxford, 1989) are liberally referenced, as are hundreds of modern sources. The volume concludes with a chronological list of more than 350 standard titles on English usage and a select bibliography.

The prose in this work is readable, interesting, witty, and lively. Although it will be controversial because it takes issue with long-held scholarly judgments on usage, it will be very helpful for modern writers who desire to write correctly but unpretentiously. This resource is highly recommended for public and academic libraries. High-school librarians may also want to consider purchase because of the accessibility of the prose and the focus on modern usage.

Scholastic Children's Thesaurus. By John K. Bollard. 1998. 256p. illus. index. Scholastic, $15.95 (0-590-96785-1). DDC: 423.

Scholastic First Dictionary. Ed. by Judith S. Levey. 1998. 224p. illus. index. Scholastic, $14.95 (0-590-96786-X). DDC: 423.

Scholastic Treasury of Quotations for Children. By Adrienne Betz. 1998. 256p. index. Scholastic, $16.95 (0-590-27146-6). DDC: 082.

Each of these three new sources from Scholastic approaches language in a different way.

Scholastic Children's Thesaurus has more than 500 entries, containing 2,700 words, to help children write more precisely. Each entry has a headword and its part of speech, printed in green caps, followed by a definition. Two to six synonyms (in purple) and their definitions follow. An adjoining column gives one or more example sentences. Sentences are designed to illustrate typical use and construction. For example, the order of synonyms for the headword leave is depart, exit, withdraw, desert, and abandon. Occasional colored boxes give additional information. Illustrations, generally one per double-page spread, are drawings that illustrate sample sentences. Although descriptive and often humorous, they seem to function primarily to enhance page appearance. The index lists all words, and the headword under which each is found; antonyms are also referenced. Prefatory material consists of a two-page introduction for adults, and a five-page guide for children.

This is an attractive source, with words appropriate for elementary-school-age children. The strongest feature is the format, paralleling defined terms with example sentences. HBJ Student Thesaurus [RBB N 1 91] has more words, but defines only the generic concepts, with example sentences to illustrate shades of meaning. American Heritage Children's Thesaurus [RBB D 1 97] also has more terms, but with little more than a listing of synonyms.

Scholastic First Dictionary is a true dictionary, with guide words, pronunciations, multiple meanings, and forms of the main entry given as well as definitions and example sentences. There are two columns per page; type is very large. Guide words are printed in blue, entry words in green; the headword and its variants are bolded. Most pages have two or three colored pictures, almost all photographs. Pictures are more consistently informative than in other dictionaries for younger users, but the choice of what to illustrate seems arbitrary.

The intended audience is children ages six to nine, but definitions could be read to and understood by younger children. A two-page introduction explains dictionary use. The pronunciation system seems unnecessarily complex, and inconsistent with dictionary conventions. For example, ab-suhnt is the pronunciation for absent, her-uh-wuhn for heroine. The pronunciation of safe is sayf, but that for hide is hide. Accents are called stressed syllables. Concluding the work are very brief segments (one page or less) on word creation, plurals, homophones, parts-of-speech, and measurements. There is an index to picture labels.

Word choice seems appropriate, with mostly concrete nouns and some verbs. Parts of speech are not labeled, although a back page ("How Words Work in Sentences") introduces the topic. Definitions and example sentences are clear. Other, similarly titled volumes, American Heritage First Dictionary [RBB S 1 94] and Kingfisher First Dictionary [RBB N 1 95], are more elementary.

In Scholastic Treasury of Quotations for Children, 1,200 quotations are arranged within approximately 75 broad topics (e.g., Wealth and Poverty, Food, Humor, Prejudice), and within topic by author/creator. A lengthy biographical index gives a thumbnail sketch of each author, and refers to the topic(s) where the author's works are quoted. Authors cited range from Hatshepsut to the Delany Sisters, Judy Blume to Charlotte Bronte, traditional proverbs to the Reagans, the Bible to Alcoholics Anonymous. A four-page introduction gives the child-reader reasons to read and use quotations, as well as an explanation of how to use the source. Boxed sections in the text occasionally add more information about a quotation or an author. Very occasionally a quotation has an explanation. The format is quite readable, with a lot of white space on each page. The quotations, generally quite brief, are not aimed specifically at children. Many would require discussion for understanding, and most could be used as a basis for discussion.

It is doubtful how many children would consult quotation books "to add style and energy to [their] own words...," or for any of the other reasons given in the introduction. More perceptive older children—and adults—could enjoy browsing for ideas and turns of phrase. However, teachers and parents might need to help children make connections with the wit and wisdom in quotations. If the well-equipped children's collection requires a quotation book, this could well be it. The format, the biographical index/dictionary, and the diversity of authors all commend it. Adult ESL students and new readers might find this a good introduction to quotation books.

These three reference sources are attractive, with inviting covers. Although none is a must purchase, all are worthy of consideration, and could add depth to existing elementary school and public library children's room collections. Each could also be considered for family or classroom purchase.

The Canadian Oxford Dictionary. Ed. by Katherine Barber. 1998. 1,707p. appendixes. Oxford, $35 (0-19-541120-X). DDC: 427.3.

Oxford has another winner on its hands with its latest entry in the dictionary marketplace. The new Canadian Oxford Dictionary (COD) is an instant classic. This is a well-researched, comprehensive study of Canadian English incorporating words and terminology from Canada's diverse ethnic cultures and its every region. From the surprisingly not uniquely Canadian eh to chesterfield, jambusters, pencil crayon, poutine, and squid jigger, COD explores, defines, and explains in classic Oxford English Dictionary manner—scholarly but not pedantic, clear but not simplistic—all that makes Canadian English unique.

There is also an encyclopedic aspect to COD as it includes very short biographies of more than 800 well-known Canadians and 5,000 "internationally significant" individuals. More than 6,000 geographic locations and features, both Canadian and worldwide, are also defined, as are important historical events. Pronunciation of words is based on surveys and daily use. Does one pronounce schedule as "shedule" or "skedule"? Either could be "eether" or "eyether." Spelling variations are also noted: theatre or theater, labour or labor. It must be noted that although this is meant to be a Canadian dictionary, with 2,000 uniquely Canadian words and uses, it is clearly international in its scope, with U.S., British, and Australian English also making up some of the more than 130,000 entries. The emphasis is on how terms and words would be used in a Canadian context.

The work is the result of more than five years of research, using well-known Canadian lexicographers as well as experts in ethnic languages and their idiomatic use in Canadian English. Contributors and project team members are listed just after the table of contents. There is a short history of Canadian English and its growth and change from Loyalist American English and the evolution of Aboriginal, Inuit, and ethnic words into Canadian English. At the end of the dictionary are several appendixes: a six-page style guide; a list of all prime ministers and governors general of Canada; weights, measures, and notations; and alphabets in the Arabic, Hebrew, Greek, and Russian.

The layout is easy-to-read and easy-to-use: two columns per page, with entries in boldface for ease of searching and boldface headers on every page. Pronunciations and examples of how a word is used in everyday language ensure a thorough study of any term or word. The seven-page "Guide to the Use of This Dictionary" is thorough and clear.

This is a first edition and a completely new work for Oxford University Press. *The Canadian Oxford Dictionary* is a highly recommended reference tool for academic institutions that include programs in Canadian studies, or the study of the English language, as well as those U.S. public libraries found along northern borders. It can go almost without saying that every Canadian library—school, public, academic, and special—must have at least one copy of this indispensable guide to Canadian English on its shelves.

The Cassell Dictionary of Slang. By Jonathon Green. 1998. 1,316p. bibliog. Cassell, $37.50 (0-304-34435-4). DDC: 427.03.

The Oxford Dictionary of Slang. By John Ayto. 1998. 474p. index. Oxford, $27.50 (0-19-863157-X). DDC: 427.03.

These two new dictionaries take different approaches to the topic of slang.

Eric Partridge's *A Dictionary of Slang and Unconventional English* (Routledge, 1984) has been a reference classic from the first edition in 1937 to the eighth edition published in 1984, five years after his death. Jonathon Green is a contemporary British lexicographer who fills the bill (slang for *to satisfy*) with a new, comprehensive 65,000-term dictionary from Cassell that may replace Partridge's work as a current classic.

In the introduction Green defines *slang* as the "language of the rebel, outlaw, despised, marginal and young" that is usually an insult or obscenity. The creation of slang is a continuous and current process. (Perhaps it is not surprising that slang dictionaries are often missing from the shelves of high-school and college libraries!) The author believes it is his task "to display language, not moralize on it." Therefore, he spells out anything and everything. Racial slurs usually include the phrase "a derogatory term for . . ." Green notes that if all slang that is offensive to someone was noted as such, then the phrase "not derogatory" should be used instead.

Green includes words from the seventeenth century to the present with slang from all English-speaking areas: U.S., U.K., Canada, the Caribbean, New Zealand, Australia, and India. Each entry includes the part of speech, date of use, and definition. In a volume of this size it would be impossible to cite each source, so instead, Green includes a bibliography of more than 200 books and numerous newspapers, comics, films, television scripts, and even Internet sites.

What education and entertainment one receives in perusing this slang dictionary! Included are current terms (*awesome, hacker, veg*); historical terms (*cabbage-head, gin-trap*); geographic terms (*Treasure State* [Montana], *Mob Town* [Baltimore]); phrases (*open a can of worms, to; send mail by Netscape, to*); Australian terms (*emu-bobber*); British terms (*Covent Garden nunnery, Cadberry alley*); and, of course, all the popular expletives, and more words pertaining to sex or bodily functions than anyone would think possible.

Green does not slight American slang, but for a scholarly and comprehensive U.S. slang resource, the *Random House Historical Dictionary of American Slang* (1994–97) will be the definitive work when completed (the third and last volume has not yet been published). *The Cassell Dictionary of Slang* is highly recommended as an affordable, one-volume work for high-school, public, and academic libraries. It is the cat's meow!

The Oxford Dictionary of Slang is also written by a British author, John Ayto. It is based on *The Oxford Dictionary of Modern Slang* [RBB Ap 15 93] but is arranged by topic, beginning with "The Body and Its Functions."

Each topic is then subdivided. "Behaviour, Attitudes and Emotions" has forty-nine subdivisions: "Surprise," "Anger," "Violence," "Honesty," etc. Fortunately, there is an index if a user doesn't care to browse through the horse-racing slang, for example, to find the definition of a *no-hoper*.

This thesaurus has more entries than *The Oxford Dictionary of Modern Slang* but far fewer (10,000 words) than the Cassell dictionary. Each entry includes the date of what Ayto believes is the earliest appearance of the word. The origin and an illustration of the use of the word is usually taken from the *Oxford English Dictionary* or its files. Although there are numerous names for particular body parts, it is good to know that there are also more than 75 slang words for *excellent*, listed chronologically from *tip-top* in 1755 to *crucial* in 1987.

This thesaurus might be incorrectly compared to *The Thesaurus of Slang* (rev. ed., Facts On File, 1997), which is not topically arranged and does not include date of origin or illustration of use. Though *The Oxford Dictionary of Slang* appears more British than the Cassell dictionary, it should still be useful for most libraries and provide entertainment for anyone over ten! If a library can only afford one, *The Cassell Dictionary of Slang* is worth much more than its reasonable price of $37.50.

The Cambridge French-English Thesaurus. By Marie-Noelle Lamy. 1998. 338p. appendix. illus. indexes. Cambridge, $69.95 (0-521-56348-8); paper, $24.95 (0-521-42581-6). DDC: 443.

Students of French learn the basics of grammar and vocabulary, but, unless they spend time in France or have other opportunities to immerse themselves in the language, they do not pick up the nuances of native speakers. This volume offers students at an intermediate or advanced level a guide to more sophisticated French usage.

Unlike most thesauri, this one is organized thematically. Fifteen major categories such as Position, Movement, and Travel; The Natural Environment; and Emotions, Feelings, and Attitudes are further divided into 142 more precise subdivisions: Direction and Distance; Animals; Positive and Negative Feelings; etc. Each subcategory is numbered. The section Knowledge and Thought Processes serves as an example. It begins with a sidebar explaining the difference between the verbs *savoir* and *connaitre*, and a list of idioms using each one. This is followed by related expressions, explaining which are ironic, slang, or informal. The section is then divided into categories such as Ways of Knowing and Finding Out, Thinking, and Differentiating and Identifying, with several more specific topics listed under each. All words, phrases, and examples are translated. Information provided for each headword may include synonyms, idioms, quotations, glosses, grammatical information, "false friends," pitfalls for English speakers, and differences between American and British English. Sidebars and even the occasional illustration are used to further clarify meanings.

Specific information on commonly used slang and vulgarisms appears throughout the book. An explanation of the routine informal use of the verb *emmerder* and its components to indicate boredom, and variations of *foutre* and its less vulgar substitute *ficher* to indicate irritation will help users who wish to use colloquial French correctly. The section on communicating electronically contains important vocabulary relating to computers, fax machines, and telephones.

The book concludes with a section called Conversational Gambits which provides common expressions needed to introduce people, ask for things, conduct routine business, and write both personal and business letters. A verb conjugation chart and alphabetical English and French word indexes complete the volume. *The Cambridge French-English Thesaurus*, a bridge between the classroom and real life, is a useful source for all libraries where there is interest in the French language. The paperback version is inexpensive enough for the personal libraries of serious students.

Science

The Cassell Dictionary of Science. By Percy Harrison and Gillian Waites. 1998. 512p. appendixes. illus. Cassell; dist. by Sterling, $35 (0-304-34483-4). DDC:.

Designed for high-school and university students, this new dictionary explains key terms taken from all areas of science and technology, in approximately 10,000 alphabetically arranged entries. Authors Harrison and Waites are a science teacher and a biochemist, respectively.

Concentrating on scientific concepts encountered in daily life, coverage is general in the areas of math, computers, astronomy, earth sciences, and environmental science; physics, biology, and chemistry are dealt with in more detail. Articles range from short definitions of words to more lengthy pieces on fundamental concepts and issues, some with explanatory black-and-white diagrams. Cross-references lead readers to related terms. Seventeen appendixes complete the dictionary; these list common measures, conversion factors, chemical elements, amino acids, and more. British spellings reflect the book's origins. Metric and International Standard measurement systems are used throughout.

Slightly more expensive and three years older, Larousse Dictionary of Science and Technology, edited by Peter Walker [RBB D 1 95], contains 49,000 entries, 500 illustrations, and 25 appendixes. Cassell defines the Internet but not the World Wide Web, while Larousse leads readers from the Internet to the Web. Reference collections will probably stick with Larousse, but student and personal libraries will be well served by Cassell.

The Facts On File Encyclopedia of Science, Technology, and Society. 3v. By Rudi Volti. 1999. 1,158p. bibliog. illus. index. Facts On File, $225 (0-8160-3123-1). DDC: 503.

In 900 alphabetically arranged entries, this title aims to be "a presentation of the social settings in which science and technology have emerged, been developed, and put to use." It is not a technical encyclopedia, per se, but the entries can contain some technical information. It includes articles on a wide range of topics, such as the origin and chemistry of cheese, the historical development of software, and the rise and fall of drive-in movies. The entry on gunpowder "explodes" the myth of its Chinese origins. The focus is on science and technology successes, but there are notable failures as well. For example, *polywater* was a new form of water "discovered" by a Soviet scientist in 1961; after much international scrutiny, its properties were shown to be caused by contaminants. Examples of other entries include *airbags, arches and vaults, Bhopal, bubonic plague, cholesterol, eyeglasses, nylon, quark, resource depletion, space probe,* and *wheel.*

Entries were written by more than 90 contributors, almost all of whom have academic affiliations. Most entries are at least a page; a number (e.g., *cloning*, DNA) are more than three pages. Both U.S. customary and metric units are used for measurements. *See also* references and, in some cases, suggestions for further reading are listed at each entry's end. Occasionally, these citations are older. For example, the suggested reading at the end of the AIDS article is from 1989. There is a 13-page bibliography in volume 3. The index that concludes each volume is cumulative but refers only to page numbers, not volumes.

In the crowded field of science encyclopedias, this title is less technical than McGraw-Hill Encyclopedia of Science & Technology [RBB S 15 97] or Van Nostrand's Scientific Encyclopedia [RBB My 1 95], but its focus on society and science will give it a niche in public libraries or with freshmen or sophomore undergraduates, particularly nonscience majors.

The International Encyclopedia of Science and Technology. 1999. 471p. illus. tables. Oxford, $49.95 (0-19-521531-1). DDC: 503.

Aimed at the secondary-school or college student, this work is Oxford's version of a general science encyclopedia. It contains more than 6,500 entries covering all the disciplines of the sciences throughout history. In addition to scientific topics and theories, more than 850 biographies of important scientists are included. Because of such ambitious coverage, this work is really more of a scientific dictionary than encyclopedia. Entries are alphabetically arranged and are very short, rarely more than a couple of sentences. With such little space devoted to each entry, the encyclopedia provides only the most superficial coverage of any given topic.

In addition to the alphabetical entries, there is a 60-page chronology of science. Students can use the chronology to study the development of various scientific disciplines throughout the ages. The real strength of this work is in its illustrations, which are clear and colorful and enhance the entries in the text. Other one-or two-volume general science encyclopedias, such as the McGraw-Hill Concise Encyclopedia of Science and Technology (4th ed., 1998) or Van Nostrand's Scientific Encyclopedia (8th ed., 1995), provide more complete coverage (but no biographies) and will continue to be the standard sources for this type of information. However, the low price and excellent illustrations in the Oxford volume make it a fine ready-reference companion for those other sources.

McGraw-Hill Multimedia Encyclopedia of Science and Technology. CD-ROM. 1998. McGraw-Hill, $995 (0-07-853074-1). DDC: 503.

System requirements: Windows 3.1 *or* 95; 4 MB RAM (8 MB *preferred*), 10 MB *hard disk space.*

Take a couple of premier print scientific reference sources, digitize the text, add some multimedia applications, link it to the Internet, and what do you get? A surprisingly bad science multimedia encyclopedia. Given the great educational potential of a multimedia version of McGraw-Hill Encyclopedia of Science and Technology, the results as demonstrated in this product do not merit its purchase.

Certainly, the source material for this product is excellent. McGraw-Hill Encyclopedia of Science and Technology [RBB S 15 97] and McGraw-Hill Dictionary of Scientific and Technical Terms (5th ed., 1993) are the first sources to which most patrons and librarians turn when looking for scientific information. The encyclopedia is clearly written and understandable to the nonspecialist, without compromising its scientific content. The dictionary provides brief yet accurate definitions for scientific terms in all subject areas. For the multimedia encyclopedia, short biographical entries of 250 famous scientists have been added. A study guide consisting of a hierarchical approach to the disciplines of the sciences was also created. While the CD-ROM uses the full text from all of these sources, several problems arise from the way they were adapted to the electronic environment.

The search software allows the reader to find information either by browsing through the list of headings or by conducting a keyword search of the text. When browsing, the reader can select from encyclopedia articles, dictionary entries, biographies, or articles from the study guide. Hotlinks within the entries jump directly to related articles. However, these links go only to the encyclopedia entries and do not allow a reader to link from an encyclopedia article to a dictionary definition or a biography.

Keyword searching only covers the text of the encyclopedia and does not retrieve dictionary or biographical entries. Search results may be displayed either in alphabetical order or rank based upon word frequencies, providing the most relevant entries first. The software does allow users to bookmark articles for faster future retrieval, and all search results may be printed or copied to disk.

The default typeface of the display is very large. This makes for easy reading, but causes problems when looking at mathematical formulas or chemical structures. Often, the entire formula or structure does not appear in the window, requiring the user to scroll up and down. It is possible to reduce or enlarge the text at any time, but this must be repeated every time a new window is opened.

McGraw-Hill makes a point of advertising the illustrations, graphics, and animations that are included in the multimedia encyclopedia. Unfortunately, these do not come anywhere near to living up to their hype. While the print encyclopedia has 13,000 illustrations, the electronic version includes only 1,400. There are no illustrations for the biographical entries and most of the illustrations for the encyclopedia articles are simple line drawings that have been extracted from the print version. A few entries do have color photos, including most of the chemical elements. Unfortunately, many entries that would greatly benefit from color photos—such as various articles relating to astronomy, plants, and animals—have no illustrations at all. When illustrations are used, they may be viewed within the text or in a separate window by selecting the appropriate button. Links within the text often give the illusion that there may be more illustrations that are not shown, but they always open the same ones.

In addition to static illustrations, animations are used in 66 entries. These consist of moving drawings with an audio soundtrack, and they provide enhancement to the text that cannot be reproduced in the print volumes. However, other entries that could greatly benefit from visual or audio enhancement have no such animation. This feature has great potential to create a true multimedia encyclopedia, but has been applied only in a highly selective number of entries.

No science Web sites are directly linked to the product—instead, what the user is offered is the option of searching the Web through three search engines: Excite, Lycos, and Infoseek. The user enters the search terms into the software and the program then loads the user's Web browser, zgoes to the appropriate search engine, and finds the topic of interest. It is not possible to bookmark Web sites, nor are Web searches included in the search history. Since it only offers three search engines and no direct links, the encyclopedia's Internet link is less flexible and more cumbersome than searching the Internet directly.

It is unfortunate that this product cannot be recommended. Its source material is of the highest quality, but its transformation into the multimedia environment is disappointing. At a cost of just under $1,000 for a single user, it is priced beyond the reach of most libraries and individuals. For most users, general multimedia encyclopedias make much better use of multimedia at less than one-tenth the price. Unless a lot of improvement is seen in future versions of the CD-ROM, libraries should retain their print editions of the *McGraw-Hill Encyclopedia* and *Dictionary*.

DK Nature Encyclopedia. 1998. 304p. glossary. illus. index. DK, $29.95 (0-7894-3411-3). DDC: 508.
The DK Science Encyclopedia. rev. ed. 1998. 448p. glossary. illus. index. DK, $39.95 (0-7894-2190-9). DDC: 503.
DK Ultimate Visual Dictionary of Science. 1998. 448p. glossary. illus. index. DK, $29.95 (0-7894-3512-8). DDC: 503.

DK has a reputation for putting information in a format that is visually pleasing, textually accurate, and terse. They have done it again with these one-volume encyclopedias.

Within each encyclopedia, each section begins with a short introduction to the subject and then, using illustrations and short paragraphs, goes into more detail to explain specific topics. Cross-references lead to entries on related subjects. Generally, each topic is covered on a double-page spread, half of which is illustration (labeled photographs and diagrams). The typefaces vary in size: the first paragraph is larger, the text slightly smaller, the captions smaller still. A glossary and index complete each volume.

Sections are broad in scope. In DK *Nature Encyclopedia*, the "How Living Things Work" section begins with the cell and covers photosynthesis, respiration, and reproduction. Also covered are growth and development, movement, communication, and migration. The ecology section covers every type of ecosystem and discusses the relationship between humans and nature. The plant and animal chapters include information on every major plant and animal group. Librarians are often hard pressed to locate an easy-to-understand explanation of scientific classification—the presentation in this encyclopedia is excellent. It begins with one animal and moves up the classification ladder by showing how more and more species are included. Subsequent pages discuss each group in more detail, and many entries have "profile" boxes highlighting a particular species of animal or plant from the group.

The *DK Science Encyclopedia* is a revised version of *Dorling Kindersley Science Encyclopedia* [RBB D 1 93]. It features more than 280 main entries and 1,900 subentries grouped under subjects such as matter, materials, weather, and space. The section on space has been updated to include information on Voyager 1 and 2, although "Using Computers" contains nothing about the World Wide Web. A "Factfinder" section has charts, tables, and maps.

DK *Ultimate Visual Dictionary of Science* covers just about every major concept and historical development in science. It is divided into chapters that cover nine broad areas of science, such as physics, life sciences, and medical science. Each chapter begins with a table of contents that lists the topics covered, followed by a history of their development and a time line of important discoveries. The chapters range in length from 18 pages ("Mathematics") to 58 pages ("Life Sciences and Ecology"). A "Useful Data" section has such information as units of measurement and physics formulas. A four-page "Biographies" section has very brief biographical profiles; no women are mentioned, not even Nobel Prize winners such as Barbara McClintock. The illustrations are beautifully reproduced and meticulously labeled; of particular note are the illustrations of wave behavior, the functional areas of the brain, and stellar life cycles. The photographs of ancient/historical items are fascinating and add to the wonder of our modern methods. The time lines will be a boon to students who are often assigned time-line projects.

The three titles cover many of the same topics but use completely different text and illustrations. One of the chief differences is the way in which content is organized. *Ultimate Visual* is arranged by scientific discipline, while *Nature* and *Science* take a less academic approach, grouping topics under broad categories likely to be of interest to younger readers—weather, how living things work. *Ultimate Visual* often presents information in a way that is more complex and detailed. *Nature* and *Science* each cover animal classification in two pages, but *Ultimate Visual* covers it in four, relying less on illustrations and more on tables. Cross-references in *Ultimate Visual* appear in bold type within the text, instead of in separate "find out more" boxes.

Nature and *Science* are designed for children ages eight and up, but, as in other DK publications, the page layout, small print, and vocabulary level may make them confusing and difficult for younger readers. Both are suitable for upper-elementary and middle-school children and will serve as good beginning points for more in-depth research. *Ultimate Visual* will be infinitely useful to older students and adults who want a detailed overview of science.

Scientists, Mathematicians, and Inventors: Lives & Legacies: An Encyclopedia of People Who Changed the World. Ed. by Doris Simonis. 1999. 244p. appendixes. bibliog. illus. index. time lines. Oryx, $69.95 (1-57356-151-7). DDC: 509.2.

This is the first of a projected four-volume biographical series called Lives and Legacies, aimed at students in high school through college. The first volume presents biographies of 200 men and women. As stated in the introduction, subjects were selected on the basis of work that had significant influence on society in general or on scientific disciplines in particular, influence that extended beyond a lifetime or work that extended beyond the limits imposed on these individuals (e.g., women and minorities) by contemporary society.

Although coverage extends back to Pythagoras, nearly 75 percent of the subjects are people who lived in the last 200 years. Entries are alphabetically arranged, and each usually includes an illustration of the person, followed by a one-page synopsis of the "Life and Work," and "Legacy." Each of the essays is signed by one of the nine contributors who worked on the volume. Each entry also contains a short time line showing the world events juxtaposed with major events in the biographee's life and a further reading list of between two and six items.

There are several appendixes. One, "Highlights in the History of Science, Mathematics, and Invention," gives major events starting with B.C.E. and continuing through 1990, with the introduction of the Microsoft Corporation's Windows computer operating system or GUI (graphical user interface) system. This is followed by a list of biographies arranged by country and a list of biographies arranged by scientific discipline. A topically arranged bibliography and an index complete the work.

As always, readers might question some of the selections. If Bill Gates is chosen as a modern giant of technology, why not include Steve Jobs, too, who brought the GUI to market years before Gates in the form of the Macintosh computer. Despite the book's claim of highlighting women inventors, scientists, and mathematicians, there are only 20 of them profiled among the 200 biographies. But a more important question is whether libraries need another volume that profiles important scientists. Many of these individuals are also covered in greater detail in Marshall Cavendish's *Biographical Encyclopedia of Mathematicians* [RBB D 15 98] and *Biographical Encyclopedia of Scientists* [RBB My 15 98], among other recent titles. Features unique to the Oryx volume are the summary of each scientist's legacy and the time lines that place events in each scientist's life in the context of world history. Recommended for school and public libraries that serve the high-school level and up and need additional coverage in the area. Future titles in the Lives and Legacies series will cover artists, writers, and musicians; philosophers and religious leaders; and government leaders, military rulers, and political activists.

Biographical Encyclopedia of Mathematicians. 2v. Ed. by Donald R. Franceschetti. 1998. 640p. illus. indexes. Marshall Cavendish, $149.95 (0-7614-7069-7). DDC: 510.

Marshall Cavendish has published a biographical encyclopedia of more than 170 alphabetically arranged entries, with all the information students need for reports: pictures, time lines, and personal details, as well as professional facts. Intended for grades seven and up, the text explains difficult concepts and theories in terms that are not too technical. Each entry begins with a chronology of important events in the person's life and career. A photograph or portrait is included for most of the subjects. Several paragraphs cover early home and school life. Entries are generally two to four pages in length and close with bibliographies of primary and secondary sources. Sidebars, each with its own bibliography, highlight theories or significant achievements.

Each volume has a table of contents for the volume and a cumulative index. The second volume has a "Country List" that groups mathematicians by country. This list also identifies women and U.S. mathematicians belonging to specific ethnic groups. In addition, there is a list of mathematicians by "Areas of Achievement." Also in volume two are a glossary and a time line. Both volumes have a pronunciation key, and pronunciations are included in the text.

Similar in format is Marshall Cavendish's *Biographical Encyclopedia of Scientists* [RBB My 15 98]. There is some overlap between the two sets, but it is minimal. Only 10 percent of the mathematicians also appear in *Scientists*. Although almost 40 percent of the *Mathematicians* authors worked on both sets, most of them wrote different articles, and those that covered the same person for both sets wrote very different texts because of the change in focus. Another resource for the high-school audience is Gale's *Notable Mathematicians* [RBB Ag 98], which covers 303 mathematicians, including approximately twice as many women and ethnic Americans. In general, Gale has more extensive bibliographies, while Marshall Cavendish has more added features, such as illustrations and sidebars, to support the text. Approximately 125 people are covered in both the Gale and the Marshall Cavendish sets. Scribner's four-volume *Biographical Dictionary of Mathematics* (1991), which reprints articles from the 16-volume *Dictionary of Scientific Biography*, is more scholarly.

School libraries that require writing in their math curricula will want this well-designed set from Marshall Cavendish. It is also recommended for public libraries.

Outer Space. 12v. 1998. 768p. glossary. illus. indexes. Grolier, $269 (0-7172-9179-0). DDC: 520.

Each of the volumes in this set designed for elementary school and up covers a different aspect of space, from the solar system in volume 1 to satellites and probes in volume 12. Other volumes treat the moon, the stars, the planets, and space exploration. The set is extremely attractive, loaded with color photos, charts, and diagrams, and set off with colorful sidebars and headings.

Information is clearly organized and presented. An introduction and table of contents for each volume precedes the text. Unfamiliar words and phrases are defined in context; in addition, every volume has a glossary of 50–75 words. Unusual in a source for this age group are the number of cross-references to related information throughout the set. The set index is repeated in each volume.

There is some duplication of information. Both volume 8 (Space Travel) and volume 12 (Satellites and Probes) discuss NASA's recent emphasis on "doing more with less," although in slightly different contexts. Volume 8 says the first test of this new philosophy was a series of missions to Mars begun in 1996; volume 12 says it was the Clementine space probe launched in 1994. Occasional language may be difficult for younger readers: "note the solar prominence along the limb of the sun." Most material is U.S.-oriented, although cooperation with the Russian space program is described and European and Japanese astronauts are mentioned. Information is fairly up to date.

Much of the information is available elsewhere, although not always presented so attractively. If there is strong demand for brief coverage of these topics for students at the upper-elementary and middle-school levels, this set should be considered.

Encyclopedia of the Solar System. Ed. by Paul Weissman and others. 1999. 992p. appendix. bibliog. charts. glossary. graphs. illus. index. tables. Academic, $99.95 (0-12-226805-9). DDC: 523.203.

By bringing together the latest information about the solar system, this title makes an important contribution to our understanding of our planetary neighborhood from the Sun to the Kuiper Belt and beyond. As astronaut Sally Ride says in the foreword, "It represents our current state of knowledge on the origin, the evolution, and the fascinating components of our solar system."

The contributors are world-renowned scholars in their fields. The book starts with the solar system in relation to the Milky Way Galaxy, and proceeds outward from the Sun to the terrestrial planets (Mercury, Venus, Mars, and Earth) and on to the giant planets. There are three chapters on the fascinating satellites of Io, Titan, and Triton. There also are chapters on solar-system dynamics, planetary impacts, planets and the origin of life, and extrasolar planets. Each chapter includes an outline, cross-references to other chapters, and a glossary. The index includes 4,500 terms. The book is written at the level of college astronomy, with intensive technical writing and quality black-and-white and color photographs. Equations and charts will require the reader to have taken at least calculus to understand the concepts presented.

The encyclopedia incorporates recent discoveries obtained by spacecraft about other residents of the solar system. An example is Janus and Epimetheus, two moons of Saturn. They are almost in the same orbit, and every four years the inner satellite overtakes the outer satellite and they exchange orbits, starting the four-year chase over again.

Two small criticisms are that the indexing is adequate but not outstanding, and some of the photos are repeated. As an example of the indexing, the chapter "Chaotic Motion in the Solar System" discusses Kepler's laws in relation to the three-body problem, but there is no reference to this discussion under *Kepler's laws* in the index. An extraordinary photo of an object that "skipped out of the atmosphere" in 1972 appears in three places. In one place the object is called a fireball, and in another place it is called a bolide. One caption describes it as having 1013 to 1014 Joules of energy, and the other describes it as being one-million metric tons. In any case, it was lucky that it did not strike the earth, and it is hard to believe that it was photographed.

These are minor problems with a book of this scope and breadth. As an added feature, there is also a Web site available at http://www.academicpress.com/solar/. The Web site features author-recommended links to topics discussed in the chapters, including links to the authors' home pages. The spectacular NASA *Atlas of the Solar System* [RBB Ag 97] has more photographs but less text than *Encyclopedia of the Solar System*, which is recommended for academic and large public libraries serving an astronomy clientele.

Q Is for Quantum: An Encyclopedia of Particle Physics. By John Gribbin. 1999. 545p. bibliog. illus. Free Press, $35 (0-684-85578-X). DDC: 539.7.

This dictionary by a well-known science popularizer provides good A–Z coverage of the field of quantum mechanics. Unlike many other science dictionaries, it covers more than concepts and terms. There are entries for people (*Feynman, Richard Phillips; Huygens, Christiaan; Oppenheimer, Robert*), places (*Brookhaven National Laboratory, Fermilab*), and historical highlights (*Manhattan Project*). Most entries are a few sentences, although biographies are generally longer, and some entries (*relativity, string theory, time travel*) cover several pages. There are ample cross-references. Some entries include suggested further readings; several of these are other books by Gribbin. Following the entries is a bibliography that lists the books referred to in the text, together with others; the more technical titles are indicated with an asterisk. The volume concludes with time lines of birth dates of famous scientists, key dates in physical sciences, and key dates in history.

The book's audience ranges from the interested layperson to undergraduate physics majors to professional physicists. It is narrower in scope than *Macmillan Encyclopedia of Physics* [RBB Ap 15 97] or *McGraw-Hill Dictionary of Physics* (McGraw-Hill, 1997). However, Gribbin's approach makes a difficult topic accessible even for those who don't have a science background. Recommended for large public and academic libraries.

Chemical Elements: From Carbon to Krypton. 3v. By David E. Newton. 1999. 686p. bibliog. illus. indexes. UXL, $84 (0-7876-2844-1). DDC: 546.

Designed especially for students in middle school, but also appropriate for high school, this three-volume introduction to the chemical elements meets its stated objective of providing "a valuable source of fundamental information for research reports, science fair projects, classroom demonstrations," and supplemental textbook information. The 112 elements of the periodic table are arranged alphabetically by chemical name, with the exception of elements 101–112, which are discussed under the entry *transfermium elements*. Although the entries vary in length (e.g., *actinium* is three pages long, *carbon* is twelve pages), each follows the same format. The first page outlines "basic information about the chemical element: its chemical symbol, atomic number, atomic mass, family and pronunciation." It includes a diagram of an atom with the electrons arranged in energy levels outside the nucleus and the number of protons and neutrons indicated inside the nucleus. The entry then discusses the element's discovery and naming, physical and chemical properties, occurrence in nature, isotopes, methods of extraction, important compounds and uses, and health effects. Sidebars within the entries highlight commonly used terms, well-known products, interesting facts, and scientists.

Access to the entries is provided by three tables of contents: by chemical name, by atomic number, and finally, by family group. A cumulative index in each volume provides still another means of access. The volumes also include a time line of the elements by year of discovery and a bibliography. The bibliography suggests print sources and Web sites on chemistry in general and on individual elements. Most of the print sources are copyrighted in the 1980s and 1990s, with many appropriate for the set's age group. More than 200 black-and-white illustrations and photographs, with three eight-page color-photo inserts, comprise the set's visuals. The black-and-white illustrations and photographs are often murky. The "Words to Know" sections function as a glossary and may prove useful for a science vocabulary lesson.

Chemical Elements fits in nicely with other titles for this age group. Grolier's *The Elements* [RBB Ja 1 & 15 97], with its wonderful color photographs, does not discuss all the elements. Oxford's *Guide to the Elements* [RBB D 1 96] discusses all the elements, but the layout is not as report-writing friendly. Information on elements can be found in *McGraw-Hill Encyclopedia of Science & Technology* (8th ed., 1997) and *Van Nostrand's Scientific Encyclopedia* (8th ed., 1994), but these are more appropriate for advanced-placement students. Given the reasonable price, consider purchasing one set for reference and two or three for circulation at report-writing time. Recommended for school and public libraries.

The Atlas of Global Change. Ed. by Lothar Beckel. 1998. 160p. glossary. illus. index. Macmillan, $90 (0-02-864956-7). DDC: 550.

That the often negative consequences of global change should result in a series of beautiful photographs and illustrations is both disturbing and intellectually stimulating. The accompanying text in this book, which was first published in Europe in 1996, is also double-edged: sometimes sensational and other times dryly factual. The maps, based on satellite images, are works of abstract art until one looks closely at the planet's open wounds and scars caused by human activity, weather, fire, volcanism, and pollution. While the words describe the history and current events depicted in the maps and photographs, the pictures speak even louder.

Following an introduction that discusses the development and impact of satellite photography, the book is divided into two broad sections: one covering Earth in general, and the other covering Europe. Within this division, individual sections describe some facet of the global condition—events, man-made constructions, weather, oceans, erosion, etc. Topics covered include plate tectonics, the expansion of the deserts, distribution of clouds, the hole in the ozone layer, distribution of vegetation, and Europe's network of waterways. Each section presents a map or a series of maps, often followed by a few pages that focus on more specific conditions or phenomena. For example "Earthquakes and Volcanism" discusses Mt. St. Helens and the volcanoes of the Hawaiian Islands. The section called "The Earth Endangered by Storms" discusses sandstorms over the Persian Gulf and flooding in Bangladesh. Text is illustrated by tables, charts, and photographs, in addition to maps. The vivid colors are sometimes too close in shade and hue to show the finer gradations being depicted in many of the digital maps. The book concludes with a brief glossary and an index.

Although the emphasis is on Europe, this is a global book with examples from all continents and regions of the world. The large world maps keep reinforcing the connectedness of all parts of the planet, and the changes being discussed. Expensive but worth the price, and highly recommended for most libraries.

Sciences of the Earth: An Encyclopedia of Events, People, and Phenomena. 2v. Ed. by Gregory A. Good. 1998. 901p. bibliogs. illus. index. maps. Garland, $150 (0-8153-0062-X). DDC: 550.

With 135 international contributors, this well-documented and illustrated overview of the history of earth science provides insight into "both the questions of tradition and of change in knowledge of the Earth." It is volume three in the Garland Encyclopedias in the History of Science series; the Board reviewed volume 1, *History of Astronomy*, in the April 15, 1997, issue of RBB, and volume 2, *Instruments of Science*, in the June 1 & 15, 1998, issue.

The preface points out that this is not a true encyclopedia of earth sciences—rather, its goal is "to provide coherent and understandable accounts of what has been accepted as knowledge of earthly occurrences, even if those earlier ideas appear strange or fabulous to today's science." Most of the more than 230 articles deal with the history of ideas and research about Earth; examples are *tides, before Newton,* and *underwater research, early history of.* There are also articles relating to institutions and groups that have influenced earth science, such as Woods Hole Oceanographic Institution and the Jesuits, and articles on the relationship between practical knowledge and geoscience, such as *mining and knowledge of the earth* and *weather modification.* Historians will find discussions of various issues and concepts that have helped shape the history of science; for example, *Lakatos's idea of scientific research programs* and *Popper's ideas on falsifiability.* The focus is on Western science, with some discussions that look at other cultures throughout the world. Biographies are not included since they are adequately covered in the multitude of biographical dictionaries and encyclopedias. Illustrations are clear, crisp, and described in detail. There are both comprehensive name and subject indexes, as well as a categorical listing of the entries. The bibliographies are extensive, providing the reader much to turn to for additional information.

This is a landmark multidisciplinary work that brings together articles that cut across geography, geology, geophysics, chemistry, meteorology, astronomy, marine geology, and medicine. It is a fascinating set that will spark debate among scientists and curiosity among laypeople. There has been so much written about the earth, both fact and fiction, that having a resource such as this will certainly help bring concepts, ideas, and theories together. It will also form the basis for future research in many of the areas that are discussed. Highly recommended for all academic libraries and larger public libraries.

The Encyclopedia of Hurricanes, Typhoons, and Cyclones. By David Longshore. 1998. 288p. appendixes. bibliog. charts. illus. index. maps. tables. Facts On File, $45 (0-8160-3398-6). DDC: 551.55.

This volume gives the reader an informative and interesting look at some terrifying and destructive weather phenomena. The history and chronology of the great storms form the major part of the book, but the human, and often tragic, side of the story is not neglected. Included is information on storms that occurred from the colonization of the Americas through 1997.

The 350-plus entries cover hurricanes, cyclones, and typhoons by name; storm-related terms (*advection, pressure gradient, storm stage*); descriptions of locations where storms frequently occur; biographies; and related topics, such as *animals and tropical storms*. The first entry for each letter is a list of storms whose names have begun with that letter since the practice of naming storms began, and the name cycle through the year 2000 for the North Atlantic, Caribbean, and North Pacific Oceans. Entries for individual storms provide details on the path of the storm, the dates of the storm, the severity, size, and wind speeds, and the resultant destruction of both lives and property. Storms of outstanding severity may warrant longer treatment, with a day-by-day chronology. Hurricanes Carmen (1974), Gordon (1994), and Joan (1988), among others, are treated in this manner.

The book is amply illustrated with photographs, maps, charts, graphs, and line drawings. The black-and-white photographs convey the ravages of the great storms and, in some instances, show the storms themselves. Maps and charts that illustrate the path of a storm are particularly helpful for the reader. Within the articles, terms in all caps guide the reader to related entries. If a topic does not merit a full treatment, a *see* reference refers the reader to the appropriate entry. Four appendixes follow the A–Z entries: "Hurricane Safety Procedures," "A Chronology of Hurricanes, Typhoons, Cyclones, and Tropical Storms," "Tracking a Tropical Cyclone," and "List of Named Hurricanes, Typhoons, Cyclones, and Tropical Storms." A fairly extensive bibliography and an index complete the volume.

The Encyclopedia of Hurricanes, Typhoons, and Cyclones is a companion to the previous Facts On File publication *Encyclopedia of Earthquakes and Volcanoes* [RBB Ap 15 94]. Like the earlier volume, it is intended for the general reader and provides an excellent overview of natural disasters, rather than an exhaustive look at every recorded hurricane and typhoon. High-school and public libraries, particularly those in Hurricane Alley, will want a copy for their reference shelves.

Dinosaurs of the World. 11v. Ed. by Chris Marshall. 1999. 704p. bibliog. glossary. illus. index. Marshall Cavendish, $329.95 (0-7614-7072-7). DDC: 567.9.

This profusely illustrated set consists of slim volumes (approximately 64 pages each) that will appeal to its intended audience—children in elementary and middle school. With pages consecutively numbered, the first 10 volumes contain more than 200 articles on dinosaurs and related topics. Volume 11 has been designated the "reference" volume, and features a brief history of the earth, time lines, a list of famous fossil sites and digs, dinosaur family trees, brief biographies of 24 dinosaur hunters, museums with pertinent collections, and a section called "Things to Do," which lists resources and activities appropriate and accessible to this age group. The list includes books, reference works, CD-ROMs, clubs, magazines, science kits and games, TV programs, videos, and a few Web sites.

All of the first 10 volumes begin with the same "Tree of Life," a two-page spread illustrating the evolution of life. This is followed by the articles, arranged alphabetically by dinosaur name (*Abelisaurus—Zephyrosaurus*) or topic (*bony fish, eggs and babies, rocks,* etc.). Entries reflect current research (through early 1998), and acknowledge errors and wrong assumptions or interpretations that were once commonly held. Written by a team of specialists, most of the articles run across two facing pages, with an occasional three-or four-page entry, and feature, in addition to text, a one-or two-sentence summary; a "fascinating facts box" describing pertinent digs, how this dinosaur compares to modern animals, etc.; a "Dinofacts" information panel of vital statistics (size, weight, food, habitat, locator map, skeletal details, etc.); and "Check These Out," which are cross-references to related articles in the set. Each entry also features a color illustration of its dinosaur, portrayed in an action pose, situated in its proper environment. The text acknowledges the controversy concerning what color dinosaurs may have been, and emphasizes that the illustrations are interpretations. Unfortunately, the bindings are so tight that some visual details are swallowed in the gutter, disrupting those illustrations that span two pages.

Additional user-friendly features include a "How to Use this Set" introduction; a glossary that provides easy-to-understand, one-sentence descriptions; a pronunciation guide that is simple to decipher; a geographical index divided by continent, country, and state; and a comprehensive index.

This is the only multivolume reference source currently in print on the topic of dinosaurs, and one of the few comprehensive works aimed at this age group. Recent discoveries and current research have rendered many standard sources obsolete, so the need for this new publication is apparent. Public libraries will want to pair this with adult titles such as *Encyclopedia of Dinosaurs* [RBB N 1 97] or *The Complete Dinosaur* (Indiana Univ. Press, 1997). School libraries that already own the less comprehensive *Ultimate Dinosaur Book* (Dorling Kindersley, 1993) will want to update. Because of its extensive coverage and currency, *Dinosaurs of the World* is a worthwhile addition. The text will be accessible to interested upper-elementary-school students, and the illustrations will attract a much younger crowd. Recommended for public, elementary, and middle-school collections.

Encyclopedia of Genetics. 2v. Ed. by Jeffrey A. Knight and Robert McClenaghan. 1999. 598p. bibliogs. charts. glossary. index. illus. tables. Salem, $200 (0-89356-978-X). DDC: 576.5.

This clear, well-written guide to an area of emerging importance in science and policy will be useful to undergraduates and the general public. Topics include bacterial genetics, classical transmission genetics, developmental genetics, genetics engineering and biotechnology, human genetics, immunogenetics, molecular genetics, and population studies. The articles strive to be objective, even in the face of controversy. The articles on sociobiology and the human cloning debate are examples.

There are 172 signed, alphabetically arranged entries, ranging in length from 1,000 to 3,500 words. Contributors, listed at the beginning of volume 1, have university affiliations or are identified as independent scholars. Articles begin with a quick summary of the entry, including field of study, significance of the topic, and key terms. *See also* references and suggestions for further reading are listed after the body of the entries. The topics and bibliographies are very current to the time of publication. Following the A–Z entries are a "Time Line of Major Developments in Genetics," brief biographical entries of important geneticists, a glossary, a general bibliography, a category list of entries, and an index. More than 200 black-and-white photographs and illustrations accompany the text, along with charts, diagrams, and tables.

The audience for the *Encyclopedia of Genetics* is less the biological researcher and more the public with a general understanding of science and the issues it raises. It is less specialized than *The Encyclopedia of Bioethics*, edited by Warren T. Reich [RBB O 15 96]. The *Encyclopedia of Molecular Biology*, edited by John Kendrew and Eleanor Lawrence (Blackwell Science, 1994), and *Molecular Biology & Biotechnology: A Comprehensive Desk Reference*, edited by Robert A. Meyers (VCH, 1995), are excellent sources of genetic information. Another source is KEGG: *Kyoto Encyclopedia of Genetics and Genomes* (Kyoto, Japan, GenomeNet, 1998–), which is a full-text molecular and cellular biology project from the Japanese Human Genome Program [http://www.genome.ad.jp/kegg/]. These are written more with the practicing scientist in mind. The *Encyclopedia of Genetics* is recommended for both smaller and larger academic and public libraries.

Wildlife and Plants of the World. Ed. by Deborah Evans and Leon Gray. 1998. 1,096p. bibliog. illus. index. maps. Marshall Cavendish, $329.95 (0-7614-7099-9). DDC: 578.

This is an expanded and updated edition of *Wildlife of the World* [RBB My 15 94]. The emphasis is still on animals, but the set now also includes microorganisms and fungi (e.g., *bacterium, fungus*); plants (*fern, pine, soybean*); and biomes (*rain forest, suburban habitat*). Entries in these new areas make up about 25 percent of the more than 400 articles. Some important plants, such as banana and cacao, do not have entries.

The information is arranged alphabetically in 16 volumes, with the seventeenth volume containing the indexes as well as essays defining the various organisms, plants, and animals. The books are easy to use. Volume 1 contains a section on classifying organisms and a table of contents for the entire set. At the beginning of each volume is an introduction to the kingdoms into which living things are classified. Each entry has the same arrangement. Color-coding indicates the type of organism being described (purple for bird, orange for fish, etc.). Some of these colors are too similar; green indicates invertebrates, and a slightly different shade of green indicates plants. Brief text is accompanied by a distribution map, a "key fact" box providing essential details, colored photographs, and some detailed drawings. *See also* references are provided. In some cases, broad topics are illustrated with very specific examples. For example, the *cactus* distribution map shows only the habitat of the Saguaro cactus, although there are many hundreds of cactus species.

For animal entries, much of the text is unchanged from the 1994 edition. In a few entries, the key facts are revised to reflect changes in status; two kinds of zebras, for example, are now endangered rather than threatened. The Board noted in its earlier review that there were entries for specific types of whales (*humpback whale, white whale*) but no entry *whale*; the revised edition does have a four-page *whale* entry. The glossary that was repeated in each volume now appears only in volume 17. The bibliography is now two pages instead of one. A "Biomes Index" has been added to the geographic, classification, scientific names, and general indexes.

The set will be useful for research by upper-elementary and middle-school students. Libraries that own the 1994 edition may not want to add this one, especially if they have other resources that cover plants.

The Kingfisher First Animal Encyclopedia. By John Farndon and others. 1998. 160p. illus. index. Kingfisher, $16.95 (0-7534-5135-2). DDC: 590.

This slim encyclopedia is aimed at satisfying the very young reader's first attempt at animal research. The 155 entries are arranged in alphabetical order, from *aardvark* to *zebra*, and are illustrated with just fewer than 1,000 color pictures, including some photographs. The animals are those most likely to be encountered by young children in picture books, zoos, or their own backyards. There are also entries for larger groups (*baby animal, mammal, reptile*) and for some topics related to animal behavior, such as communication and migration. Each topic is covered in one page, with text consisting of a brief description of the animal in bold type, and captions for each picture. The print size is readable and appealing to the elementary user.

For some animals, such as butterfly and frog, an illustration of the life cycle is provided, with numbers to help students see the various stages in sequence. Each page includes "Find Out More," which functions as a *see also* reference. Fact boxes contain added facts and figures, but are missing for some animals. Parents, teachers, and librarians will welcome step-by-step activities and projects that are included with animal topics that lend themselves to arts-and-crafts projects. A glossary and index add value to the volume as a reference tool.

Similarly-named volumes, The Kingfisher First Encyclopedia of Animals (1994), with 400 entries, and The Kingfisher Illustrated Encyclopedia of Animals [RBB O 15 92], covering more than 2,000 animals, are geared toward older children. Children ages five through eight will have a visual adventure with this new Kingfisher volume, which will answer the basic requirements of animal reports, though further research may be required on most animals. Recommended for school and public libraries.

The Simon and Schuster Encyclopedia of Animals: A Visual Who's Who of the World's Creatures. Ed. by Philip Whitfield. 1998. 616p. appendix. illus. index. Simon and Schuster, $50 (0-684-85237-3). DDC: 590.

The subtitle "a visual who's who of the world's creatures" best summarizes the scope of this interesting reference book. In the introduction, general consultant Philip Whitfield explains that the book "sets out to provide a comprehensive catalog of the staggering range of animal types within the vertebrate group." Using this criterion, the entries progress from those with highly developed vertebrae (i.e., mammals) through those with "simple rudiments of vertebral structure" (i.e., fish). Within these broad classifications, animals are then grouped by family. Whitfield points out that it is impossible to represent every vertebrate species in a single-volume work, but that grouping by family allows for greatest representation.

Each section begins with a brief overview and includes a cladogram which charts possible phylogenetic relationships among animals in that classification. Each animal is pictured in a full-color drawing. All entries begin with capsule information on name (both scientific and popular); range (general location where the creature lives); habitat (the creature's specific environment); and size. Length is given in both English and metric measurements. In some cases, additional measurements are provided (one for body and one for a tail and/or wingspan). Because the pictures are not drawn to scale, these measurements are important. If an animal is on the Red List of Threatened Animals produced by the IUCN (World Conservation Union), a code appears next to its name; this code is explained in the introduction. In addition to the vital facts, each entry includes a description that is brief but gives essential information. An appendix has a detailed listing of the animals as classified in the text, and an index gives access by both popular and scientific names. The book was originally published in England, which may be why no entry was provided for the spotted owl, an endangered bird that has been at the center of controversy over logging in the U.S. There are no entries for domesticated animals.

This is one of the few comprehensive single-volume reference tools available for purchase on the subject. It is an attractive book that nonscientists will appreciate and enjoy. Although it does not provide enough information for report writing, it's a good ready-reference source for school and public libraries.

Encyclopedia of Birds. 2d ed. Ed. by Joseph Forshaw. 1998. 240p. bibliog. illus. index. Academic, $34.95 (0-12-262340-1). DDC: 598.03.
Encyclopedia of Fishes. 2d ed. Ed. by John R. Paxton and William N. Eschmeyer. 1998. 240p. bibliog. illus. index. Academic, $34.95 (0-12-547665-5). DDC: 597.03.
Encyclopedia of Mammals. 2d ed. Ed. by Edwin Gould and George McKay. 1998. 240p. bibliog. illus. index. Academic, $34.95 (0-12-293670-1). DDC: 599.03.
Encyclopedia of Reptiles & Amphibians. 2d ed. Ed. by Harold G. Cogger and Richard G. Zweifel. 1998. 240p. bibliog. illus. index. Academic, $34.95 (0-12-178560-2). DDC: 597.803.

These four volumes provide extensive information about their subjects, and follow the same basic format, beginning with a general introduction; an explanation of the classification system; a historical overview; a look at habitats, adaptations, and behavior, and a section about endangered species. The major portion of the text is devoted to kinds of birds, fishes, mammals, and reptiles and amphibians arranged by orders. Each entry has been authored by an expert in the field, so readers are provided with accurate and detailed information. The various contributors include scientists and curators from universities and museums around the world.

Chapters generally include a "key facts" box that contains a "conservation watch"; a distribution map; sidebars ("Why do whales run aground?"; "Sex reversal in parrotfishes and wrasses"); and text that describes the various families. Length ranges from one page for *lanternfishes* to nearly 40 pages for *snakes*. The text is informative but not too technical. The books are highly illustrated, with a mix of full-color photographs and detailed drawings, often taking up more than half the page. The birds volume, as an example, has more than 200 photographs and more than 150 original paintings, diagrams, and maps. Changes from the first editions, which were published in Australia, include updated statistics, new conservation information, and redrawn distribution maps. The text has been revised to reflect the latest taxonomic classifications.

Though not as comprehensive as the standard *Grzimek's Animal Life Encyclopedia* (now unfortunately out of print), these four volumes provide more up-to-date information. Another recent title, *The Simon and Schuster Encyclopedia of Animals* [RBB O 15 98] attempts a comparable breadth of coverage in a single volume, but has less detail. Marshall Cavendish's *Wildlife and Plants of the World* [RBB Mr 1 99] is arranged alphabetically instead of according to scientific classification, and is suitable for a younger audience. Older students who need detailed information for reports will find a complete and accurate investigation in the volumes under review, but their particular strength is the splendid illustrations. High-school, public, and academic libraries needing to fill out their collections on animals will want to consider one or more of these attractive and affordable books.

Medicine, Health, Technology, Management

Alt-HealthWatch. Internet database. 1997. SoftLine Information, Inc., 20 Summer St., Stamford, CT 06901, $1,795/yr. For information, call 203-975-8292 or visit [http://www.slinfo.com]. (Last accessed March 16, 1999.)

With interest in alternative medicine at an all-time high and the National Institutes of Health establishing an Office of Alternative Medicine, the need for information in this subject area is increasing. Finding journal literature on alternative and complementary therapies is a challenge. Alt-HealthWatch is a full-text and image database that contains English-language periodicals, peer-reviewed journals, academic and professional publications, consumer magazines and newsletters, research reports, and association newsletters in alternative health fields. These publications cover complementary, alternative, and integrated approaches to health and wellness in both human and veterinary medicine.

The database is cumulative with quarterly updates and access to seven years of back issues. The current contents include approximately 46,000 articles and 7,500 images. Both a Web and a CD-ROM version (for $1,495 per year) are available. This review was done with the Web version using a Pentium II PC.

Using Alt-HealthWatch is easy. The menu allows searching by words in article (keyword), title word, subject, publication name, publication date, author, type of article, and type of publication. Users may employ Boolean operators, truncation, and adjacency operators to refine the search. A sidebar has options for sorting, printing/downloading, and help screens. Pull-down menus for each search option open complete lists of terms used in the category (types of articles indexed, subject headings, publication titles, etc.). One can scroll through them to browse or type in a term and go to a specific section of the list. After executing a search, the total number of items retrieved is displayed. Citations are listed in reverse chronological order. Clicking on a citation leads to a display with the publication's logo at the top of the screen followed by the full text of the article. Clicking on the journal logo provides complete subscription information.

Search results may vary depending on the strategy used. A search using the title words *breast cancer* and *alternative therapies* yielded two citations in the peer-reviewed *Alternative Therapies in Health and Medicine*. The same search using the subject heading *complementary and alternative therapies* produced thirty citations. Using the terms *back pain* and *chiropractic* as article words resulted in 334 citations, while the terms *back pain* and *yoga* produced two as title words, none as subject headings, and 92 as article words. Search terms are highlighted in the article text.

The range of publications indexed is quite broad. There are approximately 160 titles, including consumer magazines such as M*ind, B*ody, S*pirit M*agazine; newsletters such as N*utrition Action Health Letter;* peer-reviewed journals such as *Acupuncture in Medicine;* and professional journals such as M*assage and Bodywork Quarterly.* These reflect the diverse interests of alternative health practitioners and clients.

*Alt-HealthW*atch is a unique source. There is nothing else that provides systematic coverage of alternative medicine. It is a welcome addition to academic and health science libraries. Consumer health and large public libraries with sufficient funding should also consider it.

The Complete Directory for People with Rare Disorders, 1998–99.
Ed. by Leslie E. Mackenzie. 1998. 850p. index. Grey House, $190 (1-891482-03-3); paper, $165 (0-939300-98-2). DDC: 362.1.

This directory from the National Organization of Rare Disorders (NORD) covers more than 1,000 rare conditions, which are defined as those that affect fewer than 200,000 people in the U.S.

There are four parts to the directory. The first defines and describes the disorders, which are listed alphabetically. The entries in this section also refer the user to entries for pertinent organizations or agencies. Unfortunately, the referring statement (repeated under each entry) is long and confusing; a simple *see also* would have sufficed.

The other three sections list disease-specific support groups, umbrella organizations that serve a wide range of disorders, and government agencies serving the needs of those suffering with a rare disorder. Organization entries include a service description, contact information, and a list of publications. In the case of umbrella groups, the disorders the agency is concerned with are listed. There are a keyword and a name index.

A random sampling of the disorders included showed that they are defined in the M*erck Manual.* The added value of this directory is the link to the associations. NORD has a Web site at rdb.com but no definitions or information are given online; users must order a report at a cost. The National Institutes of Health's Office of Rare Diseases Web site ord/ provides only links to other sites, and neither site provides quick access to information about disorders. Large public libraries (especially those specializing in consumer-health information) and hospital patient libraries that need more than a M*erck* definition will find this a useful resource in directing users to support groups or agencies dealing with a rare disorder.

Encyclopedia of AIDS: A Social, Political, Cultural, and Scientific Record of the HIV Epidemic. Ed. by Raymond A. Smith. 1998. 601p. bibliogs. glossary. illus. index. Fitzroy Dearborn, $125 (1-57958-007-6). DDC: 362.1.

Today, understanding HIV/AIDS can still be a challenge for the nonspecialist. Smith, a research scientist at the HIV Center for Clinical and Behavioral Studies at the New York State Psychiatric Institute, is to be commended for undertaking the Herculean task of systematically organizing, synthesizing, and contextualizing an enormous body of information on the global HIV/AIDS crisis for a general readership. The encyclopedia provides a record of the first 15 years of the epidemic; it takes as its starting point the summer of 1981 and continues its coverage through the summer of 1996. The contents cover eight broad domains: basic science and epidemiology, transmission and prevention, pathology and treatment, impacted populations, government and activism, policy and law, culture and society, and the global epidemic.

The 250 signed entries are arranged alphabetically. Entries cover many of the most crucial dimensions of the HIV/AIDS epidemic prior to 1996. Examples include *bathhouse closure, disclosure, gene therapy, homeless populations, long-term survivors and non-progressors, marches and parades, needle-exchange programs, public assistance, queer theory, religious faith and spirituality, testing debates, underground treatments,* and *visual arts.* Each entry is followed by lists of related entries, key words (for use in online searches), and suggestions for further reading. The entries were written by 181 contributors from more than a dozen countries on five continents. Smith notes that all contributors were asked to write their entries from the perspective of the "mainstream consensus" that has emerged over the past 15 years regarding the causes and nature of the epidemic. Similarly, authors were asked to avoid writing entries that "indulge in polemics or advocate one point of view to the exclusion of all others."

Considerable added value is provided by a multipart resource guide designed to help readers who wish to update information and seek out further information beyond what is covered in the encyclopedia. Included are U.S. publications on HIV/AIDS; U.S. federal and state government documents; international English-language periodicals on HIV/AIDS; major North American HIV/AIDS information centers, libraries, and subject collections; major U.S. HIV/AIDS organizations; major HIV/AIDS contacts in the United Kingdom and Canada; major international HIV/AIDS organizations; and Internet resources (Web sites, search engines, and electronic bulletin boards). A short list of commonly used terms and abbreviations, as well as notes on editors and contributors, and an index of nearly 20 pages conclude the volume.

This volume is unique because of its multidisciplinary approach to HIV/AIDS. Well organized, well researched, and well written, it is also without competition. T*he* AIDS D*ictionary* [RBB S 15 98], also published in 1998, is a more traditional dictionary of the words and phrases that define the epidemic. The E*ncyclopedia of* AIDS is perfect for reference (academic, public, and high-school) collections. It is also recommended for personal libraries, although the Board acknowledges that price may be a deterrent for that market. Specialists and those seeking more rigorous articles on many of the topics covered will, of course, be better served by the scholarly journal literature in a variety of disciplines.

Technology in Action: Science Applied to Everyday Life. 3v. By Phyllis Engelbert. 1998. 523p. bibliogs. chronology. glossary. illus. indexes. UXL, $79.95 (0-7876-2809-3). DDC: 603.

This set is designed to present "a comprehensive overview of many technologies that are relevant to the lives and future careers of students." There are 64 articles grouped into eight chapters: "Communication," "Electronics and Computers" (volume 1); "Energy," "Food and Agriculture," "Health and Medicine" (volume 2); "Civil Engineering," "Manufacturing and Materials," and "Transportation" (volume 3). Each volume begins with a table of contents for the entire set, a chronology, and a glossary.

The chronology is 33 pages long and includes a time line running along the bottom of each page. This section makes it easy for students to see how long it took for technology to develop in the early centuries of civilization, and how rapidly we have progressed since the 1800s. The text of the chronology mentions each of the inventions and developments that are addressed in the main articles. The pages in the set are consecutively numbered; the comprehensive index in each volume refers to both the volume and page numbers.

In each chapter, a page-long introduction and chronology of relevant inventions and discoveries precede the articles. The articles range from 5 to 15 pages; most are 8 to 10 pages long. Illustrations include diagrams as well as photographs. There are also numerous portraits of scientists and inventors. Gray boxes provide extra information—specific inventions, trends, new developments, and other important facts. Terms that might be unfamiliar are frequently clarified or defined within the text. The articles discuss the history of each technological achievement from earliest time to the present, so the reader sees how much time and effort go into scientific advancement—invention is not just a matter of "Eureka! I've found it." Future applications are discussed as well. Articles also provide biographical profiles, highlighting in particular the contributions of women and African Americans. Most of us know that Thomas Edison was the mind behind modern electrical technology, but we are made aware of the invaluable contributions of Lewis Latimer, the son of an escaped slave, who invented improved carbon filaments for light bulbs and wrote the first textbook on incandescent lighting. Each article concludes with a bibliography. Gale's *World of Invention* [RBB Jl 1 94] is a frequently cited source, as are *The Timetables of Technology* (Simon and Schuster, 1993) and David Macauley's *The Way Things Work* (Houghton Mifflin, 1988).

When a student needs more information than is found in *The Way Things Work,* this is the set to have on hand. Technology is explained in terms that any middle-or junior-high-school student will understand and most adults will appreciate. An excellent resource for public and school libraries.

Free or Low Cost Health Information. Comp. by Carol Smallwood. 1998. 344p. appendixes. indexes. McFarland, paper, $39.50 (0-7864-0309-8). DDC: 610.

Here is a directory of more than 1,400 nonprofit organizations, plus a few companies, that provide free or inexpensive (under $15) printed materials on health-related topics. The primary audience is "librarians and teachers for the vertical file and curriculum." Organizations are listed under approxomately 700 topics, which are arranged alphabetically, from *abdomen* to *yellow fever*. A listing of the topic headings appears in the table of contents. They cover age and gender groups (*adolescent health, women's health*); other categories of persons and groups (*lesbian health issues, veterans*); parts of the body; vitamins and minerals; drugs; pollutants; diseases and conditions; disabilities; and medical specialties and procedures. Other categories cover environmental, ethical, and social issues.

Some topics are not clearly differentiated. There is no apparent difference between *alcohol and driving* versus *drinking and driving*, yet different organizations and resources are listed under each, and no cross-references are provided, even in the index at the end of the book. Similarly, *smoking* is not linked to *tobacco*, except in the index. Another example is *organ transplants* versus *transplants*, confusing because it is organs that are transplanted. One of the vaguer topical headings is *institutions*, because almost every organization listed could be considered an "institution." Under this heading are listed Consumer Information Center-6A and National Health Information Center.

Listings include the agency name, address, telephone and fax numbers four publications, with title, price, number of pages, and a brief annotation. Only print materials are cited. Some agencies are listed under more than one category, with different resources highlighted in different listings.

The volume concludes with an index, which, in addition to the topical headings, also includes entries for all the agencies listed, plus some cross-references. A few headings have entirely too many page references and should have been modified with contextual or explanatory subheadings. For example, 75 page references are listed under the index term National Organization for Rare Disorders, Inc.

Despite its problems, this volume does achieve the author's goal of providing help to librarians, teachers, and the general public who wish to find inexpensive or free publications "when there is little or no money available for purchases." Since the directory will go out of date quickly, and since a great deal of free health information is now available online, e-mail addresses and URLs would have been a useful feature.

Informacion de Salud para los Consumidores. Ed. by Alan M. Rees with Irene Affranchino-Miniello. 1998. 536p. appendixes. indexes. Oryx, $74.95 (1-57356-166-5). DDC: 610.

Hispanics are the most rapidly growing segment of the U. S. population. They will comprise 15 percent of the total population—39 million people—by the year 2000. Although 70 percent of Hispanics live in California, New York, Florida, and Texas, libraries in all parts of the country serve Spanish-speaking patrons. The availability of health information that is accurate and up to date in Spanish is an ongoing concern. This volume brings together current Spanish-language materials for lay readers.

Editor Rees is a medical-information specialist. He worked with a medical translator to prepare this volume, which compiles and reprints Spanish-language publications from government and private agencies. Selections are derived from approximately 300 documents from 50 sources: federal and state government agencies, voluntary health organizations, pharmaceutical companies, and other organizations. The emphasis is on topics that are priorities for government health policies: AIDS, cancer, heart disease, diabetes, nutrition, pregnancy, childhood immunization, substance abuse, lead poisoning, and communicable diseases. While these cover a wide range of interests, there are still major gaps in what is available for Spanish speakers.

The book is arranged in 32 chapters, alphabetically by subject in Spanish. (A miscellaneous chapter includes publications that do not fit well within the assigned subject areas.) Within each chapter, the full text of Spanish-language publications on given topics is reproduced along with a citation so that one may order it. Two appendixes contain a description of the Physician Data Query (PDQ) program of the National Cancer Institute, and a directory of sources for Spanish-language health publications. The directory entries contain only the name and address of the organization. Three indexes—title, agency, and subject—complete the text. The agency index lists private and government agencies in separate sections.

The preface of the book appears in both Spanish and English. The table of contents, chapter headings, publication titles, and agency names and source titles in the index are presented bilingually. The subject index is only in Spanish. These features make the book easy to use for staff who may not know Spanish and patrons with limited English. This is a welcome addition to consumer-health collections in libraries serving Spanish speakers. It is valuable for both reference and collection development.

The Cambridge Encyclopedia of Human Growth and Development. Ed. by Stanley J. Ulijaszek and others. 1998. 486p. appendix. bibliogs. illus. index. Cambridge, $95 (0-521-56046-2). DDC: 612.6.

Human growth and development are complex processes that can be studied in many ways. This encyclopedia, containing articles written by physicians, anthropologists, and psychologists with academic appointments, uses a multidisciplinary approach to explain the changes that happen during the course of life.

The book begins with a general introduction and a history of the study of human growth. The signed articles are organized into parts by broad subject area: Measurement and Assessment, Patterns of Human Growth, Behavioral and Cognitive Development, the Human Lifespan. Each part has an introductory overview essay. The articles within cover more specific topics, such as growth disorders, migration and changing population characteristics, nutrition, and aging. *See* references appear as article numbers within parentheses in the text. *See also* references are in a box at the end of each article. Photographs, charts, tables, and drawings augment the text. Three appendixes offer brief biographies of major scientists in the field, a glossary, and an extensive bibliography by subject. An index and a detailed table of contents provide access to the material.

The articles are written at a very technical level with British spelling, but educated lay readers will be able to understand them. Many interesting topics not covered in other sources appear here—the comparative development of mammals, dental development, the effects of war and famine on growth, and prematurity and development. *The Cambridge Encyclopedia of Human Growth and Development* will be most useful for academic health-sciences and social-sciences collections, but large public libraries where there is sufficient interest will also want to consider it.

Under the Microscope: The Human Body. 8v. 1998. 384p. glossary. illus. index. Grolier, $219 (0-7172-9265-7). DDC: 612.

This set introduces young readers to the anatomy and physiology of the human body. Each slim volume covers a different topic: heart, skeleton, digesting, making life, breathing, senses, muscles, and brain.

A one-page introduction to the body system begins each volume. This is followed by double-page spreads presenting information on the system as a whole, and on its various components. For example, the skeleton volume not only covers the entire human skeleton but also the ankle, elbow, leg, and arm bones. The concise text is fitted in among the many drawings (including diagrams and cutaways), photographs, and examples of microphotography. The editors have chosen to emphasize the microphotography feature by titling the series "Under the Microscope," and there are many examples of X rays and various types of scans. However, the drawings are far more illustrative for a young audience which uses pictures to interpret text. The illustrations are beautifully detailed and clearly labeled.

The set is well done. Information is logically organized, and the vocabulary is accessible to children grades three to five. Each volume has a glossary, and new words are also defined the first time they are used in the text. Elementary-school and public libraries may want to consider this set for assignment demands, with the caveat that upper-elementary students may need more comprehensive sources.

The Consumer's Guide to Herbal Medicine. By Steven B. Karch. 1999. 240p. appendixes. glossary. illus. index. Advanced Research, $29.95 (1-889462-06-3). DDC: 615.03.

Television ads for herbal medicines are beginning to appear as frequently as those for over-the-counter drugs. The effectiveness of the advertising and the public's growing interest in "natural" remedies have caused sales to soar astronomically. It is not surprising that guides to medicinal herbs have also proliferated. There is now even a *PDR for Herbal Medicines* [RBB Mr 1 99].

This attractive consumer-oriented guide reviews 67 of the most popular medicinal herbs, including chamomile, echinacea, garlic, ginseng, and St. John's wort. Recommendations of Germany's Commission E, a group of scientists and researchers appointed by the German Federal Health Agency to study the safety and effectiveness of herbs, are cited as the authority for the information presented.

Each two-to three-page entry contains an illustration of the plant. Full botanical and common names are given as well as the plant's geographic origin and the documented and legendary history of its use. Proven effects (based on recent research data), potential problems, warnings, and safe dosage amounts are included. Warnings are given about the use of certain herbs that, although safe for consumption, could have serious consequences for users with specific medical conditions.

Consumers are encouraged to become educated about the remedies they use so that they recognize relevant information on packaging labels. The author emphasizes the importance of knowing a product's botanical name and the part of the plant used to produce the effective remedy as well as what percent of the herb is actually contained in the product. The discussion of the FDA's position in the regulation of herbal medicines and chapters explaining the basic biology and chemistry of the most popular groups of herbal products are clearly written and arm consumers with important knowledge that will be useful in making decisions.

Other features include an alphabetical list of herbs and the ailments for which they are used, another list of ailments and the appropriate herbal treatments, and a glossary. Appendixes cover herbal combinations approved by Commission E, a list of unproved and potentially dangerous herbs, a guide to searching *Medline*, and a brief annotated list of reference sources.

Because the FDA provides little guidance in the area of herbal medicines, this volume fills a need by giving an informative overview based on the best existing authority. Because the author has chosen to limit the scope of the contents to only the most popular herbal supplements, the guide will complement more comprehensive sources such as the PDR volume or *The Encyclopedia of Medicinal Plants* (DK, 1996) by providing quick access to the most frequently requested information.

Encyclopedia of Native American Shamanism: Sacred Ceremonies of Northern America. By William S. Lyon. 1998. 468p. bibliog. illus. index. maps. ABC-CLIO, $65 (0-87436-933-9). DDC: 615.8.

A continuation of the author's *Encyclopedia of Native American Healing* (ABC-CLIO, 1996), which focused on powers used for healing, this new title examines "all the other various ways in which medicine powers are manifested" among Native Americans of North America.

In A–Z format, the volume includes names, techniques, paraphernalia, and results of various medicine ceremonies; concepts; acclaimed shamans; motifs and themes; and pertinent anthropological terms and scholars. The researcher will find entries for *amulet*, *Deganawidah* (renowned shaman of the pre-Columbian period), *lahatconos* (a Wintu initiation dance for novice shamans), *rain-making ceremonies*, *Sea Lion* (a Haida shaman), *swadash* (a type of Skokomish medicine power), and *vision quest*. Entries range in length from a paragraph or two to seven pages for *war medicine*, and include, when relevant, literal translation, tribe or tribal grouping, and culture area as well as cross-references and citations to source material. Much of the text consists of direct quotations from original sources. Since this volume and its companion are designed to complement each other, there are *see* references to terms defined in *Encyclopedia of Native American Healing*. Maps, illustrations, a bibliography of sources, an "Ethnobotanical Bibliography," and an index add reference value. According to Lyon, only around 15 percent of the sources referenced in this encyclopedia are also listed in the earlier volume, because "each encyclopedia focuses on a different aspect of the known literature on shamanism."

Though information on shamanism can be found in other more general titles on Native North Americans, this volume provides the most in-depth treatment. Highly recommended for public and academic libraries, especially where *Encyclopedia of Native American Healing* is already part of the collection.

Medicinal Plants of the World: Chemical Constituents, Traditional and Modern Medicinal Uses. By Ivan A. Ross. 1999. 418p. bibliog. glossary. illus. Humana Press, $99.50 (0-89603-542-5). DDC: 615.

As interest in alternative medicine continues to grow, sifting through the rumors and claims of nonstandard therapies can be a confusing process. Garlic, it often seems, will cure just about anything; and aloe's uses seem unlimited. In this new volume, Ross, a biologist with the U.S. Food and Drug Administration, cuts through the claims and gives the historical uses and documented effects of 27 plants that are widely used throughout the world. Whereas *The Encyclopedia of Medicinal Plants* (DK, 1996) offers a discussion of hundreds of plants and their preparation, and the excellent *Encyclopedia of Natural Medicine* (2d ed., Prima, 1998) offers detailed advice on treating illness, Ross' goal in this volume is to provide a summary of the systematic and scientific information about the most widely used medicinal plants.

The first chapter is dedicated to plant nomenclature and description. The discussion is accented by abundant illustrations. Each of the succeeding chapters is dedicated to a particular medicinal plant. Entries begin with a listing of common names for the plant from around the world, followed by a botanical description and details of the plant's distribution and origin. Next comes a list of the traditional uses of the plant in various countries. Each use is documented with a citation to an entry in the extensive bibliography. Then there is a listing of the chemical constituents that indicates the part of the plant (e.g., root, leaf, or stem) and concentration of the constituent. Perhaps the most valuable part of each entry is the final section, where Ross provides an extensive listing of the pharmacological effects and activities of the plant. Typically, this includes numerous effects, such as antifungal and antibacterical activity, and a toxicity assessment. Like the list of traditional uses, this comprehensive discussion is very well documented. One color plate of each plant is provided in a separate section. An index to all common names precedes a glossary of terms and a 67-page bibliography, which primarily contains citations to journal articles.

Ross has done an outstanding job of gathering information from a wide variety of sources and synthesizing it into a readable and systematic discussion. No other single volume brings such depth and intense research to the systematic understanding of the uses and effects of the plants discussed. The delivery is fairly technical and will be most accessible to readers with some background in botany and pharmacology. As a resource that summarizes a huge amount of published information on medicinal plants, this volume belongs on the shelves of medical and botanical libraries. Large public libraries and academic libraries, especially those supporting graduate programs in the health or botanical sciences, may also want to consider this title.

PDR for Herbal Medicines. 1998. 1,246p. bibliog. illus. index. Medical Economics, $59.95 (1-56363-292-6). DDC: 615.

The growing popularity of herbal medicines has generated a need for reliable information about them. Because they are not regulated by the Food and Drug Administration, they are not subjected to rigorous tests and clinical trials. Manufacturers may claim that herbal preparations do wondrous things, but they cannot market them for the diagnosis, treatment, cure, or prevention of any disease in the U.S. Consumers who want scientific information on herbal products do not have many sources to use. *PDR for Herbal Medicines* is one of the few books that offers such data.

By using the findings of the German Regulatory Authority's herbal watchdog agency, known as Commission E, the editors have compiled information based on an intensive examination of peer-reviewed literature. Approximately 300 common botanicals have been studied by this commission. In addition, they have included information from an exhaustive literature review conducted by the PhytoPharm U.S. Institute of Phytopharmaceuticals. This provides data on about 300 more herbs not covered by the Commission E reports.

Organized like the other members of the PDR family, the book begins with several indexes. The scientific and common name index is an alphabetical listing of all profiled botanicals by both their scientific and common names. The scientific names are in boldface, and the common names are in regular type. All common names are repeated in italics under their respective scientific names, making it easy to find a plant. The indications index lists symptoms and conditions alphabetically in bold type. Under each one, herbs deemed effective by Commission E are listed in Roman type, while those that have not been approved appear in italics. The therapeutic category index organizes the herbs alphabetically by drug class—analgesics, hair-growth stimulants, otic preparations, and so forth—listing both verified and folk uses together. The side-effects index is an alphabetical list of reactions, in boldface, with the herbs causing them listed underneath (e.g., *apathy—cannabis sativa* [*marijuana*]). The next index, the drug/herb interactions guide, is an important and useful feature. Here, alphabetical lists of drugs and herbs are coupled with lists of products that interact with them. One discovers that a patient taking antithrombolytic drugs, for example, should not take Ginkgo biloba because it increases the effects of the drugs. Following the indexes is an herb identification guide, with color pictures of 350 common medicinal plants listed by their Latin names.

The main part of the book is the herbal monograph section, containing profiles of more than 600 medicinal herbs listed alphabetically by their Latin names. Each profile includes the names of the plant, a detailed botanical description, actions and pharmacology, indications and usage, contraindications, precautions and adverse reactions, overdosage, dosage, and a bibliography of technical literature. The majority of articles are in German. A glossary and directories of poison control and drug information centers in the U. S. complete the work.

PDR for Herbal Medicines fills a genuine need in reference collections. It complements sources such as *Encyclopedia of Medicinal Plants* (DK, 1996), which has more illustrations and cultural and historical background information about herbal medicine. *Herbal Drugs and Phytopharmaceuticals* (Medpharm/CRC, 1989) contains technical manufacturing specifications. *Medicinal Plants of the World* [RBB F 15 99] provides chemical constituents as well as much more coverage of both traditional and modern uses but includes only 27 of the most widely used plants. *PDR for Herbal Medicines* provides the necessary information for using herbs safely and belongs in all medical reference collections.

The AIDS Dictionary. By Sarah Barbara Watstein. 1998. 318p. appendixes. bibliog. index. Facts On File, $45 (0-8160-3149-5); paper, $24.95 (0-8160-3754-X). DDC: 616.97.

Although the outlook for those infected with HIV has improved with new treatment options, AIDS is still an incurable disease affecting people all over the world. There is a need for current material that explains this complex illness to lay readers. *The AIDS Dictionary* is a new source that is useful for ready reference and introductory research.

The work contains approximately 4,000 alphabetical entries ranging in length from one sentence to three pages. They cover a wide range of medical, psychosocial, ethical, legal, and health-care topics, for example, *benefit, coenzyme 910, fetish, malaria, protease inhibitor, sadomasochism safety, T-cell count,* and *transmission*. Entries explain the material in a clear and nonjudgmental manner. *See* references and the use of small capitals for terms within articles that have their own entries refer users to related areas. A bibliography, list of abbreviations, statistical table of HIV cases and deaths, and list of agency telephone numbers and Web sites complete the text.

The AIDS Dictionary does not have the depth of comprehensive sources such as the second edition of *The AIDS Knowledge Base* (Little Brown, 1994), but it does provide quick definitions of a wide variety of terms and promote awareness of the problems facing people with HIV. It is a good starting point for those doing research on AIDS. Public, health-sciences, and patient-education libraries will want to own a copy of this source.

The Encyclopedia of Infectious Diseases. By Carol Turkington and Bonnie Ashby. 1998. 400p. appendixes. bibliog. glossary. index. Facts On File, $50 (0-8160-3512-1). DDC: 616.9.

Infectious diseases are an integral part of human existence. While colds may cause temporary discomfort, epidemics have changed the course of history. With new viruses emerging and spreading rapidly, an understanding of infection is vital. This new encyclopedia provides an introduction to this interesting field of medicine.

Alphabetical entries ranging from one sentence to five pages in length form the main part of the book. These cover a wide range of topics: infectious organisms (*arenavirus, streptococcus*), types of disease (*encephalitis, pneumonia*), specific diseases (*hepatitis C, scarlet fever*), drug classes (*cephalosporins, penicillin*), preventive measures (*immunization, vaccine*), and miscellaneous subjects (*pets and infectious disease, World Health Organization*). Cross-references in small capitals appear within or at the end of entries. Articles on diseases include etiology, history, symptoms, diagnosis, treatment, complications, and prevention.

The encyclopedia is written in lay language. It contains a good deal of useful, practical information. The article on food poisoning has detailed charts on the proper cooking, serving, and storing of food. The article on vaccine provides recommended immunization schedules for adults by age, health, and job. There is, however, no schedule of childhood immunization.

A glossary provides brief definitions of biomedical terms. There is some overlap with the main text here. A series of appendixes provides information on drugs used to treat infectious diseases, home disinfection, health organizations, disease hotlines, health publications, and Web sites. There is also an extensive bibliography of current professional and lay books and articles.

The Encyclopedia of Infectious Diseases is an excellent source for ready reference and overview information. For greater depth, one can consult *Current Medical Diagnosis and Treatment* (Appleton, annual), *The Cambridge World History of Human Disease* [RBB N 1 93], or *Merck Manual of Medical Information Home Edition* (Merck, 1997).

The Gale Encyclopedia of Medicine. 5v. Ed. by Donna Olendorf and others. 1999. 3,442p. bibliog. charts. illus. index. Gale, $499 (0-7876-1868-3). DDC: 616.

Current, accurate medical information in lay language tends to lack depth. Librarians rely on one-volume medical guides and then use professional-level sources for further background. These may be difficult for lay readers to understand. *The Gale Encyclopedia of Medicine* is a five-volume, consecutively paged set that bridges the gap between basic consumer sources and specialized medical texts. An advisory board of physicians and librarians worked with contributors who are health-care professionals and medical writers to produce the encyclopedia

Approximately 1,500 alphabetical entries cover 905 disorders and conditions, 235 tests and procedures, and 325 treatments and therapies. The latter include common drugs listed by generic name with the brand names given in the article. Alternative health is covered, too. There are articles such as *aromatherapy, Chinese medicine, homeopathy,* and *meditation*. Entries on specific diseases and conditions include information on alternative treatments that may be useful.

The entries range in length from one to three pages. All are signed, and all have brief bibliographies and lists of organizations for referral. Entries on diseases and conditions include definition, description, causes and symptoms, diagnosis, treatment, alternative treatment, prognosis, and prevention. Those on tests and procedures have a definition, purpose, precautions, description, preparation, aftercare, risks, and normal and abnormal results. Each entry has a shaded box with a list of key terms and their definitions. Black-and-white photographs, line drawings, and charts augment the text. The charts provide very useful information, such as the comparative effectiveness of various contraceptives.

The articles are quite comprehensive and easy to understand. Diseases are well covered. There are general articles on subjects such as cancer and sexually transmitted diseases as well as separate entries for each individual cancer and disease. Hepatitis A, B, C, D, and E each have an entry. The articles on operations such as adrenalectomy and hysterectomy explain the advantages and disadvantages of the various surgical approaches. Endoscopic procedures (e.g., cystoscopy) are described in detail so that patients will know what to expect. Users who desire more detailed information about anatomy and physiology will have to consult other sources, but these are readily available in most reference collections. The article on menopause seems to contain contradictory information on when physicians recommend that women begin hormone replacement therapy.

The Gale Encyclopedia of Medicine is more comprehensive than sources such as the single-volume *Mayo Clinic Family Health Book* (2d ed., Morrow, 1996) and the three-volume *Magill's Medical Guide: Health and Illness* [RBB O 1 95]. It is a welcome addition to consumer health and public library collections.

Johns Hopkins Family Health Book. Ed. by Michael J. Klag and others. 1999. 1,657p. appendixes. charts. illus. index. HarperCollins, $49.95 (0-06-270149-5). DDC: 616.

Every page (including the endpages) of this book is filled with information vital to maintaining good health at every stage of life. Developed in conjunction with an advisory board of more than 100 Johns Hopkins' health professionals, the resource focuses on family health issues with a goal of educating health-care consumers to become informed participants in their own care and that of their families.

Organized into five major areas, the guide begins by covering the basic components of good health—diet, exercise, safety, and disease prevention. This is followed by an examination of health issues specific to each life stage from conception to death. Another section covers body systems and disorders. The function of each system, as well as associated disorders, their causes, symptoms, treatment, and prevention, is described. This section is enhanced by a "Color Atlas" illustrating various body systems, conditions, and poisonous plants. Part 3, "First Aid and Emergency Care," provides clear instructions, accompanied by illustrations, from handling simple cuts and bruises to more life-threatening emergencies. Guidance on choosing a health-care provider, a discussion of health-insurance options, issues surrounding death and dying, treatment options, and patients' rights are covered in a section called "Taking Charge of Your Health Care." Each section includes information about related professional and support organizations.

The appendixes contain a medication directory of the 80 most commonly prescribed drugs. Each drug's generic name, purpose, and side effects are provided. There are a glossary of commonly used medical terms, growth charts, a list of laboratory tests and their normal values, and sample forms for living wills and advance medical directives. The alphabetical index highlights symptoms in red and main entries in boldface.

The clearly written text is supplemented throughout by more than 300 two-and four-color illustrations, photographs, sidebars, diagrams, charts, and graphs. Cross-references guide the user to all related information.

This outstanding work truly reflects the reputation of its institution of origin. It includes information on the latest advances in treatment for erectile dysfunction, HIV, specific cancers, and other diseases and conditions, as well as in-depth discussion of genetic testing and cancer research. Each topic is thoroughly explained in language that can be understood by the layperson. The text, illustrations, extensive coverage of universal health issues, and timeliness of the information serve to make this title a strong contender in the field of consumer health guides. The somewhat older *Columbia University College of Physicians and Surgeons Complete Home Medical Guide* (3d ed., Crown, 1995) and *The Mayo Clinic Family Health Book* (2d ed., Morrow, 1996) are also very useful; all three have unique features. The *Johns Hopkins Family Health Book* is highly recommended for public libraries and hospital libraries providing consumer health information.

Stress A–Z: A Sourcebook for Facing Everyday Challenges. By Ada P. Kahn. 1998. 378p. bibliog. index. Facts On File, $40 (0-8160-3295-5). DDC: 616.9.

Designed as an overview of stress-related topics, this dictionary-style work provides selective coverage of various aspects of stress. The author has taken a holistic approach in selecting topics to include. Among them are absenteeism, aging, culture shock, domestic violence, downsizing, environment, hot flashes, information anxiety, relocation, stuttering, weekend depression, and writer's block. The author emphasizes what people under stress can do for themselves using alternative techniques, self-help, and self-healing, although she does also cover the pharmacological approach.

There are more than 500 entries, with an average length of 400–500 words. The longest entry, *depression*, covers almost six pages. Many of the entries include *see also* references. Many are also followed by contact information for agencies and organizations, such as the National Association of Anorexia Nervosa and Associated Disorders. Where applicable, the source(s) of information for the topic covered is also included at the end of the entry. A 14-page bibliography at the end of the volume includes works consulted arranged by topics, such as addictions, alternative therapies, cancer, and divorce.

This resource is not intended to provide complete information on any one stress-related topic, but as an overview it would be a helpful addition to almost any reference collection, including medical libraries, public libraries, high-school libraries, and academic libraries.

Dictionary of Space Technology. 2d ed. By Joseph A. Angelo. 1999. 487p. appendixes. illus. tables. Facts On File, $50 (0-8160-3073-1). DDC: 629.4.

There have been many developments in space technology since the first edition of this work was published back in 1981. The *Challenger* disaster, the Hubble Space Telescope, the Mars Pathfinder mission, and numerous other achievements and failures are all covered by this new edition. Similar to the first edition, the 3,000 alphabetical entries range in length from a single sentence to several pages, with most of the longer entries devoted to various missions or destinations. Although space programs from all nations are included, the emphasis is clearly on the U. S.

Entries are written for the general adult reader or student and do not rely heavily on mathematics for their explanations. The author is unashamedly a space enthusiast, and the writing sometimes reflects this position by promoting space exploration. Black-and-white diagrams and a few photos accompany some of the entries. Considering the availability of excellent public domain images related to space exploration, the quality of the illustrations in this work is disappointing. Appendixes list units of measure, conversion factors, and Web sites related to space exploration. Despite its poor illustrations, this work will be a useful tool for anyone interested in space exploration. A good companion on the reference shelf is *Who's Who in Space* (3d ed., Macmillan, 1999), which has astronaut biographies. Recommended for high-school, public, and academic libraries.

Encyclopedia of Women in Aviation and Space. By Rosanne Welch. 1998. 286p. bibliog. illus. index. ABC-CLIO, $65 (0-87436-958-4). DDC: 629.13.

Intended for high-school level and up, this encyclopedia profiles the women who pioneered the realm of flight for their gender. The introduction highlights some of these women and their specific accomplishments and obstacles. Many of the entries, such as Amelia Earhart and Mae Jemison, will be familiar to readers. Others, such as Katherine Stinson, the first woman to fly the U.S. mail, and Tamara Pamyatnykh, a World War II Russian bomber pilot, are less well known. The entire range of aviation is covered, so that there are entries for balloonists, commercial airline pilots, test pilots, skydivers, and aviation company executives, as well as astronauts and early aviation pioneers.

More than 250 entries, arranged alphabetically, vary in length from one column to several pages and are written in a conversational style. Biographical profiles, which make up most of the text, focus on aviation and related events in the subjects' lives, with only brief information concerning early lives. It would be helpful to have birth and death dates noted at the beginning of the entries instead of mentioned within text. For a number of the subjects, no birth or death dates are provided at all. Photographs, scattered throughout the book, offer readers a further glimpse of these women. In addition to biographical entries, some related topics are included. Among these are *Atlantis space shuttle*, *Tailhook sexual harassment scandal*, and *Women's Airforce Service Pilots* (WASPS). Each entry includes cross-references and bibliographic references. Full citations are contained in the bibliography at the back of the volume, which also includes organizational sources. Print resources include books, magazine articles, and Web postings. An index concludes the volume.

Information on many of these women can be found elsewhere. A number of the astronauts, for example, are profiled in *American Women in Science: 1950 to the Present* (ABC-CLIO, 1998). However, this volume provides a fresh perspective on their contributions by situating them within the context of other flight pioneers. It will be appropriate for high-school, public, and academic libraries needing materials for women's studies or to balance the information on men in aviation and space.

The Horse Encyclopedia. By Josee Hermsen. 1998. 312p. appendix. illus. index. Firefly, $19.95 (1-55209-305-0). DDC: 636.1.

This is the English-language edition of a fact-filled guide to the world of horses, originally published in The Netherlands. There are two main sections: one covering breeds of horses and the other dealing with the care of the horse and equestrian activities. Fifty breeds of horses and ponies are described in terms of their origins and physical characteristics. A color photograph accompanies the description of each breed. The section on breeds is followed by "Caring for Horses and Equestrian Sports," which includes an explanation of confirmation points, charts illustrating colors, leg and facial markings, and habits and characteristics of specific breeds. There are definitions of equestrian terms as well as sections on equipment, feeding, grooming, hoof care, equine diseases and disorders, and stable requirements. Training and riding basics, dressage terminology and exercises, show jumping, and driving are covered.

Although the focus of the book is European, there is a chapter on Western riding; and North American breeds are included. An appendix lists foundation sires and other well-know sires, and there is an alphabetical index.

The encyclopedia does a good job of covering the broad spectrum of information of interest to horse lovers. Although *The Horse Encyclopedia* is not as lavishly illustrated as Dorling Kindersley's *Encyclopedia of the Horse* [RBB D 1 94], almost all of the short but informative descriptions and explanations are accompanied by photographs, and young readers especially will find the format appealing. Both *International Encyclopedia of Horse Breeds* and *International Encyclopedia of Horses and Ponies* [both RBB N 1 95] cover more breeds, while *The Horse Dictionary* [RBB N 1 95] covers more related terms. *The Horse Encyclopedia* is recommended for school and public libraries needing another resource on the topic.

A Companion to California Wine: An Encyclopedia of Wine and Winemaking from the Mission Period to the Present. By Charles L. Sullivan. 1998. 368p. bibliog. illus. maps. tables. Univ. of California, $39.95 (0-520-21351-3). DDC: 641.2.

Some of those who settled California were winemakers who imported European varietal grapes to start their vineyards. Today California is among the world's top five wine producers and its top-quality products easily rival those of Europe's fine wineries. Anyone interested in wine history and lore will find *A Companion to California Wine* to be a useful guide.

Unlike standard consumer and tourist guides, this book's focus is geographical and historical. The alphabetical entries range in length from a few sentences to one page. They include all producers and wineries of historical importance (*Gallo, Inglenook*), place names (*Sonoma County, Stag's Leap*), grapes (*Cabernet, Chardonnay, Zinfandel*), wine types (*claret, sparkling wine*), technical terms (*fermentation, pest control*), and organizations (*Bureau of Alcohol, Tobacco, and Firearms; Wine Institute*). Cross-references appear in small capitals. Photographs, maps, and charts augment the text. Entries for counties include maps and charts of the amounts and types of grapes produced each year. Articles on technical processes explain them as they are used in the wine industry. An interesting entry on libraries provides the addresses and telephone numbers of California academic and special libraries with important wine collections. A bibliography, list of oral histories, list of sources for used wine books, and an index complete the book.

Although patrons concerned with evaluating and purchasing wines for consumption or collection will be better served with standard resources such as *The New Sotheby's Wine Encyclopedia* [RBB D 1 97] or Steven Koplan's *Exploring Wine* (Van Nostrand Reinhold, 1996), those interested in the colorful history of California's wine industry will find an excellent introduction here. Recommended for academic, special, and public libraries serving patrons interested in California history and/or wine.

The Wellness Nutrition Counter: The Essential Guide to Complete Nutritional Information for Over 6,000 Foods and Products. By Sheldon Margen and others. 1998. 479p. index. tables. Random, $34.95 (0-8129-3038-X). DDC: 641.2.

By the editors of the University of California at Berkeley *Wellness Letter* and the Wellness Nutrition Center, this is a welcome addition to consumer-oriented nutrition guides as an explanation of the importance of knowing what's in the foods we eat. Written in language that is clear and nontechnical, the volume is well laid out and easy to understand. Perhaps the most important information can be found in the opening sections, which explain the basics of a healthy diet, including the building blocks of nutrition, nutrient needs, 15 keys to a healthy diet, and how to read a food label.

The text is divided into three sections. "Vitamins and Minerals" describes the individual nutrients and provides a list of leading sources of each. "Foods, General" supplies the nutritional values of whole fresh and nonbranded foods based on the USDA Handbook 8 used by nutrition professionals. "Foods, Brand Name" includes nutritional data that come from the manufacturers on a variety of brand-name products, including the offering of fast food restaurants such as Burger King and Domino's Pizza. The weakest section is the index, which seems to be missing subjects contained in the book, such as Wendy's. And readers may be confused by the fact that mineral and vitamin contents of foods in the brand-name section are given as percentages of the RDI (Reference Daily Intake, the information that appears on manufacturers' food labels), while in the other sections they are expressed in terms of an average serving.

This volume is the only good alternative to the nutrition standard *Bowes and Church's Food Values of Portions Commonly Used* (17th ed., Lippincott, 1998). Although similar in cost to *Bowes and Church's*, this new resource seems to be more consumer-friendly. Neither volume does a very complete job of giving nutritional data for restaurants, but this information can be found for 37 national chain restaurants in *Fast Food Facts* (5th ed., IDC Pub., 1998).

Overall, *The Wellness Nutrition Counter* is recommended for most libraries. As consumers become more health conscious, books of this type will become even more popular. The price is right for all libraries. A good popular selection.

The Encyclopedia of Parenting Theory and Research. Ed. by Charles A. Smith. 1999. 501p. bibliog. index. Greenwood, $95 (0-313-29699-5). DDC: 649.

The market is flooded with parenting howto books, but a volume covering the theories and research related to parenting is long overdue. This encyclopedia, edited by an expert from the School of Family Studies and Human Services at Kansas State University, offers more than 240 entries on a variety of issues that illuminate the nature of the relationship between parents and children. Arrangement is alphabetical, but nine main categories or clusters are identified: child activity, child outcomes, child states, parent behaviors, parent state or context, external or community factors, system issues, resources, and people. The introduction provides a list of entries grouped into these categories, with no entry appearing more than once. Although it is possible to dispute where any single entry has been listed, the editor states in his preface that the categories are for convenience and have fluid boundaries and considerable overlap.

Entries, of approximately 1,000 words each, were written by more than 160 experts from a wide range of backgrounds including medicine, human development, psychology, education, learning, behavior, and counseling. Some of the individual entries include *feminism, Hispanic/Latino parents, mediation, motor development, problem solving, siblings* and *single parents*. The indexing is extensive. A general bibliography containing some of the classics in the field is included at the end of the book. Each contributor's entry contains a list of bibliographic references specific to the individual article. Entries are very well written and act as a good review of the literature and research related to the topic.

The target audience for this encyclopedia includes parents, educators, teachers, researchers, health and mental health professionals, community educators, librarians, and others interested in parentchild relationships. Smith is maintaining a Web site, *The WonderWise Parent* ([http://ksu.edu/wwparent/]) in anticipation of adding additional terms for a second edition. Overall, this encyclopedia provides a good summary of what is known about parenting and parentchild relationships. Highly recommended for academic libraries and public libraries with community interest in these areas.

Encyclopedia of Small Business. 2v. Ed. by Kevin Hillstrom and Laurie Collier Hillstrom. 1998. 1,061p. bibliogs. index. Gale, $395 (0-7876-1864-0). DDC: 658.02.

This outstanding, unique, one-stop source for relevant, in-depth articles on small-business topics is intended for entrepreneurs and owners/managers from a variety of backgrounds. The Hillstroms, who run an editorial services business, have developed the encyclopedia in recognition of the trend that suggests small business enterprises will continue to grow in size, number, and importance.

Arranged alphabetically, more than 500 one-to-four-page essays discuss current issues such as advertising on the Web, DSS (decision support systems), employee leasing, Internet commerce, and variable pay. All aspects of owning and managing a small business are covered, from managing money (*accounts payable, budgets and budgeting, seed money*) to managing people (*absenteeism, Family and Medical Leave Act, organizational chart*). Other articles explain various business-related concepts and practices: *downsizing, franchising, total quality management*. Each article is followed by a list of bibliographic citations, and often cross-references. Within the articles, bolded terms denote words or phrases that have separate entries.

The index found at the end of volume 2 contains an alphabetical list of subjects, names of institutions, organizations and associations, key government agencies, and relevant legislation. This detailed index is a highlight of the encyclopedia and adds greatly to the set's accessibility. Reference librarians, small-business owners/managers, scholars, and teachers will enjoy using EOSB and will find the information they need quickly and easily. The Board's only quibble is the price, but quality costs. Perhaps Gale could throw in an annual update for a year or two after purchase?

Fine Arts, Decorative Arts, Music

The Grove Dictionary of Art Online. Internet Database. 1998. Grove, call 1-800-221-2123 or visit |http://www.groveart.com| for subscription information. (Last accessed April 2, 1999.)

Launched in November 1998, the electronic version of the monumental *Dictionary of Art* |RBB D 15 96| is exactly that. *The Grove Dictionary of Art Online* (GDAO) makes use of the more obvious advantages of an electronic format. Thousands of links to additional images, additional articles, and full-text-searching capability make GDAO a fine alternative to the print version.

The Web site is graphically crisp, elegant, and easy to negotiate. From the main menu, users can select Introduction, Articles A–Z, Search, Indexes, and Appendixes. These choices are in a frame that is accessible while most sections of the GDAO are being consulted. The introduction is similar to that in the print version, providing its full text in electronic format with the same table of contents (alphabetization, illustrations, bibliographies, appendixes, and index) in clickable format. In some cases, differences between the print and electronic versions are explained. For example, the section on illustrations explains that all illustration references in the printed version have been retained, that all maps and drawings commissioned for the printed dictionary are available online, that there are links to images available elsewhere on the Internet, but that illustrations that appear in the printed dictionary but for which electronic reproduction restrictions apply are not presently available online.

Clicking the Articles A–Z category takes the user to the beginning of the article list, but columns in the left-hand navigation frame with letters A–Z (one column with uppercase and the other with lowercase letters) provide a more direct route to headwords. Choosing the uppercase letter connects to the first letter of the headword, and choosing a lowercase letter will take the user to the second letter in the headword. For example, a user searching for the article on Pre-Raphaelitism would choose the uppercase letter P to go to the beginning of the list of articles beginning with P, then the lowercase r to go to a list of articles with headings beginning with Pr.

Articles are accompanied by three buttons: Contents (a clickable outline), Images (either captions for illustrations in the print set or external image links), and Abbreviations (to search for the full form of the abbreviations used for locations of artworks, periodical titles, and so forth). Articles are identical to that in the print *Dictionary of Art*. The advantages, of course, are the ability to link directly to related articles and cross-references and being able to print or download articles. GDAO's other advantage is the ability to link to images available on external Web sites. There are now more than 10,000 Web links to museums, galleries, and collections. For example, the article about Pre-Raphaelite painter Sir Edward Burne-Jones includes links to 23 images ranging from a drawing of unknown date of a fragment of an ancient frieze to *The Magic Circle*, a gouache on paper executed in 1882, housed at the Tate Gallery, and made available on the Tate Gallery's Web site. The print version includes only two illustrations. The article for graphic artist M. C. Escher, a perennial favorite with secondary and college students, is unillustrated in the print edition, but the electronic version includes links to 13 images, most from the National Gallery of Art in Washington, D.C. Because linking to images takes the viewer from the Grove site to other Web sites, content at each location varies. Artists' most famous works are sometimes missing from the list of links. For example, the popular *Hylas and the Nymphs*, by Victorian artist J. W. Waterhouse, graces many dormitory rooms but is not among the images included in the list of links attached to the Waterhouse article. The 13 Escher images are not among the best known or the most frequently requested.

Besides providing external links, the Images button enables users to view captions of the illustrations that appear in the print set. Not all of the illustrations are available in the online version; picture frame icons indicate those that are—mainly maps, line drawings, and diagrams. Works of art that are captioned may or may not also be represented in the external links. For example, the article on Georgia O'Keeffe in the print set includes an illustration of *New York with Moon*. The online version does not include an illustration of this work, but does include links to 15 other O'Keeffe works in eight collections, each presented in the context of the collection.

GDAO is updated on a monthly basis. A list of additions and enhancements, called "new site developments," is available on the GDAO Web page. Because this list is accessible to both subscribers and nonsubscribers, it is not hyperlinked; it would be useful if subscribers could link directly from "new site developments" to the pertinent articles. New articles and links added for February 1999 include an article on Chris Ofili, winner of the 1998 Turner Prize, and images for Ingres, van Gogh, and Van Eyck. A recent partnership with the Bridgeman Art Library Online, representing more than 750 museums and other collections worldwide, will provide an additional 100,000 images by the end of 1999. There are currently no images available for Chris Ofili or for several other controversial artists (e.g., Robert Mapplethorpe) and subjects (*censorship*, *performance art*). The article *erotic art* includes only one image, of Gustave Courbet's *The Sleepers*. GDOA is probably not in danger of being monopolized by those desiring access to frisky images.

Searches can be done by article heading, full text, contributor, caption, or combinations of these. A full-text search for *tattoo* retrieved 90 references. In addition to the major *tattoo* article, these included geographical areas or cultural groups (*Japan*, *Maori*), a reference to tattooing within the article on erotic art in ancient cultures, tattooing in the context of graffiti art, and artists influenced by tattooing (e.g., English painter Peter Blake and Moroccan painter Ahmed Cherkaoui). The search term is highlighted within the article for easy identification. Hits are ranked from highest to lowest, with rankings given in percentages. Search Tips details simple searches, including searching for a phrase, truncation, and combining terms. More advanced searches can include combining multiple words in phrases or searching for words in more than one field. About 25 hits per page are displayed, with the option to click on numbered pages at the bottom of the list to move forward and backward through the list.

A link to a list of Help categories is available in the navigation frame at all times. Help is clear, straightforward, and covers most of the questions that arose during the Board's trial of GDAO. The list of contributors is the same as that in the print version, without hyperlinks. This is an example of a lost opportunity for value added beyond the print version. Links could easily have been made to existing Web pages of contributors.

Although it may be possible to locate many additional images in various nooks and crannies of the Web and in art books, GDAO provides the additional context and authority of links to museums and other collections that may offer more information about the piece, the artist, related works, and sometimes even an opportunity to acquire a print or poster of the piece. *The Grove Dictionary of Art Online* is a fine alternative to the print set, with its full-text searching and expanding image collection. Although it does not yet exploit the Web format as much as it could, it is still a valuable resource for academic and large public libraries. Grove is offering a discount price to libraries that own the print version.

Encyclopedia of Comparative Iconography: Themes Depicted in Works of Art. 2v. Ed. by Helene E. Roberts. 1998. 1,400p. bibliog. illus. indexes. Fitzroy Dearborn, $250 (1-57958-009-2). DDC: 704.9.

Many art reference sources identify works of art by title, artist, or medium. Identification on the basis of theme or subject has always been more problematic. It is also an approach that many students, teachers, and other library users interested in art wish to pursue. Reference sources taking this approach tend to be narrow in focus, such as those on religious iconography or depictions of saints. *Encyclopedia of Comparative Iconography* (ECI) expands the scope of the thematic guide to art to include mythological, biblical, and literary themes that have been represented in art of all periods and media. Roberts is editor of *Visual Resources: An International Journal of Documentation* and the book series *Documenting the Image* (Gordon and Breach).

ECI includes 119 signed, alphabetically arranged essays on actions (*harvesting*, *kiss/kissing*), situations (*upside down*, *widowhood*), and concepts (*whiteness*, *calumny*). Entries were written by 42 prominent contributors, most of whom are faculty in art history, classics, archaeology, or literature at universities in the U.S. Many of the contributors are full professors, department chairs, and authors of their own books. Among them are Diane Apostolos-Cappadona, author of The Encyclopedia of Women in Religious Art [RBB S 15 97].

Each essay is divided into sections on motifs and iconographic narratives that constitute subdivisions of the essay. For example, drunkenness/intoxication includes sections on Dionysius/Bacchus; Lapiths and Centaurs; the drunkenness of Noah, Judith, and Holofernes; and artists and alcohol in the twentieth century and in China. The essay addresses narratives that are the sources of the images, historical background, symbolism, variations in presentation, and how the theme evolved over time. Each section includes references to works of art depicting the theme. These are also listed by section and then in chronological order in a list of Selected Works of Art at the end of the essay. The theme Bacchanales and Related Subjects, for example, is depicted in 15 works from the Barberini Faun (c. 220 B.C.) to Picasso's Feast of the Fauns (1957). These references include artist, title, medium, date, and location (if known). Each essay includes one full-page black-and-white photograph illustrating a representative work of art. The Feast of the Fauns, for example, illustrates drunkenness/intoxication. A list of further reading includes books and periodical articles.

Seven indexes to terms discussed in the entries increase the likelihood that the user will find references to the subject being sought. An Index of Ancient Mythological and Historical Personages, Places, and Concepts, and an Index of Judeo-Christian Personages, Places, and Concepts help the user who is interested in a particular place or the narratives of particular characters, but isn't sure how themes relating to them are categorized. These are followed by an Index of References to the Bible and Other Sacred Books; an Index of Other Cultures, Religions, and Mythologies; an alphabetical Index of Artists and Works of Art; and an Index of Authors, Literary Texts, Composers, Filmmakers, and Folktales, which includes references from classical to contemporary, including Aesop, Benjamin Franklin, the musical Hair, and Walt Disney. A final Index of Other Names and Terms includes topics that appear in the essays but are not themselves mythological, religious, or literary, such as brothels, dogs, and puzzles.

In addition to the further reading included with each essay, the encyclopedia provides a bibliography of approximately 300 reference books in English and other European languages. The list includes the classics upon which scholars have traditionally relied for thematic information, such as Gertrud Schiller's Iconography of Christian Art (New York Graphic Society, 1971), George Ferguson's Signs and Symbols in Christian Art (Oxford, 1954), and James Hall's Dictionary of Subjects and Symbols in Art (Harper, 1979).

Editor Roberts points out that "there is no other reference book that uses the comparative method to describe the use of iconography in art that is organized from the point of view of actions, situations, or concepts rather than by the personages in mythical, biblical, or literary narratives." There is no doubt that many users seek access to artwork by subject and that few tools exist to aid them in their quests. Most users seeking simple depictions of an object (a snake or a volcano) have found Marsha Appel's Illustration Index I–VIII (Scarecrow, 1980–1998) useful. Those pursuing Christian iconography have relied on Schiller's Iconography of Christian Art. This comprehensive, two-volume work still sets the standard for Christian iconography with, for example, more than 80 pages and numerous reproductions devoted to the Crucifixion, as opposed to seven pages and one reproduction in ECI. The broad thematic arrangement and comparative analysis of classical and contemporary, as well as Christian themes, make ECI a complementary resource to Schiller.

There is also no doubt that ECI is thorough, scholarly, and effectively arranged with its numerous access points. Its lists of selected works of art for each theme are especially valuable, as this feature is not offered in some sources, such as Ferguson and Hall. The extent of its usefulness will depend on whether the desired subject is among the 119 themes included. The encyclopedia will be less useful to those trying to find artwork depicting literal subjects such as snakes or teapots—and any art librarian can tell you that there are requests like this—than for those seeking conceptual discussions of broad themes. These users will find ECI a treasure (discussed under abundance and luxury). Highly recommended for art, academic, and large public libraries.

Nineteenth-Century European Art: A Topical Dictionary. By Terry W. Strieter. 1999. 300p. bibliog. index. Greenwood, $90 (0-313-29898-X). DDC: 709.

This alphabetically arranged topical dictionary, containing approximately 750 entries, is a selective survey "of the major art movements, works of art (notably in painting and sculpture), art themes, people, and events of the period from 1789 to 1914." It also covers European historical developments that "impinged on the art community." The author, a professor of art history, has produced a highly readable text for college and university students.

Entries range in length from a sentence (calligraphic line, eclecticism, engraving) to two pages (music, theme of; Renoir, Pierre-Auguste). Each entry on a work of art contains its date and current location, a description of the work, and the context in which it was created. Asterisks are used to direct readers to other related entries in the dictionary, and there are numerous see references. Following entries in which specific artists, artworks, or art movements are mentioned, examples of artworks are given, with sources, set off in parentheses, where pertinent illustrations can be found. These references are specific and detailed, employing either page number, figure number, or color plate number, depending upon which designation is used in the source work. An approximately 125-entry bibliography and a detailed index conclude the volume. More specific and narrower in scope than the authoritative Oxford Dictionary of Art [RBB O 1 97], this succinctly written, cleanly laid out dictionary gives concise information, clear definitions, and precise, useful references for in-depth research. Recommended for academic and large public library collections.

Oxford Dictionary of Twentieth-Century Art. Ed. by Ian Chilvers. 1998. 528p. Oxford, $40 (0-19-211645-2). DDC: 709.04.

Covering every person, movement, or topic pertinent to twentieth-century art is the aim of Chilvers' newest addition to Oxford's group of art reference books. A revised and abridged edition of Harold Osborne's Oxford Companion to Twentieth-Century Art (1981), it also draws on the revised edition of The Oxford Dictionary of Art [RBB O 1 97]. One-fourth of 1,700 entries do not appear in either previous work, and those that do have been updated and expanded. The volume is geared to the general reader and includes information on painting, sculpture, and graphic and other visual arts. Architecture, design, photography, and the applied arts are not included.

Based almost entirely on secondary sources, the alphabetically arranged entries cover artists who were alive in the twentieth century but exclude those whose main influence was in the nineteenth century. No artist born after 1965 has an individual entry. Entries are mainly biographical; entries about movements, styles, or artistic techniques include their historical background, main proponents, and an assessment of their influence or importance. The work is sprinkled with anecdotes that flesh out the facts, and is chiefly concerned with art and artists in English-speaking countries, particularly Britain and the U.S. Clearly marked cross-references add to the usefulness of the book, and the brevity of the entries (the shortest is four lines, the longest six columns) enables ready access to facts. There are no illustrations. Page numbers are difficult to use, as they are located at the top inside gutter of each page.

This work will be useful for ready reference or browsing, and the clear, well-written entries will aid both library users and librarians. Those libraries that wish to update the Oxford Companion to Twentieth-Century Art, or that find the brief entries in The Oxford Dictionary of Art not meaty enough, will want to add this to their collections. Recommended for high-school, public, and academic libraries.

A Dictionary of Architecture. By James Stevens Curl. 1999. 833p. bibliog. illus. Oxford, $45 (0-19-210006-8). DDC: 720.

Compiled by an architectural historian, this wide-ranging work is intended for the lay public and beginning researchers. The author has written several other books, primarily on British architecture.

Alphabetically arranged, more than 5,000 entries are presented in the familiar two-column per page Oxford Companion format. Coverage is from ancient Egypt and Babylonia to the present. In addition to definitions of terms, there are entries for styles, types of buildings, regional movements, and major architects, from Filippo Brunelleschi to Helmut Jahn. Entries treat the English-speaking world, Europe, and Latin America, but there are no entries for the architecture of individual countries. There is, however, peripheral coverage of Asian, Oriental, and Colonial architecture. The compiler states that no comprehensive attempt was made to cover Buddhism, China, India, Islam, and Japan except when there had been influence on Western architecture.

Entries range in length from one line to two pages, often with brief bibliographical citations of further information sources. (Full citations can be found in the extensive bibliography at the end of the dictionary.) An asterisk next to a name or term indicates an entry under that heading. Approximately 200 clear black-and-white line drawings of architectural details and plans support selected definitions. The dictionary concludes with a 71-page bibliography of more than 2,500 in- and out-of-print titles, the majority of which are in English, although other European-language material is found.

This is a straightforward work that should quickly become a staple reference source in libraries serving architectural beginners and scholars wanting quick information. Beginners will be satisfied with the basic entries, and advanced readers will be led to further material in the extensive bibliography. Its closest competitor, the familiar *Penguin Dictionary of Architecture*, has been expanded and is now called *The Penguin Dictionary of Architecture and Landscape Architecture* (5th ed., 1998). Another recent work, *Illustrated Dictionary of Architecture* [RBB S 1 98], focuses more on technical and stylistic elements. The Oxford volume is recommended for high-school, public, and academic libraries that do not already own the Penguin dictionary or that need an additional one-volume reference source on architecture.

Illustrated Dictionary of Architecture. By Ernest Burden. 1998. 261p. illus. index. McGraw-Hill, $49.95 (0-07-008987-6); paper, $29.95 (0-07-008988-4). DDC: 720.

Illustrated Dictionary of Architecture is a compilation of more than 5,000 photographs and drawings in nearly 1,500 entries that define the technical and stylistic elements of both current and historical architecture. Some definitions stand alone, but most are accompanied by at least one illustration.

Terms are arranged alphabetically. Definitions of similar elements are clustered together under one heading, for example, *geodesic dome*, *interdome*, *melon dome*, and *bellshaped dome* are all included under *dome*. All terms are listed in the alphabetical index at the end of the volume. Throughout the volume, *see* references guide the user to the correct term or cluster of terms.

Definitions are brief, generally no more than one or two sentences for most elements. The clear photographs and drawings, all in black and white, convey the definitions of the elements better than hundreds of words could. Often more than one illustration is used to show variations. *Doorway*, for example, has six photographs of different historical and modern examples. The buildings used to illustrate architectural elements are not identified as to date, location, or architect.

Two or three small black-and-white photographs are not enough to give more than the most general idea. There are no entries for architects. More comprehensive resources include *Dictionary of Architecture and Construction* [RBB O 1 93] and *The Penguin Dictionary of Architecture* (4th ed., Penguin, 1991), not to mention the 34-volume *Dictionary of Art* [RBB D 15 96]. However, *Illustrated Dictionary of Architecture* is very useful in making clear just what is meant by terms such as *crocket ornament*, *impost*, and *rustication*. It is an excellent resource for interested laypeople as well as professionals in the field and is recommended as a ready-reference tool for public, academic, and high-school libraries.

The World Encyclopedia of Comics. 7v. Rev. ed. Ed. by Maurice Horn. 1999. appendixes. bibliog. glossary. illus. indexes. Chelsea House, $245 (0-7910-4854-3). DDC: 741.5.

Updating a comprehensive reference classic (originally published in 1976), this second edition adds some 200 new entries to the original 1,200 as well as revising 600 entries that appeared in the first edition. A large proportion of the new entries comes from areas of the world that were underrepresented in the 1976 edition: Asia, Africa, and Eastern Europe. The purpose is the same as that stated in the foreword to the first edition: "to cover the entire field of comic art in all of its aspects—artistic, cultural, sociological and commercial—on a global scale." The book's format remains largely unchanged, even though the content has been thoroughly revised.

The 31-page essay on the history of comics that focused on the U.S. in the previous edition has been updated and broadened to include coverage from all over the world. This is followed by a revised world chronology of comic art, updated through 1997, and an unchanged extended essay analyzing comics as art.

The main body of the work consists of the alphabetized entries of comic strips and the creators and producers of comics. On almost every page, Horn has inserted black-and-white relevant examples of comic strips; and in this edition, he has substituted newer or more illustrative examples of comic art. An appealing and thoroughly revised 80-page section of color comic art reproduction appears in volume 3. Revisions and expansions of other essays by the book's contributors (such as a history of newspaper syndication), a glossary, a bibliography, and several appendixes (including the Code of the Comics Magazine Association of America and the "official facsimile of excerpts from the record of the U.S. Senate Subcommittee of the Committee on the Judiciary to Investigate Juvenile Delinquency" in 1954) follow the main entries.

The three indexes have been expanded to seven, allowing readers to access information by proper name, title, media, contributors' names, geographical location, illustrations in the book, and general subject.

Those libraries with the first edition of *The World Encyclopedia of Comics* should replace it with this revised version. Other academic libraries, some high-school libraries, and all but the smallest public libraries should also purchase this reference bible on a fascinating subject.

Music in the 20th Century. 3v. Ed. by Hao Huang and others. 1999. 800p. bibliog. glossary. illus. index. Sharpe, $299 (0-7656-8012-2). DDC: 780.

In this broad approach to music of the twentieth century, classical and popular genres stand side by side. Among the 500 headings included are those for performers (The Beatles, Billie Holiday, Whitney Houston, Machito, Lauritz Melchior); composers (George Gershwin, Darius Milhaud, Thelonious Monk, Carl Orff); types of music (*Colombian cumbia, electronic music, gypsy music, hard bop, highlife, opera, zouk*); places (*Cuba, the Middle East, South East Asia*); and other aspects (*film music, impressionism in music, indie bands, recording studios, rock festivals*). Most of the signed, alphabetically arranged entries range in length from one to two pages. Contributors, whose credentials are noted in the last volume, are academics and music journalists. Entries are clearly written and are appropriate for high-school level and up. Page layout is attractive, with sharp, well-chosen black-and-white photos accompanying many articles and a sidebar with reading and listening suggestions. In the last volume, a biographical digest of more than 1,000 names provides brief information on important persons and groups that did not get a full article, such as Garth Brooks, Kronos Quartet, John Lennon, and Marian McPartland. A glossary, bibliography, and index conclude the set.

Although not an essential purchase for larger libraries that may have the in-depth coverage of pricier, more specialized titles on classical, popular, and world music (e.g., *The New Grove Dictionary of Music and Musicians* [Grove, 1995], *The New Grove Dictionary of Jazz* [Grove, 1996], *The Encyclopedia of Popular Music* [RBB Ap 1 99], and volumes in the Garland Encyclopedia of World Music series), smaller libraries may find this set a useful and more affordable addition to the reference collection.

Oxford Composer Companion to J. S. Bach. Ed. by Malcolm Boyd. 1999. 626p. appendixes. bibliogs. glossary. illus. Oxford, $45 (0-19-866208-4). DDC: 780.92.

Oxford University Press is inaugurating a new series of composer companions with an impressive work on J. S. Bach. Edited by the noted Bach scholar Boyd, this first English-language A–Z encyclopedia on Bach has more than 900 entries written by 44 contributors. The contributors are well chosen, writing on their interests—Russell Stinson wrote the entry on the *Orgel-Buchlein* ("Little Organ Book") and has also completed a book on the same collection of organ chorales. The consultant editor is John Butt, who edited *The Cambridge Companion to Bach* (1997), which includes essays on Bach's life and works as well as on his influence on modern music.

The Oxford volume provides short and long entries, many with bibliographies, on aspects of Bach's life, family, pupils, and employers; musical and technical terms; and individual works. Short articles include descriptions of *cadenza fantasia*, *timpani*, and *watermarks*. There are also a number of entries for current Bach festivals and twentieth-century musicians noted for Bach interpretations, such as Glenn Gould and Nikolaus Harnoncourt.

Extensive essays cover Bach's major works (*Brandenburg Concerto*, *Mass in B Minor*) and types of compositions (*chorale*, *fugue*). One of the longest entries, *reception and revival*, surveys Bach's impact on various national musical traditions. Another discusses recordings. Black-and-white illustrations of Bach, his sons, places important in his life, a family tree, manuscripts of his works, and a map of his Germany enhance the text. Appendixes list Bach's works by category and title both with BC (*Bach Compendium*) and BWV (*Bach-Werke-Verzeichnis*) catalogue numbers. A "Thematic Overview" at the beginning of the volume lists entries by topic. There is also a brief glossary of musical terms. This volume should be considered a significant resource in the study of one of the most amazing composers who ever lived. Recommended for academic, public, and, of course, music libraries.

The Encyclopedia of Country Music. Ed. by Paul Kingsbury. 1998. 634p. appendixes. illus. Oxford, $55 (0-19-511671-2). DDC: 781.642.

Oxford University Press takes on country music in a 1,300-entry encyclopedia compiled by the staff of the Country Music Hall of Fame and Museum.

The encyclopedia is primarily biographical, but does contain some other entries such as *field recordings, jukeboxes,* Opryland USA, *western swing,* etc. Ten essays by specialists on various aspects of country music are scattered throughout the book.

The book's biographical entries include early performers like W. R. Calaway, legends like the Carter Family, newcomers like Shania Twain, and behind-the-scenes people like producer Jim Ed Norman. Each signed profile includes date and place of birth and date of death, where appropriate. The narrative mixes a varying amount of personal data with the professional careers. Important songs, recordings, contracts, tours, and other details are listed. Some entries are illustrated with black-and-white photos, and most close with a select discography.

None of the entries are very long. Hank Williams and costume designer Nudie rank about a page, Johnny Cash about one and a quarter page, and Kathy Mattea a half page. *See* and *see also* references are helpful, since there isn't an index. The entries are current through the beginning of 1998, so Tammy Wynette's death is noted. In addition to the 150 black-and-white illustrations, there is a 16-page color section of country music cover art. The book closes with appendixes of best selling records, Grammy and Country Music Awards, and other similar lists.

After a drought, the 1990s have seen a resurgence in country music publishing. However, it has been a couple of years since *Definitive Country* [RBB S 1 95] and *The Comprehensive Country Music Encyclopedia* [RBB F 1 95]. *All Music Guide to Country* [RBB N 1 97], a bio-discography, was published in 1997. Since then, old favorites like Grandpa Jones and Minnie Pearl have left us. Young performers like LeAnn Rimes have emerged. Public and academic libraries will definitely want to consider buying this volume to update their earlier titles, if they have country fans as patrons.

The Encyclopedia of Popular Music. 8v. 3d ed. Ed. by Colin Larkin. 7,000p. bibliog. discographies. indexes. Muze, dist. by Grove, $750 (1-56159-237-4). DDC: 781.64.

In its third edition, *The Encyclopedia of Popular Music* now has more than 18,500 entries, which add up to make this the most comprehensive reference work of its kind. The second edition, originally published in 1995, was called *The Guinness Encyclopedia of Popular Music* [RBB Ap 15 96] and had approximately 15,000 entries. The detail and comprehensiveness found in the new set's eight volumes (up from six) are impressive. In creating it, author and editor Larkin has truly placed the stamp of legitimacy and respect on the study of popular music. The genres of rock, country, soul, jazz, rap, folk, New Age, blues, and R & B and the music of Tin Pan Alley are all represented, but popular composers in the classical vein (Aaron Copeland, Charles Ives) are consciously omitted. The focus is upon music from or popular in the U.S. and the United Kingdom. It is impossible to be completely objective about any form of music, a subject on which contributors have likes and dislikes that inevitably come through in at least some of their writing. However, Larkin has succeeded in editing to meet his criterion: "to strike a balance between being highly opinionated and dead boring."

More than three-quarters of the entries have been enlarged, and new ones have been added. Main headings, as in past editions, cover individuals (including singers, writers, producers, actors, session players), bands, albums, films, musical theater, record labels, and concepts. Entries range in length from a paragraph or two (for some albums, stage and screen titles, and people) to one or more pages for more influential artists (Billie Holiday, George Gershwin, The Rolling Stones, Stephen Sondheim, Sun Ra) and other topics (*Atlantic Records, jazz writing*). There are numerous people and bands here that most of us have never heard of, which makes the encyclopedia fun for browsing. For individuals and groups, birth and death or formation and breakup dates are given when available, and careers are followed from early influences to albums, concert tours, and collaborations. Song titles are frequently mentioned, and there is a mammoth song-title index in the last volume. Following each narrative is a chronological album discography (usually, but not always, complete), with original label name and date and star rating; compilation albums are listed separately. As explained in notes on style, the five-star rating system for albums (new to this edition) is different from that used in other forums. Here, ratings indicate a comparison between the various works that that performer has produced. For instance, a Heart four-star album is that much better than a Heart one-star album, but it is not necessarily the critical equivalent of a Beatles four-star album. Ratings are assigned by the editor and a few contributors and take into account critical opinion. Larkin has also begun the huge task of adding a list of videos for more recent performers, and he has added to the further reading lists appended to many entries.

For each of the 1,500 key albums important enough to rate a separate entry, the writing conveys a sense of the work's musical characteristics, critical reception, social importance, and how it reflects the performer's development at that point. Significant and hit tracks are singled out; for instance, Public Enemy's 1990 "'Fight the Power' still bites harder than just about any other track in rap's history." A list of all tracks, album release dates, and U.K. and U.S. peak chart positions are given. It would be helpful if there were a single list in an appendix of these seminal works. Although album entries contain cross-references (designated by boldface) to their creator, the reverse is not always true. For example, under *Public Enemy*, there is nothing that would tell the reader that there are separate entries for several of their works. In the next edition, perhaps boldface cross-references could be used within a performer's album listings, rather than in the text, where the album may not even be mentioned.

Film and musical entries outline plot and characters and focus on notable songs. Occasionally the words "film musical" or "stage musical" appear in parentheses following titles, but only to distinguish between two or more identical entries (e.g. *Grease*); this means that it is often hard to tell which form is under discussion until halfway through the entry. In the entry *Good Times*, the reader doesn't know until the fourth sentence that this is a Sonny and Cher film, not an album. For companies, such as Sun, Verve, and Windham Hill, we get an overview of the careers of artists who recorded for them and a sense of the musical style(s) the labels promoted. *Grunge*, AOR (adult orientated rock), and *rockabilly* are examples of entries that define musical genres, although *New Age* can't be found. Country Music Association and the Rock and Roll Hall of Fame are just two of the many institutions covered.

In the last volume, there is a bibliography by artist, which duplicates the reading lists found at the end of entries but adds publishers and dates. A bibliography by subject (blues, punk, and so forth), a list of selected fanzines (often with corresponding Web sites), and the song title index follow. A general index nearly 300 pages long and a quick reference guide to main headings conclude the set. There are several problems with the general index. The only information provided under each index entry are page numbers, but the lack of printed page ranges on the book spines, combined with the omission of a page range by volume key on the index pages, makes for a frustrating search because, for example, the reader must guess which volume contains page 4,053. On the plus side, the indexing to internal references seems to be incredibly thorough.

Spelling and typographical errors do exist, although not in noticeably large numbers. Inevitably, there are some omissions. Bobby Sherman, bubble-gum phenomenon of the early 1970s, was left out, although perhaps there is an editorial statement to be found there. Larkin does have 29,500 headwords still waiting to have entries prepared, so expect either supplements (which would be more economical for libraries) or new editions in the years to come. Problems are certainly minor, in the end, given the enormous scope of this encyclopedia. Any library that can afford the hefty price tag should have this resource in its collection on music and popular culture. Those libraries in which the previous edition has received heavy use will want to update.

Fine Arts, Decorative Arts, Music

The American Musical Film Song Encyclopedia. By Thomas S. Hischak. 1999. 522p. appendixes. bibliog. glossary. index. Greenwood, $69.50 (0-313-30737-7). DDC: 782.1.

In this companion to his earlier *American Musical Theatre Song Encyclopedia* (Greenwood, 1995), Hischak first explains the ways that film musicals in general, and specifically the use of songs in a movie, differ from stage musicals. Films need fewer songs, and they do not use songs as readily to explicate plot and character. That said, he had no problem selecting 1,760 songs from 500 film musicals, ranging from 1927's *The Jazz Singer* to Disney's 1996 animated *Hunchback of Notre Dame* and 1997's *Evita*. For the purposes of this book, a film musical is defined as having at least three songs sung by the story's characters. Songs from films based on stage musicals are not found here, unless they appeared only in the film version. For instance, "Something Good," unique to *The Sound of Music* film, is listed, but not "My Favorite Things." An appendix of famous movie songs from other sources lists song titles (e.g., "Fascinatin' Rhythm," "Ain't She Sweet") and their origin—either the name of the stage musical or the year if the song was simply a Tin Pan Alley hit.

Entries are arranged alphabetically by song title and provide the names of the lyricist, composer, singer and/or actor, character name(s), and film title and year. The author gives the context of the song (why, where, to whom it was sung) and any notable aspects of it (words, mood, rhythm, delivery). Performers who later had a hit with the number are listed. Hischak has a knack for immediately conveying the flavor of a song with just a few words: "optimistic little ditty," "chipper announcement of romance," and "pathetically cheery song of advice" are examples of his introductory statements for each entry. Browsers will find interesting facts about both the familiar and the obscure. Appendixes note alternate song titles, best-song Oscars, Oscar-nominated film musicals, and the film musicals covered in this volume. A glossary (defining such terms as *interpolation, ballad, release*), bibliography, and detailed index to composers, lyricists, singers, actors, and song and film titles are also included.

Although there are other reference works on the musical film, this one has the most comprehensive, annotated coverage of individual songs from film. Facts On File's *Hollywood Song: The Complete Film & Musical Companion* [RBB Jl 95] covers more films (7,000, including some nonmusicals) but does not devote a paragraph to each song it lists. *Encyclopedia of the Musical Film* (Oxford, 1981) describes some outstanding song titles but has a greater emphasis upon the films as a whole and biobibliographies of composers and lyricists. If all one needs are the unadorned facts, most of the songs in Hischak are listed in Lissauer's *Encyclopedia of Popular Music in America* (Paragon House, 1991). *The American Musical Film Song Encyclopedia* is recommended for comprehensive music and film collections.

Collins Musicals. By Michael Patrick Kennedy and John Muir. 1998. 416p. appendix. glossary. indexes. HarperCollins; dist by Trafalgar Square, $24.95 (0-00-472067-9). DDC: 782.1403.

Collins Opera and Operetta. By Michael White and Elaine Henderson. 1998. 478p. glossary. indexes. HarperCollins; dist. by Trafalgar Square, $24.95 (0-00-472061-X). DDC: 782.103.

The first of these volumes is an easy-to-use guide to 180 musicals, from *Floradora* (1899) to *Rent*. The introductory material provides a concise history of the development of musical theater, as well as defining the various forms of modern musical comedies (operetta musical, story musical, star vehicle, nonlinear musical, and so forth). The musicals are arranged in alphabetical order by title. Each entry provides the same information: name of musical; who wrote the lyrics, music, and book; opening date and number of performances in New York and London; principal characters; original cast members in New York and London productions; plot summary; musical highlights; a trivia section entitled "Did You Know?"; and excerpts from critical reviews. There is a recommendation of recordings, usually by the original cast, for those interested in hearing the songs. If a film version or television production has been made, that information is also provided. Brief biographies of the composers and lyricists are compiled in an appendix. There are two indexes, one for musical title and one for song title.

Arrangement is alphabetical by composer in *Collins Opera and Operetta*, which surveys more than 70 composers from the seventeenth century to the present, and more than 180 works. The introduction provides a concise historical overview of the development of this musical form from its origins in Renaissance Florence. The entries follow a similar format: the name and dates of the composer, a list of compositions, a brief biography with emphasis upon the musical career, and a synopsis of the major operas presented in alphabetical order. For each work there is a critical look at the music and its background, the highlights of the piece, and a recommended recording where available. Many works also have a box entitled "Did You Know?," which gives one or two items of trivia about the opera: for example, Gounod's *Faust* is one of the most successful operas ever written, with 1,000 performances in Paris alone in 1894; and the Cairo premier of Verdi's *Aida* was delayed because the costumes and sets were trapped in Paris during the Franco-Prussian War. In addition to a glossary, there are two indexes, one for composers and one for operas and operettas. A third index listing important characters would have been useful, but its omission does not diminish the value of the book.

There are several more comprehensive books on musical theater, including Bordman's *American Musical Theater*, 2d ed. [RBB Jl 92], Ganzl's *Encyclopedia of Musical Theatre* [RBB S 1 94], Suskin's *Opening Nights on Broadway* (Schirmer, 1990), and *More Opening Nights on Broadway* [RBB Je 97]. Opera is well served by, among other titles, *The Harper Dictionary of Opera and Operetta* [RBB Ja 15 91] and *The Viking Opera Guide* [RBB O 1 94]. *Collins Musicals* and *Collins Opera and Operetta* are informative and entertaining, and might be considered as supplemental purchases by public and academic libraries.

Songwriters: A Biographical Dictionary with Discographies. By Nigel Harrison. 1998. 643p. bibliog. glossary. index. McFarland, $125 (0-7864-0542-2). DDC: 782.42164.

Harrison pays tribute here to the people without whom there would be no—songs to sing—1,054 composers and lyricists of popular nineteenth-and twentieth-century song in the U.S. and United Kingdom. Inclusion criteria are commercial or critical success, or influence on other songwriters or performers. Performance artists who write little of their own work are not listed.

Alphabetically arranged by name, entries note dates and places of birth and death (if applicable), birth name (if it was later changed), and primary profession (e.g., rock producer, pop vocalist, C&W guitarist). Career summaries that range from a sentence or two to a lengthy paragraph give the essentials in an engaging manner. Composers from all genres of music are represented, including Tin Pan Alley, country, rhythm and blues, rap, rock, blues, jazz, and stage, among others. The longest part of each entry lists chart compositions by song title, date, and peak rank on U.S. and U.K. charts; albums by title, date, and rank; compilations; and hit versions of the subject's works by other performers. For some composers, such as Irving Berlin or Burt Bacharach, entries can run more than two pages.

The real strength of this work is these chart listings; no other reference work provides such detailed information gathered under the original songwriter's name. For longer biographies of songwriters, patrons may be referred to David Ewen's *American Songwriters* (H. W. Wilson, 1987), or more general works, such as *The Guinness Encyclopedia of Popular Music* [RBB Ap 15 96]. An excellent index to songs, albums, people, and groups mentioned within entries allows one to find who wrote *Bird in a Gilded Cage*, or to determine the front man for the group Simply Red. For all music reference collections.

Who's Who in Opera: A Guide to Opera Characters. By Joyce Bourne. 1998. 457p. appendix. illus. index. Oxford, $35 (0-19-210023-8). DDC: 782.1.

Compiled by the associate editor of the *Oxford Dictionary of Music* (Oxford, 1984), this biographical dictionary of characters also contains brief plot synopses.

Coverage is from Monteverdi to the present and includes more than 2,500 characters from 279 major works. Each entry is arranged alphabetically by character name and places the character in the context of the plot. The creator of the role is noted, with the year of first performance. Minor characters are treated in a sentence or two, while entries for major characters may cover several pages. In addition to their main entry, 27 characters, including Brunnhilde (from Wagner's *The Ring*), Leporello (from Mozart's *Don Giovanni*), and Violetta (from Verdi's *La Traviata*), are the subjects of essays by noted interpreters of the role, directors, or critics. Each of the special essays is accompanied by a murky black-and-white photograph of a performer in appropriate costume, but the poor quality of the illustrations makes them of little value.

There are two appendixes. The first provides brief biographies of 26 of the authors of the special essays, and the second is an index of composers, with a list of their operas and characters that are entered in the main work.

This clearly written and arranged volume will be a useful information source in any library with readers interested in opera.

Performing Arts, Recreation

The Princeton Review Guide to Performing Arts Programs. By Carole Everett and Murial Topaz. 1998. 516p. appendixes. Random, $24.95 (0-375-75095-9). DDC: 790.2.

Here is a resource that provides descriptions of more than 700 colleges, high schools, and summer programs in music, drama, and dance. Coverage is international. Each entry has contact information and a description of the institution, including institution type, enrollment, entrance requirements, course information, costs and financial aid options, application information, housing options, and services and facilities. Some entries include the names of instructors, choreographers, and notable alumni.

In addition to information about performing arts programs, the book provides guidance in choosing a program. The first five chapters offer specific information on both the decision-making and the application process and include special chapters for actors, dancers, and musicians; addresses for performing arts organizations; and sample resumes. Programs are grouped into high-school, college, and summer programs, with the summer programs further divided into dance, drama, and music. Within these groups, individual programs are listed by state. Appendixes include lists of books and periodicals, addresses for performing arts organizations, and sample resumes.

Coverage is not comprehensive. One notable omission, for those interested in music programs in the Northwest, is the Cornish Music Institute in Seattle. The lack of a detailed index makes it cumbersome to look up individual programs that may or may not be included. Nonetheless, this is a useful resource for researching and applying to performance arts programs across the U.S. and abroad. Recommended for high-school and public libraries.

Dictionary of Television and Audiovisual Terminology. By Moshe Moshkovitz. 1998. 208p. McFarland, $39.95 (0-7864-0440-X). DDC: 791.45.

Television has a language that is often so specific and idiosyncratic that general dictionaries prove insufficient. This book began when Moshkovitz was teaching a college-level technology course and decided to compile a list of some common terms. That list eventually grew into the more than 1,500 words and phrases defined here, "the terms used by professionals in everyday work and professional publications of the television and telecommunications industry worldwide." Terms related to both video and audio are included.

The dictionary is arranged in strict alphabetical order with acronyms filed as words and numbers filed as spelled. The definitions are clear and often have examples or descriptive information. The terms included span the breadth of the field: characteristics (*hue, hum*), individual roles (*gaffer*), equipment (*delay distribution amplifier*), devices (*edit controller, standards converter*), technologies (DVD), and many acronyms (B-Y, EOT, MIDI). Not all the terms are technical; there are definitions for *jingle, promo,* and *superstation*. There are also some terms from electronics and computer science. Although most definitions are brief, some, such as *lens* and *studio*, take up nearly a page. *Camera (video)* is more than two pages in length. The type font, page layout, and paper assist in lightening the dense nature of longer definitions. Recommended for libraries with television/audiovisual collections and for those that collect subject-specific dictionaries.

Encyclopedia of Chinese Film. By Yingjin Zhang and Zhiwei Xiao. 1998. 472p. bibliog. illus. indexes. Routledge, $140 (0-415-15168-6). DDC: 791.43.

As the note at the beginning of the text indicates, the aim of this volume is to provide "comprehensive coverage of Chinese film in its historical, cultural, geo-political, generic, thematic, and textual aspects." The contributors include film critics and scholars.

Part 1 offers six essays on Chinese, Hong Kong, Taiwanese, and "transnational" cinema, as well as Chinese film in the West and foreign films in China. These essays, which are signed, provide a sense of the development of film from its introduction (in China and Hong Kong in 1896, in Taiwan in 1900); the way each country's history influenced the subject matter; the flow of film between mainland China, Hong Kong, and Taiwan, which led to the notion of transnational cinema; and the growth of Western films in China. For many readers this is the first opportunity to learn about the challenges faced by the film industry in China, including the lack of control on the importation of Western films and the desire to develop a new cinematic language that differed from the classic Hollywood story.

Part 2 consists of alphabetically arranged entries on genres, topics (e.g., *propaganda and film*), persons (directors, actors, producers), and themes, as well as 300 individual films. Some of these, such as *Farewell My Concubine*, may be familiar to American audiences. The film entries provide the title in English with the Chinese title in parentheses, director, actor(s), studio, date of release, synopsis, and awards. Most entries conclude with brief annotated lists of resources for further reading. A classified contents list at the beginning of the volume and copious cross-references facilitate use.

The volume ends with a bibliography, a list of selected Web sites, and a glossary showing Chinese characters for all the proper names listed in the indexes, along with pinyin romanizations and English equivalents. Three indexes list titles, names, and studios.

Another recent book, McFarland's *Chinese Filmography* [RBB N 15 97], has entries for many more films but restricts its coverage to the output of studios in the People's Republic of China from 1949 to 1995. The wider-ranging Routledge volume is recommended to persons interested in international film as well as Chinese specialists who see in the medium another opportunity to study Chinese culture. It would be an asset in any university or large public library that offers a collection of or concentration in film or Asian studies.

Femme Noir: Bad Girls of Film. By Karen Burroughs Hannsberry. 1998. 656p. bibliogs. filmography. illus. index. McFarland, $75 (0-7864-0429-9). DDC: 791.43.

The film noir, according to Hannsberry, is recognized by its somber mood and tone; cynical heroes and villains; and visual elements like looming shadows, foggy nights, and rain-swept streets. Most of these films were produced during the 1940s and 1950s. The "femmes" of film noir are the actresses featured in these movies, and this book recounts the personal and professional stories of 49 of them.

Each entry begins with a striking black-and-white studio portrait set off by a black border and captioned with the entrant's name in large print. An essay ranging in length from 7 to 15 pages follows, providing a biography and an account of film roles. One, and sometimes two, publicity stills often accompany the text. Entries are finished off with a "Film Noir Filmography," in which the director, producer, cast, month/year of release, and running time of each film are listed. The references that follow are usually citations of magazines and newspaper articles, and, in a few cases, books.

Who are the femmes of film noir? Lauren Bacall, Joan Crawford, Ida Lupino, Barbara Stanwyck, and Gene Tierney are among the quintessential types. Less familiar are Peggy Cummins, Hope Emerson, Coleen Gray, Ella Raines, and Helen Walker. A few actresses better known for other kinds of film roles—Ava Gardner, Rita Hayworth, Marilyn Monroe, Jane Russell, and Lana Turner—are included because each appeared in at least a few noir films. A bibliography of several pages and an index by personal name and film titles completes a work suitable for reference and performing-arts collections in academic and large public libraries.

The Film Festival Guide: For Filmakers, Film Buffs, and Industry Professionals. By Adam Langer. 1998. 264p. index. Chicago Review Press, paper, $16.95 (1-55652-285-1). DDC: 791.43.

If you have patrons who welcome the thought of spending day and night in darkened rooms, eyes glued to the big screen, this book will help them find their next fix. Author Langer is a filmmaker who compiled this directory to film festivals worldwide when he could not find such data gathered in one location. Chapters include "Best of the Fests" (Langer's personal favorites), followed by chapters on North American, European, Asian, African and Middle Eastern, Australian, and South American festivals. Within chapters on geographic areas, there are two lists arranged alphabetically by festival name, one for detailed entries and one for brief entries. It would be more convenient to search an integrated list.

Detailed entries note place, time (e.g., first week of November), background (a descriptive paragraph giving the flavor of the fest), major award winners (although the year is not specified), number of films, celebrity sightings, ticket prices, and, for filmmakers, how to enter a film, contact information, and deadline. Brief entries have an address and often include phone, fax, e-mail, URL, and entry deadline and/or date of festival. Everything's here, from the big and famous (Cannes) to the small and specialized (Insect Fear Film Festival). Six interviews with festival directors are scattered throughout, and a final chapter is a guide to the best art-house movie theaters in more than 100 cities worldwide. The index follows the same arrangement as the rest of the book, with the various festivals grouped under chapter titles. An index listing all the festivals in a single alphabet would be a useful feature in the next edition; as it is, there is no way to locate the Insect Fear Film Festival without first knowing that it takes place in North America (Champaign-Urbana, Illinois, to be exact). Also useful would be a detailed geographic index. Although the book is arranged in broad geographic areas, it is not possible to look up more specific locations, such as Pennsylvania or France. Despite these shortcomings, any library with travel or film reference collections will want to consider adding this guide.

Guide to American Cinema, 1930–1965. By Thomas Whissen. 1998. 424p. appendixes. bibliogs. index. Greenwood, $79.50 (0-313-29487-9). DDC: 791.43.

Guide to American Cinema, 1965–1995. By Daniel Curran. 1998. 512p. appendixes. bibliogs. index. Greenwood, $79.50 (0-313-29666-9). DDC: 791.43.

The goal of Greenwood's Reference Guides to the World's Cinema series is to give "a representative idea of what each country or region has to offer to the evolution, development, and richness of film." These volumes cover 65 years of film production in the U.S., from the emergence of talking pictures through the release of *Toy Story*.

Whissen, a professor emeritus of English at Wright State University whose previous works include *Classic Cult Fiction* [RBB Je 1 & 15 92], considered such criteria as the availability of printed sources on a film or individual, professional recognition through awards or critical acclaim, notoriety, and contemporary appeal in selecting the actors, actresses, directors, and films featured in his guide to the early years. In addition, he included some films because they are cult classics or his personal favorites. For the volume covering the later years, Curran, a screenwriter, calls his selection process "purely subjective."

Entries appear in a single alphabetical sequence. Articles on individuals combine biographical and critical information and include filmographies, while those on films provide the date of release, the genre, and brief credits in addition to a lively narrative, blending descriptive elements with quotations from promotional materials and critical commentary. All entries in Whissen include a section listing awards and honors, and a bibliography of two or three books. Bibliographies are missing from many of the entries in Curran, though he does list some stage and television appearances for the actors he includes, as well as the names of sequels in his entries on films. Whissen's filmographies are more complete, extending into the 1990s, while Curran includes only selected "key" pre-1965 films for actors such as Paul Newman and Sidney Poitier. Additional features in Whissen include directories of film schools and film archives and museums, and a list of film festivals. In Curran, separate appendixes list films in the guide by year, notable producers and screenwriters with lists of credits, major studio releases by year, Academy Award winners, and films listed in the Library of Congress National Film Registry. Both volumes include selected bibliographies. There are no cross-references between related entries, but the indexes provide good access to people and films mentioned throughout the guides.

On the whole, both authors' selections are sound and understandable, and people and films missing from one volume can often be found in the other. Although there is little duplication, some actors, such as Marlon Brando and John Wayne, are discussed in both. Some areas are not sufficiently covered. For example, Whissen ignores animated features; thus, there are no entries for such Disney masterpieces as *Fantasia* and *Snow White and the Seven Dwarfs*. Curran has an entry for one Disney animated feature, *Beauty and the Beast*.

Looking at the two volumes side by side, with their slightly different approaches and emphases, illustrates one of the difficulties of publishing books in series without tight editorial control. The reference value of both would be enhanced if they could be used as a set, with the same kinds of information included in the entries, the same appendixes, and a cumulative index. Nevertheless, both are entertaining and informative, and both would be good additions to academic and large public library collections.

Hollywood Stunt Performers: A Directory and Filmography of Over 600 Men and Women, 1922–1996. By Gene Scott Freese. 1998. 280p. bibliog. filmography. illus. index. McFarland, $48.50 (0-7864-0511-2). DDC: 791.43.

This directory lists more than 600 men and women who have created the exciting action scenes in the movies. The work is risky, the compensation is low, the career span is limited, and the recognition is minimal. A few performers, such as Jock Mahoney and Branscombe Richmond, have graduated from stuntman to featured actor. The book is an attempt to alert movie fans to the names of those performers who have created memorable moments in films.

Using an A–Z arrangement, the book lists stunt performers who have at least ten major theatrical releases. Minimum personal information is given: a birth year, membership in a professional organization, doubling for a star, ethnic group, relationship to others in the industry, etc. Some entries do not give any personal information, just a listing of film credits.

It is difficult to know who the intended audience is for this book. The lack of addresses does not help the fan who wishes to contact a performer. Although film students may find it helpful for identifying performers in specific films, that task is made difficult by the fact that the index includes only a limited number of movie titles to help direct the reader to a performer. For the most part, the index is a listing of stars and refers the reader to stunt doubles. One can look up Kevin Bacon in the index, for example, and be led to the entry for Gary Jensen. There is nothing in Jensen's entry, however, to identify the films in which he played Bacon's double.

Black-and-white photographs, usually scenes from films, are included. The introduction provides a good overview of the profession, explaining the difficulties of finding work in the field and sustaining a career. A listing of stunt organizations is provided in an appendix. A bibliography concentrating on the technical aspects of films should be helpful for further research. Academic libraries serving film programs or large public libraries with comprehensive film collections might find this a helpful resource for identifying obscure performers.

On the Air: The Encyclopedia of Old-Time Radio. By John Dunning. 1998. 822p. bibliog. index. Oxford, $55 (0-19-507678-8). DDC: 791.44.

As he did in *Tune in Yesterday: The Ultimate Encyclopedia of Old-Time Radio* (Prentice Hall, 1976), Dunning here provides a storehouse of information about the people and programs of radio's Golden Age (1930s, 1940s, 1950s). The storehouse, however, has been thoroughly remodeled and refurbished. The amount of material covered has been considerably expanded and its presentation carefully reorganized.

Some 1,500 radio shows, listed in alphabetical order, are described in concise articles linked with an extensive system of cross-referencing. The cross-referencing is crucial, because someone looking for *Ozzie and Harriet* or *Sam Spade* will need to know that both programs are listed in the main part of the text under *The Adventures of . . .* . The articles vary in length, from the briefest of paragraphs (*The Billie Burke Show* and *Linda's First Love*) to several pages (*The Lone Ranger* and *The Mercury Theater of the Air*). Each program entry consists of title and broadcast history (including exact starting and ending dates, day and timeslot, network, announcer, sponsor, etc.). This is followed by an essay that often imparts all manner of detail, or, in the case of those short entries, a capsule description of the program.

Although the majority of the articles are about individual programs, there are also a number of survey articles, such as *sports broadcasts*, *concert broadcasts*, and *news broadcasts*. Here, too, the cross-referencing is essential in order to find information about a specific program that might fall under one of those categories and is not listed separately. There is an extensive bibliography, which will be of great help to those wishing to pursue the subject further.

In the electronically connected world of today, it is hard to imagine a time (not so long ago) when there was but one medium of electronic information. The rich detail in this solid work helps convey the flavor of that earlier time. Devotees of classic television shows may be surprised to find out that such programs as *Father Knows Best*, *Our Miss Brooks*, *Queen for a Day*, and *Sky-King* all started as radio programs. A worthy addition to most reference collections, this volume is an interesting portrait of a time when radio was more than background music or xenophobic talk shows. Another recent publication, the *Historical Dictionary of American Radio* [RBB Ag 98], covers a wider range of topics related to radio but has far less coverage of individual programs.

Plunkett's Entertainment & Movie Industry Almanac. Ed. by Jack W. Plunkett. 1998. 626p. appendixes. charts. indexes. Plunkett Research, P.O. Drawer 541737, Houston, TX 77254-1737, $149.99 (0-9638268-6-7). DDC: 791.4023.

Job seekers and financial investors sit high on the list of targeted audiences for this almanac—right alongside generalists, students, newcomers to the field, and seasoned industry analysts. In order to compile "the only complete guide to the entertainment and media industry," the editors have combined a directory of selected U.S. entertainment and media corporations with many other facets of the entertainment/multimedia field—a general overview of the entire entertainment/multimedia industry, career descriptions and outlooks for each related occupation, business trends, new products and technologies, international developments, and a host of statistical data. Aspects from advertising and budgeting, broadcasting and film production, retailing, gambling, and the Internet are examined.

The bulk of the almanac consists of "The Entertainment & Media 400," described as "our unique grouping of the biggest, most successful corporations in all segments of the American entertainment & media industry." Although the company profiles are quite detailed, the statistical and financial data are not current (usually 1996), and warnings appear throughout stating that numbers may have changed since publication. The corporate profiles are fairly standard but do include data about salaries and employee benefits, as well as making mention of women and/or minority officers or directors, advancement potential for women/minorities, and hiring and growth plans. These profiles are accompanied by several indexes, including rankings by industry group; geographical location; subsidiaries, brand names, and affiliations; and "hot spots for advancement for women and minorities" (based on company track records).

Career information comprises another substantial portion of the almanac. Detailed descriptions and discussions of careers and occupations in the entertainment and media field are adapted from *The Occupational Outlook Handbook*. Approximate salaries, training, education, licensing, employment projections, and more are all covered.

Much of this information can be found elsewhere but not in a single volume devoted to one industry. This resource is highly recommended for public, academic, and career-oriented libraries. Business libraries will want to consult other sources in order to obtain timely financial data. Plunkett publishes a number of other business and career guides, including *Plunkett's InfoTech Industry Almanac* [RBB Je 1 & 15 96].

The Reel Middle Ages: American, Western and Eastern European, Middle Eastern and Asian Films about Medieval Europe. By Kevin J. Harty. 1999. 316p. bibliog. illus. index. McFarland, $78.50 (0-7864-0541-4). DDC: 791.43.

The Middle Ages conjure up images of knights, castles, dragons, and fair maidens, brought to life by filmmakers from the earliest days of cinema to the end of the twentieth century. Harty has taken approximately 600 films and created a work that will benefit a wide audience.

The preface and introduction explain why a film such as *Dragonheart* was included and *Conan the Barbarian* excluded. Confining his selection to films about the European Middle Ages, Harty includes films from Japan, China, and India that fit his criteria. Certain stories have been told over and over, such as Joan of Arc, which was first filmed in 1897. Perhaps one of the greatest strengths of this work is the coverage of a large number of silent films. Wisely, Harty decided not to include Shakespearean films, which have been covered in other resources.

The filmography section gives the title of the film, alternate titles, production company, director, producer, and cast members. A synopsis of the film, which varies in length from a few sentences to several paragraphs, outlines the plot. An analytical or comparative section, which may address accuracy, point of view, production qualities, and other pithy observations, follows the summary. A bibliography of reviews, periodicals, and books with full citations completes each entry. A number of photographs are included. Major films such as *The Adventures of Robin Hood* starring Errol Flynn get the full treatment, including a photograph of Flynn. Full-length animated features, such as Disney's *Hunchback of Notre Dame*, receive equal treatment with nonanimated works. *Monty Python and the Holy Grail* is deemed "perhaps the funniest movie set in medieval times."

The bibliography provides a solid list of film resources. The index is especially useful, indicating both the entry number of each film and the pages on which other references to the film can be found. Numbers in boldface indicate pages with photographs.

A work such as this is important on a number of levels. It is a key work on how filmmakers have handled the Middle Ages, an excellent resource for teachers trying to locate good films on a particular medieval event, and a collection development tool to build a film library. It is also interesting to browse. Recommended for public and academic libraries.

The Sci-Fi Channel Encyclopedia of TV Science Fiction. By Roger Fulton and John Betancourt. 1998. 669p. Warner, paper, $15.99 (0-446-67478-8). DDC: 791.45.

TV-land has featured science fiction for 50 years, and one channel has certainly embraced the genre: the Sci-Fi Channel. This reference work covers more than 200 U.S. and British television series over the past five decades (up to spring 1998). It is based on Roger Fulton's *Encyclopedia of TV Science Fiction*, of which the latest edition was published by Boxtree in Britain in 1997. The U.S. version expands on the original, and is cowritten by sf author Betancourt.

The book encompasses more than the classic sf titles. Fantasies such as *She-Wolf of London* and *Xena: Warrior Princess*; time-travel programs such as *Quantum Leap* and *Time Tunnel*; even comedies such as *Get Smart* and *I Dream of Jeannie* are included because they contain science fiction elements. Because coverage is so broad, depth is sometimes lacking.

Each alphabetically arranged entry describes the series and usually lists each episode; about 10 percent of entries also describe each episode and list the cast and director. Credits for each series include the regular cast, production details, number and duration of episodes, B/W or color, and starting date. Entries vary in length from a half-page (*Tattooed Teenage Alien Fighters from Beverly Hills*) to more than 10 pages (*Star Trek*). In general, British programs tend to get greater coverage—*Space: 1999* creator Gerry Anderson's TV puppet shows, such as *Fireball XL5* and *Terrahawks*, are described in particular detail. A few series such as *The Adventures of Superman* are mentioned only briefly because other sources treat them in depth. *American Science Fiction Series of the 1950s* [RBB O 1 98], for example, devotes more than 60 pages to Superman. Sixteen pages of black-and-white photos complement the text. Around 40 short-lived series are given four-line coverage at the end; most are BBC productions. Disappointingly, no bibliography or index enrich the volume.

This volume appears to be designed for American audiences that might not have access to the original British volume. Its strength is its broad coverage; consult other works, such as the aforementioned *American Science Fiction Series of the 1950s*, for detailed treatment of specific series. Useful for public libraries with sf and TV readership.

Women Filmmakers and Their Films. Ed. by Amy Unterburger. 1998. 573p. appendix. bibliogs. illus. indexes. St. James, $110 (1-55862-357-4). DDC: 791.43.

Unlike other reference sources on people involved in the fine arts, drama, and cinema published by St. James (*Contemporary Artists*, *Contemporary Dramatists*, etc.), *Women Filmmakers and Their Films* consists of entries not only on women working in "behind-the-camera" cinematic jobs but also on films these women have helped make or direct. The scope is broad, encompassing women filmmakers from 34 countries, from the beginning of the cinema to the present.

Each of the 190 biographical entries consists of very brief biographical data, a complete filmography (with bolded cross-references for films that are treated in a separate entry), a short bibliography of published material by and about the entrant, and a one to three-page biocritical essay on the filmmaker. The selection of entrants represents a strong cross-section of women who have made significant contributions to the cinema, from early pioneers such as Alice Guy (1873–1968) and Lois Weber (1882–1939) to Jane Campion, Jodie Foster, and Penny Marshall.

The 60 entries on particular films include production information, names of cast and crew, a short bibliography of works on the film, awards won, and a one to two-page critical essay written by a film expert. The films selected for separate entries are generally movies that have been critically acclaimed, but there are some questionable inclusions and some serious omissions. Nora Ephron's feel-good film *Sleepless in Seattle* is included but not Barbra Streisand's *Yentl*. Penny Marshall's lightweight comedy *Big* has a separate entry but not her much more dramatic film *Awakenings*. Two of Leni Riefenstahl's films (*Triumph of the Will* and *Olympia*) are covered in separate entries, but there are no separate entries for films by Elaine May and Jodie Foster (although they are both covered in biographical entries).

Many large, clear black-and-white stills accompany both the film entries and the biographical entries. Prefacing the book's main body of entries are a short chronology about the historical and contemporary contributions of women in the cinema and two informative introductory essays on the history and current status of women filmmakers. Indexes include listings by nationality and occupation of the entrant, an award index, a film title index (with films in bold indicating separate film entries), and a selected list of distributors of women-made films.

This volume succeeds in highlighting the influence of women filmmakers and providing useful, accurate information on important moviemakers often excluded from other reference sources. It is recommended for academic libraries, large public libraries, and specialized film collections. In addition, high-school libraries supporting courses in filmmaking and film history should consider this informative reference source.

Women in Horror Films, 1930s. By Gregory William Mank. 1999. 403p. appendix. illus. index. McFarland, $45 (0-7864-0553-8). DDC: 791.43.
Women in Horror Films, 1940s. By Gregory William Mank. 1999. 393p. appendix. illus. index. McFarland, $45 (0-7864-0464-7). DDC: 791.43.

Mank has written several books about horror films, demonstrating a love for the genre. In these two volumes he treats the women who appear in these films in both starring and supporting roles. These actresses, such as Helen Chandler, Elsa Lanchester, and Fay Wray, portrayed heroines, femme fatales, misfits, and even monsters. They came from different backgrounds and achieved different levels of fame.

The format of both books is identical. Twenty-one actresses are covered in each volume, for a total of 42. The method of arranging the entries is not clear; it is neither alphabetical nor chronological. Photographs, both glamour shots and movie stills along with some posters, are included. Entries, which can be as long as 25 pages, cover the actress's life and work, with extended coverage of her career in films. Some of these women, such as Miriam Hopkins, made only one or two horror films, and others became typecast and appeared mainly in this genre, often in "B" pictures. The author interviewed the actresses if possible, friends and relatives if not. Each entry concludes with a complete filmography. Each volume ends with an appendix listing outstanding performances, based upon a poll of directors, writers, and producers. Categories include best performance by an actress as a horror heroine (Zita Johann in *The Mummy* in the 1930s volume, Evelyn Ankers in *The Wolf Man* in the 1940s volume), best monster, best supporting actress, best "voluptuary," most beautiful, and Mank's all-time favorite performance. An index of names, films, and so forth completes each volume.

Biographical information on these movie stars can be found in other sources, especially film biographies. What makes these volumes unique is the author's approach. Mank concentrates on the horror films and reports anecdotes, news stories, gossip, and the actresses' own memories of working on these films. Certain themes emerge. The women were underpaid in comparison to the male actors. Almost everyone loved Boris Karloff and respected Bela Lugosi. Sexual harassment was definitely a problem for many of these women, and some left the business because no redress was possible.

Mank has done a wonderful job of bringing these actresses to life for the reader. These two volumes are recommended for film reference collections in academic and large public libraries.

International Dictionary of Modern Dance. Ed. by Taryn Benbow-Pfalzgraf. 1998. 891p. bibliog. illus. indexes. St. James, $160 (1-55862-359-0). DDC: 792.8.

This biographical dictionary eschews ballet and social dance to concentrate on the dance form that blossomed in the twentieth century. Originating in popular theatrical performances, this form was influenced by the theory of expansive movement advocated by Delsarte, eventually receiving the name "modern dance."

The dictionary provides information on dancers, choreographers, teachers, companies, designers, writers on dance, national overviews, and selected important dances. The Western world is emphasized, but coverage is global. The 425 clearly written entries are arranged alphabetically. Adjacent to roughly half of the personal and dance-company entries are clear black-and-white photographs, large enough to show detail. The typical pattern for personal entries is: field(s) of activity; *Who's Who* type biography with dates, education, career highlights, and awards; chronological listing of specific works; writings by and about; and an essay on the subject's contribution to modern dance. Written by subject specialists, the signed essays are long enough to provide insight.

Preceding the main part of the dictionary are a five-page chronology of notable developments in modern dance, a list of contributors, and a list of entries. Concluding the volume are a four-page bibliography of books (almost all in English) on modern-dance topics, a breakdown of persons and companies by country, a classified index of entries under appropriate subjects, and brief identification of contributors.

The *International Dictionary of Modern Dance* amplifies the modern-dance coverage found in Oxford's six-volume *International Encyclopedia of Dance* [RBB My 1 98]. There appears to be little overlap. Of the 49 entries in the As and Bs in the dictionary, only about 10 also receive coverage in the Oxford set, among them Alvin Ailey American Dance Theatre, Gertrud Bodenwieser, and Butoh, a Japanese "dance-drama." Although libraries with general collections can skip it if they have already added the Oxford work, *International Dictionary of Modern Dance* will be useful in any public, academic, or special library where dance and the performing arts are of interest to readers.

The Tap Dance Dictionary. By Mark Knowles. 1998. 240p. bibliog. McFarland, $45 (0-7864-0352-7). DDC: 792.7.

During his career as a dancer, teacher, and choreographer, the author collected tap-dancing terminology, steps, combinations, and stories about their provenance. His teacher, Louis DaPron, was his inspiration for starting this project, the source of much of his information, and the originator of the notation for writing down how the steps are done. Knowles' later research consisted of searching old books and articles for names of steps, and personal interviews with people in the tap field. Primarily a record of steps, this volume does not have entries on performers or other aspects of the field. It will not teach readers how to tap. It does, however, give the basic information necessary for dancers to perform the steps, from *A,B,C Step* to *Zink*.

Tap steps can be named for the way they sound when danced, the way they look, the person who created them, or the place they originated. Many tap steps have several names, and these are cross-referenced. Entries are broader than just tap. A few terms come from ballet but are used in tap dancing (*cabriole, pas de Basque*). Entries explain and describe many ballroom dances (*boogie woogie, bunny hop, rumba, waltz*), folk dances (*clog dancing, polka, schottische*), and African American dances (*black bottom cake walk*). Some entries include brief historical information.

This unique reference book will be a welcome addition to academic libraries supporting curricula in dance and theater arts, and public libraries with comprehensive dance collections. While concentrating on notation, it also sheds some light on a slice of the history of popular dance in America. Other libraries may purchase as needed.

World Encyclopedia of Contemporary Theatre, Volume 5: Asia/Pacific. Ed. by Don Rubin. 1998. 536p. bibliog. illus. index. Routledge, $140 (0-415-05933-X). DDC: 792.625.

This latest volume in the proposed six-volume set lives up to the high standards set by the previous volumes and continues to allow each country to define its own theatrical profile through the eyes of a native author. In a few cases where information has been hard to come by, the editorial staff has authored an entry. The time period covered is 1945 to the second half of the 1990s, a real challenge for the editors due to ever-changing political landscapes. This Asia/Pacific volume covers 30 nations as far west as former Soviet republics like Turkmenistan and Izbekistan, to Iran in the southwest, Mongolia in the north, New Zealand in the far south, and numerous islands in the South Pacific as far east as French Polynesia.

The majority of the entries follow the basic format established in the earlier volumes: background material; structure of the national theater community; artistic profile including companies, dramaturgy, directing and acting, music and dance; theater for young audiences; puppet theater; design; theater space and architecture; training, criticism, scholarship, and publishing. Each entry includes a brief bibliography, with a lengthier one appearing at the end of the volume. Illustrations pepper the text and add welcome visual authentication to the content. India and Australia receive the most coverage. Sixteen nations are covered in briefer overviews, among them Papua New Guinea, Tajikistan, and Vietnam. Singapore is covered in an overview essay while Hong Kong is treated in the entry on China. Except for a brief historical introduction, the entry on Korea deals only with the south. As in earlier volumes, there are several introductory essays at the beginning of this volume, covering theater in the area in general. Authors of these point out that many young people are turning to television, film, and technology, and away from the folk cultures that produced traditional performing art in their nations. Many essays stress the secularization of dance, drama, and puppetry, which had sacred and religious roots.

This is an excellent place to begin scholarly research on historical and contemporary theatrical activity in this part of the world. The editors claim the encyclopedia is a "theatre library for every country but the reader's own," and is for "sophisticated professionals from abroad," assuming that it is not scholarly enough for a country's own researchers. However, because the encyclopedia is rich in specific detail—naming individuals, troupes, and forms, and giving dates, background material, influences, and analysis of evolution and change—it represents at least a starting point for any researcher, no matter how sophisticated. Because the success and failure of theatrical arts within each country reflect the socioeconomic/political culture of the time, and because the authors have pointed this out, citing specific events and influences, all of the volumes serve as a rich resource for scholars in many fields other than theater.

Previously published are *Volume 1: Europe* ($165, 0-415-05928-3), *Volume 2: The Americas* ($140, 0-415-05929-1), and *Volume 3: Africa* ($140, 0-415-05931-3). *Volume 4: The Arab World* ($140, 0-415-05932-1) will be published in 1999. Each volume includes its own index, but volume 6 (also coming next year) will contain a cumulative index as well as a bibliography. Recommended for academic and large public libraries.

The New Dickson Baseball Dictionary. Rev. ed. By Paul Dickson. 1999. 579p. bibliog. illus. Harcourt, $35 (0-15-100380-7); paper, $20 (0-15-600580-8). DDC: 796.357.

One would not think that a mere game, a sport, and not even a world sport at that, could be the basis for a lexicon of some 7,000 terms. Could the same be true for other games or team sports, such as soccer, which is played around the world and has a pedigree at least as old? It does not seem possible, unless languages other than English are taken into account. The game of baseball has, for various reasons, always stimulated more and better writing than rival sports. Baseball has been known as the more thoughtful of the mass sports, with writers waxing eloquent about its balletic grace, its convoluted rules, its strategies, and its lack of a time clock. The many colorful figures who have played and coached the game, and announcers such as Dizzy Dean, who made famous the word *slud*, only add to the mix.

Readers will enjoy the scope of this dictionary, a revised edition of *The Dickson Baseball Dictionary* (Facts On File, 1989). It is intended to represent the "words, phrases, and slang expressions that define the game." There are definitions not only for *designated hitter, ground ball,* and *unassisted triple play* but also for *Black Sox, Cactus League,* and *Lou Gehrig's disease*. No term has been included unless the author could collect at least two examples of its use. He identifies which terms are archaic, uses cross-references, and points out parts of speech. First use, etymology, a note on usage, and extended use in the language of everyday life may be given, along with pungent quotations. Besides the language of baseball, the book covers the lingo of its poor relation, softball. Dickson obviously knows his subject, but he could have used the services of an editor who is also a fan. Occasionally players are misnamed (Gary Maddux for Greg Maddux of the Atlanta Braves).

The book includes a brief thesaurus, a list of baseball abbreviations, and a partially annotated bibliography of works on baseball terminology, all of which add to its reference value. Illustrations consist of photographs and drawings from the game's storied past.

The Baseball Encyclopedia (10th ed., Macmillan, 1996) provides a record of player, team, and league statistics; and *The Cultural Encyclopedia of Baseball* [RBB D 15 97] covers the customs, folklore, and social significance of the sport. Dickson's focus on language is unique. As the author of several other books on baseball, and some others on words, he has shown himself to be one of the better sports lexicographers in terms of clarity of definitions and currency. The result of his efforts is an engrossing, highly readable reference book that could well become a standard in the public library.

Literature

Literature Resource Center. Internet database. 1999. Gale, call 1-800-877-GALE or visit [http://www.gale.com] for subscription information. (Last accessed April 6, 1999.)

Available since last fall, Gale's *Literature Resource Center* (LRC) is a literature reference database offering biographical, bibliographical, and contextual information for the undergraduate researcher. Integrating content from Gale's *Contemporary Authors* (CA), *Contemporary Literary Criticism* (CLC), and *Dictionary of Literary Biography* (DLB) databases, plus other selected sources, this is the one-stop resource for information on authors, their works, criticisms of their works, and various other aspects of their writing. Material on 90,000 authors is available.

The database offers eight major search categories: Author, Title, Genre, Literary Movement/Time Period, Literary Themes, Essays on Publishing Companies, Essays on Literary Topics, and Custom Search. The first two are standard searches of the full text of the database to find the biographies, criticisms, and related essays. The third and fourth categories allow the searcher to find authors associated with a particular genre (from 89 listed) or movement/time period (from 88 listed). For example, one can focus a search on authors of the Irish Literary Renaissance and retrieve 16 hits (up from five when we looked at LRC last fall), from Austin Clarke to William Butler Yeats. The fifth category, Literary Themes, searches for authors and works associated with various themes ranging from *abandonment* to *Zionism*. Essays on Publishing Companies provides company histories, taken from various volumes of DLB. Essays on Literary Topics consists of entries on (mostly early) literary topics, as opposed to authors, covered in DLB—*The Anglo Saxon Chronicles, Carmina Burana,* for example. It is in Custom Search mode that the researcher can combine all of the above searching modes with each other and with other categories, such as Nationality, Ethnicity, and Year of Birth. Some of these added categories are not complete. For example, *Portuguese* is not listed on the Nationality menu, so that a researcher would not be able to do a Nationality search to find Jose Saramago, the 1998 Portuguese Nobel Laureate for Literature. Custom Search also allows individual searching of the CA, CLC, and DLB databases. *Merriam Webster's Encyclopedia of Literature* is searchable from a button in the sidebar.

Information in LRC varies from author to author. For some, only entries from *Contemporary Authors* are provided. For others, the database offers a variety of resources. There are 2,400 authors (with plans to add more) who have been selected for in-depth coverage by Gale editors and an advisory panel. As an example, the Board did a search under Daniel Defoe. His Author Resources Page opens with a portrait and a brief summary listing his nationality and genres and the literary movements and time period to which he belonged. The links offered under Defoe are biography, lists of Defoe's works, criticism (reprinted from *Reference Guide to English Literature* [2d ed., St. James, 1991] in addition to several scholarly monographs and journals), Internet links, overviews of Defoe's works ("summaries, explication, and other information about" individual Defoe works, reproduced from several sources, including Gale's *Characters in Young Adult Fiction* [1997]), further resources (including, for example, the bibliographies of works about Defoe from DLB), hyperlinked lists of other authors who wrote on similar themes, and full-text journal articles. The Internet resources were "reviewed and selected by a team of Internet researchers using specific editorial criteria." There are six Web sites listed for Defoe; currently, LRC provides links to more than 2,500 sites. The final search option under Defoe links to 17 full-text journal articles, many from the Information Access database. Among the 20 or so journals whose articles are accessible in the current iteration of the database are *Studies in Contemporary Fiction, Poetry,* and *World Literature Today*. Journal coverage is 1995–98.

We also did a search on a contemporary author, Bebe Moore Campbell. Her Author Resources Page has fewer links than Defoe's—no overviews or Web sites. One problem with drawing information from the *Contemporary Authors* database is that not all the CA entries are up-to-date. The most current title in Campbell's list of works is *Your Blues Ain't Like Mine*, published in 1992. We did find information on later titles such as *Brothers and Sisters* and *Singing in the Comeback Choir* in the links to journal articles (in this case, *Publisher's Weekly* reviews).

LRC is one of the most user-friendly resources of its kind. The ability to search across so many of the Gale lines with one search engine is by itself a major selling point. Access to the many other pieces of information, including Internet resources and full-text journal articles, makes the product even more useful. Libraries that cater to undergraduate researchers, in particular, would be remiss not to add this to their electronic database collections. Future plans include integrated content from several Macmillan databases, including the Scribner Writer series and Twayne's author series; updated author biographies and bibliographies; discussion groups on the 2,400 most-studied authors; additional author portraits; and links to holdings.

Poem Finder on the Web. Internet database. Roth, pricing beginning at $600 (single user, single site). Call 1-800-899-ROTH or visit [http://www.poemfinder.com] for subscription information. (Last accessed April 1, 1999.)

Now there is a Web version of *Poem Finder*, which was first made available on CD-ROM in 1991. The content is very impressive: 50,000 full-text poems, 600,000 citations, 12,500 source references, and more. It indexes poetry from 3,000 anthologies, 4,500 single-author works, and 5,000 periodical issues.

Four search options are available from the main menu: Basic Search, Advanced Search, Subject Navigator, and The Year's Best Poetry. The search algorithms seem to deal with plurals and apostrophes adequately. In Basic Search, the user enters a term and qualifies it by title, text, author, or subject. Results, which are displayed 50 at a time, consist of poem title (generally listed in alphabetical order) and author. We did a Basic Search under the subject *funerals* to find the title of the W. H. Auden poem made so popular by the film *Four Weddings and a Funeral*. Selecting *Twelve Songs*: 9. *Funeral Blues* from the results list led us to a record made up of author name, title, first line, last line, date, and subject headings. A Reference link took us to a screen listing four titles in which the poem is anthologized (with page numbers). Clicking on Auden's name took us to another page with a brief author record (name, birth and death dates, nationality) and a Poem link that led to a list of all the Auden poems that are indexed in the database. For many poems, there is also a link that leads to the full text; these are indicated with asterisks next to the author's names in the Results list.

Advanced Search allows the user to search for terms in a number of areas within three categories—poem (e.g., *poem author, poem first line, poem original language*), author (e.g., *author nationality, author birth date*), and book reference (e.g., *book reference by title, book reference by publisher*). The user can also use Boolean operators to combine searches. Advanced Search works best when terms are searched within just one of the three categories; the example in Help is *Emily Dickinson* in the *poem author* area AND *love* in the *poem subject/classification* area to find a list of Dickinson love poems. Users are warned that searches that combine categories may fail. When we tried the search *love* in the *poem subject/classification* area AND *American* in the *author nationality* area, the program retrieved all love poems but ignored the criterion *American*. Advanced Search can be useful when queries are quite specific, but most users will find Basic Search adequate to their needs.

Another way to search is Subject Navigator, an index of 12 general topics, such as nature, people, and the family, with numerous subcategories. This may be of interest to the general user who has time to explore but may not be as useful as a reference tool to find specific poems. Finally, The Year's Best Poetry is an ongoing anthology presenting new full-text poems. When we last looked, there were 193 poems from 1998; 1999 poems were due to start appearing this spring.

There is much to like about *Poem Finder*, but there are also several annoying features. The main menu is completely displayed at the top of every page, making it necessary to scroll down a full screen to see any results. The search options should be displayed across the top and perhaps again at the bottom, but most of the page should be results. Users would be better served if information were contracted to a page per poem, instead of having separate pages for full text (if available), poem links, and book references. Multiple layers can lead to user frustration, especially if the Internet connection is at all shaky. When one retrieves a long list of results, there is no link back to the beginning of the list—say, from the fifth page of hits (251–300)—except by clicking on the browser's Back button five times. Advanced Search can be cumbersome because of the need to limit searches to the same category; and subject searching in Basic and Advanced Search can be a problem because the user must guess which subject headings the database uses (*17th century* or *seventeenth century*?).

The breadth of poetry is fascinating and as the database grows will become even more useful. The Board very much likes the content and its many potential uses. However, this is an expensive database for many smaller libraries, which must balance potential use and ease of use with cost. It would be worth the money if the organization and presentation were improved. For libraries that limit each patron's time online, the extra pages and potentially slow page-loading time are problematic. Those that charge for printing may also encounter complaints, unless patrons are sufficiently delighted to find long-sought-after poems. We recommend that potential buyers evaluate the demo as well as read reviews.

Encyclopedia of Folklore and Literature. Ed. by Mary Ellen Brown and Bruce A. Rosenberg. 1998. 766p. bibliogs. illus. index. ABC-CLIO, $99.50 (1-57607-003-4). DDC: 803.

Coeditors Brown and Rosenberg successfully address an enormous topic in this single volume. They've assembled alphabetically arranged, signed essays from more than 130 independent and university scholars from around the world to provide access to a vast field of study. The goal is to examine the relationship between folklore and literature.

Many of the 350 entries treat individual authors like Chinua Achebe, in whose fiction folklore serves "as a reminder of identity, as a call to identity, and as a basis for a revitalized nation." Each contributor brings his/her own knowledge and experience to the analysis of the subject of an entry; however, there is remarkable continuity and easy readability among them. Not all entries are laudatory. The one on Maya Angelou is an objective view of an author whose work has been praised and criticized but who has enlarged "a personal narrative to encompass the rich and complex experience of African America." Margaret Atwood, Geoffrey Chaucer, Bob Dylan, and Herman Melville are among the others discussed. Coverage ranges from Aesop to modern times. In addition to authors, there are entries for scholars, theorists, and teachers.

Forms such as archetype, epic, fakelore, and riddle have entries, as do specific works, such as *Canterbury Tales*, *Iliad*, and *King Lear*. Latino, Native American, Scandinavian, Scottish, and Russian literatures receive attention, along with genres of tales specific to certain cultures, such as the tall tale of the U.S., the romancero of Spain, the minnesang of Germany, and the jataka of Japan. Various methods of studying literature and important themes (*Robin Hood, trolls, wandering Jew*) receive treatment.

There are a few entries for Asian authors and themes, but basically the work concentrates on European and Western themes, including classical Greek and Roman. Cross-referencing between entries is good, and each entry includes a brief bibliography. An introductory overview of folklore's relationship to literature is worthwhile as background material. The introduction is preceded by an alphabetical list of entries, and a list of entries by category (authors, works, scholars/movements, concepts/themes, themes/characters). The work done by influential folklorists Antii Aarne and Stith Thompson to identify recurring tale types and motifs is cited in brackets throughout the text.

A number of the same topics are covered in other reference books on folklore. However, this volume adds something new by focusing on the complex ways in which folklore forms the basis of and continues to influence literature. It will serve as a handbook for undergraduate college students and the general reader, and is recommended introductory reading for all folklore collections.

Encyclopedia of World Literature in the 20th Century. 4v. 3d ed. 1999. 3,500p. bibliog. illus. indexes. St. James, $575 (1-55862-373-6). DDC: 803.

Based on a German work, the second edition of *Encyclopedia of World Literature in the 20th Century* was published between 1982 and 1984 by Frederick Ungar, with a supplement from Continuum in 1993. With

2,300 entries, St. James' third edition is a comprehensive survey of the significant international literary activity from 1900 to the present. Its assessment and appreciation of the growth and variety of world literature are appropriate for both general and scholarly readers.

Every author entry consists of four parts: a headnote that lists vital statistics; the body, which includes both a biographical sketch and a critical assessment of the author's work; a list of further works that are not mentioned in the body of the entry; and, finally, a bibliography of select secondary sources. National literature and literary movements are covered in separate articles that contain uppercase cross-references to the author articles within the four volumes. Authors were selected for inclusion based on an evaluation of critical recognition by an international board of advisors from an impressive list of colleges and universities. Each country represented has its own advisor. To maintain its international scope, many U.S., British, and European writers who are well-known in the English-speaking world are treated as part of national survey articles in order to include more writers from less-familiar literatures.

The amount of revision in the entries varies. Entries for some, such as J. R. R. Tolkien, are the same in both editions. In some cases, such as the entry for Maya Angelou, the essay is unchanged but the bibliography has been updated. Other entries, such as Margaret Atwood and Wole Soyinka, have revised essays. And finally, some entries are entirely new, among them Martin Amis, Russell Banks, Ellen Gilchrist, Jamaica Kincaid, and Arundhati Roy. A nationality index has been added to the last volume.

A significant number of writers included in these volumes have not had their works translated into English, and for them, *Encyclopedia of World Literature in the 20th Century* is the first source of reference for English-speaking readers. This inclusive and authoritative guide is appropriate for all academic and larger public libraries. Those that own the previous edition will probably want the update.

A Multicultural Dictionary of Literary Terms. By Gary Carey and Mary Ellen Snodgrass. 1998. 184p. index. McFarland, $29.50 (0-7864-0552-X). DDC: 803.

Including the popular buzzword *multicultural* in a book title almost assuredly boosts sales to libraries. The compilers of this new guide to literary terms justify titling it *multicultural* by noting that they include foreign language terms and offer examples from writings representative of a wide range of nationalities, cultures, and eras. Carey, an editor of Cliffs Notes, and Snodgrass, author of *Encyclopedia of Southern Literature* [RBB Ap 15 98] and various other reference sources, state in their preface to this slim volume that their intent is to "present terms essential to a thorough, comprehensive study of world literature, including print literature as well as stage drama."

Although the dictionary includes only 468 entries, the actual number of terms it defines is higher because many are treated within more general articles; for example, *stream of consciousness* is defined under *point-of-view*. The lack of cross-references from such terms to the appropriate entry is a major deficiency. Some entries indicate pronunciation, and many provide *see also* references to other entries. Definitions vary from excellent to barely adequate, for, in a number of cases, the compilers' penchant for listing illustrative works and authors takes precedence over exposition. In fact, the work's real distinction lies in its exceptional number of illustrative examples drawn from a broad chronological, geographical, and cultural spectrum and covering nonfiction works as well as novels, poetry, and other imaginative writings. Writers cited range from Akhenaten to Marie de France to Sonia Sanchez, and, although many canonical authors are represented, contemporary figures, such as Margaret Atwood, Barbara Kingsolver, and Michael Ondaatje, receive strong emphasis. This feature could be especially helpful to teachers seeking to go beyond the established canon in selecting works for their students to study, but the lack of an index to authors and titles cited hampers that kind of use. Following the dictionary section are lists of winners of major literary prizes, a 10-page chronological chart of significant works of world literature, and a brief bibliography. The index covers terms that are accorded separate entries as well as those defined or simply mentioned in other entries.

Unfortunately, this work falls far short of the comprehensiveness alluded to in its ambitious goal. It ignores major literary groups, movements, and periods, such as the Agrarians, the Harlem Renaissance, and Restoration comedy; and it omits many important terms and concepts, among them, *georgic*, *light verse*, and *mise-en-scene*. On the other hand, it does include some terms not generally found in similar works (*dog drama*, *happening*, *lauda*) and also encompasses a smattering of literary terms from other cultures (*corrido*, *makta*, *Ritterdrama*). Librarians attracted by the wide variety of examples in this work should be aware that Ross Murfin and Supryia M. Ray's *Bedford Glossary of Critical and Literary Terms* (Bedford Books, 1997), a dictionary containing more than 700 entries, also identifies examples from diverse nationalities and cultural groups. Emphasizing literature of the Western world, Murfin and Ray achieve a better balance between explanation and example, and they include an index to the authors and works cited. In addition, libraries on small budgets will continue to be well served by such standard sources as William Harmon and C. Hugh Holman's *Handbook to Literature*, seventh edition (Prentice Hall, 1996) and Karl Beckson and Arthur Ganz's *Literary Terms: A Dictionary*, third edition (Noonday, 1989).

The Oxford Dictionary of Twentieth Century Quotations. Ed. by Elizabeth Knowles. 1999. 482p. indexes. Oxford, $30 (0-19-860103-4). DDC: 808.88.

Knowles, managing editor of Oxford Quotations Dictionaries, has chosen 5,000 quotations from the twentieth century, using 1914, the year World War I broke out, as the starting point. These quotes are from writers and others alive in or after that year and come from political movements, songs, poetry, advertisements, television, sound bites, and even online sources. Earlier events that have continued to echo down the century, such as the sinking of the *Titanic* in 1912, are included. Coverage is international, although emphasis leans toward British sources.

Quotes are arranged alphabetically by the author of the quote. Special sidebars (e.g., "Film lines," "Last words," "Misquotes," "Official advice") add interest and variety; it would be helpful to have these listed in the table of contents. Author names are followed by dates of birth and death (where known) with a very short description. Where needed, cross-references are provided to quotations about that author elsewhere in the text. Within the author entries, quotations are separated by literary form and then arranged alphabetically by title. Primary sources are listed first, followed by other writers' works and biographies. Authors covered range from W. C. Fields and Paul McCartney to Bella Abzug and J. Robert Oppenheimer, with many others represented. Each quotation is accompanied by contextual information, if needed, and always a note as to the source. Two indexes, subject and keyword, provide additional access to users when an author is not known or when a quote for an occasion is needed.

Quotation books abound, and smaller libraries probably need only standard general titles, such as Bartlett's *Familiar Quotations* [RBB N 1 92], now in its 16th edition; and *The Oxford Dictionary of Quotations* [4th ed., RBB D 1 92]. Larger libraries can expand their collections by adding titles, such as *The Oxford Dictionary of Twentieth Century Quotations*, that are more specialized. Knowles and her project team have produced an authoritative overview of social, political, cultural, and scientific concerns of the century. This fun and enlightening quotation source is recommended for high-school, public, and academic libraries.

Beacham's Encyclopedia of Popular Fiction. v.9–11. Ed. by Kirk H. Beetz. 1998. 1,276p. appendixes. indexes. Beacham, $153 (0-933833-48-2). DDC: 809.3.

These are the latest additions to the set published in 1996 [RBB Mr 1 97] and are intended, according to the publisher, as another step toward a "goal of compiling a comprehensive encyclopedia of popular fiction." *Popular fiction* here is broadly defined. It is not just current best-sellers (short stories as well as novels) but those from earlier in this century as well as late in the last. The three volumes under consideration offer analyses of a variety of works: those of "authors in the core set who have published new works or whose older works were not included earlier; contemporary authors who were not included in the core set and additional nineteenth and early twentieth century authors." The base set, an updated edition of *Popular Fiction in America* (1986), consists of three volumes of biography and eight volumes of analysis; these new volumes continue the analysis series.

The signed critical essays, most written by academic specialists, are arranged by title and offer a social context for the work and discussions of themes, characters, techniques, literary precedents, and related titles. Ideas for group discussions are also offered, and in many instances adaptations (audiobooks or films) are noted. The length of the essays varies from two pages to nearly ten. Some of the contemporary writers now represented are Alice Adams, William Peter Blatty, Laura Esquivel, and Charles Frazier. Writers from the nineteenth and early twentieth centuries now included are Charlotte Bronte, E. M. Forster, Thomas Hardy, Dorothy Parker, and Jules Verne.

Special features include an appendix grouping themes by title and one grouping titles by themes or social concerns. There is also a cumulative index (covering the entire set) of authors with analyzed titles. The location of biographical information in the original set is noted; and, for authors new to the set, a reference is made to the Beacham Web page [http://www.BeachamPublishing.com], where additional information may be found. A cumulative master index of authors and titles is also provided. Useful for high-school classroom discussions as well as public library book-discussion groups, this set will also serve academic institutions that support classes in popular culture. The access to updated information via the publisher's Web site is an attractive feature. Recommended for high-school, public, and academic libraries where needed.

Black Authors and Illustrators of Books for Children and Young Adults: A Biographical Dictionary. 3d ed. By Barbara Thrash Murphy. 1999. 513p. appendixes. bibliog. illus. indexes. Garland, $65 (0-8153-2004-3). DDC: 809.

Black Authors and Illustrators of Books for Children and Young Adults offers 274 biographical sketches in its third edition. Each entry is arranged alphabetically by author's and illustrator's surname. Those using pen names are listed accordingly, with the pen name as the entry heading. The selection of writers was based on a questionnaire sent to publishers, and on to authors and illustrators. Much-studied writers such as Paul Lawrence Dunbar and Alice Walker are included, along with such popular and prolific contemporary figures as Walter Dean Myers and Jerry Pinckney; and Mahji Hall and Nancy B. Williams, for each of whom only a single book is listed. Each entry ranges in length from a paragraph to two pages and includes such information as year and place of birth, influences, approaches to writing and or illustrating, achievements, awards, and a selected bibliography of works. Photographs of the authors or illustrators are included when available.

An appendix of sample book covers and jackets is included, followed by an appendix listing books that have received awards or honors. An alphabetical listing by state of bookstores and distributors provides the user with an added resource for acquiring books that are cited in the text. Two indexes complete the volume, one an alphabetical listing of included books by title and the other an alphabetical listing of included authors and illustrators.

Librarians who are familiar with this resource will be glad to see it updated. It covers some writers not included in other reference works; only 17 are also found in the recent *Lives and Works: Young Adult Authors* [RBB My 1 99], for example. Although the sketches are brief in many instances, the volume provides a beginning resource guide for the young-adult researcher. An inexpensive but important tool for public libraries and elementary-and middle-school collections.

Encyclopedia of the Novel. 2v. Ed. by Paul Schellinger and others. 1998. 1,613p. bibliog. indexes. Fitzroy Dearborn, $270 (1-57958-015-7). DDC: 809.3.

It takes an encyclopedia to fully capture and track the twists and turns that the novel has taken on its road to becoming the most popular literary form. Imagine a two-volume, crisply written, elegantly framed source that is truly encyclopedic, and you have an understanding of much of what has been accomplished here. Strikingly enough, a quick scan of the literature points up that there has been little published to compare with this book for some time.

Presented here, in language packed with meaning and of a clarity that makes the book accessible to scholars and lay readers alike, are some 650 very satisfactory essays. There are entries not only on classic novels and great novel writers but also, as the editor says, "types of novels, on technical and formal aspects of novels," as well as criticism, theory, and influences. Because the work's stated intent is to emphasize the novel as genre, many writers are treated as integral parts of larger entities. Entries for individual authors, including Chinua Achebe, Henry Fielding, Carlos Fuentes, Thomas Hardy, and Virginia Woolf, discuss lives and works, but more space is given to explaining the writer's role in the development of the genre.

The hard choices as to which individual authors and books should be given their own entries were of course made by the editor, with the help of about 20 advisors, all associated with distinguished academic institutions here and abroad. The larger entries are thematic, for example, *adventure novel and imperial romance*; *Caribbean novel*; *English novel*; *magic realism*; *tense in narrative*. Though most of the contributors and advisors are affiliated with universities of North America, Britain, and Australia, the development of the genre in the rest of the world is given its due (*African novel*, *Chinese novel*, *Southeast Asian novel*, and others). A look at the notes on the contributors shows them to be very well qualified, with positions in higher education as professors of English or other languages and usually with numerous books and articles to their credit. Their essays range in length from one full large-format two-column page to four or five pages. Material is presented in alphabetical order, and finding information is made easier by the use of appropriate *see* references. Entries contain *see also* references to related entries, lists of further reading, and in the case of authors, lists of novels and a brief biographical summary. Some longer entries are subdivided by time periods.

The set concludes with title and general indexes. The title index contains all titles mentioned in the encyclopedia, even those listed in the "novels by" section of individual writer entries but not actually discussed.

A bibliography of seven pages (approximately 200 reference books in English or in translation from other languages) is divided into three parts: "General Sources for Research"; "Historical and Genre-Based Criticism, Narratology and Other Theoretical Approaches to the Novel"; and "The Novel in Its Regional Contexts" (subdivided geographically). Among the sources listed are such scholarly seminal works as E. M. Forster's *Aspects of the Novel* (Harcourt, 1927), *The Cambridge History of Italian Literature* (Cambridge, 1996), and Ian Watt's *The Rise of the Novel* (Univ. of California, 1957).

Encyclopedia of the Novel will help students, professors, and the avid reader to identify, evaluate, appraise, and perhaps enjoy the defining writers, novels, and themes. This work is a felicitous melding of the interests of the novel-reading multitudes and the critics who analyze the genre. Its acquisition should be a high priority for academic and large public libraries.

Literary Lifelines. 10v. 1998. 2,560p. illus. index. Grolier, $319 (0-7172-9211-8). DDC: 809.

Literary Lifelines is a tool without a real focus. Its purpose seems to be to put authors into some kind of chronological context and show how they relate to other authors; 1,000 authors are featured.

The selection of writers is marvelous. It includes writers from the classical era (Aeschylus, Virgil), the Middle Ages (Chaucer), the Renaissance (Machiavelli), the eighteenth and nineteenth centuries (Voltaire, the Brontes, Wordsworth), and contemporary figures (Rita Dove, Ian Fleming, Ellery Queen, John Updike, Sam Shepard). It is also culturally diverse, covering Chinua Achebe, Naguib Mahfouz, Wu Chengen, and others. Many genres are covered, too—novelists, playwrights, poets, short story writers. From the standpoint of authors selected, a good start was made; it can be difficult to find information on some of these authors in reference sources designed for students.

It is the entries themselves that are inadequate. Each entry is two pages. The first page features several paragraphs about the author, accompanied by an illustration of the author, an illustration representing a book cover or some other relevant object or scene, and a list of works. The illustrations are unattractive and uninformative. Users could easily live without them and would have benefited instead from more text. The second page of each entry starts with a list of authors related, either by time period, genre, or nationality, to the writer being covered. Following this list is a chronology of world events that correspond to the author's life span, illustrated with small dark sketches. There seems to be no logic to the events that are represented. Often they have no apparent relevance to the author's life. The chronology for Alexandre Dumas, for instance, lists the invention of the McCormick reaper and the opening of the Erie Canal. Neither of these events appears in the chronology for Charles Dickens, who lived at the same time. It's difficult to understand why the reaper and the Canal are more relevant to Dumas than Dickens.

Each volume ends with a glossary of literary and historical terms. The index is well done, offering access by author, genre, title, and country.

Despite its breadth of coverage, this set provides too-little useful information, and the illustrations are not an enhancement. Not recommended.

Asian American Literature: Reviews and Criticism of Works by American Writers of Asian Descent. Ed. by Lawrence J. Trudeau and others. 1999. 536p. bibliog. illus. index. Gale, $99 (0-7876-0296-5). DDC: 810.9.

Asian American Literature was created in response to suggestions from college, public, and high-school librarians who saw a need for an anthology of critical writings on the works of Asian American authors in the same format as Gale's other publications, *Black Literature Criticism* [RBB D 15 91], *Hispanic Literature Criticism* [RBB Jl 94], and *Native North American Literature* [RBB Ap 15 95]. The more general Gale literature series, *Contemporary Literary Criticism* and *Twentieth-Century Literary Criticism*, both cover many Asian American authors, but this new volume provides its audience with a more concentrated approach to the topic.

The volume includes entries for 45 American and Canadian authors from the fields of poetry, fiction, drama, essay, autobiography, and children's literature, arranged in alphabetical order. Both pioneering authors such as Edith Eaton (Sui Sin Far), whose 1912 collection of stories, *Mrs. Spring Fragrance*, was the first book about Chinese American life published by a writer of Chinese ancestry, and emerging ones, such as Korean American Chang-Rae Lee, are included, providing readers with a wide range of authors that represent a diversity of voices as well as a variety of historical periods. Entries are generally more than 10 pages long and contain a short introduction, a list of major works in chronological order, reviews and criticism either excerpted or reprinted in their entirety, annotations to the essays, bibliographic citations to the essays, and, finally, a bibliography of further readings. There are also citations to entries in other Gale publications. Most entries include a portrait of the author. A complete index of all titles discussed concludes the work.

This companion to Gale's other titles on writers of specific ethnic backgrounds is a worthwhile purchase for public, high-school, and undergraduate collections.

Contemporary Southern Writers. Ed. by Roger Matuz. 1999. 442p. index. St. James, $140 (1-55862-370-1). DDC: 810.9.

Southern writers are identified as writers born and raised in the South or who have lived and worked in the South for a significant part of their lives. The defining characteristic is their experience of living there rather than necessarily that the South or southern themes are a focus of the works. Names one would expect to find are here—James Dickey, Shelby Foote, Walker Percy, Eudora Welty. But the scope also includes mystery writer Sue Grafton, born and educated in Kentucky, but not a "southern" writer unless you count the southern California landscape of her detective. *Contemporary* is defined as those writers living in the late 1990s or, if recently deceased, who published new works in the 1990s. Writers of poetry, fiction, drama and nonfiction are included, 244 in all.

Entries have brief biographical data, a list of publications, and a critical essay. Many of the entries include a comment from the writers on their own work. References to critical studies are usually, but not always, included. Supplementary materials to the alphabetical entries include a time line of southern literary history and a title index. An index categorizing entries by literary form might also be useful. Some of the signed essays are overall critical assessments of the writers' works and themes; and others, more a series of summaries of novels or other works.

Information on the better-known authors in this book is available in other places. Most are included in Gale's *Contemporary Authors* if not their *Dictionary of Literary Biography*. St. James Press also publishes several reference books on contemporary writers, including the sixth edition of *Contemporary Poets* (1996), the sixth edition of *Contemporary Novelists* (1996), and the fifth edition of *Contemporary Dramatists* (1993). One expects a certain amount of duplication and spinning-off these days with reference publishers. Although most of the *Contemporary Southern Writers* entries seem to be, except for the basic information, newly written, at least one entry, that for poet Henry Taylor, is identical to that in *Contemporary Poets*. The entries on novelists Larry McMurtry and Richard Ford are by different authors than those in *Contemporary Novelists*. However, essentially the same ground is covered, and that brings up the question of how necessary yet another book of this type is. As noted, most of the subjects can be found in other literary biographical dictionaries, and the treatment of the writers is not as in-depth as that in the more selective *Contemporary Poets, Dramatists, Essayists, and Novelists of the South* (Greenwood, 1994). Although the information here is perfectly acceptable, up-to-date, and suitable for large public and academic libraries, most can probably live without it.

Encyclopedia of American Literature. Ed. by Steven R. Serafin and Alfred Bendixen. 1999. 1,305p. bibliogs. index. Continuum; dist. by Gale, $150 (0-8264-1052-9). DDC: 810.

This is a one-volume snapshot of the current canon of American literature, its development, its luminaries, and its legacy of "commonality and diversity." It is intended as a comprehensive survey of literature from colonial times to the present, "that is by definition American in scope."

The editors, one an editor of other important reference works such as titles in the Dictionary of Literary Biography series and the other the founder of the American Literature Association, have gathered more than 300 contributors to write 1,100 biographical and critical articles and 70 topical essays. The former vary in length and coverage depending on the prominence of the subject (for example, F. Scott Fitzgerald earns more than twice the space as Isaac Asimov), but they have the same basic elements: birth and death dates and places, a critical examination of the subject's life and works, a summary paragraph that justifies the subject's inclusion in the encyclopedia, and a brief bibliography of further reading. The topical entries are much more focused on the development and influence of a genre, region, or theme. Examples are *African American literature*, *the detective story*, *language and dialect*, *modernism*, and *the South*. The entry on science fiction is about 1,500 words and surveys the history of the genre, beginning with the early versions (Mary Shelley and Jules Verne) before focusing on the genre's development in America from Hugo Gernsback's *Ralph 124C 41+* (1911) to Gregory Benford's *Cosm* (1998). Index entries are primarily personal names, although some groups of writers (*cyberpunk fiction, writers of; expatriates*) are also listed. For individuals, index entries provide birth and death dates in addition to page numbers.

This volume is less comprehensive than *The Oxford Companion to American Literature* [RBB O 1 95], now in its sixth edition. *Oxford* has more than 5,000 entries and includes characters, titles, and more topical entries, in addition to authors. Entries in *Encyclopedia of American Literature*, on the other hand, are generally longer: almost a page for Grace Paley, as opposed to seven lines in *Oxford*; five pages on *romance*, which *Oxford* covers in 15 lines. Both volumes treat authors not found in the other. *Encyclopedia of American Literature* is a worthy addition to literature reference collections in academic and public libraries.

Lives and Works: Young Adult Authors. 8v. 1999. 869p. bibliogs. illus. index. Grolier, $255 (0-7172-9227-4). DDC: 810.8.

From Douglas Adams to Paul Zindel, this set provides information designed to meet the needs of middle-school students, although it could be used at the high-school level as well. More than 250 writers are covered, the classic (Louisa May Alcott, Edgar Allan Poe, William Shakespeare), as well as the modern. Arranged alphabetically by writer, each entry averages three pages and describes the writer's life and works. A quotation from one of the works and a black-and-white photograph accompany the text. At the end of each entry, one finds a selected list of the writer's works and, in some cases, a few titles about the writer and a Web site address for further information.

Information about a writer's life includes date of birth, education, and family history. In the discussion of the works, emphasis is on character development and prevalent themes. If other writers who have their own entries are mentioned (e.g., Arthur Conan Doyle and Nathaniel Hawthorne in the entry on Poe), their names appear in boldface. Each volume has a separate table of contents and a master index for the entire set. In addition to names and titles, the index includes some subject headings, such as *African-American writers*, *autobiographies*, and *social issues*. Only volume and page numbers are listed under these headings, not writers or works. This creates a challenge for the student who, looking under *humor* or *racism*, is faced with turning to more than 20 different pages and trying to find information that is relevant.

This set has a broader range than Scribner's *Writers for Young Adults* [RBB O 15 97], although it covers far fewer authors, of course, than Gale's *Authors and Artists for Young Adults* or *Something About the Author*. Libraries that hold other reference works on young adult authors may not need this new set, but it is recommended for school and public libraries that need additional resources on the topic.

Literature

Native American Literatures: An Encyclopedia of Works, Characters, Authors, and Themes. By Kathy J. Whitson. 1999. 295p. bibliog. illus. index. ABC-CLIO, $65 (0-87436-932-0). DDC: 810.9.

The author of this guide is an associate professor of English at Eureka College in Eureka, Illinois. More than 300 entries are arranged in alphabetical order by author, title, character name, theme, or significant historical event. The literary entries have analysis of the character, plot, themes, and autobiographical elements of the work or character. The biographies give the authors' tribal affiliations and analyze their lives as they relate to their work. Portraits are frequently included, and many of the thematic entries also have evocative black-and-white photographs. Entries range in length from a paragraph or two to slightly more than two pages. There are extensive cross-references.

The writing is outstanding, fluid, and dynamic. Whitson delves into the psyches of the authors and characters of the literature that is born of the diverse Native American experience. Her love and understanding of the works is evident. There are several common elements: divided families and abandonment, alcoholism and depression, involuntary dislocation from the ancestral culture and nonacceptance from the culture into which these real and fictional people are supposed to be "adopted." Also common are character types such as disaffected youth in search of their birth culture and wise people who guide them on their journey.

In her introduction the author states that she attempts to "provide summary and interpretive information on those texts that would most likely be read and studied by high-school students and college undergraduates." She also states, "In no way does this volume attempt to be comprehensive." There are entries for approximately 40 authors, from Samson Occom (b. 1723) to Sherman Alexie and Louise Erdrich. There is no entry for Susan Power, although there is extensive coverage of her 1994 novel, *The Grass Dancer*. Whitson does not analyze books marketed specifically to the YA audience, such as Michael Dorris' *Morning Girl*, *Guests*, or *Sees Behind Trees*, that are likely to be taught in high schools; she does not even mention the prolific and popular YA author Jamake Highwater. Although the bibliography is useful for further research, a complete list of works by the authors treated would have been helpful, as would a list of authors by tribal affiliation.

Gale's *Native North American Literature* [RBB Ap 15 95] covers 78 writers but does not have separate discussions of titles, characters, and themes. Garland's *Dictionary of Native American Literature* [RBB Ap 15 95] contains scholarly essays arranged by historical period. This new title is an excellent addition to literary criticism for the reference sections of public and academic libraries. Many high-school libraries will find it useful and affordable, too.

The Oxford Companion to Canadian Literature. 2d ed. Ed. by Eugene Benson and William Toye. 1998. 1,199p. Oxford, $65 (0-19-541167-6). DDC: 810.03.

This edition of *The Oxford Companion to Canadian Literature* (the first was published in 1983) has added more than 300 new entries, and its preface states that most entries have been modified and edited to capture up-to-date information. In nearly 1,200 pages, the book features entries that vary from a quarter page to more than ten pages in length. This is a worthy survey, including a wealth of information on all aspects of Canadian literature, from the erudite Robertson Davies to popular contemporary genre writers such as mystery writer Gail Bowen and science-fiction writer Spider Robinson.

The many thematic essays are well written and provide enough information to develop a basic level of knowledge about a subject. There are essays on French and English children's literature, Acadian writers, drama, and the novel in both French and English; a major article on criticism; and a number of entries on the literature of various ethnic groups, including Italian-Canadians and Caribbean-Canadians. All entries are signed and contributors' affiliations are listed at the beginning of the book. There are plenty of *see* and *see also* references; in addition, names and terms within entries are capitalized to indicate that they appear as separate entries. Some entries include a few bibliographic references.

The scope of this volume is impressive. It includes not only information about writers and poets but also publishers, publishing houses, themes and symbols in Canadian literature, and essays on individual works that stand out as landmarks in the field. It is the kind of reference work one can "dip into" for interest or use as a quick reference tool to begin a research assignment. The *Companion* is a must for all Canadian high-school, public, and academic libraries. This is also a necessary work for colleges offering Canadian literature and Canadian studies curricula, as well as those large public libraries where there is interest. Highly recommended.

Encyclopedia of American Poetry: The Nineteenth Century. Ed. by Eric L. Haralson. 1998. 536p. bibliogs. indexes. Fitzroy Dearborn, $125 (1-57958-008-4). DDC: 811.

This one-volume encyclopedia is intended as a companion to the Library of America anthology *American Poetry: The Nineteenth Century*. More than 1,000 poems from nearly 150 American poets are included in that collection published in 1993. Haralson, who served as a researcher on the Library of America project, conceived of this reference companion to provide accounts of the lives, writings, and other achievements of more than 100 of the poets anthologized. Entries are substantial, ranging from three pages to more than ten in the case of poets like Emily Dickinson. In addition to furnishing biographical information, each entry is also a critical essay, discussing the poetry as well as the literary and historical significance of the poet. As a companion to the anthology, the essays include specific references to volume and page numbers in the anthology where the reader can find many of the verses under discussion.

Cross-references to other poets in the encyclopedia are indicated in the entries by bold face. At the end of each entry a reference list includes selected works of the poet as well as suggestions for further reading. A few topical essays, on American Indian poetry and popular poetry, for example, are also included. The entries are signed, and contributors, primarily academics, are listed in an appendix. Both a general index and a title and first line index are included.

The range of the inclusions is great—the well-known poets, such as Dickinson, Emerson, and Longfellow, are accompanied by those better known for other pursuits—John Quincy Adams, Nathaniel Hawthorne, Edith Wharton—as well as very minor figures and the forgotten and the forgettable. Many writers popular in their day and significant in that context no longer appear in literary reference works or anthologies. Since many authors who have been marginalized or left out of the American literary canon are being rediscovered, it is perhaps for these poets that this encyclopedia will prove most useful. Two entries that follow each other are cases in point. John Townsend Trowbridge was a popular and prolific writer in his time, primarily a novelist, especially of books for boys but also of some narrative poetry and light verse. The entry here acknowledges that he was a very conventional poet and that he has dropped from the public eye. His significance lies in his role as friend and critic of Whitman. In any case, while Trowbridge has brief entries in the *Oxford Companion to American Literature* [RBB O 1 95], and in the venerable *Allibone's Critical Dictionary of English Literature* (Lippincott, 1858–1871), as well as in some other older literary reference works, he is not featured in Gale's widely used *Dictionary of Literary Biography* series, nor has he ever turned up in Gale's *Nineteenth Century Literary Criticism* set. Certainly his poetry is not included in *Guide to American Poetry Explication* (G. K. Hall, 1989).

The next entry is for a poet almost unknown in his own day, Frederick Goddard Tuckerman (1821–1873). Tuckerman, a recluse like Emily Dickinson, was rediscovered in the 1930s and critically acclaimed. Still, as the contributor notes, he remains a fairly obscure figure. He also does not appear in the Gale series noted above or in Scribner's *American Writers* set. The long essay here, with close attention to the poetry itself, will prove very useful to any student interested in this poet.

As the editor notes, while this reference work is an ideal companion to the Library of America anthology and will be useful as such, it also stands alone as a comprehensive reference work for students, teachers, and scholars. It will be valuable in academic and large public libraries or anywhere that found the anthology itself an essential purchase.

Contemporary African American Novelists: A Bio-Bibliographical Critical Sourcebook. Ed. by Emmanuel S. Nelson. 1999. 530p. bibliogs. index. Greenwood, $95 (0-313-30501-3). DDC: 813.

The past 20-odd years have seen the emergence of a significant body of African American fiction. Providing reliable, thorough, and up-to-date biographical, critical, and bibliographic information about that literature for advanced scholars, undergraduates, and general readers is the stated goal of this work.

The 79 profiled writers include major novelists, such as Toni Morrison and John Edgar Wideman, as well as such lesser-known writers as Steven Corbin and Dawn Turner Trice. The word *contemporary* in the title is somewhat elastic. Although most of the writers featured have written in the past thirty years, several had their most prolific period in the 1940s and 1950s. And although each author has written at least one novel, some of them are better known for their poetry, plays, or nonfiction. Forty-one of the writers are women.

Entries range from 4 to 19 pages, with most encompassing 5 pages. Each author's profile begins with a short biography. A discussion of the writer's major works and themes follows, with an overview of the critical reception in both popular and scholarly journals. Each entry concludes with a bibliography that lists the works of the profiled author and secondary sources for further investigation. The bibliographies are not completely up-to-date. Although novels published as recently as 1998 are included in several entries, others, such as Bebe Moore Campbell's *Singing in the Comeback Choir* and Gloria Naylor's *Men of Brewster Place*, are not, perhaps because they were published too late in the year. The bibliography for Alice Walker ends unaccountably in 1992.

The stated purpose of this book is to be a "scholarly guide to the lives, works, and achievements" of the writers profiled. Some of the entries accomplish this, with thorough, perceptive analysis, although others are cursory, providing little insight into the subject covered. The benefit of a compendium such as this is that a number of authors are covered in one handy volume, and some may be hard to find elsewhere. For more prominent writers, both general readers and scholarly researchers will be better served by other resources, such as Gale's *Contemporary Authors*.

An F. Scott Fitzgerald Encyclopedia. By Robert L. Gale. 1998. 472p. bibliog. index. Greenwood, $85 (0-313-30139-5). DDC: 813.

Three publishing events in 1998 reflect the place F. Scott Fitzgerald—chronicler for the *Jazz Age*, a term he invented—continues to hold in the American literary firmament. First, there was the publication in January of Mary Jo Tate's *F. Scott Fitzgerald A–Z* (Facts On File, 1998). Second was the publication on July 20 of the list of the 100 best English-language novels of the twentieth-century. This list, by Modern Library's editorial board (a panel of 10 scholars and writers), selected two of Fitzgerald's novels—*The Great Gatsby* (number 2) and *Tender Is the Night* (number 28). The third event is the publication of the title under review, by Professor Emeritus Robert L. Gale (University of Pittsburgh).

In entries from *Abbot, Hamilton* ("Ham") (a character in *The Love Boat*) to "*Zone of Accident*" (a story published in 1935), Gale covers all Fitzgerald's works and named fictional characters; and biographical sketches of his family, friends, and associates are included. Entries range in length from a single sentence to nearly three pages for Fitzgerald, Zelda and *The Great Gatsby*. Longer entries include bibliographies.

While Gale's *An F. Scott Fitzgerald Encyclopedia* and Tate's *F. Scott Fitzgerald's A–Z* are complementary volumes, the placement and detail of certain materials differ widely. Gale's chronology is quite brief and precedes the A–Z entries; Tate's chronology, following the alphabetical entries, is far more extensive. Tate includes some 70 black-and-white illustrations; there are none in Gale. Tate does not attempt, as does Gale, to list all minor characters. With respect to major works (e.g., *The Great Gatsby*), Tate begins with a summary of the writing, publication, and critical reception of the work, then summarizes the novel chapter by chapter. Gale's approach is to first list the characters, then summarize the plot. Gale concludes his volume with a bibliography listing 29 titles of general works from the 1960s to 1995. Tate provides an appendix indexing entries by topic, such as characters, people, and places. An extensive five-part bibliography follows, including numerous subtopics in most of the parts.

Both volumes will undoubtedly be useful to general readers, students, and scholars. *An F. Scott Fitzgerald Encyclopedia* is recommended for high-school, public, and academic libraries, but smaller libraries that have already acquired Tate's *F. Scott Fitzgerald A–Z* may find they have sufficient coverage.

An Encyclopedia of British Women Writers. Rev. ed. Ed. by Paul and June Schlueter. 1998. 741p. index. Rutgers, $60 (0-8135-2542-X); paper $28 (0-8135-2543-8). DDC: 820.9.

This is an enlarged edition of *An Encyclopedia of British Women Writers* published by Garland in 1988. The number of entries has been increased by half again as much (from 400 to 600), and many, if not all, of the original articles have been revised or reworked. Although most of the entries are for British women writers from the eighteenth century to the present, an effort was made to include women writers of the medieval and Renaissance periods as well. The preface addresses the question of who is to be considered "British," for place of birth is not the only criterion. Those born elsewhere but residing in Great Britain for a considerable amount of time, those born in other countries of the British Commonwealth who emigrated to Great Britain, and those born in Great Britain who eventually emigrated to the U.S. are all included.

The alphabetically arranged, signed articles range in length from a few paragraphs to a few pages. Dates and places of birth and death and names of parents and husbands and other names under which the subject wrote are provided at the beginning of each entry. The articles offer both biographical detail and critical appraisal. Each entry ends with a list of sources for further information (reference works, books, and sometimes articles). The cross-referencing is very thorough, an important consideration because many women writers wrote under pseudonyms, titles, or married names. These references are found in the main part of the text and also in the index.

Other helpful features are a list of abbreviations used in citing reference works and one of abbreviations used in citing periodicals. Coverage is wide and represents familiar and unfamiliar figures of literary accomplishment. Here you will find not only Sylvia Plath and Beatrix Potter but Margaret Paston (1423–1482) and Violet Paget (1856–1935) as well. Scribes from Eliza Acton (1799–1859) to E. H. Young (1880–1949) are well served by this solid reference work. Reference collections in literature and women's studies alike will find this to be a great resource, especially for those embarking on studies of particular writers not usually represented in standard literary biographical sources. Recommended for academic and large public libraries.

Twayne's English Authors on CD-ROM. 1998. G. K. Hall, $995 (0-7838-1716-9). DDC: 820.

Twayne's United States Authors on CD-ROM. 1998. G. K. Hall, $995 (0-7838-1714-2). DDC: 810.

Twayne's World Authors on CD-ROM. 1998. G. K. Hall, $995 (0-7838-1718-5). DDC: 809.

Minimum requirements: Windows 3.x or Windows 95, 16 MB of free hard drive space, and 16 MB of RAM.

The famous Twayne's series on authors was previously released on CD-ROM under the title *DiscLit* and was published by OCLC. This time, G. K. Hall is publishing the CD-ROM version on its own. Once again, the full text of its various series appears on the disks, although without the enhancement of additional OCLC records that appeared on *DiscLit*. *American Authors* features 201 titles from the series; *English Authors*, 194; and *World Authors*, 193.

The system uses Netscape Navigator to view the titles and run the retrieval software. Having Navigator as a front-end is nothing new, but there is no option to bypass the Navigator installation if it is already on the system, which is frustrating. All three CDs have the same interface as well as the same printed instructions. A TCP/IP stack (an Internet protocol) must be installed on Windows 3.1 and 3.11 machines; Windows 95 includes a TCP/IP stack that is compatible. The program uses the ClipPrint print utility, which allows selective printing off parts of a screen, thereby providing slightly better control of printing than Navigator alone offers.

The main menu of the program has three choices. In Depth Search opens a form to fill in author's name, genre, sex (of author), keywords, time period, and, in the case of the *World Authors* disk, nationality. The genre, sex, and time period options have pull-down menus to select choices from; the others are free text. Boolean operators may be used within fields (AND is the default), as can internal or external truncation. Oddly, phrases are searched by using single quotation marks only, rather than the more conventional double quotation marks. Once a search is keyed in, results are displayed on a book-chapter-by-book chapter basis for keyword searches or by table of contents hyperlinks for other searches. Clicking a hyperlink brings up the full text of the corresponding book chapter, with searched words appearing in boldface type. There is also a citation at the bottom of each chapter's screen—most welcome for an electronic work and an idea more publishers should implement. The retrieval system generally works, though the Board discovered for one search (author: *Cleary*, keyword:

dogs) that out of the eight hits, two contained only the singular *dog* rather than the requested plural form.

The second search option, Authors A–Z, is a straightforward listing of all titles on the CD. Clicking on a link will lead to the table of contents for that book. The final search option, Research Ideas, is little more than a broad topical listing for authors. The *United States Authors* disk, for example, lists Early American Writers, 1492–1800, Poets, and Women Writers, among others, with each section leading to appropriate books. Some authors are missed in this search option. The *United States Authors* disk fails to list Anne Bradstreet, Willa Cather, or Amy Lowell under Women Writers, while the *English Authors* disc fails to list Ngaio Marsh or Iris Murdoch—the latter not appearing in any category whatsoever.

Although using the Navigator interface means less of a learning curve for most users, it is peculiar that this program is very Internet-like in another way—it is exceedingly slow, even on a Pentium with a 20x CD-ROM drive. The Main Menu, which contains several images, is annoyingly slow to load, and simply navigating from screen to screen after executing a search can be slow, too.

Finally, there is the issue of price. Each disk, to be sure, constitutes a significant savings when compared to buying some 200 printed volumes that contain the same text, and a considerable amount of shelf space is saved as well. But since the Twayne's works are monographic in nature and almost entirely devoted to just one author, patrons are likely to find it easier just checking out the volume of their choice rather than searching for all relevant information on disk. It is only when patrons wish to compare one author to another or are doing something on genre that the full-text retrieval capabilities of this program will be of benefit. Libraries will have to determine if the price of these compilations is justified by likely use in their collections. Also, many of the Twayne's volumes are badly dated, and the CD-ROM versions do not update them. Among the more dated volumes are those for John Cheever (originally published in 1979), Doris Lessing (1965), Norman Mailer (1978), Wole Soyinka (1967), and Gore Vidal (1968). The result is that more recent critical assessments do not appear for each author, nor any coverage of more recent works penned by that author. Electronic reference titles that simply reprint books may have been appropriate when CD-ROMs were first gaining in popularity, but users expect more today—especially at $1,000 each.

The Columbia Dictionary of Quotations from Shakespeare. Ed. by Mary and Reginald Foakes. 1998. 516p. indexes. Columbia, $50 (0-231-10434-0). DDC: 822.3.

This highly selective compilation of approximately 3,700 quotations is by a UCLA professor emeritus of English (and contributor to *The Shakespeare Quarterly*) and his late wife. It uses the modern-spelling text of *Riverside Shakespeare* (Houghton, 1974), whereas the standard work, Stevenson's *Home Book of Shakespeare Quotations* (Scribner, 1937; repr. Macmillan, 1987), with some 90,000 quotations, is based upon the revised Globe edition (1911). Like Stevenson, Foakes is arranged alphabetically by topic with numerous *see also* and a few *see* references; but unlike Stevenson, its considerably fewer topics are not subdivided. Among topics in Foakes but not Stevenson are anti-Semitism, exorcism, homelessness, last words, misogyny, and politics.

The strength of Foakes lies in its annotations to most quotations, providing explanations of changes in meaning or style since Shakespeare's day. Stevenson's annotations, on the other hand, are frequently devoted to the number of times a word or phrase was used by Shakespeare; much less frequently do they explain meanings. Whereas Stevenson concludes with a very full index and concordance, the title under review has four indexes: character, play, poem, and keyword.

The Columbia Dictionary of Quotations from Shakespeare complements Stevenson's *Home Book of Shakespeare Quotations* by its approach to annotations—an emphasis on explaining changes in meaning since Shakespeare's time—and the inclusion of character, play, and poem indexes, and a solid keyword index. It is recommended for high-school, public, and academic libraries that do not own Stevenson but want to provide more coverage of Shakespeare than is afforded by general quotation dictionaries. It may also be considered a useful supplemental title for libraries owning Stevenson.

Pronouncing Shakespeare's Words: A Guide from A to Zounds. By Dale F. Coye. 1998. 744p. appendixes. bibliog. indexes. Greenwood, $99.50 (0-313-30655-9). DDC: 822.

How should today's actors, teachers, and readers of Shakespeare pronounce *lineament* (*Romeo and Juliet*, act 1 scene 3, line 83)? Is there a difference between the preferred U.S., Canadian, and U.K. pronunciations of *Rosaline*, a character in the same play? What is the pronunciation of *shrowd* (meaning harsh) in the poem *Venus and Adonis*? And compare/contrast the U.S.-, Canadian-, and U.K.-recommended pronunciations of *Adonis*. These are typical examples in what the compiler (an assistant professor of English at the College of New Jersey) terms a straightforward guide to "all the words in Shakespeare's plays and poems which the average college student or actor might find difficult to pronounce." It is not about how Shakespeare might have pronounced his words. It is, rather, a guide to how the words are pronounced today, based on a survey of American, Canadian, and British Shakespearean scholars for their recommendations as well as research in dictionaries and other linguistic works. More than 3,400 words are treated, including uncommon words, common words whose pronunciation varies, words stressed differently in current English, proper names, and foreign phrases. *The Riverside Shakespeare* (1974) was chosen as the basic text.

The introduction discusses various problems with modern English pronunciation, including losing rhymes and maintaining the meter. Each play appears in alphabetical order. Characters and places in the play are listed first, with other words listed by scene in the order in which they appear. Following the plays, six poems appear in A–Z order. Many word entries provide brief definitions as well as pronunciation guidelines. Preceding the entries for plays and poems are two helpful lists, one of the most common "hard" words in Shakespeare (which are not included in the individual play entries because they occur so often) and one of the most common reduced forms.

The volume concludes with five appendixes, of which appendix A (common words with more than one standard pronunciation in today's English) may be the most useful, a bibliography, an index of words, and a subject index (British English, received pronunciation, New England pronunciations, Welsh accent, etc.). *Pronouncing Shakespeare's Words* is an authoritative resource that will undoubtedly be extremely useful to actors, students, teachers, and general readers of Shakespeare. Recommended for academic, public, and high-school libraries, though its price may put it out of reach for some.

A Jane Austen Encyclopedia. By Paul Poplawski. 1998. 411p. bibliogs. illus. index. Greenwood, $75 (0-313-30017-8). DDC: 823.7.

As the creator of numerous memorable characters ranging from the lively and intelligent Elizabeth Bennet in *Pride and Prejudice* to the slyly obsequious Mrs. Norris in *Mansfield Park* to the dashing but duplicitous Frank Churchill in *Emma*, Jane Austen has always had a large and devoted following that admires her scintillating wit, mastery of repartee, and sense of irony. A recent spate of film and television adaptations of her works, and the publication of three Austen biographies in 1997, have attracted scores of new readers to this beloved British writer. Thus, the time was ripe for this encyclopedia, the nucleus of which is a dictionary containing entries for Austen's works, her characters, and selected family members.

Articles on Austen's major novels average 12 pages and include a detailed synopsis of the plot, publication information, a list of characters, and bibliographical references to critical sources. Character entries vary in length, but each provides a perceptive and finely honed description of the individual. Also notable are two general articles—*criticism*, which surveys selected critical and biographical writings on Austen, and *themes and concerns*, which discusses four thematic elements central to her works. Other features include chronologies that cover Austen's life and writings and outline major historical and literary events from the middle of the eighteenth century through 1820, a section of illustrations, a list of Austen's works, and extensive secondary bibliographies.

The detailed index covers names and titles noted in both the chronology of Austen's life and the dictionary entries. A useful section under the heading *themes and concerns, keywords* provides references to mentions of topics such as dancing, health and sickness, social climbing, and theatricals. Unfortunately, these references can be misleading; for instance, the subentry *wit and wittiness* guides the user to the entry for Mary Bennet, who is decidedly lacking in this regard, but it does not refer to Elizabeth Bennet, one of the wittiest of Austen's characters.

This compilation reflects meticulous research and a thorough knowledge of Austen's writings. However, Poplawski, a senior lecturer in

English at Trinity College Carmarthen in Wales, could have increased its value by including articles on Austen's settings and associates, and on specific topics and themes; by providing a filmography of television and motion-picture productions of Austen's novels (or, at least, by mentioning film adaptations in entries for her works); and by acknowledging major Austen resources on the Internet, such as the wealth of material available through the Jane Austen Information Page at [http://www.pemberley.com/janeinfo/janeinfo.html/]. Because it lacks these and other elements, this book is not the definitive reference work on Jane Austen. Earlier guides, such as J. David Grey's *The Jane Austen Companion with a Dictionary of Jane Austen's Life and Works* (Macmillan, 1986) and F. B. Pinion's *A Jane Austen Companion: A Critical Survey and Reference Book* (Macmillan, 1973), offer better coverage of Austen's world and her themes and settings, while George L. Apperson's *A Jane Austen Dictionary* (C. Palmer, 1932; repr. R. West, 1977) continues to be useful for identifying places, people, and titles mentioned in her writings. However, Poplawski's encyclopedia provides excellent plot summaries and character sketches, and it will be a valuable addition to high-school, public, and academic libraries.

Science Fiction Writers: Critical Studies of the Major Authors from the Early Nineteenth Century to the Present Day. 2d ed. Ed. by Richard Bleiler. 1999. 816p. bibliogs. illus. index. Scribner, $125 (0-684-80593-6). DDC: 823.

In his introduction, editor Bleiler discusses the difficulty of defining science fiction as a genre and deciding which authors to include. This book takes a critical look at 96 writers ranging from Mary Shelley to Pat Murphy (b.1955), encompassing the "most important and influential" authors in the science fiction field from the early nineteenth century to the present day. The writers were chosen because they have played an important role in the development of the science fiction genre. With a few exceptions, only American and British writers are discussed. Unlike the first edition, which had chronological arrangement, this one uses a dictionary arrangement with names appearing in alphabetical order. Each signed entry includes biographical information, critical analysis, and a selected bibliography of primary and secondary works. Most entries include a portrait.

This edition has more than 24 new entries, and most of the original articles have been updated and revised, often by the original authors. Some popular authors whose works are considered fantasy rather than science fiction have not been included. Although C. S. Lewis's *Out of the Silent Planet* and *Perelandra* are discussed at length, his Narnia books are dealt with in only a brief paragraph and with no analysis. On the other hand, the article on Ursula K. LeGuin covers her Earthsea series in some detail. The length of each article varies depending upon the contribution the author has made and the number of books that are analyzed. The volume concludes with a brief general bibliography and an index of titles and names.

This is a valuable reference tool that will be useful for general interest as well as for reports about an author. Recommended for high-school, public, and academic libraries. Libraries owning the first edition, which was published in 1982, will want this update.

The Oscar Wilde Encyclopedia. By Karl Beckson. 1998. 456p. bibliogs. illus. index. AMS, 56 E. 13th St., New York, NY 10003-4686, $125 (0-404-61498-1). DDC: 828.

This encyclopedia, which is the first to concentrate on Oscar Wilde, offers information on Wilde's art and personal life, the social mores and cultural trends of his time, and the persons who had a significant role in his life. Other entries offer details on literary movements, such as aestheticism; or fashion and theater; or selected symbols, such as the green carnation, a signal of decadence in the 1890s. Karl Beckson is a professor of English at Brooklyn College, City University of New York.

Entries are arranged alphabetically, and the majority are devoted to Wilde's writings. Wilde's works cover a wide range of forms—essays, poetry, reviews, drama, fiction. Each work has a separate entry, with bibliographic details (first appearance; if published; subsequent revisions; inclusion in a collected volume). For more important works, the background, sources, and critical reception are discussed, and the location of manuscripts is noted. Many poems that were not published in Wilde's lifetime are included, even if they were never completed. Often the plot of a fictional work is provided, and in the case of a play, the production details. Although some literary entries are brief, the discussions of major works such as *The Importance of Being Earnest* and *The Picture of Dorian Grey* are lengthy and thorough. Among the more interesting entries that deal with other aspects of Wilde's life and career are those on the prison years, the American lecture tour (with complete schedule), and the biographical entries on George Bernard Shaw and Constance Wilde. Under *newspapers and periodicals*, there are several pages on the wide variety of papers in which Wilde published, from the penny *Pall Mall Gazette* to *Lady's World*.

This volume provides a chronology and an introduction by Wilde's grandson, Merlin Holland. There is no general bibliography, although many entries include scholarly references for further reading. *See* reference guide the reader to appropriate entry headwords. The general index, with main entries designated by page numbers in boldface, integrates names, title, subjects, and places. The illustrations are sparse but at times helpful in giving a sense of place (Wilde's Reading Prison cell) or providing a face (Yeats in the 1890s) to a familiar name.

Whether the reader is a student, or a specialist in the writings of Oscar Wilde, or just interested in English literature of the late nineteenth century, this easy-to-use and very readable volume will satisfy interests and provide answers. It should complement such works as *Oscar Wilde: An Annotated Bibliography* (Greenwood, 1993) and is recommended for academic and large public libraries.

Reference Guide to Russian Literature. Ed. by Neil Cornwell. 1998. 972p. index. Fitzroy Dearborn, $125 (1-884964-10-9). DDC: 891.7.

Cornwell, professor of Russian and comparative literature at the University of Bristol, has assembled an impressive reference work for Russian literature. There are no entries for literary terms, concepts, or movements, although 13 introductory essays do "give coverage to most periods, topics, and genres of Russian literature." Authors included have been limited to Russians and non-Russians writing in Russian, all of whom are creative literary figures rather than critics, philosophers, or theorists. Names have been transliterated according to Library of Congress rules and are arranged alphabetically. A few anonymous works of literature are included, interfiled with authors by their English-language title. In choosing which writers to include, the editor professes a bias toward the nineteenth and twentieth centuries "and, to some extent, towards contemporary authors."

Each of the more than 250 author entries begins with brief biographical information and a wonderful bibliography of primary works, including English translations, arranged by date of publication and grouped by genre when appropriate. Citations to critical studies are also listed. Introductory essays about the authors are provided and are followed, in many cases, by critical assessments of selected individual works; almost 300 titles are covered. Essays for both authors and works are approximately 1,000 words long. All essays are signed by the scholars who wrote them. Often, the essays on individual titles have been written by different scholars, thereby allowing for a broader scholarly assessment of the writer and his or her works.

Preceding the introductory essays are alphabetical lists of the writers and works included, a chronological list of writers, a general reading list, a chronology of significant events, and a glossary. The volume concludes with a title index, followed by notes on the contributors.

Other English-language reference tools are available. The essays in the revised edition of *The Cambridge History of Russian Literature* (Cambridge, 1992) offer lengthier treatment of periods in Russian literary history. Mention of specific authors or works is part of a larger narrative and not provided in separate entries. In addition to entries for authors, *Handbook of Russian Literature* (Yale, 1985) includes literary concepts, movements, and figures important in the history of Russian literature who are not creative literary writers themselves. It does not have separate entries for literary works. The *Modern Encyclopedia of Russian and Soviet Literature* (Academic International Press, 1977–), while not yet complete, casts its net far and wide to include the literary output of the former Soviet Union, treating non-Russian authors writing in languages other than Russian. Finally, *Dictionary of Russian Women Writers* (Greenwood, 1994) limits its coverage to women.

In addition to covering writers, such as the poet Gennaai Aigi, not found elsewhere, the chief contribution of *Reference Guide to Russian Literature* is the inclusion of critical essays on specific titles. These provide the reader with in-depth analysis not usually found in literary reference works. Of course, no single reference work can include everything; ownership of several of the titles mentioned in this review affords broader coverage. Highly recommended for large public and academic library collections, especially those supporting programs in Russian language and literature as well as comparative literature.

Encyclopedia of Arabic Literature. 2v. Ed. by Julie Scott Meisami and Paul Starkey. 1998. 896p. bibliogs. index. Routledge, $290 (0-415-06808-8). DDC: 892.7.

It's probably safe to say that until Najib Mahfuz won the Nobel Prize for Literature in 1988, few people other than specialists could name a single Arabic author. As this new encyclopedia reveals, Arabic literature has a much older and richer tradition than most of us know.

The editors, both scholars in Middle Eastern studies, have brought to completion a project begun in the early 1980s. The work was originally conceived as a biographical dictionary of Arab personalities, then as a dictionary of writers, then as a handbook modelled on the Oxford Companions. It has entries on "the most important authors, works, genres, key terms, and issues in the Arabic literary tradition—classical, transitional, and modern." Entries are arranged alphabetically and vary in length from a few sentences to more than eight pages (for *Alf layla wa-layla*, or the *Thousand and One Nights*). Among the longer entries are those for genres, such as *historical literature* and *prose, non-fiction, medieval*. Most of the entries are devoted to writers, ranging from Aristotle, regarded by many Islamic philosophers as the first teacher, to al-Araj Wasini, an Algerian novelist born in 1954. A sample of other entries shows the diverse coverage—*books and bookbinding, artistic prose, Al-Jarida* (an important newspaper), *censorship in Arabic literature, Tunisia*.

Most entries end with lists of further reading, some of which are fairly extensive. The bibliography appended to *Spain*, for example, lists more than 30 items, many in languages other than English. Appendixes include a glossary and dynastic tables. Access is aided by *see* and *see also* references as well as a general index.

The four-volume *Cambridge History of Arabic Literature* (Cambridge, 1983–92) takes a more in-depth approach. This encyclopedia will be useful for students of Middle Eastern culture and philosophy, as well as literature, and should be a welcome addition to any academic or large public library.

Geography, Biography

Chronology of World History. 4v. Rev. ed. By H. E. L. Mellersh. 1999. 3,200p. indexes. ABC-CLIO, $375 (1-57607-155-3). DDC: 902.

This set is the latest revision of volumes that have gone through numerous printings since their first appearance in the 1960s and were most recently issued by Simon and Schuster in 1994. The copyright page of each volume states that these books are "extensively revised and updated" editions of the previously issued titles: *Chronology of the Ancient World, Chronology of the Expanding World,* and *Chronology of the Modern World* [RBB O 15 95], though they fail to mention *Chronology of the Medieval World*, which was also part of the last revision. ABC-CLIO published an abridged version of the Simon and Schuster volumes, called *Chronology of World History, Compact Edition*, in 1996.

Content has been completely rewritten, and a new page design makes this version more attractive and easier to read. Coverage of the twentieth century has been expanded. The first volume now embraces both the ancient and medieval worlds, from prehistory to A.D. 1491; and the period previously dealt with in volume 4, from the mid–eighteenth century to 1992, has been expanded into two volumes, one covering 1776–1900 and the other covering 1901–1998. The volumes are arranged in strict chronological order with date spans for each section ranging from an entire millennia in the first volume to individual years in the last two. The preface to each volume states that the entire chronology "contains over 70,000 entries," a number verified by a sampling by the Board. Within each date span, entries are grouped within four main categories (Politics, Government, and Economics; Science, Technology, and Medicine; Arts and Ideas; and Society) and up to 25 subcategories. A number of these subcategories—Colonization, Computing, Ecology, Everyday Life, Human Rights—reflect a shift from the 1994 version, which generally tended to emphasize politics and literature. Also new are several topical "mini-chronologies," such as "Rise of Islam (610–756)," "The Automobile (1862–1900)," and "New Food Products (1904–98)." These are compiled from related entries scattered throughout the set. Each chronological section also includes a listing of births and deaths of "noteworthy people" within the span of years covered. In the previous edition, these lists provided only names and dates; but now each person gets a descriptive sentence. Each volume concludes with an index of people and events plus a separate titles index listing various works of art or literature. Unfortunately, as with the previous revision, there is no cumulative index.

One problem with virtually any chronology is the relative lack of background information for some entries. In this set, although most entries are longer than those in its predecessor, they are still quite brief when compared to, for example, Grun's *Timetables of History* (Simon & Schuster, 1991) or the much more verbose *The People's Chronology*, by James Trager (Holt, 1992). In volume 1, for example, it is stated that in 1274 "the examination system is abandoned in South China," with no explanation of what the examination system was. Volume 4 reports that in 1986 the A320 Airbus was "the first commercial aircraft to use a 'fly-by-wire' system," with no explanation of what that phrase means in aviation. More disappointing is the inconsistency with which specific dates of events are given. At no time, for example, are exact opening dates of movies given or the exact dates of operatic premieres. The "Sports" section for 1981 notes that "Mairzy Dotes . . . wins the inaugural Japan Cup at Fuchu racecourse," but fails to note the exact date, while a chronological listing for the same year notes the specific date (August 30) that "John Henry . . . wins the first Arlington Million horse race." One series of outright errors was spotted in the third volume, where it is stated that in 1890 "Anatole France publishes his novel *Thais*, based on the opera by French composer Jules Massenet"; while under 1894 it is noted that "*Thais*, by the French composer Jules Massenet," premieres and "is based on a novel by the French writer Anatole France published in 1890." The latter entry, of course, is the accurate one, as the novel preceded the opera.

Although coverage of other cultures has been expanded, there is still a distinct European–North American emphasis. With the exception of the first volume, well under 10 percent of the entries in the set deal with events taking place outside of Europe or the U.S. Larger libraries, even those that own the 1994 version, may wish to consider this set, because on size alone it covers more events than any other general chronology. Smaller libraries will likely find *Timetables of History* or *The People's Chronology* adequate for their needs.

Encyclopedic Dictionary of Conflict and Conflict Resolution, 1945–1996. By John E. Jessup. 1998. 887p. bibliogs. index. Greenwood, $175 (0-313-28112-2). DDC: 903.

Examining conflict among nations and peoples and the various methods of resolution, this volume has A–Z entries on the people, places, and events which have played prominent parts in the conflicts of the late twentieth century.

Though there are no separate entries for the U.S. and the former Soviet Union, the majority of the world's countries are included. Entries range in length from a sentence or two to five or six pages. Each entry for a country consists of a brief historical overview from ancient to modern times, with emphasis given to those events of recent years that fall within the scope of the work. Biographies for prominent leaders from both ends of the political spectrum treat only those life events that touch on conflict, violence, or conflict resolution. Treaties, agreements, and accords between various countries and groups are also detailed. Although most of the agreements contained in this volume were put into place during the time period covered, some, like the Monroe Doctrine, are still in effect and are still invoked to warn foreign countries against new world entanglements. Entries such as *Pueblo Incident* and *Iran-Iraq War* discuss the causes and results of the conflicts.

In the introductory section, the author reviews his criteria for choosing the subjects he covers. Much of the information appeared in an earlier Greenwood publication, *The Chronology of Conflict Resolution: 1945–1985* (1989), but here is reformatted so that a particular person, place, or event is the focus of each entry. This allows for a fuller exposition of the background details of the events and the people who have played a primary role in them. *See* and *see also* references direct the reader to correct entry headings and related entries. All spellings are westernized, followed by the alternative spelling where available. Entries may be followed by suggested readings. An index of major names, places, events, and concepts completes the work.

Congressional Quarterly's *International Conflict: A Chronological Encyclopedia of Conflicts and Their Management, 1945–1995*, published last year, covers similar ground, providing summaries of 292 international conflicts. The chronological arrangement leads to some disjointed discussions and makes it necessary to refer to multiple entries to get a comprehensive overview of a recurrent dispute or of the events affecting a specific country or region. *Encyclopedic Dictionary of Conflict and Conflict Resolution, 1945–1996* contains much useful information in an easily accessible format. This volume would work well in answering ready-reference questions and in directing the reader to more in-depth works. Recommended for academic and large public libraries.

The Encyclopedia of Political Revolutions. Ed. by Jack A. Goldstone. 1998. 580p. bibliog. illus. index. maps. Congressional Quarterly, $125 (1-56802-206-9). DDC: 903.

Over the past 500 years, almost every country in the world has been touched by revolution, either directly through events occurring within their own boundaries or through influences that spread from neighboring countries. In more than 300 entries, this encyclopedia provides a fascinating and thorough review of revolutions around the globe since A.D. 1500, beginning with the Italian city-state revolutions of the Renaissance and progressing to movements that are still continuing today, like the Kurdish revolts.

Defining *revolution* as an event that used irregular procedures aimed at forcing political change within a society and that had lasting effects on the political system of the society in which it occurred, the encyclopedia encompasses topics such as the Civil Rights and women's rights movements and the Indian and Pakistani independence movements as well as the American Revolution, the French Revolution, and the Spanish civil war. The volume includes biographies of more than 70 leaders, including Susan B. Anthony, Gandhi, Martin Luther King Jr., Hitler, and Robespierre, chosen because their influence spread beyond their own countries. Concepts important to an understanding of why revolutions occur and the influence they have had on political and social history are also the subject of essays. These essays, such as *anarchism, ethnic conflict, liberation theology, religion,* and *terrorism,* help the reader understand recurring themes and underscore the veracity of editor Goldstone's opening quotation: "the more things change, the more they remain the same."

Articles are authored by scholars, mostly from the U.S. and England; are signed; and include *see also* references and bibliographies. Arrangement is alphabetical by subject, and length varies from one to five pages. At the beginning of the volume are an alphabetical list of articles, with their contributors; and a list of contributors, with their articles. A list of articles by subject divides the content into three broad areas—biographies, concepts, and events; more-detailed subject access is provided by the index. A time line, also at the beginning of the volume, charts revolutionary events for the period covered.

A more popular treatment of similar topics can be found in Facts On File's *Encyclopedia of Revolutions and Revolutionaries* [RBB My 1 96]. *The Encyclopedia of Political Revolutions* is recommended for academic and larger public libraries. Congressional Quarterly has also issued a paperback volume, *Who's Who in Political Revolutions* ($29.95, 1-56802-461-4), which reprints the biographical entries and the time line.

Oxford Encyclopedia of World History. 1998. 775p. chronology. illus. maps. tables. Oxford, $30 (0-19-860223-5). DDC: 903.

This reference source was drawn from the two world history volumes of the multivolume *Oxford Illustrated Encyclopedia* (Oxford, 1988). Articles were enlarged and updated, and new ones were added. The volume has approximately 4,000 brief entries arranged in an alphabetical format, covering prehistory to current events. There are many biographies of world leaders, such as Winston Churchill, and others important to the development of ideas, inventions, and discoveries, such as Aristotle, Einstein, and Magellan. There are histories of each country and a short table giving the country's capital, area in kilometers and square miles, population, currency, religions, ethnic groups, languages, and international organizations. These country profiles are generally quite current. *Northern Ireland* mentions the 1998 Good Friday agreement, and *Cambodia* mentions the 1998 death of Pol Pot. Appropriately placed throughout the text are 50 maps and 50 portraits, engravings, and tables. Rounding out the volume is a 27-page chronology of world events.

There are numerous single-volume works similar to *Oxford Encyclopedia of World History.* Three of the more recent are *The Hutchinson Dictionary of World History* (ABC-CLIO, 1993), *Larousse Dictionary of World History* [RBB N 1 94], and *Macmillan Concise Dictionary of World History* (Macmillan, 1983). The first work has 5,000 entries; 70 maps; many appendixes of leaders, organizations, and disasters; plus a world chronology. The second has 7,500 entries, 36 maps, 40 tables, and no illustrations. The last has 10,000 entries and no maps or illustrations. The Oxford volume has the advantage of containing current information, useful country facts, and illustrations. This well-organized and up-to-date book will be useful for ready reference in high-school, public, and academic libraries.

Great Misadventures: Bad Ideas That Led to Big Disasters. 4v. By Peggy Saari. 1998. 730p. chronology. illus. indexes. UXL, $99 (0-7876-2798-4). DDC: 904.

This resource presents 100 events from ancient to modern times that reflect "human error, greed, and poor judgment." Its goal is to "show that success can also involve failure, triumph can encompass defeat, and human beings are inspired by self-interest as often as they are motivated by selflessness."

The set is divided into four themed volumes, made up of 25 events that are arranged chronologically. Each entry describes the event and discusses its historical background and significance. A few references are given for further reading. Sidebars within entries contain biographical profiles or highlight various related facts and issues. Black-and-white photographs, illustrations, and maps complement each entry. Each volume carries the same annotated table of contents, time line of important events, and cumulative index.

Volume 1, *Exploration and Adventure,* covers events such as the Children's Crusade (1212), the Donner Party Tragedy (1846–47), and the Mount Everest climbing disaster (1996). Volume 2, Science and Technology, looks at, among other events, the sinking of the *Titanic* in 1912 and the outbreak of mad cow disease in 1996. In volume 3, Military, one finds such events such as the fall of Athens (415 B.C. to 413 B.C.) and the Bay of Pigs Invasion (1961). Volume 4, Society, examines as examples of misadventure the Triangle Shirtwaist Company fire (1911) and the nerve gas attack on the Tokyo subway system (1995). Most of the entries provide a fresh slant on events. For example, the entry on Christopher Columbus focuses on his settlement of the New World, poor administrative skills, cruelty to the native population, and his later years. Some events, such as the Tonya Harding–related assault on Nancy Kerrigan, are not on par with most entries (e.g., the accident at Chernobyl, Watergate) in terms of historical importance.

It is common for resources at this level to use parenthetical definitions for words and terms that might be unfamiliar. However, in this set the parenthetical definitions are intrusive and often unnecessary, for example, "Paris (the capital of France)"; "American Revolution (1775–83; a movement by American colonists to gain independence from Britain)." Students in the targeted grades are expected to be familiar with many of these terms. There are a few problematic definitions. In the chapter on the Battle of Verdun, storm troopers are defined as "members of an elite, private Nazi army"; but the battle took place during World War I, and the Nazi army didn't come to power until the 1930s.

Despite some problems, this resource is attractive both in terms of layout and price. Although its title might draw browsers, the set should receive a workout at report-writing time in middle, junior, and senior high schools. Teachers might find it a useful supplement to textbook materials. Recommended for school and public libraries.

Encyclopedia of Historians and Historical Writing. 2v. Ed. by Kelly Boyd. 1999. 1,562p. bibliogs. indexes. Fitzroy Dearborn, $275 (1-884964-33-8). DDC: 907.2.

Designed for the "informed reader" rather than the specialist, this encyclopedia includes writers from non-Western cultures as well as the Western canon. The entries, arranged alphabetically, consist of three types of essays—on individuals, nations or geographical areas, and topics. The topics were suggested by 19 advisors and prepared by approximately 400 contributors. Within some entries there may be chronological arrangement. Each entry is signed and followed by *see also* references and an often extensive bibliography or further reading list. Biographical entries include brief biographical notes. Length ranges from half a page to more than 12 pages for *United States: Nineteenth Century.*

A list of advisors and contributors and an introduction, "Rethinking History," can be found at the beginning of volume 1. Both volumes provide alphabetical and thematic lists of entries and a chronological list of historians. The thematic list groups entries by region and periods (*Europe, medieval*, for example) and topics, from *art history* to *women's and gender history*. The chronological list begins in 551–479 B.C.E. with Kong-zi (Confucius) and concludes with Australian historian Marilyn Lake (1947–). Volume 2 concludes with a title index, a "Further Reading Index," and notes on contributors and advisors. The title index provides access to the principal writings listed in the entries on individual historians. The "Further Reading Index," arranged by author, leads the reader to citations in the bibliographies.

The choice of entries reflects a global intellectual culture that has led to new branches of history and debate: social history, with influences from anthropology and sociology; gender studies; and metahistory, to name a few. The encyclopedia leads the reader both to familiar historians, such as Edward Gibbon and Plutarch, and to the less well known, such as Fernando Ortiz, the founder of Afro-Cuban studies. There are essays on slavery, ancient and modern; Vietnamese chronicles, which are an important source of Vietnamese history from the Tran dynasty (1225–1400) onward; the study of crime and deviance; and labor history. Notable historians or history writers from places as far-flung as Iceland and India are given coverage. Another recent title, Garland's one-volume *Global Encyclopedia of Historical Writing* [RBB D 15 98], has a similarly broad perspective; but entries are generally briefer and coverage is more selective. Only a few living historians are included, for example, while the Fitzroy Dearborn set has entries for more than 200, among them Stephen Ambrose, Eric Foner, Peter Gay, Elaine Pagels, and Simon Schama. *Encyclopedia of Historians and Historical Writing* is a worthy addition to the reference collections of large public and academic libraries.

A Global Encyclopedia of Historical Writing. Ed. by D. R. Woolf. 1998. 1,047p. bibliogs. index. Garland, $175 (0-8153-1514-7). DDC: 907.

This encyclopedia considers historiography, or the practice of writing about the past. It examines writing about the past in general, as well as current and recent writing about a particular period, person, or topic. The word *global* in the title reflects the editor's efforts to cover a wide range of topics and categories and to move from a Western emphasis to include representatives of non-Western cultures. Volume 1 consists of an introduction, information on contributors, and entries A–J. Volume 2 contains entries K–Z and the index. The editor, who is a professor of history at Dalhousie University in Halifax, Nova Scotia, has written extensively on modern historiography and rhetoric. The contributors were drawn from colleges and universities throughout the world.

The coverage consists of brief biographical entries on individuals (*Boorstin, Daniel*; *Gibbon, Edward*) or individual genres (*business history, urban history*); longer surveys of the historiography of periods or regions (*Renaissance, historiography during the*; *Soviet historiography*) and articles on approaches or concepts (*Annales school*; *revolution, as historical concept*). An interesting entry, *computers and historiography*, examines the impact of new technology on historical writing and research. As explained in the introduction, the work is representative rather than comprehensive. Space constraints dictated that coverage be selective, and only a few living historians are included. Also in the interests of economy, internal cross-referencing is not complete, although there is a comprehensive index. Each entry is followed by a bibliography. In the case of biographical entries, the bibliography cites both primary texts and secondary references.

Whether the reader is a student, teacher, or simply one interested in the writing of history, this scholarly encyclopedia provides a wide range of information and is recommended for academic libraries. Public libraries with research collections in history will also find it a valuable tool.

DISCovering Nations, States, and Cultures. CD-ROM. 1998. Gale, $600 (0-7876-0559-X). DDC: 909.

System requirements: Windows 3.1 *or higher*; 4 MB RAM (8 MB *or more recommended*).

DISCovering Nations, States, and Cultures is a program designed to help users understand all the world's nations and cultures. Its target audience is high-school students and teachers, although anyone interested in broadening cross-cultural understanding will find it useful.

The CD-ROM contains information on 200 nations, The 50 U.S. states (plus Washington, D.C., and U.S. dependencies), 12 Canadian provinces and territories, and nearly 500 cultural groups. Searches are simple and can be done four ways—Culture, Place, Full Text, and Picture Gallery. Culture and Place searches can be executed either by entering search criteria or scrolling down an alphabetical list. Place search also has a clickable map. More refined searches can be conducted from the Main Menu. Entries are similar to what one would find in the print sources from which much of the content is drawn—*Worldmark Encyclopedia of Cultures and Daily Life* [RBB My 1 98], *Worldmark Encyclopedia of the Nations* (9th ed., 1998), and *Worldmark Encyclopedia of the States* (4th ed., 1998). Each entry includes a historical overview and current information about the economics, politics, geography, and environment of the culture or area. The more than 1,650 illustrations include official flags and seals, regional maps, and photographs that describe the everyday lives of diverse inhabitants. There are links to related documents and images. Cultural differences and similarities are the focal points, and comparisons are easy due to the standardized format of the entries and a "context bar" that allows searching each entry by subject categories, such as Climate, Judicial System, and Balance of Payments. Tables enhance understanding, and some are hard to find elsewhere. For example, in the entry for Brazil there is a table that lists the newspapers of that country and indicates their political bias.

The command buttons and the toolbar are easy to use, even for novices. Users can print or download all or parts of documents—libraries can customize the setup to limit printing and downloading. Because the default illustration (usually the official flag) and the search results box and other tools take up the left half of the screen at all times, the user sees relatively little text at once. Some of the tables cannot be read at one viewing. It is easier to "Print All" and scan the hard copy than to scroll through numerous screens.

Libraries that own the *Worldmark* encyclopedias already have much of this information in a form that is more convenient for ready reference. The CD-ROM offers conceptual linkages that make it especially useful for a classroom setting.

Encyclopedia of Conflicts since World War II. 4v. Ed. by James Ciment. 1999. 1,400p. appendixes. bibliog. glossary. illus. indexes. maps. M. E. Sharpe, $399 (0-7656-8004-1). DDC: 909.82.

The world has undergone dramatic change since World War II, especially in the importance of regional conflicts to the peace and security of all nation-states. Before the end of the cold war, these conflicts were mostly held in check by the two major world superpowers, except where they boiled over in Vietnam, Angola, Hungary, and Nicaragua. There was always the fear that a spark from one of these conflicts would unleash a third world war. With the end of the bipolar hegemony and superpower control over client states, regional conflicts are at center stage in the world today.

Encyclopedia of Conflicts since World War II is a multivolume resource that attempts to describe and analyze approximately 150 important post-WWII conflicts. The set is divided into three sections. "Roots of War" contains introductory essays illuminating the various causes of the conflicts, such as border disputes, cold war confrontations, coups, and ethnic and religious clashes. Chapters include "Cold War Confrontations," "People's Wars," and "International Arms Trade." This is followed by 11 regional maps. "Alliances and Treaties" describes the various diplomatic efforts at resolving the conflicts, including NATO (North Atlantic Treaty Organization), OAU (Organization of Africa Unity), and the Warsaw Pact. The final section contains the A–Z arrangement of the conflicts themselves, from *Afghanistan: Soviet Invasion, 1979–1989* to *Zimbabwe: Struggle for Majority Rule, 1965* Entries in this section, as well as in "Alliances and Treaties," are generally between four and ten pages long. Each entry is signed and includes a three-to ten-item bibliography. *See also* references refer the reader to related articles in the set.

Appendixes include brief biographies of the most significant individuals referred to in the conflicts; a glossary with definitions of key organizations, groups, and terms; and a general bibliography. There are three indexes: a general subject index, a biographical and organizations' names index, and a geographical index.

The cost of this set is well in line with most reference sets of like quality. It provides more in-depth treatment than dictionary-style reference sources such as *The Penguin Encyclopedia of Modern Warfare: 1850 to the Present Day* [RBB F 15 92]. Because of the potential for future conflicts in the regions of the world described in these volumes, the discussions should continue to serve as useful background information. *Encyclopedia of Conflicts since World War II* is an important contribution to the understanding of the historical and political condition of the world today and is a recommended purchase for any public, academic, or high-school library that wants to help users understand these local disputes.

The Columbia Gazetteer of the World. 3v. Ed. by Saul B. Cohen. 1998. 4,500p. Columbia Univ., $750 (0-231-11040-5). DDC: 910.

Last year saw the publication of two good geographical dictionaries: *The Houghton Mifflin Dictionary of Geography: Places and Peoples of the World* [RBB Mr 15 98], covering more than 10,000 places, and *Merriam-Webster's Geographical Dictionary* [RBB Ag 97], with more than 48,000 entries. Now comes the long-awaited successor to the classic *Columbia Lippincott Gazetteer of the World*, published in 1952. Dwarfing the 1997 titles in size and coverage, the *Columbia Gazetteer* contains 165,000 entries, including 30,000 new entries which reflect the dramatic changes in the world over the past 40-plus years. The new gazetteer will assume its predecessor's place as the definitive English-language encyclopedia of places and geographical features, and will be an essential reference for all types of libraries that can afford its price tag.

Gazetteer entries were selected to provide maximum coverage of places and features while achieving a balanced profile of each country. Accordingly, there are 21 entries for Andorra, 3,742 for Japan, and, in a nod to its largest potential market, 40,000 for the U.S. In addition to political subdivisions and physical features, the gazetteer includes entries for national parks, monuments, resorts, airports, ports, dams, nuclear plants, military bases, shopping malls, theme parks, and mythic places. Entries include information on the following, where appropriate: demography; physical geography; political boundaries; industry, trade, and service activities; agriculture; cultural, historical, and archeological points of interest; transportation lines; longitude, latitude, and elevations; distance to relevant places; pronunciations; official local government place names; and changed or variant names and spellings. Length varies from a few lines for small towns to more than a page for most countries.

Editor Cohen is university professor emeritus at Hunter College of the City University of New York and one of the world's most distinguished geographers. He was assisted by an editorial board of 150 geographical scholars from all over the world, who not only reviewed material for accuracy but also wrote new entries and developed pronunciation systems.

The Columbia Gazetteer focuses strictly on the alphabetical arrangement of places; there are no appendixes or maps as are often found in geographical dictionaries. The three volumes contain copious amounts of information, useful not only for finding the location, population, spelling, or pronunciation of a specific place but also for discovering its history and political, economic, and social conditions. Accordingly, students, travelers, businesspeople, the press, and researchers will all find this title valuable, and it is recommended for all libraries. Given the price, smaller libraries that already own the newest edition of *Merriam-Webster's Geographical Dictionary* may find that title sufficient for their needs.

Explorers: From Ancient Times to the Space Age. 3v. Ed. by John Logan Allen and others. 1999. bibliog. illus. index. maps. Macmillan, $275 (0-02-864893-5). DDC: 910.

The logical organization of this set will appeal to both the middle-grade student and the adult researcher interested in exploration from ancient times to the space age and its impact on the civilizations of the world. The first volume contains the complete table of contents for all three volumes, the list of maps, and introductory essays. Volume 3 supplements the text with a glossary, lists of explorers by nationality and by area of exploration, a bibliography, and a complete index. The bibliography is divided into general works and works listed by region; an asterisk denotes titles written for young adults. Students will appreciate the alphabetical listing of the entries, which affords quick information retrieval, as well as the introductory essays, which offer an enhanced perspective. These include "The Technology of Exploration," which discusses tools, maps, and vessels; "Causes and Effects of Exploration"; and "The History of Exploration," which contains a time line.

Profiles of 333 men and women make up most of the set's content, arranged alphabetically from *Acuna, Cristobal de*, a Spaniard who published the earliest account of the Amazon, to *Zheng He*, a fifteenth-century Chinese naval commander. Among others who are included are astronauts Neil Armstrong and Valentina Tereshkova, naturalists John James Audubon and Charles Darwin, President Theodore Roosevelt, and conqueror Alexander the Great. Entries are between one and seven pages long. The margin of each page is used to present headnotes, define terms used in the text, and, in many cases, provide portraits. Also in the margin is a background design taken from ancient maps; though attractive, this can be distracting. Fifty of the entries contain maps. *See also* references help the reader navigate the text, and each entry concludes with a few suggested readings. An added feature is the inserts of full-color plates in each volume; the rest of the set is in two colors.

There are a number of other resources available for students on the topic of explorers. The 10-volume *Grolier Student Library of Explorers and Exploration* [RBB Ap 15 98] is organized according to topic, such as voyages to Asia and Australia and the exploration of the North and South Poles. Color illustrations are generously placed throughout the text. UXL's four-volume *Explorers and Discoverers* [RBB My 1 95] and its two supplements, based on Gale's *Explorers and Discoverers of the World* (1993), profile more than 200 individuals in entries that are three to five pages in length. The reading level of both the Grolier and UXL sets is slightly lower than Macmillan's. For an older group of students, Salem Press has recently published *Explorers*, which compiles articles from Magill's Great Lives from History series. *Explorers: From Ancient Times to the Space Age* is an attractive choice for middle school and up and is recommended for public and school libraries that need another resource on the topic.

Travel Legend and Lore: An Encyclopedia. Ed. by Ronald H. Fritze. 1998. 443p. bibliog. illus. index. ABC-CLIO, $65 (0-87436-759-X). DDC: 910.4.

Travel is as old as civilization itself and nearly as fascinating. This volume focuses on the people, places, events, creatures, expectations, beliefs, and occurrences found and described in the tales of travelers. Ancient mythologies are steeped in travel lore, with tales of the Gilgamesh, the Hyperboreans, and Odysseus, all covered here, as are such historical travelers as the Crusaders, Marco Polo, and the Barbary pirates. Legends surrounding the mysterious geographic regions of lost continents and disappearing islands (Atlantis, Avalon, the Flyaway Islands); strange waterways, such as China's Grand Canal and the well-known Seven Seas; and vanished civilizations (Tartarus and Sybaris) are among the nearly 200 topics explained here. Amazons, centaurs, and mermaids are a few of the creatures described. The European explorers of the fifteenth and sixteenth centuries, lured by stories of the East, added still another dimension of legend and lore with their extraordinary accounts of explorations and discoveries in the New World. The Straits of Magellan, the Fountain of Youth, and El Dorado were just a few of the sources of later legends. The Erie Canal, wagon trains, stage coaches, and railroads were among the wellsprings of North American lore.

By no means exhaustive, but comprehensive in scope, *Travel Legend and Lore* serves as a solid introduction to the subject. The entries span all continents and civilizations up to, but not including, the twentieth century. The articles range from just a few lines to five pages, with the average length being one to two pages. Where appropriate, each entry contains cross-references to other articles within the encyclopedia as well as suggested additional readings. A bibliography and index round out the volume. The nonscholarly language makes the text suitable for high-school level and up. Recommended for high-school, public, and academic libraries and anyone with a strong sense of historical imagination and adventure.

The Book of the World. Rev. ed. 1998. index. Macmillan, $465 (0-02-864966-4). DDC: 912.

This new edition of the massive *Book of the World* was not available in time to be included in "An Evaluation of Current World Atlases," which was published in the January 1 & 15 issue of RBB. Now that the revised edition is out, it is understandable that the publisher calls it a revised rather than a second edition. Revisions to the maps are minimal: the changing of *Zaire* to *Democratic Republic of the Congo*, the reversion of Hong Kong into China, the new capital of Bolivia (Sucre), and a few name changes for cities in Armenia, India, and Russia. Based on user input, mistakes have been corrected, including correctly labeling Lake George and Schroon Lake, New York (although Schroon Lake is not in the index). Statistics for countries have been revised in the "Data and Facts" section. This section lists brief, basic information on population, life expectancy, GNP per capita, illiteracy, etc.

Sections unchanged in the revised edition include the 264 pages of maps from the database of the famous cartographic institute, Bertelsmann; more than 40 pages of satellite photographs of different environments (e.g., coral reef [Maldive Islands], rift valley [East Africa], glacier [Aletsch Glacier]); and the full-page satellite photographs of the Mississippi Delta, Anti Atlas Mountains in Morocco, and other stunning geographic features of the world. Although the index has 100,000 entries, there still are familiar place-names that are not listed (Marblehead, Massachusetts; Thun, Switzerland; Montalcino, Italy). Libraries that are interested in a larger index of place-names still need to use the *Times Atlas of the World* (ninth ed., Times, 1994) with its 200,000-term index-gazetteer. A new edition of the Times atlas will be out later this year.

The Book of the World depicts the world as a beautiful place and illustrates how modern technology benefits the publication of a book. This is a comprehensive atlas and also provides an education in geography. Libraries that have the first edition [RBB Jl 96] will have to decide if minimal changes warrant buying the revised edition. Any library without the first edition should certainly consider purchase of this fantastic atlas.

DK Student Atlas. 1988. 160p. illus. index. DK, $19.95 (0-7894-2399-5). DDC: 912.

The Reader's Digest Children's Atlas of the World. Ed. by Colin Slade. 1998. 128p. illus. index. Reader's Digest, $22.99 (1-57584-156-8). DDC: 912.

Here are two new atlases for children, similarly arranged. Both have introductory material that includes easy-to-follow instructions on the use of the atlas, followed by information about maps and mapmaking, with directions on how to read a map. In both atlases, this section is followed by a series of maps on such topics as the physical world, weather and climate, and population. After this introductory material, there is a basic consideration of each continent, followed by two-page spreads for various regions, such as western Canada and northeastern U.S.

Where the atlases differ is in the maps themselves, and in the accompanying information. The more than 50 digital maps in the Reader's Digest atlas are generally large-sized and brightly colored, showing major cities and some physical characteristics. Small pictures of buildings, natural features, crops, wildlife, etc., are placed within each map. There is some gutter loss. Each map is accompanied by several captioned pictures of famous places, events, and customs; a locator map; and population statistics. Text boxes contain "amazing facts," projects, and quizzes. The DK atlas, designed for children ages 10 and up, has maps that are smaller but also much more detailed, similar to what one would expect to find in a standard atlas for adults. Each map is accompanied by smaller thematic maps showing industry, population, farming and land use, major landscape features, environmental problems, and climate.

Each atlas concludes with a glossary and an index. In addition, the Reader's Digest atlas has a 16-page "World Fact File" providing essential, up-to-date facts about each country, with pronunciation guides and small colored pictures of flags.

Both atlases are attractive and reasonably priced. The Reader's Digest volume, though not an in-depth tool, is an informative browsing atlas for ages 8 to 13, and would be a good choice for family use. The DK atlas has more reference value and is appropriate for an older and more sophisticated audience. Both are recommended for school and public libraries.

The National Geographic Satellite Atlas of the World. 1998. 222p. illus. index. National Geographic, $50 (0-7922-7216-1). DDC: 912.

This book is not a world atlas in the true sense. It contains about 400 satellite images and maps of the earth taken by a variety of U.S. and foreign government agencies, institutions, and organizations. The introductory material provides information on the history of satellites and how they work. The first section of the atlas has two current foldout maps of the physical and political world followed by thematic world maps on tectonics, vegetation, climate, oceans, population, and El Nino. The rest of the volume is divided by continent, beginning with North America and ending with Antarctica. Each section has a physical and political map of the continent and a series of satellite images showing land forms, forces of nature, human impact, and cities. The images are all excellent representations; examples include a 3-D view of Los Angeles, a Russian satellite image of Vatican City, jet contrails over Germany, an area in Mali affected by the tsetse fly, the resemblance of Tasmania to southeastern Australia in a Landsat photo, and the infamous ozone hole over Antarctica. Small locator maps indicate the cities and features that are shown in the photos. In addition to the index, duplicate world maps on the inside of the front and back covers provide page numbers for the various locations that are illustrated in the photos.

The Macmillan series of the world atlases, *The Book of the World* (Rev. ed., 1999) and *Planet Earth* (1996), contains some satellite images, but the *National Geographic Satellite Atlas* is the only volume that concentrates solely on satellite imagery. This is an excellent addition to any library reference collection or the personal libraries of people interested in the impact of humans or nature on this planet.

African Biography. 3v. Ed. by Virginia Curtin Knight. 1999. 602p. bibliogs. glossary. illus. index. maps. UXL, $84 (0-7876-2823-9). DDC: 920.067.

This attractive set meets the needs of middle-and high-school students for information about prominent Africans of the past and present. Its 75 biographees have been selected to be "representative of people by region, race, sex, and field." Entries are limited to sub-Saharan Africans and run 6 to 10 pages, containing essays that cover personal and professional accomplishments, lists of titles for further reading, photographs, and a locator map. Introductory material at the beginning of each volume includes a list of entries by nationality and field, an overview of African history, a glossary, and a time line of African history. A bibliography and set index are repeated at each volume's end. The indexing is thorough, and each bibliography includes periodicals as well as books.

Students will easily locate specific individuals (arranged alphabetically from *Achebe, Chinua,* to *Yaa Asantewa*) or be able to find people of interest by browsing. Writing style is concise and clear, and words are often explained in context even when they are also in the glossary. Even troublesome or cruel situations and people are described. However, the work does have a few limitations. Admittedly it's difficult to decide whom to include. Despite the effort to be representative, most entries represent black male political figures, with a few women and whites (among them Frederik Willem de Klerk, Nadine Gordimer, and the Leakey family) included. Even so, Liberian Samuel Doe and Congolese Laurent Kabila are missing. Were sports figures specifically excluded? South African golfer Gary Player and Kenyan runners such as Kipchoge Keino are known worldwide. The editors acknowledge that women are underrepresented; only a dozen or so of the 75 people profiled here are women.

Much of the information on contemporary individuals is already available in other sources, including Gale's series Contemporary Black Biography. Still, this print set is so attractive that some repetition may be overlooked. In addition, it is a good source for finding information on somewhat obscure individuals from the past—for example, Adelaide Smith Casely Hayford, a Sierra Leonean who was born in 1868 and worked to promote the education of African women; Mansa Musa, fourteenth-century emperor of the Mali kingdom; nineteenth-century explorer and slave trader Tippu Tib. Recommended for school and public libraries.

American National Biography. 24v. Ed. by John A. Garraty and Mark C. Carnes. 1999. Oxford, $2,500 (0-19-520635-5). DDC: 920.073.

Stanley N. Katz, president emeritus of the American Council of Learned Societies (ACLS), says in his foreword to *American National Biography* (ANB) that it is "the major reference work of American biography of our generation," a statement that is hard to dispute. It is a worthy rival to ACLS' *Dictionary of American Biography* (DAB), and will stand with the British *Dictionary of National Biography* as a major reference work for many years to come. In spite of the change in publishers (DAB was published by Charles Scribner's Sons), ACLS has maintained continuity with the older work by appointing Garraty, the editor of DAB supplements four through eight, as the general editor of ANB. With Carnes, professor of history at Barnard College, Garraty has drawn together thousands of scholars to produce a tremendous work of biographical reference. Some of the leading scholars of our time cover the lives of people they have researched; for example, Ann D. Gordon writes on Susan B. Anthony; Stephen Ambrose on Dwight D. Eisenhower; and Arthur M. Schlesinger Jr. on Adlai Stevenson.

DAB was first published between 1926 and 1937 when history was narrowly focused on the lives of the "great," generally defined as famous white men. The lives of women and ethnic minorities were largely ignored. The various supplements tried to redirect this focus in recent times, but did little to address the basic need for an update to the old DAB. The general editors of ANB note this, and have expanded the scope of the work accordingly. There are entries for 17,450 men and women, all of whom died before 1996, with a few, such as Leif Erikson and Huron spiritual leader Deganawidah, from the precolonial era. As stated in the preface, "priority was given to persons, especially women and minorities, about whom new information or new ways of interpreting data had become available." Of the 16 Native American religious leaders profiled in ANB, only four also appear in DAB. Among the women covered in ANB but not in DAB are Hawaiian queen consort Emma, Thomas Jefferson's slave and putative mistress Sally Hemings, revolutionary heroine Deborah Sampson, and editor and antilynching activist Ida B. Wells-Barnett. The term "American" is defined, very loosely, as someone whose significant actions occurred while a resident in the U.S., or whose life or career directly influenced the course of American history—Christopher Columbus, Enrico Fermi, Thomas Mann, to name a few. In addition, the editors have made a point of including some "ordinary" people, such as Martha Ballard (1735–1812), a midwife whose diary is an important source for historians. The entry for Rose Philippine Duchesne, a French Catholic missionary, notes her beatification in 1940 but not her canonization in 1988.

The essays, which range in length from 750 to 7,500 words, are arranged alphabetically by last name and are copiously indexed. The final volume contains an index of the people who are the subject of entries, an index of entries by contributors, index by place of birth (meaning state) within the U.S., an index by place of birth outside the U.S., and an index by occupations and "realm of renown" (*geophysicists, painters, political figures*, etc.). Some of the categories are unexpected: *chewing gum industry executives, occultists, puppeteers*. There are index headings that list Native Americans (*American Indian leaders, American Indian religious leaders*), but for the most part people are indexed by type of activity rather than cultural group. The essays themselves have a format familiar to researchers used to DAB. They open with a brief biographical statement, continue with chronological details of the person's life with emphasis on key achievements and essential details of private lives, and conclude with an evaluative paragraph putting the person's life in historical perspective. Each essay has a descriptive bibliography listing and discussing source material, including personal papers and obituaries.

If ANB covers a subject that appeared in DAB, the biography is rewritten to take into account new historical methods and current research. For example, the life of President Andrew Johnson gets a shorter, more focused essay in ANB than in DAB. Where the latter tends to ramble, the former delivers a portrait of a president who, on the surface, failed, but who, in reality, kept the South a "white man's country" for another three generations. Both discuss Johnson's impeachment trial at length, but ANB looks more at the reasons for the failure of the impeachment, while DAB deals more with the outcomes. The ANB entry for Susan B. Anthony is longer than that in DAB and reflects more current attitudes and scholarship, including the work done by contributor Ann D. Gordon in compiling Anthony's papers.

One major difference between ANB and DAB is that DAB's coverage ends in 1980. Recently, Scribner's launched a new set, *The Scribner Encyclopedia of American Lives* (SEAL), of which volume 1 [RBB Ja 1 & 15 99] treats Americans who died between 1981 and 1985, and volume 2 treats those who died between 1986 and 1990. A contemporary figure that is covered in both ANB and SEAL is John Belushi. Each essay on him provides details not found in the other; the SEAL entry includes a photograph. An influential figure of contemporary Americana not yet included in SEAL is Richard Nixon. Nixon earns a long entry in ANB, detailing his career as both vice-president and president of the U.S. The essay is a balanced portrait of a skillful politician brought down by his own weaknesses. Almost a third of the essay deals with the Watergate affair, looking closely at the investigation and impeachment process. It discusses controversial theories, such as the one that suggests John Dean organized the entire incident. The entry ends with Nixon's slow rehabilitation as an elder statesman.

It is important to note that DAB still includes many individuals not found in ANB. However, with its coverage of people excluded from DAB, and its updated treatment of many others, ANB is an essential addition to the reference collection of any large public and academic library, even if the library already has DAB on its shelves.

Dictionary of World Biography: The Ancient World. 1998. 997p. bibliogs. illus. indexes. Salem/Fitzroy Dearborn, $125 (0-89356-313-7). DDC: 920.02.

The current profusion of biographical encyclopedias and dictionaries reflects our growing fascination with the lives of the famous and influential. Often, biographical reference resources are narrowly focused on a specific country or group. Gale's new edition of the *Encyclopedia of World Biography* [RBB My 1 98] provides comprehensive international coverage. Now the *Encyclopedia* is joined by the *Dictionary of World Biography*, an update of Salem's Great Lives from History series.

The Ancient World is the first of the *Dictionary's* projected 10 volumes. This new collection rearranges the Great Lives entries: as the title of the first volume suggests, the *Dictionary* is chronologically arranged, as opposed to the prior geographic arrangement. Other sets in the series, scheduled to be published between now and June 1999, are *The Middle Ages* ($125, 0-80356-314-5), *The Renaissance* ($125, 0-89356-315-3), *The 17th and 18th Centuries* ($125, 0-89356-316-1), *The Nineteenth Century* (2v., $195, 0-89356-317-X), and *The 20th Century* (3v., $295, 0-89356-320-X). There is a price break for purchasing the entire collection.

The Ancient World has 261 essays (43 of which are new) that look at the lives and works of individuals who died before 450 A.D. Each of these essays is between 2,000 and 3,000 words long. Following ready-reference information about birth, death, and accomplishments, they examine an individual's early life and then discuss in more detail the portion of his or her life that makes them important. The essays conclude with a summary placing the person in historical perspective and are appended with an updated, annotated bibliography of further readings. Following the A–Z entries are indexes by area of achievement, geographical location, and name. A comprehensive index for all volumes will be available at the conclusion of the series.

Compared with Gale's *Encyclopedia of World Biography*, the *Dictionary of World Biography* will cover many fewer people, although *The Ancient World* does include individuals not found in the Gale set. The *Dictionary* has longer articles on some figures, such as Marcus Junius Brutus and Caligula; however, the article on Buddha is twice as long in the *Encyclopedia* and provides a more detailed look at Buddha's philosophy, teachings, and modern significance. The *Dictionary's* chronological arrangement will allow readers quicker and easier access to specific time periods. Since the volumes in the series can be purchased separately, libraries can choose to fill gaps in their coverage of particular periods without investing in the entire 10-volume set. Nevertheless, libraries that have purchased the more comprehensive Gale *Encyclopedia* may wish to direct their resources elsewhere, especially if they already own the Great Lives from History series.

Encyclopedia of World Biography on CD-ROM. Version 1.0. 1999. Gale, $975 (0-7876-2939-1). DDC: 920.

System Requirements: Windows 3.1 *or higher*; 8 MB RAM; 5 MB *available hard disk space*.

This biographical-information source contains 7,200 entries and 5,700 portraits on an easy-to-install CD-ROM. Biographies of renowned personalities from all over the globe and all fields of endeavor are supplemented with lists of additional sources. Content is based on the second edition of *Encyclopedia of World Biography* [RBB My 1 98] and its supplement.

New users will quickly be searching by name, subject, place (of birth or death), works (novels, plays, poems, films, or paintings), or keyword(s). Sophisticated users can use Boolean logic or do custom searches, filling in one to fifteen fields such as occupation, birth year, birthday, birthplace, death month, nationality, ethnicity, and awards. Browsing is possible through Search by Name, Search by Subject, Search by Place, Search by Works, Multimedia (portraits) or Timeline. Timeline is an exceedingly useful and unique feature that enables searching by year. When a year is selected, a Historical Context window pops up on the left of the screen with a brief listing of world events occurring during that year; on the right is a list of events that took place in the lives of individuals profiled in the encyclopedia. For example, entering the year 1432 pulls up "Gonzalo Cabral discovers the Azores" in the Historical Context window, accompanied by events from the lives of painter Rogier van der Weyden and humanist Nicholas of Cusa. Clicking on one of these events leads the user to a full biographical entry. Search by Subject is also very useful. The user can either enter a subject or select from an extensive index. Subject headings range from the general (*abdications, abolitionists, mathematicians*) to the very specific (*authors, Japanese-screenwriters*; "I Love Lucy"; *Reims, council of* [1148]; *rice* [*cereal*]). Another useful feature is the Trails button on the tool bar, which keeps a record (up to 40) of what has been searched.

Although much of the information is the same as in the print *Encyclopedia of World Biography*, we found differences in many of the entries we checked. A list of works, including 1998's *Street Lawyer*, has been added to the entry on John Grisham, and his portrait on the disc is in color instead of black and white. A portrait has been added to the entry for Palestinian nationalist George Habash. The bibliography in the entry for Bernadine Healy, former head of the National Institutes of Health, has been expanded. Although there is an entry for 1997 Nobel literature prizewinner Dario Fo, we found nothing on 1996 winner Wislawa Szymborska. It is not clear how often the disc will be updated.

Page design is clean and uncluttered. Text is on the right, and an enlargeable portrait and search results window are displayed on the left. Entries are hyperlinked, making it easy to move from one to another. Documentation, which consists of a user's manual and a Help card, is detailed and clear.

This terrific reference will be useful in school and public libraries. It is very easy to use, navigate, download, and print. One drawback is, of course, cost. On the other hand, the CD-ROM is less expensive than the print *Encyclopedia of World Biography* and does not take up shelf space. Patrons will enjoy searching this biographical collection.

Heroes and Pioneers. 1998. 414p. bibliog. glossary. illus. index. Macmillan, $75 (0-02-865059-X). DDC: 920.02.
Scientists and Inventors. 1998. 390p. bibliog. glossary. illus. index. Macmillan, $75 (0-02-864983-4). DDC: 509.2.
Tycoons and Entrepreneurs. 1998. 350p. bibliog. glossary. illus. index. Macmillan, $75 (0-02-864982-6). DDC: 332.
Villains and Outlaws. 1998. 361p. bibliog. glossary. illus. index. Macmillan, $75 (0-02-865058-1). DDC: 909.

Macmillan Reference is known for providing excellent material on a scholarly level. Recently, they have recognized the long-standing need for resources accessible to young adults by rewriting several of their classic encyclopedias and dictionaries. These four titles, part of the Macmillan Profiles series, rely heavily on entries found in other Macmillan and Scribner titles, such as *Dictionary of American Biography* (volumes 9 and 10, 1964), *Encyclopedia of Religion* (1987), and *Encyclopedia of the American West* (1996); although some of the profiles are new and were especially commissioned. As stated in the preface to *Scientists and Inventors*, "the article list was based on the following criteria: relevance to the curriculum, importance to history, name recognition for students, and representation of as broad a cultural range as possible." For some volumes, the article list "was refined and expanded in response to advice from a lively and generous team of high-school teachers and librarians."

Each book has more than 100 profiles, a glossary of important terms, and an index. The profiles are one or two pages in length (a few are longer) and generally include a photograph or portrait, at least one quotation by the individual, other quotations about the person, and a time line of his or her achievements. Occasional sidebars of related information are interspersed throughout each volume and listed in the table of contents. Examples are "Habitat for Humanity International" in the Jimmy Carter article in *Heroes*; "The Progress of Printing" in the Johannes Gutenberg article in *Scientists*; and "The Pullman Strike" in the George Pullman article in *Tycoons*. Another good feature is the inclusion of definitions of words in boldface on the page where they appear. The words in the glossaries are not the same as the words defined in the text.

The profiles are interesting and fun to read. They try to relay the truth about the individual, especially those who have become almost legendary (Galileo, Lawrence of Arabia, Tokyo Rose, Belle Starr). The editors did a fair job of making the volumes representational by gender, nationality and ethnic group, and time period. It is heartening to see several religious leaders in the *Heroes* volume.

On the critical side, there are no pronunciation guides for the names or the defined terms. In many cases, this does not matter, but for the few where it does matter, the omission is glaring. Some closer editorial scrutiny is needed, too. In the *Scientists* volume, there is a quote in French in the profile of Edward Jenner that has no translation. Also in *Scientists* there is a possible conflict in the article on Stephen Hawking. The time line states, "1992: NASA discovers ripples in the fabric of time"; but the article text says, "In 1992, NASA announced . . . 'ripples' in the fabric of space." In *Tycoons*, J. Paul Getty is referred to correctly as Jean Paul in the entry heading but incorrectly as John Paul in the text. Although women seem to be adequately covered in the other three volumes, they are underrepresented in *Tycoons*. Yes, Oprah Winfrey and Madame C. J. Walker are there, as are rancher Juana Briones, Motown executive Suzanne De Passe, and one or two others; but surely there are other prominent women entrepreneurs who could have been included. Why not Helen Gurley Brown, Coco Chanel, Leona Helmsley, Estee Lauder, Mary Kay, or Lillian Vernon? The suggested reading lists would be more useful at the end of each entry rather than the volume.

Information on many of the people profiled in these volumes is available elsewhere, most notably in various sets from UXL, such as *Outlaws, Mobsters, and Crooks: From the Old West to the Internet* [RBB N 1 98]; and *Scientists: The Lives and Works of 150 Scientists* [RBB Ap 1 97] and its supplements. The UXL titles are appropriate for a slightly younger audience. On the whole, the Macmillan Profiles series will be useful in libraries that serve young adults, grades seven and up. The information is good, and the features are excellent. Teachers and students will appreciate having these portraits available, and the price is right for most library budgets. Eight additional titles are scheduled to be published this year.

Notable Black American Men. Ed. by Jessie Carney Smith. 1999.1,365p. bibliog. illus. indexes. Gale, $90 (0-7876-0763-0). DDC: 920.71.
Notable Black American Scientists. Ed. by Kristine Krapp. 1999. 349p. bibliog. illus. indexes. Gale, $75 (0-7876-2789-5). DDC: 509.2.

These two new titles from Gale will be welcome additions to most library collections.

Notable Black American Men is the companion to Jessie Carney Smith's *Notable Black American Women* (1992) and *Notable Black American Women, Book II* (1996), which have become standard reference sources. It profiles 500 men, from poet Jupiter Hammon (b. 1711) to Tiger Woods. Subjects were chosen from an initial list of 2,500 because they met certain criteria, including important contributions to business, the arts, social justice, government, and scholarship. Emphasis seems to be on "firsts"—the first black man elected to public office in a state, the first black man to sing at the Metropolitan Opera, the first black man to receive a college degree, etc.

Each entry begins with birth and death dates and a few words describing the subject's major fields of endeavor, followed by a biographical essay, a list of references, and, in some cases, a note on collections of source material. Entries vary in length, depending on the importance of the individual and the amount of information available. Martin Luther King Jr. is covered in six pages, and artist Grafton Tyler Brown (1842Cornish (1795–1858) are each covered in one. Profiles highlight influences and obstacles as well as achievements. Current addresses are provided for subjects who are living. Approximately 400 photographs accompany the entries; the portrait found in the entry for Louis Wade Sullivan, Secretary of Health and Human Services during the Bush administration, is obviously an error. The volume concludes with a geographic and occupation index, along with an index of people, places, events, institutions, and other terms contained in the entries.

As the Board noted in its review of *Notable Black American Women* [RBB Ap 15 92], the real value of this volume lies not so much in covering well-known figures but in bringing to light more obscure individuals like explorer Matthew A. Henson (1866–1955), believed to be the first person to reach the North Pole; and Charles H. Parrish Sr. (1859–1931), who was born a slave and became a university president. There is also fresh perspective to be gained by examining the lives of men such as James Baldwin, Frederick Douglass, and Michael Jordan within the context of the struggles and achievements of those who are not so famous.

Almost 30 of the men who are profiled in *Notable Black American Men* are also covered in *Notable Black American Scientists*. In all, *Scientists* has entries for 254 scientists, inventors, and physicians, 58 of whom are women. The format of the two volumes is similar, except that there is a time line at the beginning of *Scientists*, and most entries include a few writings by as well as about the subject. There are gender and field of specialization indexes in addition to the general index. Entries in *Scientists* are generally shorter and less detailed; for example, the entry on physicist Warren Elliott Henry is less than half as long as his entry in *Men. Scientists* lists only two sources in the Henry bibliography, but *Men* lists eight.

Again, the value of the book lies in its profiles of not-so-well-known figures who have made significant contributions to science. George Washington Carver and Mae Jemison are familiar names, but how many people have heard of Garrett A. Morgan (1877–1963), who invented the gas mask and the traffic light; or Susan Smith McKinney Steward (1847–1918), the first black female doctor in the state of New York? A curious omission is George Cleveland Hall, described in *Notable Black American Men* as "one of the leading African American medical practitioners in the country at the turn of the century." *Notable Black American Scientists* expands the coverage of Oryx's *Distinguished African American Scientists of the 20th Century* [RBB F 15 96], which profiles 100 men and women and is frequently cited as a source for entries in the Gale volume.

Both of the titles under review are highly recommended for school, public, and academic libraries. *Notable Black American Men*, in particular, is indispensable for most collections, especially where its companion volume on women has been heavily used. It can be supplemented with Gale's Current Black Biography series for more coverage of today's popular figures and news makers.

The Scribner Encyclopedia of American Lives. v.1. Ed. by Kenneth T. Jackson and others. 1998. 930p. bibliogs. illus. index. Scribner, $125 (0-684-80492-1). DDC: 920.073.

This volume marks the official break in Scribner's tradition of publishing supplements to the *Dictionary of American Biography* (DAB), and also, perhaps, the beginning of some confusion on the part of library patrons. As readers may know, DAB was published under the auspices of the American Council of Learned Societies. ACLS announced the launch of a new work, *American National Biography*, due for release in 1999 and published by Oxford University Press. Scribner's was allowed to publish supplements to DAB covering individuals through 1980, though supplements nine and ten of that work were not published under ACLS auspices. Following a 1997 court order, however, no publisher may use the DAB name. *The Scribner Encyclopedia of American Lives* (SEAL), covering Americans who died between 1981 and 1985, thus marks the first volume in Scribner's new series.

Notwithstanding the lack of the DAB name, SEAL bears a great deal of resemblance to the work it continues to update—not surprising, since it retains the editorial hand of Kenneth T. Jackson, professor of history at Columbia University, as did supplements nine and ten of DAB. As the preface points out, however, there are several enhancements. SEAL has a photograph of most subjects, a subject listing by occupation in the back of the volume, and a brief opening description for each subject outlining key achievements. This is a particularly refreshing change. Whereas DAB would simply open with the subject's name, birth and death dates, and a word or two summarizing his or her occupation or avocation, the present volume elaborates with a full paragraph highlighting claims to fame.

SEAL features 494 entries for people who died between January 1, 1981, and December 31, 1985, written by 332 different contributors. Final judgment of whom to include in the volume was made by an advisory board. The preface indicates that future volumes will cover five-year periods, much like previous DAB supplements. Entries range from just about a column in length (for Lazar Margulies, developer of the IUD), to around four pages (for General Omar Nelson Bradley). Among others profiled in these pages are Count Basie, John Belushi, Roman Catholic Cardinals Cody and Cooke, McDonald's founder Ray Kroc, Jessica Savitch, and Orson Welles. All entries conclude with brief annotated bibliographies. The photographs are a welcome addition, but the date of the photograph is not always given. The photos for actress Selma Diamond and writer E. B. White are both dated as being taken in 1960, but the photos for college football coach Paul "Bear" Bryant and actor William Holden have no dates at all.

Libraries that have invested in DAB will clearly want to add this reasonably priced volume to their collections, and will likely want to continue to add future supplements. Volume 2, available in December 1998 but not received in time for this review, covers individuals who died between 1986 and 1990, among them Ted Bundy, Huey Newton, and Geraldine Page.

Genealogical Encyclopedia of the Colonial Americas: A Complete Digest of the Records of All the Countries of the Western Hemisphere. By Christina K. Schaefer. 1998. 204p. bibliogs. illus. index. Genealogical Publishing Co., $22.50 (0-8063-1554-7). DDC: 929.097.

Written by a genealogist for genealogists at all levels, this volume fills a significant research void. "Colonial Americas" refers to "the period of colonial history from the beginning of European colonization in the Western Hemisphere up to the time of the American Revolution"; that is, from 1492 to 1775. In the cases of Latin America and the Caribbean countries, the scope extends to include their independence dates in the early 1800s. Throughout the encyclopedia, the underlying assumption that its readers are skilled researchers is evident. This is clearly a road map to sources of information and not an instructional guide.

The volume opens with a fairly detailed chronology of colonial history, suggested readings, and dates of the first European colonial governors in America. The next five chapters are devoted to each of the major geographic areas (Latin America, Caribbean, U.S./New England and the 13 colonies, other U.S. states with pre-Revolutionary settlements, and Canada) and outline the types of records that exist and where to find them. The brief colonization history of each area supplies the proper historical terminology needed for requesting material. The organization of each chapter varies, depending on the kinds of records that are available. States with more extensive records are divided into separate sections for statewide, county, and town resources. In addition to census records and land deeds, parish, missionary, viceroyalty, notorial, municipal, and military records are among the major types of obtainable records. Web sites for major record repositories are noted. Maps and bibliographies are interspersed throughout the text. The closing section of the book is devoted entirely to resources obtainable from the parent countries.

Affordably priced and easy to use, this is one reference book not to be overlooked. A must purchase for public and academic libraries as well as specialized libraries having substantial local-history/genealogy collections.

History

From Aristotle to Zoroaster: An A to Z Companion to the Classical World. By Arthur Cotterell. 1998. 496p. chronology. illus. index. maps. Free Press, $30 (0-684-85596-8). DDC: 930.

Less scholarly and less detailed than *The Oxford Classical Dictionary* [RBB My 1 97], this is a small dictionary of the civilizations and persons of the classical period, from 600 B.C. through A.D. 600. It was originally published in Great Britain as *The Pimlico Dictionary of Classical Civilizations* (Pimlico, 1998). Unlike most works of this type, it includes material on the civilizations of India and China as well as the Greco-Roman world. The author has written a number of other books on classical civilizations.

Most of the more than 250 entries are about individuals, places, and empires and dynasties and range in length from approximately half a page to nine pages. The information given in conceptual entries, such as *administration* and *drama*, allows for some comparison between cultures. Each entry ends with cross-references to related entries. Documentation is very limited, consisting only of one or two books listed at the end of each entry. The illustrations are mostly decorative and rarely serve to illustrate concepts.

The A–Z section of the volume is followed by a chronology that displays major events in the Mediterranean region, divided by "west" and "east." Another time line lists events in west Asia, India, and China. Nineteen simple maps were created especially for this volume. The index lists only names and subjects without their own entries in the body of the work.

As a classical dictionary, this is basically one author's overview and is of limited reference value. Greece, Rome, and Persia are better covered in a traditional classical dictionary such as *The Oxford Classical Dictionary*. However, libraries with limited resources on Asian and Indian history of the classical period may find this volume to be useful.

History

Handbook to Life in Ancient Egypt. By Rosalie David. 1998. 416p. appendix. bibliog. illus. index. maps. Facts On File, $45 (0-8160-3312-9). DDC: 932.

This is an ambitious book—a summary of a civilization that lasted more than 5,000 years. For the most part it succeeds. In 11 chapters, David, a respected Egyptologist, surveys Egypt from predynastic times through the arrival of Islam, although the work concentrates on the period before the establishment of the Greek Ptolomies as the royal line. Arrangement is thematic. The first chapter surveys the history of Egypt, historiography, and the various dynasties. The second chapter covers geography, the Nile and its inundations, and agriculture. The third chapter covers society and government and describes the nature of kingship, local government, and the substantial bureaucracy that kept Egypt running.

Religion and funerary beliefs and customs are covered in the fourth and fifth chapters. Egypt had a rich and complex religious life, both public and private, and the chapter on "Religion of the Living" samples it generously. The next chapter explores the changes in the cult of the dead over time and gives a graphic description of the mummification process and the status of those who did the work.

The chapter on architecture describes how the pyramids were built, including a description of how the workforce was recruited, organized, and paid. There are also sections on the building of palaces and temples and town planning. The chapter on "Written Evidence" begins with a cursory description of how Egyptian writing was deciphered. The art and technique of writing, writing materials, and the education of the professional scribes are summarized. There is a brief glance at religious and secular literature, but none is quoted.

Although Egypt was a peaceable and self-contained place, in time the kingdom grew to an empire. To do that, and to secure building materials and trade in what Egypt did not mine or grow itself, it needed an army and a navy. Chapter 8 describes the Egyptian military and includes a short section on the Medjay, nomads from the Nubian desert who were enrolled in the police force. "Foreign Trade and Transport" and "Economy and Industry" could probably have been one chapter, as they overlap extensively. Transport problems are discussed as are foreign sources of materials, and the various domestic industries including glassmaking, jewelry, and food production. "Everyday Life" looks at the Egyptians outside the royal family, what they ate, who they were, and what they did for amusement.

Each chapter cites relevant sources from the bibliography. Many of the citations are to academic journals or books which may not be available in public libraries. Besides the bibliography, the volume concludes with a chronological table, a list of museums with Egyptian collections, and a detailed index, essential given the book's arrangement. Black-and-white photographs, drawings, and maps complement the text.

Because of the attempt to survey 5,000 years of history in about 400 pages, chapters and sections tend to be cursory. The chapter on daily life will not be much help to a student with a homework assignment, but in conjunction with something like John Romer's *Ancient Lives: Daily Life in Egypt of the Pharaohs* (Holt, 1984) it can be useful. Some topics overlap chapters, including descriptions of the Medjay, construction practices, and the donkey. One curious omission is cats, which were first domesticated in Egypt and were pets and rat-catchers throughout Egyptian history.

This volume is a companion to *Handbook to Life in Ancient Greece* [RBB Ag 97] and *Handbook to Life in Ancient Rome* (Facts On File, 1994). Recommended for high-school and public libraries, especially those serving students who get that annual ancient Egypt assignment. Lower-division undergraduates should find it useful as well.

Ancient Greece and Rome: An Encyclopedia for Students. 4v. Ed. by Carroll Moulton. 1998. 752p. bibliog. illus. index. maps. Scribner, $350 (0-684-80507-3). DDC: 938.

Scribner has revised its college-level *Ancient Writers: Greece and Rome* (1982) and *Civilizations of the Ancient Mediterranean: Greece and Rome* (1988) to provide us with an attractive encyclopedia for younger students. With a glimpse into the relevance of Greek and Roman history and their impact on Europe and the Americas, these four volumes cover the period from 2,000 B.C. to 529 A.D. The volumes are arranged alphabetically, with volume 1 containing a table of contents that lists the maps, color plates, and entries for all four volumes.

The encyclopedia features almost 500 entries ranging from a few short paragraphs to more than 17 pages for *Greece, history of*. Entries provide explanations of each subject, as well as references to related topics found within the four volumes. On each page, in the left margin, one can find definitions of terms that might be unfamiliar to users, along with sidebars and time lines. Following the entries in volume 4 is a list of suggested readings grouped under 11 subject areas, including culture and society, myths and legends, biography, and fiction. A "Timeline of Ancient Greece and Rome" is repeated at the beginning of each volume.

Covering a wide range of topics, the entries provide students with a basic understanding before they move on to more in-depth sources such as Facts On File's *Handbook to Life in Ancient Greece* [RBB Ag 97] and *Handbook to Life in Ancient Rome* (1994). Most public and school libraries will want to add this set to their reference collections because of the lack of similar resources designed especially for students at the middle-to high-school level.

The Oxford Companion to Classical Civilization. Ed. by Simon Hornblower and Antony Spawford. 1998. 792p. bibliog. chronology. illus. maps. Oxford, $49.95 (0-19-860165-4). DDC: 938.

The past few years have seen a tremendous growth in the number of popularly written one-volume titles on classical civilization, such as *Encyclopedia of the Ancient Greek World* [RBB N 1 95], *Encyclopedia of the Roman Empire* [RBB Je 1 94], and *Handbook to Life in Ancient Greece* [RBB Ag 97]. These titles were all published by Facts On File, but the present volume brings with it the hefty reputation of Oxford University Press. *Oxford Companion to Classical Civilization* (OCCC) is designed to "make available to an even wider readership the essential material from . . . the *Oxford Classical Dictionary* [RBB My 1 97] . . . but in a cheaper and less weighty format." There are more than 700 entries in OCCC, as opposed to more than 6,200 in the parent work. Omitted are entries thought "too technical or recondite," as well as the bibliographies concluding each entry. Other entries, however, are retained intact from the *Classical Dictionary*. A major addition is more than 140 illustrations and 16 color plates. Other additions are a thematic listing of entries, a select bibliography, a chronology, and maps.

A sampling of articles from both the parent *Classical Dictionary* and the present work reveals that articles retained are, as the preface asserts, unchanged from the earlier work with the exception of the exclusion of bibliographies. Many articles, however, were cut. The letter L, for example, has 257 entries in the *Classical Dictionary* (not including entries that were predominately cross-references), while the same letter has but 28 entries in OCCC. The letter R has 102 entries in the *Classical Dictionary*, while there are but 18 in OCCC. Among the entries dropped from this volume are *Ravenna*, *Red Sea*, *rhapsodes*, and *Rutilius Claudius Namatianus*.

Although the title is intended for a more general reader than its parent work, readers will still have to confront a variety of abbreviations when looking at entries. H*ades*, for example, begins "son of Cronus and Rhea (Hes. *Theog*. 453–56) and husband of Persephone (*Od*. 10 491), is 'Lord of the dead' (*Il*. 20. 61) and king of the Underworld." The general reader will probably have to consult the table of abbreviations at the beginning of the volume to understand which classical works are cited.

Such entries, however, make OCCC a cut above and will satisfy the interested layperson who found the Facts On File works perhaps too general. Libraries that purchased *The Oxford Classical Dictionary* will be able to pass up this volume unless they have a decided need for more works in the genre, as the addition of illustrations alone will not justify the purchase of a work that is essentially the same. Other public, secondary, and academic libraries wishing to further increase their ready-reference collection in the area of classical studies can certainly not go wrong with this reasonably priced volume.

Almanac of World War I. By David F. Burg and L. Edward Purcell. 1998. 350p. bibliog. illus. index. maps. Univ. of Kentucky, $22 (0-8131-2072-1). DDC: 940.3.

From two historians comes this interesting reference work on World War I. The book begins with an introduction by William Manchester, followed by an essay detailing world events leading up to the start of the war. The bulk of the text is arranged chronologically by year and date, listing almost daily occurrences from 1914 through 1918.

There are approximately 1,084 entries for days of the war in which significant events occurred. Entries vary from one sentence to a page in length. The work is international in scope, covering political and military happenings from around the world. Scattered throughout the text are around 75 black-and-white photographs and drawings and six maps, appropriately placed. Eighteen sidebars cover topics such as poison gas, artillery, tanks, songs of war, and the literature of the war. These sidebars vary from a half to a full page in length.

The chronology is followed by biographies of 74 prominent political and military figures, arranged alphabetically. Each biographical entry provides birth and death years, and about half a page of text. This is followed by a select bibliography that lists approximately 109 monographs.

There is really nothing comparable to this volume. Other works, such as *The Dictionary of the First World War*, by Stephen Pope [RBB F 1 96], have an alphabetical arrangement that provides easy ready-reference access. In contrast, *Almanac of World War I* allows users to identify diverse significant events that happened on a particular day, and place them in context. Recommended for academic, public, and high-school libraries.

The Pacific War Encyclopedia. 2v. By James F. Dunnigan and Albert A. Nofi. 1998. 704p. appendixes. bibliog. charts. illus. maps. Facts On File, $125 (0-8160-3439-7). DDC: 940.54.

More than a chronology of battles and campaigns, this source provides background material that allows the reader to comprehend the factors, developments, and results of World War II's Pacific Theater of Operations (PTO). The authors are a military analyst for NBC and an author of numerous books on military history.

Entries are arranged alphabetically and include the expected people (military personnel and politicos from all sides, as well as persons such as Charles Lindbergh and Ernie Pyle), places (Manchukuo, Melbourne, Nagasaki, Timor, etc.), and events (Battle of Iwo Jima, Port Chicago mutiny). Entries such as *black Americans in the Pacific War*, *prisoners of war*, *sunglasses*, and *torpedoes* cover other aspects of the conflict. Throughout the text, tables are used to provide information on such topics as casualties, troop strength, and weapons, and to compare resources and losses in the PTO with those in the European arena and with those in other wars. Especially interesting are tables that address logistical matters, such as food rations, and those that compare personnel, such as Allied and Japanese aces. Less heroic aspects of the war are discussed in entries such as *altitude sickness*; *friendly fire*; *Pearl Harbor, the doomed survivors*; and *Tokyo Rose*. Entries generally range in length from a paragraph to around five pages for *deception* and *American citizens, relocation of*, with most being less than a page. Longer entries include citations to one or more references. Entries for individual battles and campaigns were kept short because the authors "wanted to focus . . . on matters not usually covered in standard histories."

A 75-page chronology follows the entries, and there is a nine-page bibliography (including Web sites). A nice feature for today's researchers is the table of Modern Equivalents of Notable Pacific War Place-Names. Another is the table of Code Words and Code Names. There are numerous illustrations from the National Archives.

Well written, albeit with an admitted American perspective, this is a useful source that many will enjoy reading and browsing for background material that enhances understanding. Recommended for high-school, public, and academic libraries as a good starting point for more in-depth research.

People of the Holocaust. 2v. Ed. by Linda Schmittroth and Mary Kay Rosteck. 1998. 508p. bibliogs. illus. index. UXL, $49 (0-7876-1743-1). DDC: 940.53.

Understanding the Holocaust. 2v. Ed. by George Feldman. 1998. 458p. bibliogs. illus. index. UXL, $49 (0-7876-1740-7). DDC: 940.53.

Voices of the Holocaust. 2v. Ed. by Lorie Jenkins McElroy. 1998. 493p. bibliogs. illus. index. UXL, $49 (0-7876-1746-6). DDC: 940.53.

Each of these two-volume sets geared toward middle-school students offers information on different aspects of the Holocaust. While all three use vocabulary appropriate to the intended audience, *Voices* relies on primary sources to educate readers while *People* offers biographical profiles and *Understanding* provides background and context by describing events. Each attempts to place people and events in historical perspective and to show their impact.

The volumes are formatted with wide outside margins where each set places informative captions to their black-and-white photographs and illustrations. *Voices* also uses this area for its glossary, giving definitions of unfamiliar terms that are indicated within the text by bold print. The brief glossaries in *People* and *Understanding* are found at the beginning of each volume. Related information is presented in boxes or sidebars; the boxed text is difficult to read because of the gray barbed-wire design background. All three sets include a time line that covers the period from before the Holocaust up to 1998, and an index. *People* and *Voices* offer bibliographies of further reading at the end of each entry. The bibliographies include current and classic adult and young-adult titles. In *Voices*, bibliographies contain fiction and nonfiction books only, while *People* also includes print and electronic encyclopedia articles and Internet sites. In *Understanding*, a bibliography is repeated near the end of each volume and includes general histories, aliases, nonfiction titles on specific topics, and works of fiction, as well as a list of organizations.

People contains 60 alphabetized biographies, ranging in length from 6 to 10 pages, of Nazi perpetrators, victims, world leaders, resisters, and rescuers. Most entries have a photo or drawing of the subject and include birth and death dates. Most of the information concerns the subject's relevance to the Holocaust. Sidebars contain short biographies of people related to the main biographee, as well as other related information. In addition to the expected (Adolf Eichmann, Anne Frank, Simon Wiesenthal), biographees include Eva Braun, anti-Semitic radio personality Father Charles Coughlin, Varian Fry ("America's Schindler"), Benito Mussolini, General George Patton, and Pope Pius XII.

Understanding is arranged in 14 chapters that survey topics such as Jewish life in Germany before the Holocaust, the rise of the Nazi Party, life in the ghettos, the death camps, the trials that followed the war's end, and contemporary views.

Voices includes 34 excerpts from essays, diaries, newspaper articles, letters, and court transcripts. Many of them are primary-source documents, such as the *Protocols of the Elders of Zion*, the Nuremberg Laws, and Anne Frank's diary. Other pieces, excerpted from novels or personal narratives, include *Summer of My German Soldier*, *Schindler's List*, and *Playing for Time*. The set is divided into six chapters dealing with various aspects of the Holocaust, such as anti-Semitism and resisters. Each chapter contains a historical overview, followed by four to seven excerpts. Each excerpt is accompanied by background information, a discussion of "what happened next," and various relevant facts. Sidebars include a brief biography of the author and information on related issues and events

For the middle-school library or public-library young-adult collection looking for introductory material on the Holocaust, these sets will be suitable. The information is accessible to all readers, yet the sets give enough in-depth material to be used as research tools and may serve as the impetus for students to go a step further and read the entire works excerpted or listed in the bibliographies. The three titles form UXL's Holocaust Reference Library and may be purchased separately, or as a set ($132, 0-7876-1739-3) that comes with a cumulative index to all six volumes.

Who Was Who in the Napoleonic Wars. By Philip J. Haythornthwaite. 1998. 320p. bibliog. illus. Arms and Armour; dist. by Sterling, $34.95 (1-85409-391-6). DDC: 940.2.

Haythornthwaite is a prolific author of military history with many titles of English, American, and especially Napoleonic interest to his credit. This latest monograph surveys approximately 888 individuals who were important during the period of the French Revolution through the Napoleonic reign. An occasional entry will survey more than one person; for example, the entry for poet AndreChenier also includes information on his brother, Marie-Joseph-Blaise Chenier. Included within this survey is the War of 1812, involving the U.S. and many American figures, such as Andrew Jackson, John Jay, and Francis Scott Key. The majority of the subjects surveyed are military figures, but prominent politicians and some cultural luminaries are covered, as well as a few women. Arrangement is alphabetical by name. Appropriately placed throughout the text are about 306 black-and-white portraits and pictures of individuals. Also, approximately 25 half-tone pictures of historical events are scattered throughout the volume, adding mood to the entries but little else.

A typical entry provides the person's name in bold letters with birth and death years. More specific death dates are frequently cited within the text. Most entries are about one-third page in length. A random survey determined that about half of the entries have a short bibliographic citation at the end referring to predominantly English-language works. There are only a few citations to periodicals. At the front of the book is a Footnote References page providing bibliographic information for citations within the text.

There are few comparable books. One excellent resource is *Dictionary of the Napoleonic Wars* by David G. Chandler (Macmillan, 1979). With approximately 1,200 entries, Chandler's title covers battles as well as persons, and has nine in-depth essay entries of 2,000 to 7,000 words in length, as well as an extensive bibliography. For academic and large public libraries that do not own Chandler, *Who Was Who in the Napoleonic Wars* is worth considering.

World War II: An Encyclopedia of Quotations. Ed. by Howard J. Langer. 1999. 449p. appendix. bibliog. illus. indexes. Greenwood, $75 (0-313-30018-6). DDC: 940.53.

Langer has authored several other books on quotations, including *American Indian Quotations* [RBB N 15 96] and *The History of the Holocaust: A Chronology of Quotations* (Aronson, 1997). His latest is an excellent collection of quotations dealing with World War II. International in scope, the work provides 1,554 quotations, drawn from a variety of sources. Appropriately placed throughout the text are approximately 17 photographs.

The first 12 chapters are arranged by type of person quoted, from "The War Leaders" to "Civilians," and then alphabetically by name. A typical entry has a short introductory paragraph providing biographical and historical information including birth and death years of persons. The remaining chapters cover other sources, including movies and songs. There are numerous cross-reference to other citations, designated by the symbol "q.v." Quotations taken from monographs have their titles cited but no page numbers. There is a bibliography of approximately 214 titles cited in full bibliographic format. An appendix lists quotations by category. There are two indexes, one of individuals and the other arranged by subject. All quotations are numbered consecutively, thus enabling users of the indexes to quickly locate appropriate entries.

A number of these quotations can be found in more general sources, such as *The Oxford Dictionary of Twentieth Century Quotations* (reviewed on this page). Although there are dozens of reference books on quotations, there are only a handful that deal with war. *Dictionary of War Quotations* (Free Press, 1989), *Warrior's Words* (Sterling, 1992), and *Words on War* (Prentice Hall, 1990) include quotations from World War II and will probably be sufficient for smaller libraries that own them. *World War II: An Encyclopedia of Quotations* is much more extensive in coverage for its time period. It is a unique resource that should be popular in academic, public, and high-school libraries.

World War II: A Student Companion. By William L. O'Neill. 1999. 384p. appendixes. bibliogs. illus. index. maps. Oxford, $35 (0-19-510800-0). DDC: 940.53.

World War II in Europe: An Encyclopedia. 2v. Ed. by David T. Zabecki. 1999. 1,920p. appendixes. bibliogs. glossary. illus. indexes. maps. tables. Garland, $195 (0-8240-7029-1). DDC: 940.53.

Here are two works covering one of the greatest conflicts in history, each designed for a different audience.

World War II: A Student Companion is part of Oxford's Student Companion to American History series, written for ages 12 and up. The war is covered on all fronts, with entries on individuals, battles, military organizations, theaters, origins, weapon systems, and countries. Related issues are covered in such entries as *African Americans*, internment, isolationists, and rationing. According to the preface, "each entry is meant both to provide essential information and to lead readers on to further study by pointing to other entries, suggested readings, and significant films and videos."

Articles vary in length from two or three paragraphs to several pages. Nine pages are devoted to the longest, *strategic bombing*, but other topics also get fairly extended coverage, among them *Germany*, *Japan*, *Southwest Pacific area*, and *women*. Biographical entries begin with brief summaries of essential facts. Many articles include *see also* references and further reading lists of standard books. *Literature* and *motion pictures* have brief lists of classic World War II novels and films, respectively. A chronology, a list of museums and historic sites, and a general bibliography that includes Web sites give students additional tools to expand their original search.

For an older audience, the excellent *World War II in Europe* is volume six in the Military History of the United States series. Its perspective is that of the U.S. and its participation in the European theater. As the editor says, quoting historian John Keegan, the war is the "single biggest event in human history" and no one reference could ever adequately cover it comprehensively. What this work does quite well is provide 1,400 separate entries on the war, the events leading up to it, and its consequences and results. As the editor notes, most of the entries "easily rate their own book, and many already have."

Rather than a regular alphabetical arrangement, the encyclopedia is arranged into six major sections: "Social and Political Issues and Events"; "Leaders and Individuals"; "Units and Organizations"; "Weapons and Equipment"; "Strategy, Tactics, and Operational Techniques"; and "Battles, Campaigns, and Operations." Within each section, entries are arranged alphabetically. The reason for this arrangement, the editor says, is to make it easier for the reader who wants to focus on a particular aspect of the war. In practice, it makes for a complicated ready-reference work.

The entries, however, are well written. Each is signed by the author and, where possible, covers the new additions to World War II scholarship. Length ranges from a paragraph to four or five pages, with longer articles generally covering topics in section 6, "Battles, Campaigns, and Operations." Entries are followed by a short list of additional readings. There are 37 strategic maps at the beginning of volume 1, and these are found again in volume 2 in the "Battles, Campaigns, and Operations" section, which also has its own geographical and chronological index. Section 4, "Weapons and Equipment," includes tables of technical data. The encyclopedia has a series of appendixes, including a chronology of the war in Europe, Allied and Axis code names, and a selected bibliography, arranged by broad topic area. These are followed by an "Index of Military Units and Warships" and a general index. The indexes more than make up for the complicated arrangement mentioned previously. Another recent title, *The Oxford Companion to World War II* [RBB Ag 95], has 1,700 A–Z entries, including exhaustive essays on major countries, and covers the war with Japan as well as the war with Germany. This would be a good choice for high-school and smaller public libraries; larger libraries probably need both.

Both of these new works are highly recommended. For its intended audience, *World War II: A Student Companion* gives thorough coverage to some topics that are treated in less depth in some multivolume sets. It will be a useful addition to school and public libraries. *World War II in Europe* is an invaluable study of the Western half of the war and a worthy addition to reference collections in large public and academic libraries.

Biographical Dictionary of British Prime Ministers. Ed. by Robert Ecclesall and Graham Walker. 1998. 428p. bibliog. index. Routledge, $110 (0-415-10830-6); paper $35 (0-415-18721-4). DDC: 941.

Most Americans would probably be confused to learn that the press has criticized Britain's current prime minister (PM) for being too presidential. To the British, however, this is a damning indictment of the holder of an office that evolved out of the country's unwritten constitution and ideal of a government of collective responsibility. This work illustrates the history of this unique institution through the lives of the 50 men and one woman who have held or hold the office.

The editors, political scientists at Queens University, Belfast, have drawn on the expertise of scholars to present a series of interconnected essays on the lives and careers of the PMs. Each entry opens with an abbreviated paragraph of the PM's vital statistics and ministerial career. An extensively detailed essay follows, looking at the PM's politics, influences, career, and important policies and events that shaped his (or her) tenure. The essays also are grounded in the social and political history of the time and look at the subject's influence on the evolution of the office of prime minister.

The volume is arranged chronologically by PM, beginning with Sir Robert Walpole (arguably the first PM, from 1723–1742) to Tony Blair. The first entry not only looks at Walpole but argues why he ought to be considered the first PM and why 1723 ought to be considered the date he assumed the role. The entry on Blair notes the changes he has made in the office since assuming it in May 1997 and the implications these changes may have for future PMs. Margaret Thatcher (1979–1990) earns one of the longest entries (26 pages) as one of the most influential PMs in terms of the evolution and practice of the office. An extensive annotated bibliography of further readings follows each entry, and the entire volume is copiously indexed.

This work deserves comparison with Wilson's *Facts About the British Prime Ministers* [RBB O 1 95]. Although the current work lacks portraits and photographs that are included in the Wilson title, its essay format (as opposed to a listing of dates and facts) provides much more depth. This scholarly resource would be an excellent addition to any historical, biographical, or political science reference collection in large public and academic libraries.

The Mammoth Book of British Kings and Queens. By Mike Ashley. 1998. 544p. bibliog. charts. index. maps. Carroll & Graf, $26.95 (0-7867-0405-5). DDC: 941.

The result of some 30 years of research by a prolific writer on British royalty, this chronology provides biographical information on more than 1,000 sovereigns from approximately 100 B.C. to Elizabeth II, a period of more than 2,000 years. The volume opens with "The Royal Book of Records," consisting of such lists as the longest and shortest reigns, the youngest monarchs to die, and the oldest monarchs to be married. Ashley points out that most chronologies of the British monarchy start with Egbert (802–839). He believes, however, that there is sufficient credibility in Welsh legend to accept the authenticity of the Beli Mawr, a semi-legendary British king who was probably a historical figure, as the starting point for this survey, which is divided into three sections: "The Dark Ages" (from around 100 B.C. to around 900), "The Fight for Britain" (from around 900 to 1300), and "Uniting the Kingdom" (from 1300 to the present). Each section has numerous letter-coded subsections in order to cover all of the kingdoms and royal houses that by the Act of Union in 1707 formally brought Scotland, England, and Wales together into a United Kingdom of Great Britain and Northern Ireland.

Biographical entries, supported throughout with time lines, maps, and family trees, vary in length from a line or two to several pages. They are current to at least August 1997 and the death of Diana. Longer entries critically assess the king or queen's reign. Concluding the chronological survey is a section called "The World Around Them," containing biographies of legendary or semi-historical kings of Britain and Scotland; and charts for other kingdoms in Europe whose rulers either had some dominion over Britain or vice versa. This is followed by a gazetteer of sites with a strong royal connection, a bibliography (current to 1997), and an index.

Written in a lively style and covering more than 2,000 years and 1,000 monarchs (more than any previous compilation), *The Mammoth Book of British Kings and Queens* will be a useful resource for academic and public libraries.

Who's Who in British History: Beginnings to 1901. 2v. Ed. by Geoffrey Treasure. 1998. 1,450p. bibliog. index. maps. tables. Fitzroy Dearborn, $250 (1-884964-90-7). DDC: 941.

This alphabetically arranged biographical dictionary gives detailed listings for approximately 1,700 persons who had an impact on British history between 310 B.C. and 1901. Most of the contents were previously published as part of the eight-volume series *Who's Who in British History* (1989–97), issued in the U.S. by St. James. The series, which is organized chronologically, is itself a revision and enlargement of another series, *Who's Who in History* (Blackwell, 1961–74), which covered British history to 1837. The new oversized format is much more attractive, and some of the content has been slightly updated.

The cogent sketches both seat the subject firmly in his or her chronological setting and show the subject's effect on the times. The writing style is, for the most part, brisk and engaging, employing a rich vocabulary that targets the work for college-level research. Entries range in length from a few paragraphs to several double-column pages, with longer articles devoted to persons of relatively greater significance in terms of impact on their times. More than five pages, for example, are devoted to Alfred the Great; more than six to Henry VIII. No information is given about criteria for inclusion, and there are occasional questionable omissions. For example, while William of Ockham is cited as significant in six articles on other clerics and philosophers of his time, there is no entry for Ockham himself. Of the 1,700 people covered, only around 100 are women. By and large, however, each era is well represented by those who set the tenor of their times.

Most articles conclude with a short bibliography. Though contributors are listed on the title page, individual entries are not attributed, nor is information given on the backgrounds of the contributors or the editor. There are several points of entry. Aside from the alphabetical organization, which allows for easy location of any figure under consideration, a chronological listing and a division by 51 subject categories, ranging from academics to translators, are given at the beginning of volume 1. The opening section of volume 1 also contains an extensive reading list by era, a chronology, a glossary, a genealogical table of the Kings and Queens of Great Britain (1066–1901), and two maps of Britain showing regions, peoples, man-made features, towns, bishoprics, and monasteries referenced in the text. There are mimimal cross-references, but the comprehensive index at the end of volume 2 is very nearly a work of art, with the main article on any person noted in bold print and auxiliary references following, some with explanatory text.

Although information on the better-known figures is readily available, *Who's Who in British History* covers Britain in more depth than general resources such as *Encyclopedia of World Biography* [RBB My 1 98]. It provides accessible information across an entire 2,000-plus-year time span, and does so in an easy-to-use format. The vast amount of accurate, unbiased information contained here, combined with a pleasant prose style, make this resource worthy of purchase where British history is studied. Institutions in possession of the eight-volume series may find the two-volume version redundant.

The Arthurian Name Dictionary. By Christopher W. Bruce. 1999. 504p. bibliog. Garland, $120 (0-8153-2865-6). DDC: 942.01.

The legend of King Arthur and his knights and ladies has been around for more than a millennium. It probably began in the Dark Ages in Wales, as oral tales passed down through the years. Then it was picked up by the English, transmitted to Europe, and returned to England to be codified by Sir Thomas Malory. Meanwhile, Arthur had found a new best friend (Lancelot), a quest (the Holy Grail), and a place to live (Camelot). The Arthurian legend is best described as an amalgam of many writers' ideas, plots, themes, characters, and motifs.

To comb through 1,500 years of Arthuriana and find every name associated with it is a considerable task that Bruce has accomplished admirably. The extremely invaluable *New Arthurian Encyclopedia* (Garland, 1996) provides only 90 names (by design, it should be noted), whereas this volume has more than 5,600. It makes for both a fascinating read and a very useful reference tool. The work consists mostly of names of major and minor characters (*Arthur, Gwythyr, Tristan, Petipace of Winchelsea*), but there are also references to places, events, and things. The author has wisely made his cutoff with Tennyson's *The Idylls of the King* (1859–1886) or the volume would be twice as long because of the current proliferation of Arthuriana. Each entry is listed alphabetically and depending on the subject can be very short or quite long. The entry on Arthur is nine pages long. It looks first at his historicity and how the legend around him developed. Then it notes what the texts say about the dates of his reign, how they portray his character, what insignia he carried, and where his grave is located. Entries are fully cross-referenced with the excellent appendix on sources that lists not only author, title, and date but provides brief descriptions, some keywords, and a note on the text that was used. This is a very useful work that most large public and academic libraries should have.

Medieval England: An Encyclopedia. Ed. by Paul E. Szarmach and others. 1998. 936p. bibliogs. illus. index. maps. Garland, $135 (0-8240-5786-4).

Edited by, among others, the director of the Medieval Institute at Western Michigan University, this multidisciplinary encyclopedia is described as "an introduction to the society and culture of England from the coming of the Anglo-Saxons in the 5th century through the accession of the Tudor dynasty (1485) at the turn of the 16th century." Containing more than 700 entries by more than 300 international scholars, the volume encompasses the fields of Old English and Middle English language and literature, music and liturgy, history, and history of art. According to the introduction, it is designed to be accessible to the general reader as well as to the scholar.

Entries are arranged alphabetically and vary in length from a few lines to six or seven pages. Some longer entries are divided into subentries. *Drama, vernacular,* for example, is divided by genre, such as biblical plays and folk drama; while *liturgy and church music, history of* is divided by period. More than 170 of the entries are biographical, covering such individuals as Alfred the Great, Thomas Becket, Geoffrey Chaucer, Eleanor of Aquitaine, Margery Kempe, and Richard III. In addition, the reader will find entries for a host of topics from political history (*Battle of Hastings, castles and fortification, treason*); social history (*chivalry, marriage and marriage law*); economic history (*agriculture and field systems, fairs and markets*); and literature and the arts (*Bayeux Tapestry, Piers Plowman, satire, vaulting*). All entries conclude with a bibliography, generally divided into primary and secondary sources, and extensive *see also* references. As stated in the introduction, the content of the bibliographies "has been selected with an eye to accessibility for non-specialist readers," although a university library would still be the place to go for most of the sources.

The A–Z entries are supported by lists of kings and queens of England, archbishops of Canterbury and York, and popes, 590–1502, as well as a glossary of musical and liturgical terms. Illustrations include diagrams showing architectural terms, a number of maps copied from other sources, and black-and-white photographs. In addition to the detailed index, there is a useful list of entries arranged by topic, such as "Religious Leaders" and "Musical and Liturgical Forms."

Although similar topics are covered in other sources, most notably Macmillan's 13-volume *Dictionary of the Middle Ages* (1982–89), this nicely organized volume is unique in its focus on medieval England. In addition, it reflects more recent scholarship in a growing field. Recommended for academic and large public libraries.

Women under the Third Reich: A Biographical Dictionary. By Shaaron Cosner and Victoria Cosner. 1998. 224p. appendixes. bibliog. illus. index. Greenwood, $45 (0-313-30315-0). DDC: 943.086.

Most people, if they are aware of women during the period of the Third Reich, probably know of Eva Braun, Leni Riefenstahl, and maybe Marlene Dietrich. But many other women played very important roles both for and against the Nazi regime. This dictionary features approximately 100 women—sympathizers, resistance fighters, smugglers, writers, and entertainers—whose lives were directly affected by events during this important time period. Included are women for whom source material is available in English, or who have had their life stories published.

The entries are arranged alphabetically by the name under which the subject became prominent. The articles vary in length from a paragraph to several pages based on the amount of information and the importance of the person. The names one would expect to find, such as Anne Frank, Magda Goebbels, and Corrie Ten Boom, are represented. Other figures who are lesser known, such as Gisi Fleischmann, who worked diligently and at the risk of their lives to rescue Jews, are introduced. Physicians who worked under deplorable conditions in concentration camps, such as Lucie Adelsberger, Alina Brewda, Adelaide Hautval, and Gisela Perl, have their stories told. Ona Simaite, a librarian, tried to save Jewish children and was captured and tortured. Each entry ends with a list of source material, and additional sources are listed in the bibliography. Two appendixes identify individuals by role and by nationality. A glossary would also have been helpful, especially for the high-school audience; the term *quisling* turns up in several entries, but is never explained.

This is a unique work that should be useful in libraries with collections on women or Germany. It is recommended for public libraries and would be a good curriculum-related resource for schools. It is suitable for browsing because so many interesting individuals are covered. Although much of the information was drawn from readily available sources, such as *Contemporary Authors*, *Current Biography*, and various *Who's Who* titles, having it in one place provides the impact the authors intended: to bring to light how this controversial period in history affected women.

Encyclopedia of Contemporary French Culture. Ed. by Alex Hughes and Keith Reader. 618p. bibliogs. index. Routledge, $140 (0-415-13186-3). DDC: 944.08.

This encyclopedia, current through 1997, presents "over 700 alphabetical entries on key aspects of French culture since 1945 . . . [covering] topics which traditional reference works often neglect." The editors are university based, as are the contributors, though no subjects of specialty nor prior publications are given for any. Emphasizing cross-disciplinary concerns, and a movement "away from the . . . duo of language and canonical literature . . . to incorporate cinema, political and social institutions, gender-based studies, and critical theory," this work would be of utility to college and university students not only in French programs but in areas such as cinema studies, literary theory, or political science.

Some examples of entries are AIDS, *cinema, detective fiction, gastronomy, legal system*, Pompidou Centre and the Forum des Halles, *poststructuralism, racism/anti-Semitism*, and *student revolt of* 1986. People covered in biographical entries have contributed to the culture in a variety of ways and include, among others, Isabelle Adjani, Roland Barthes, Christian Dior, Le Corbusier, and Jean-Marie Le Pen. Lengthy articles (up to four pages) are generally reserved for such broad topics as architecture, feminist thought, and psychoanalysis. Most articles have useful cross-references either embedded or appended. Longer articles also include annotated suggestions for further reading. Many of the cited works are in French, making the book most useful as a starting point for in-depth research for those with at least reading fluency in that language. There are, however, enough English-language sources to help the monolingual researcher. In addition to the index, there is a "classified contents list" that groups topics by subject.

Coverage is generally quite thorough, especially in cultural, political, and arts-related fields. Factually correct and balanced in presentation, the encyclopedia gives a multidimensional, if pedantically written, view of current French culture. More comprehensive, if less readable, than James Corbett's nonencyclopedic *Through French Windows: An Introduction to France in the Nineties* (Univ. of Michigan, 1994), this fills a niche in cross-disciplinary studies. Recommended for academic and large public libraries.

Conflict in the Former Yugoslavia: An Encyclopedia. Ed. by John B. Allcock and others. 1998. 410p. bibliog. chronology. illus. index. maps. ABC-CLIO, $55 (0-87436-935-5). DDC: 949.703.

Here is an outstanding reference resource in which a wide array of entries deepen our knowledge of a vital contemporary issue. Three British specialists on the region have brought together 26 other colleagues, mainly from United Kingdom institutions, to provide insight on one of the major conflicts of the 1990s. The 500 entries cover political, military, geographical, historical, economic, social, and cultural matters. Biographical entries and entries on small communities caught up in the fighting help personalize the tragedy. The material is current through 1997.

The alphabetically arranged, signed entries include *see* and *see also* references. Entries are usually one paragraph but longer when necessary; *political parties* is seven pages. Twelve black-and-white maps at the beginning of the volume and many photos throughout the text add a visual dimension to the clearly written, accurate information. Although the focus is on the current period, sufficient background and analysis, such as in the article on Communist leader Tito, bring the past into the present.

An extensive bibliography includes 1998 titles; a 38-page chronology from 1941 to 1997 presents events in the country and surrounding world. This powerful resource will be useful in high-school, public, and academic libraries.

Encyclopedia of China: The Essential Reference to China, Its History and Culture. By Dorothy Perkins. 1998. 635p. bibliog. illus. index. Facts On File, $95 (0-8160-2693-9). DDC: 951.

This encyclopedia, by the author of *Encyclopedia of Japan* [RBB F 15 91], is a fairly comprehensive work on the span of Chinese history up to the present. It differs significantly from *Companion to Chinese History* (Facts On File, 1987) in its treatment of general concepts within the context of China and Chinese culture. While the emphasis is on the history, personalities, and geography of China, many entries address the significance of things such as mirrors, calligraphy, and various animals and foods.

Entries are arranged alphabetically and cover a broad range of topics, including religion, politics, Westerners prominent in Chinese history, cities, regions, the arts, and history. Copious cross-references facilitate browsing. Although main entries for Chinese words are found under the pinyin system of romanization, the older standard (Wade-Giles) is acknowledged and cross-references are provided. Thus, while the main entry for the capital of the People's Republic of China (PRC) is under *Beijing*, there is a *see* reference under *Peking*. The entries can be somewhat redundant, offering too much detail on related concepts covered in more detail elsewhere in the volume. However, the information contained in the entries is a nice blend of the scholarly, the cultural, and the commonplace. Entries for cities, for example, contain basic information of interest to travelers, such as major attractions and climate.

Following the entries, there is a bibliography of suggested readings. While brief, this is a solid and up-to-date list of relevant secondary materials for more in-depth research needs. A detailed index includes citations to main entries, tables, and illustrations. The 50 black-and-white photographs are largely decorative, and do not usually assist in the understanding of the entries. The author has included some helpful tables (e.g., the Wade-Giles to pinyin conversion table and a chronology of dynasties) which would have been more useful had they been placed at the end of the work as appendixes. No maps are included.

Given the quality and coverage of *The Cambridge Encyclopedia of China* [RBB F 15 92], many libraries may not see the need for another encyclopedia of China. However, with the ongoing changes in Chinese society, libraries may want to purchase a newer volume that discusses modern China directly. The current volume does an adequate job of bringing the reader up to date, and thus this will be a useful addition to many collections, especially in public and school libraries. A less-detailed, though much more scholarly work, covering the entire span of Chinese history is *China: A Cultural and Historical Dictionary* (Curzon, 1998), which would be a more appropriate choice for academic libraries.

Encyclopedia of the Persian Gulf War. By Richard A. Schwartz. 1998. 224p. appendixes. bibliog. illus. index. maps. McFarland, $45 (0-7864-0451-5). DDC: 956.7044.

Richard Alan Schwartz is a professor of English at Florida International University in Miami. He has authored several publications including *The Cold War Reference Guide* (McFarland, 1997). This volume on the Persian Gulf War will be of interest to the general public, students, and scholars.

More than 110 entries deal with persons, weapons, and issues of the war. The entries vary from a paragraph to several pages in length. Longer entries contain numerous subsections. For example, the nine-page entry *Diplomacy* has five subsections, including coverage of diplomacy prior to the invasion of Kuwait, after the invasion, during Desert Shield and Desert Storm, and the cease-fire negotiations. Throughout the text, there are abundant cross-references, as well as approximately 7 line maps and 23 black-and-white photographs.

The entries are followed by a 28-page chronology that covers events from 1958 through 1991. A short bibliography contains 55 items, including a joint PBS/BBC video documentary, several items from a British perspective, and a Web site. Most of the bibliography copyright dates are from 1991 to 1993, with the most current being a single entry from 1996. Rounding out the volume is an index. There are no entries in the index for illustrations or maps.

There are many books on the Persian Gulf War but only a few that are comparable to this. Two sources listed in the bibliography are *The Encyclopedia of the Persian Gulf War* by Grossman [RBB Ap 15 96] and *Persian Gulf War Almanac* by Summers [RBB My 1 95]. Both are far superior in terms of the number of maps and illustrations, and both have several hundred items listed in their bibliographies. Schwartz's volume is recommended as a supplement to the several excellent references already available.

Encyclopedia of the Vietnam War: A Political, Social, and Military History. 3v. Ed. by Spencer C. Tucker. 1998. 1,320p. bibliogs. illus. index. ABC-CLIO, $275 (0-87436-983-5). DDC: 959.7.

It ended a generation ago and is still with us. This superb reference work provides understanding and perspective of one of the greatest crises in U.S. history, and covers every conceivable aspect. The editor teaches military history at Virginia Military Institute and was an intelligence analyst during the war. The contributors are mainly history and political science professors from universities, but a number are from specialized institutions such as the Naval Historical Institute. Several contributors are Vietnamese.

There are more than 900 alphabetically arranged entries, accompanied by 149 black-and-white photographs. The first volume contains an alphabetical list of entries, 22 line maps, and entries A–M. The second volume has entries N–Z, bibliographies (nonfiction, literature, and film), a chronology of events, and a glossary. The third volume provides documents, a few statistical tables, and an index. There are more than 200 documents, from "Ho Chi Minh's Speech at the Tours Congress" (1922) to "Remarks by President Clinton in Announcement of Normalization of Diplomatic Relations with Vietnam" (1995).

The double-column entries are all signed, and each includes references for further reading, as well as *see also* references. Most of the references cited as source material, as well as the titles in the general bibliography, should be readily available. However, the only source material that exists for some of the entries is in French or Vietnamese. The articles range from a paragraph to several pages in length. They include prewar Vietnamese history, biographies, places, specific military operations, details of weapons systems, orders of battle (military units of all participants), involvement of France (both pre–and post–World War II) and other nations, and the war's impact on U.S. domestic life. The work is especially extensive on Vietnamese leaders, including those from earlier centuries, and in giving a sense of the diverse peoples in the land and how the country's specific conditions affected the war. Several biographies of U.S. leaders mention early caution signals that were not heeded.

The work is exceptionally balanced in viewing the manipulation of information by U.S. military and political leaders, the U.S. antiwar movement, and failures in South Vietnam's leadership. Defoliation, changing U.S. strategies, posttraumatic stress disorder, veterans' groups, the Vietnam Veterans Memorial, the war and the arts, and the contributions of African Americans and women are discussed in detail. An examination of articles on Buddhists, geography, the Nguyen dynasty, and the fall of Ngo Dinh Diem found them to be accurate.

Inevitably, with many contributors, there is some duplication, but the duplication is needed unless the reader is to continually refer to other entries. The entries are current, including events as recent as the March 1998 honor to a U.S. helicopter crew for stopping and reporting the My Lai massacre, and the April 1998 death of Pol Pot in Cambodia. The bibliographies (nonfiction, literature, and film) are extensive, and the 37-page chronology of events begins in 2879 B.C. and continues almost daily until April 30, 1975. The detailed 100-page index is accurate.

While there is considerable overlap with Stanley Kutler's one-volume *Encyclopedia of the Vietnam War*, published by Scribner just two years ago [RBB My 1 96], there are also important differences. Where Kutler tends toward generalization, Tucker has more extended treatment of particulars. There are 10 long overview essays in Kutler, on topics such as the antiwar movement, diplomacy, and the media, that provide useful background and context. Tucker, on the other hand, has separate entries on numerous aspects of the war that Kutler covers only within larger entries. Among these are discussions of the war's many operations—Operation Cedar Falls, Operation Game Warden, etc. Tucker's entries on individuals and battles are generally longer, and Tucker also has more coverage of people, both Vietnamese and French, who played roles in earlier Vietnamese history. Kutler has much fuller coverage of medical support systems on both sides of the war. Compared to Tucker's extensive collection of documents, Kutler includes just two.

Tucker's *Encyclopedia of the Vietnam War* is comprehensive, detailed, and highly recommended. Any high-school, public, or academic library that does not own Kutler will want to purchase this new set. Larger collections should have both titles available for their patrons.

Encarta Africana: Comprehensive Encyclopedia of Black History and Culture. CD-ROM. Ed. by Kwame Anthony Appiah and Henry Louis Gates Jr. 1999. Microsoft, $69.95 (0-7356-0057-0). DDC: 960.

System requirements: Multimedia PC with a 486DX/66 MHz or higher processor (Pentium recommended); 16 MB of RAM for Windows 95; 24 MB for Windows 98 or Windows NT Workstation; 30 MB of available hard-disk space for Windows 95, Windows 98, or Windows NT Workstation. To use Encarta Research Organizer: 5 MB of additional hard-disk space.

This new Microsoft *Encarta* product is a comprehensive multimedia encyclopedia of black history and culture. The innovative multimedia features of the *Encarta Encyclopedia*—panoramic views, videos and sound clips, and interactive maps—are used here to great advantage.

Illustrious scholars Kwame Anthony Appiah and Henry Louis Gates Jr. of Harvard University lead the editorial team, and the editorial board includes other intellectual notables such as William Julius Wilson and Nobel laureate Wole Soyinka. The writers include both academic scholars and *Encarta* staff. As the editors note, it was a dream of W. E. B. Du Bois' to produce an African encyclopedia. He conceived of an "Encyclopedia of the Negro" as early as 1909. By the 1960s, his vision was for an "Encyclopedia Africana," a scholarly project with African editorial control, written from the African point of view. This multimedia product goes back to his original conception (and certainly beyond anything Du Bois could have imagined technologically). The history, geography, and cultures of Africa are encompassed as well as the history and culture of people of African descent throughout the world, including the U.S., Latin America, the Caribbean, and Europe. Those who use the encyclopedia can explore ancient civilizations of the African continent, contemporary information on African countries, as well as the legacies of African cultures in the New World. One of the features, "Africana on Camera" (six celebrity videos), gives an idea of the scope and integrating vision of the project as well as the flash. Videos include Maya Angelou speaking about slavery, the African diaspora, and the survival of African heritages; Kofi Annan on the past and future of Africa; and Whoopi Goldberg on the meaning of race.

There are more than 3,000 articles, which vary in length from a few lines to several pages. Articles on Africa proper (approximately 1,355) and those on North America (another 1,360) are supplemented by hundreds more on the African presence in the Caribbean, Hispanic America, and the rest of the world. Multimedia features are integrated with most articles. In the entry on Ethiopia, for example, eight pages of text are supplemented with a map (enlargeable) showing its location on the continent, a picture of the flag with an audio clip of the national anthem, pictures of traditional textiles and dress, a Coptic church, farming methods, and prime minister Meles Zenawi. The article on the Afro-Brazilian religion Candomble is illustrated with seven photographs and a video of a ceremony. The article has hyperlinks to related articles, including a larger overview on African religions in Brazil and the Cuba. In all, some 84 articles have video clips. Although some videos are rather dark, their inclusion extends the meaning conveyed—truly enlivening the articles on African music or rhythm and blues, for example. The videos showing the Little Rock School integration incident or the longer videos of the Swahili Coast or the Kingdom of Kush add content to the presentation of material. There are many audio clips, most a minute or less. A few are spoken (Ralph Abernathy, Martin Luther King Jr., Rosa Parks), but the vast majority are music. It would have been a nice addition to the articles on African languages to include some sound examples. More than 1,000 pictures and photographs also supplement the text.

The articles seem quite current. Recent elections in Africa are covered as well as the 1998 bombing in Kenya. Other features of note include a Historical Timeline that depicts significant eras in the history of African peoples from B.C.E. to the present. The time line scrolls from left to right with clickable photos and sound clips. However, it is a bit awkward to use. Sidebars on many topics include excerpts from primary sources and news stories. Each article has a pull-down feature to lead to related articles, Web sites, and references for further reading. Unfortunately, many of the bibliographies are not now present. It is unclear what the updating process will be.

As in the regular *Encarta Encyclopedia*, the two-disc structure is unwieldy. The article text seems to be present on both discs, but in some cases associated media for an article require switching more than once. This may not be a problem if the set is used on a workstation with two CD-ROM drives.

The primary searching feature is Pinpointer. In a pull-down menu one can search for an article title or words in a title. A word search will retrieve all articles containing the word or phrase. This feature would be more useful if the results of the word searches in the articles were ranked in some way. For example, if a student typed in the word *Brazil* to find entries that discuss the country besides the main articles, the result would be 238 hits, but many would be like the entry on Arthur Ashe, which just happens to mention the U.S. tennis team being defeated by Brazil. A better subject expander is the Category Search. All of the articles on a region such as the Caribbean can be pulled with optional subcategories such as Sports, Daily Life, Social and Political Movements, and so forth. Other access points include a Media Gallery, which allows one to find and display all media photos, videos, sound, and maps. A search can find all media on a topic or all of a particular media.

One can print or copy an entire article or selected text, images, or captions. Other features include the ability to change the views of the page, to enlarge the text size, and to have the text read out loud. Research Organizer, a notecard and outlining tool with a tutorial on report writing, may prove useful for students.

This is a well-produced and informative product. It is suited for home use, and many libraries will want to make it available, although the equipment must also be taken into consideration. Both basic information and very sophisticated essays explore and fulfill the dream of Du Bois. Features such as Category Search and Topic Trek, which can take readers on a tour through many articles that discuss ideas such as negritude or the Harlem Renaissance, make this a learning experience beyond an encyclopedia. *Britannica Online* has longer articles on countries, *Encyclopedia of Africa South of the Sahara* [RBB Je 1 & 15 98] is more comprehensive on many aspects of the African continent, but *Encarta Africana* is a star and something that most libraries will want to acquire. Aside from the question of equipment, the price is so low for the value that no library that can run it should pass it up.

Archaeology of Prehistoric Native America: An Encyclopedia. Ed. by Guy Gibbon. 1998. 941p. bibliog. illus. index. maps. tables. Garland, $165 (0-8153-0725-X). DDC: 970.01.

There is no dearth of reference books on Indians of North America, but this scholarly encyclopedia fills a unique niche. It deals with the precontact cultures of continental North America, the area bounded by Mexico on the south, the Arctic Ocean on the north, the North Atlantic on the east, and the Pacific and the Bering Sea on the west. Although the editor writes, "the purpose of this encyclopedia is to provide an introductory overview of North American prehistory . . . ," the 750 signed entries presume a certain amount of knowledge of the field of archaeology on the part of the reader, and will be best appreciated by college students, informed laypersons, and professionals. Contributors represent university departments of archaeology and anthropology, state and federal government agencies and museums, historical societies, environmental organizations, archives, tribal councils, geology experts, and research centers.

The main body of the work is alphabetically arranged; however, the reader is encouraged to consult first the front matter in which the major culture areas and topical categories are identified: *Arctic/Subarctic*, *California*, *Eastern Woodlands*, *Great Basin*, *Northwest Coast*, *Plateau*, *Plains*, *Southwest*, *Pre-Clovis/Paleoindian*, and a General Category. An excellent "Reader's Guide" prepared by Gibbon discusses how the natural and cultural areas came to be defined and how climatic episodes affected natural life, how the glaciers receded during the Holocene period, and how the positions of sea levels and vegetation developed into "natural areas" in which precontact cultures were able to evolve. The history of North American archaeology and a discussion of dating conventions and how dates on archaeological "finds" are derived and compared are most useful.

Most of the entries deal with specific sites (*Poverty Point site*), cultures and culture areas (*Hohokam culture area*, *Koniag culture*), artifacts (*platform pipe*), archaeologists identified with specific areas and cultures (*Hrdlicka, Ales* [1869–1943]), traditions (*Pebble Tool tradition*), and general topics (*corn*, *kiva*, *Little Ice Age*, *mammoth/mastodon*). Each entry features a brief bibliography of further readings. Maps, tables, and photographs dot the text, and there is a detailed index, although not every site mentioned in the text is identified there. For example, Meadowcroft Rockshelter and the Krajacic site, both mentioned in the entry *Miller complex*, are not in the index. Location codes are given in descriptions of sites, but there is no key to what these mean.

This valuable, comprehensive work on native North American prehistory is recommended for academic and large public libraries.

Native Americans: An Encyclopedia of History, Culture, and Peoples. 2v. By Barry M. Pritzker. 1998. 868p. appendixes. bibliog. illus. index. ABC-CLIO, $150 (0-87436-836-7). DDC: 970.004.

Ten chapters on geographical regions (Southwest, California, Northwest Coast, Great Basin, the Plateau, Great Plains, Southeast, Northeast Woodlands, Subarctic, and Arctic) offer both an introduction and an overview of the tribes and nations in each area. This arrangement permits author Pritzker, a former teacher who has contributed to other works on Native Americans, to provide users with information about topographical variations and the diverse cultures and general history of each region. Each chapter starts out by defining the area under consideration, discussing the climate, and detailing the way of life of the indigenous cultures, including food, shelter, clothing, artistic expression, religious ceremonies, fundamental societal units, contact with other groups (especially Europeans), and experiences with the U.S. government. There are also an alphabetical listing of individual tribes covered and several historical photographs selected from a variety of sources (these are not the standard photographs from the Smithsonian), which enhance the text. Following the introductory material, A–Z entries treat more than 200 groups in the U.S. and Canada. These entries are divided into Historical Information (history, religion, customs, dwellings, diet, key technology, trade, art, weapons, etc.) and Contemporary Information (government, economy, legal status, daily life). Entries are well written and easy to read, and the general layout makes it easy to find pertinent information quickly.

Not generally included is information on extinct groups (although there is information about groups like the Natchez because of their importance), and there is no biographical information on specific prominent people. There are a glossary, a short general bibliography, and three appendixes that list Canada Reserves and bands; Alaska native villages, by language; and ANCSA (Alaska Native Claims Settlement Act) village corporations.

We have already seen the publication this year of the four-volume *Gale Encyclopedia of Native American Tribes* [RBB S 1 98]. Although there are many similarities between the two sets, there are also important differences. *Gale* covers more tribes in separate entries rather than as parts of larger groups. For example, more than 60 tribes of the Pacific Northwest have individual entries in *Gale*, as opposed to 17 in the ABC-CLIO work, where such tribes as the Muckleshoot, the Nisqually, and the Puyallup are all discussed in the entry *Salish, Southern Coast*. *Gale* also covers major tribes of the Caribbean, the Pacific Islands, and Central and South America, as well as prehistoric groups, such as the Anasazi. In addition, *Gale* is rich in features that make it an attractive choice for students—biographical profiles, sidebars, time lines, and excerpts from oral literature, as well as maps, a more extensive glossary, more finding aids, and many more bibliographic citations. However, *Native Americans* has information missing from *Gale*. Pritzker is more consistent in the amount of detail he provides on dwellings, diet, technology, etc.; the level of detail varies in *Gale*, where each entry has a separate author. Pritzker generally has more information on current conditions, sometimes devoting several pages to a group's contemporary life, which *Gale* may cover in a single paragraph.

Public, high-school, and academic libraries that have not acquired *Gale* will find this new title to be a good purchase. Even where *Gale* is already part of the collection, *Native Americans* is recommended as an additional source if more comprehensive coverage is needed.

North America in Colonial Times: An Encyclopedia for Students. 4v. Ed. by Jacob Ernest Cooke and Milton M. Klein. 1998. 912p. bibliog. illus. index. maps. Scribner, $375 (0-684-80538-3). DDC: 970.02.

These volumes have been adapted for middle-and high-school students from Scribner's *Encyclopedia of the North American Colonies* (1993). As in the parent set, not only are there entries examining British colonies that later became the U.S. but other European influences are included, such as the Spanish colonies in the South and Southwest and the French and Dutch colonies. The volumes are arranged in alphabetical order with a table of contents in the first volume and an index in the fourth. All four volumes begin with the same time line ranging from the first human inhabitants who crossed from Siberia to Alaska through 1867, when Russia sold Alaska to the U.S. and the Dominion of Canada was established.

The encyclopedia's 450 entries cover places, events, concepts, activities, conflicts, social and cultural life, and individuals and groups, including separate entries for Indian tribes. There are also entries, such as *diseases and disorders*, *family*, and *transportation and travel*, that cover different aspects of daily life at the time. The contributions of women, Native Americans, and African Americans are recognized. Many articles are arranged in sections that treat different groups of people; *food and drink*, for example, has sections on Native American, British colonial, African American, Dutch colonial, French colonial, and Spanish colonial foods. The articles vary in length from one or two paragraphs to several pages.

The volumes are attractively designed and easy to use. The text is arranged so that entries appear in a major column, with a minor column being used for illustrations and other supplemental information such as time lines, definitions, sidebars, and so forth. To assist the researcher, cross-references to related entries are found both within the text (words or names are printed in boldface) and at the end of the article. There are also *see* reference to pertinent maps and color plates that can be found in other volumes. Though most illustrations are in black and white, each volume contains four pages of color plates that illustrate important topics, such as daily life (in volume 1) and art (in volume 2). The bibliography in volume 4 is divided into broad topics, such as "Atlases and Encyclopedias" and "African Americans," and includes an extensive list of online resources. Many of the titles in the bibliography are university press publications. Books recommended for young readers are denoted by an asterisk.

This set retains the high level of scholarship found in the *Encyclopedia of the North American Colonies* and is recommended for school and public libraries serving middle-school and high-school students. For the upper-elementary and middle grades, Grolier's 10-volume *Colonial America* [RBB S 1 98] is a good choice.

Peoples of the Americas. 11v. 1999. 648p. bibliog. charts. glossary. illus. indexes. maps. Marshall Cavendish, $471.36 (0-7614-7050-6). DDC: 970.

This attractive and appealing set consists of slim volumes, approximately 60 pages each, that provide a country-by-country look at both indigenous peoples and immigrant groups that have settled in various regions of the Americas. Ranging from the Falkland Islands to Greenland, and considering groups that might have been present as long as 30,000 years ago through present day, this set presents an accessible ethnological approach to research for its intended audience, students in upper elementary grades and up.

Entries range from a minimum two-page spread (*Cayman Islands*, *Montserrat*) through 50 pages on Canada and more than 70 on the U.S. Each entry features a full-color relief map; an additional continent or regional map; an introduction that covers landscape, climate, and a general history; and a look at various ethnic groups, considering their religion, myths and rituals, houses and homes, clothing and adornments, language, health and education, food and drink, family life, social life, arts and crafts, and music and dance. For indigenous groups there is additional information regarding challenges to their lifestyles exerted by external influences. Larger countries are examined region by region, smaller countries as a whole. Pronunciations are provided for terms that may be unfamiliar.

Numerous color and black-and-white photos are sprinkled throughout the text, all featuring captions. Boxed inserts provide facts and figures (status, cities, population, currency, etc.), climate, and a time line. Longer entries also highlight unique practices, people, or events ("Months in the Cree Calendar," "Gauchos: Cowboys of Argentina," "The Great Gretzky").

Each volume has its own glossary, index, and lists of books for further reading. These volume-specific lists feature titles published in the 1980s and 1990s and include basic texts that would be found in most school and public library collections, such as Marshall Cavendish's *Cultures of the World* series and similar titles from Chelsea House and Children's Press.

What really makes this reference stand out is volume 11, the index volume, which begins with a comprehensive bibliography. The first section of the bibliography is an annotated list (summary, genre, style, age designation) of 30 fiction titles by authors such as Michael Dorris and Walter Dean Myers, followed by a section of nonfiction titles on individual countries. The next section is a pronunciation guide arranged alphabetically by country, which presents terms encountered in the text—*Kiowa*, *kivas*, *Kwanzaa*, for example. The "National Days" section first considers national holidays country by country, then lists them chronologically by month. This is followed by nine separate indexes. There are a biographical index, a geographic index, and an "Arts of the Americas" index. Artists, individual works, and broad terms such as *movies*, *theater*, *sculpture*, and *weaving*, as well as specialized terms such as *reggae*, *calypso*, and *the Group of Seven*, are referenced here. Next come a "Festivals of the Americas" guide, indexing general summaries as well as specific celebrations such as the Calgary Stampede and Eid ul Fitr (the feast marking the end of Ramadan); an index of "Foods of the Americas"; and indexes to "Peoples and Cultures" (ethnic groups, tribes, etc.); "Religions and Religious Ceremonies" (organized religions as well as such regional sects and orders as Amish and Rastafarians); "Sports and Games" (polo to cock fighting, and personalities such as Peleand Jim Thorpe); and, finally, a comprehensive index to the entire set.

The amount of information, logical organization, multiple access points, and attractive layout combine to create a reference tool that most school and public libraries will want in their collections. Much of this information can be culled from other resources, but this set's emphasis on ethnology will tie in nicely with curricula and texts that reflect a multicultural approach. Narrower in scope than *Peoples of the*

World: Customs and Cultures [RBB O 1 98] but much better organized and more in tune with school and report assignments, *Peoples of the Americas* will complement standard sets such as *Lands and Peoples* [RBB Jl 97].

The American Heritage Encyclopedia of American History. Ed. by John Mack Faragher. 1998. appendixes. bibliogs. illus. index. maps. tables. Holt, $45 (0-8050-4438-8). DDC: 973.

Editor John Mack Faragher is a professor of American History at Yale University and is the author of numerous award-winning histories and several reference books. He has edited an interesting new volume that covers American history from pre-Columbian times into the 1990s. This work is intended for students, teachers, scholars, and history aficionados. It is arranged alphabetically and has nearly 3,000 entries. In addition, there are approximately 500 black-and-white illustrations, including photographs, etchings, cartoons, maps, and portraits.

The work covers the standard topics of American history and also surveys once-neglected areas like American women, African and Native Americans, family history, and popular culture. Users will find entries on such diverse topics as Miles Davis, marriage, and the Nez Perce Indians. There are entries for many major cities. Nearly one-third of the text is devoted to biographies, including Supreme Court justices, signers of the Declaration of Independence, and many literary, sports, and entertainment figures. Coverage also includes fundamental Supreme Court decisions, descriptions and chronologies of all 50 states, and broad entries like *comedy, painting, science fiction,* and *television*.

Entries vary in length from a paragraph to several pages. A random sampling showed that approximately one-third of the entries are signed and contain bibliographic citations. Biographical entries give birth and death years and frequently mention important books written by the person. At the end of many entries there are numerous *see also* references, which are generally accurate. The book is quite current, mentioning the 1997 appointment of Madeleine Albright as Secretary of State, and the conviction of Timothy McVeigh for the Oklahoma City bombing. Some of the bibliographies are also quite current. However, other bibliographies are disappointing in not citing recent materials; examples are *Japanese-American Internment, Patton, Declaration of Independence,* and *Pearl Harbor*.

Assisting users throughout the text are shaded areas called Topic Guides. These guides refer users to related entries, biographies, and entries of a diverse nature for topical study. Appendixes provide the text of the Declaration of Independence, the Constitution of the United States, a time table, and several tables listing government offices and officers.

There are several fairly recent and comparable single-volume encyclopedias of U.S. history—*A Dictionary of American History* [RBB D 1 95], *The Encyclopedic Dictionary of American History* [RBB Ap 15 92], and *The Reader's Companion to American History* [RBB Ja 1 92]. *The American Heritage Encyclopedia of American History* is more current and generally combines more entries, more illustrations, and more useful appendix information. Junior-and senior-high schools, as well as academic and public libraries, should consider acquiring this reference source for their collections.

The American Years: A Chronology of United States History. By Ernie Gross. 1999. 655p. illus. index. Scribner, $95 (0-684-80590-1). DDC: 973.

General worldwide and subject specific chronologies seem to abound in the pages of *Reference Books Bulletin*, but, strange as it seems, there have been few one-volume entries for plain old U.S. history. One of the best, now in its tenth edition, is *The Encyclopedia of American Facts and Dates* (HarperCollins, 1997), by Gorton Carruth.

The most recent entry in the field is this one-volume chronology from the reputable Scribner. Its purpose, as the author states, "is an effort to give an overview of life in the United States since it became an independent nation." The time period from 1776 to 1997 is this volume's main preoccupation. A beginning chapter, "Colonial History: A Brief Overview," covers prior U.S. history in a very general way.

Each year of the chronology beginning with 1776 is divided into eight sections: "International," "National," "Business/Industry/Inventions," "Science/Medicine," "Education," "Religion," "Literature/Journalism," and "Miscellaneous." Brief paragraphs or other subdivisions follow, giving descriptions of major events. As the chronology approaches more recent times, the sections are expanded to include coverage of art and music, sports, and entertainment.

A detailed and comprehensive index enhances the volume's usefulness. Names, places, books, songs, plays, television programs, congressional acts, and poems are among the index entries. The book is nicely illustrated.

As chronologies go, this is a fairly standard tool. The major events of each year are included but not listed day-by-day, as they are in *The Encyclopedia of American Facts and Dates*. That work is more comprehensive, covering 1,000 years of American history. On the other hand, *The American Years* has illustrations and a format that students, in particular, may find easier to use. Recommended for high-school, public, and academic libraries, especially those that do not already own *The Encyclopedia of American Facts and Dates*.

The American Multimedia Archive. CD-ROM. 1998. Facts On File, $995.95 (0-8160-3845-7). Networking available. DDC: 973.

System requirements: Windows 3.1 or higher; 8 MB RAM; 20 MB free hard disk space.

Based on the publisher's *American Historical Images On File*, this program contains more than 2,000 hyperlinked images, primary-source documents, video and audio clips, time lines, and maps. The main menu allows access to the archive through 11 eras beginning with Native Societies and Colonization (to 1763) and ending with Toward a New Millenium (1970–present). Within each era, images are grouped into a number of categories including Native Americans, African American Experience, Government and Constitution, Foreign Affairs, Daily Life and Culture, Audio and Video Gallery, Historical Documents, and Timeline. The images are accompanied by full captions that provide a good overview of each topic.

Contents are also accessible through the following six categories: A Nation Divided (The Civil War), Audio and Video Gallery, Exploration and Colonial America, and Foreign Affairs. Events, such as important battles, are a major category of article. There are also many biographical articles; entries for P. T. Barnum, Yogi Berra, Janet Jackson, Madonna, Winfield Scott, and Thomas Wolfe give an indication of the wide range. But some inclusions and exclusions seem rather arbitrary: Michael Crichton and Anne Rice are included, but Emily Dickinson, Stephen King, James Michener, and Walt Whitman are not. Salvador Dali (not an American) is included, but Grandma Moses and Andy Warhol are not. Zebulon Pike, an explorer of the American West, is categorized under Foreign Affairs, while Sam Houston is mentioned only in a time line with no hypertext link to anything. The January 1998 selection of John Glenn to again become an astronaut is noted. However, the user will look in vain for Stephen Collins Foster, Hubble Space Telescope, Coney Island, and Niagara Falls, and will find Empire State Building only in the time line (with no photograph), although these are undoubtedly important elements in the American experience.

Articles are clearly written and seem most appropriate for high-school and junior-high-school students. Illustrations include a wide variety of prints, photographs, and paintings from sources including Currier & Ives, the National Archives, and the Library of Congress. A click on any illustration (already reasonably large) will increase it to nearly full-screen size. Additional features include Notepad, Bookmarks, and links to other American History Web sites.

Installation of the program was quick and problem-free. The CD-ROM uses the Logos Library System format, which, according to on-screen documentation, "is fast becoming the industry standard for multilingual electronic publishing. . ."; it is unclear to what extent this format is responsible for some of the difficulties encountered. While the hypertext capabilities are admirable and searches can be done by era, topic, word, or phrase, actually getting around the database can be difficult. The meaning of some icons is straightforward, but others are far from obvious. Several hours of use by the Board eventually decreased, but did not by any means eliminate, false steps in searching. Help screens are available, and the user can select for search tips to appear each time the program is started. Librarians who are not prepared to provide extensive training and frequent assistance to users will probably be frustrated with the program.

This product provides good basic coverage of the major topics in American history and many interesting illustrations and audio/video clips, but a good multimedia encyclopedia such as *Encarta* will provide far more articles and illustrations on most of the same, and many additional, topics with more intuitive searches, at a fraction of the cost. *The American Multimedia Archive* CD-ROM cannot be recommended as a good buy. The collection can also be purchased on four separate CD-ROMs covering different time periods and costing $299.95 each.

Colonial America. 10v. 1998. bibliog. illus. index. maps. Grolier, $299 (0-7172-9193-6). DDC: 973.2.

From *Acadia*, the French colony made legendary in Longfellow's *Evangeline*, to *Zenger, Peter*, early New York newspaper editor, topics and items related to Colonial America are arranged alphabetically throughout this set. The 13 colonies are stressed; however, colonization in some other areas, such as Florida, Nova Scotia, New Mexico, Texas, West Indies, California, Hawaii, and Alaska, is given some consideration.

Coverage for the 13 colonies is extensive although not necessarily in-depth. Among the subjects covered are reasons for colonization, growth of the colonies, leading individuals, lives of ordinary people, important events, relationships to European powers, economy, environment, fine arts, education, crime and punishment, flora, fauna, children, government, crafts, religion, slavery, farming, and the fight for independence. Native Americans and women are also covered. The more than 250 entries are generally one to six pages long and include *see also* references. Each volume opens with a table of its contents and closes with an identical bibliography of 23 titles and an identical set index. On the whole, the titles in the bibliography are well chosen. A time line would have been useful to give a sense of events.

The numerous illustrations include photographs, drawings, diagrams, and maps—all fully captioned, many in color. Sidebars offer additional informative materials; for example, different Shawnee wigwams; curing cod; excerpts of eyewitness accounts of those who lived in Colonial America.

Much of the information in these volumes can be found in a good encyclopedia, such as *World Book*. However, for upper-elementary and middle grades, this is an attractive and informative presentation of Colonial America. Recommended for school and public libraries.

The Columbia Guide to the Cold War. Ed. by Michael Kort. 1998. 366p. appendix. bibliogs. index. Columbia, $40 (0-237-10772-2). DDC: 973.9.

The decade or so since the end of the cold war has yielded a number of treatments that have proven themselves of value to libraries of various types. This work, prepared by an experienced scholar on the subject, is one of the most concise and usable handbooks available. Its pages divide into four parts. The first consists of a narrative essay that tells the story of the cold war in summary fashion, supported by documentation. The second, "Cold War A–Z," contains descriptive entries on significant topics and personages, from *Acheson, Dean Gooderham* to *Yalta Conference*. These entries average around one page in length and most are biographical. The third part presents a chronology, 1945–1991. The fourth and longest part, "Resources," is comprised of selected and well-annotated lists of several kinds of information resources. In section 1, books and articles are listed under 39 broad topics, such as "The Nixon and Ford Administrations" and "Terrorism." In section 2, additional resources are listed by type, including memoirs and biographies, archival repositories, electronic resources (CD-ROMs, microfiche, and Web sites), and films and novels. An appendix with statistical tables, and an index conclude the volume.

Students at various levels will find this work very helpful as an introductory sourcebook to the subject, an excellent starting point for further investigation and refinement of questions. A similar title, *The Cold War Reference Guide* (McFarland, 1997), has an annotated chronology but a much less extensive bibliography. The Columbia volume is recommended for high-school, public, and academic libraries.

The Gale Encyclopedia of Native American Tribes. 4v. Ed. by Sharon Malinowski and Anna Sheets. 1998. 2,604p. bibliog. illus. indexes. maps. Gale, $349 (0-7876-1085-2). DDC: 973.

This ambitious reference work, designed to be used by students, teachers, librarians, and general readers, provides historical, cultural, and current information on nearly 400 Native American groups. Although the editors attempted to secure native authors and scholars to write and review the essays, tribal affiliation and academic credentials are listed for only a few.

At first the arrangement might seem a bit awkward because entries on individual tribal and native groups are divided into 13 geographic regions as suggested by the Smithsonian Institution's classic multivolume *Handbook of North American Indians* (1988–). This means that the index is an essential access point for users with limited knowledge about Native Americans. The first volume covers the major tribal groups of the Northeast, Southeast, and Caribbean, while volume 2 deals with the groups of the Great Basin, Southwest, and Middle America. The third volume provides information about the groups of the Arctic, the Subarctic, the Great Plains, and the Plateau. The final volume deals with native groups from the Pacific Northwest, California, and the Pacific Islands. Entries on individual tribal groups are arranged alphabetically within these 13 sections. Access is facilitated by the fact that each volume, in addition to its own table of contents, lists the contents of the other volumes in the set.

The major sections begin with a signed overview essay, which varies in length from 5,000 to 20,000 words and contains information about history, culture, and contemporary issues, as well as several small black-and-white maps and photos and a bibliography. These informative overview essays are followed by signed entries on individual tribal groups. Each article is laid out with subsections containing information on the history from pre-European contact to the present, religion, language, buildings, subsistence, clothing, healing practices, customs, oral literature (with an example of a tale or myth), and current tribal issues. Special features in each entry are the sidebars that contain basic information, a time line, and profiles of important people. These sidebars make it easy to find essential information quickly. There are also a number of small black-and-white photos and a bibliography for further reading.

Each of the four volumes contains several double-page, black-and-white maps detailing the historical origins of the tribal groups, and the locations of contemporary state and federal reservations. Profiles of individuals are listed separately in each volume's table of contents, making it easy to locate biographical information. There is a cumulative general index of tribes, native peoples, pertinent famous nonnative peoples, wars and battles, treaties and important legislation, reservations, associations, and religious groups.

What makes this new Gale set unique is its coverage of tribes. The one-volume *Encyclopedia of Native American Tribes* (Facts On File, 1988) is both less detailed and less current. Another multivolume resource, *The Encyclopedia of North American Indians* [RBB S 1 97] lists a variety of topics in A–Z format. High-school, public, and academic libraries will find *The Gale Encyclopedia of Native American Tribes* a useful addition to their information on native peoples. Team it with Davis' *Native America in the Twentieth Century* [RBB D 1 94] to broaden coverage of contemporary issues.

Leaders of the Civil War: A Biographical and Historiographical Dictionary. Ed. by Charles F. Ritter and Jon L. Wakelyn. 1998. 445p. index. Greenwood, $90 (0-313-29560-3). DDC: 973.7.

This volume presents biographical essays on 47 men and women for whom the Civil War was "the major event in their lives." Each person is shown to have had an impact on the war, one that has heretofore been overlooked in some cases. Military leaders such as Ulysses S. Grant and Robert E. Lee have naturally been included, but so have political leaders, politicians, civilian leaders, businessmen, bankers, and manufacturers. Civilians who had an important effect on morale, from either side, and the women who were in "key positions to counsel and provide support" for others are also included as leaders. Among the nonmilitary figures covered are Clara Barton, Henry Ward Beecher, Varina Davis, Frederick Douglass, and Walt Whitman.

The entries, arranged alphabetically, are around 10 pages in length. Close attention is paid to influences on each leader's early life; in fact, all chapters include a discussion of whatever forces were in play during the subject's formative years. Likewise, the question of their activities after the war has not been overlooked. However, those who have been included devoted some of their greatest energies to the war, and analysis of their wartime experiences and accomplishments is the main purpose of the volume. A second purpose is to consider how the subjects have fared in history. What has been their legacy and how have they been perceived? The evolution of scholarship on each person and the views of modern historians are discussed. Each essay concludes with a bibliography, which cites primary and other source materials.

Although the title of this work refers to it as a dictionary, the lives are not treated cursorily but at some length, much as in an encyclopedia. The contributors, like the editors, are professional historians or have historical training. The essays are accurate, objective, and authoritative. More words have been written about many of these persons, and certainly about President Lincoln, than almost any other American leaders, so it is not surprising that the editors have plowed again some well-worn ground. But the scope of the entries, the particular context provided by focusing on the war, and the readability of the

Scholastic Encyclopedia of the United States at War. By June A. English and Thomas D. Jones. 1998. 192p. illus. index. Scholastic, $18.95 (0-590-59959-3). DDC: 973.

This newest offering from Scholastic joins their other one-volume encyclopedias aimed at students in the upper-elementary and middle-school grades, including *Scholastic Encyclopedia of Sports in the United States* [RBB N 15 97] and *Scholastic Encyclopedia of Women in the United States* [RBB N 15 96]. Like others in the series, it features an attractive oversize format, and includes numerous illustrations, boxed inserts, maps, time lines, and judicious use of color highlighting and bold print. A two-page introduction briefly summarizes the major conflicts that have affected the U.S., and ends with a statement regarding the costs of war and a chart of casualty figures. This is followed by 11 independent chapters, each devoted to a specific conflict, ranging from the American Revolution to the Gulf War. The longest chapters deal with the Civil War and World War II, the shortest with the Spanish-American War. Each chapter is color-coded, making access easier. A detailed index completes the volume.

Chapters follow a basic format. "Prelude to War," which creates the historical setting and defines major issues, is followed by subsections presenting major developments, including first and last confrontations, pivotal incidents, campaigns, personalities, the home front, public reaction, and so on. Each chapter ends with a description of the aftermath, which details consequences and lasting impacts of the conflict. Scattered throughout the basic narratives are all sorts of additional information: excerpts of letters from soldiers at the front, eyewitness civilian accounts, song lyrics, quotations, descriptions of uniforms, analyses of the impact of developing technologies and their affect on both weaponry and medical care, and more than 180 illustrations, including maps, photographs, reproductions of propaganda posters, and political cartoons. There is some coverage of the contributions made by women, whether as nurses, spies, factory workers, or resistance fighters. Segregated units and racial discrimination are discussed, as is the treatment afforded Native Americans, and Japanese American internment in World War II.

Authors English (who has written a number of nonfiction titles for children) and Jones have produced a worthy addition to the series. Recommended as both a curriculum supplement and a browsing selection not only for the intended audience but also for public and secondary collections serving challenged readers and students with limited English proficiency.

Scribner's American History and Culture on CD-ROM. CD-ROM. 1998. Scribner, $650 Windows (0-684-80584-7); Macintosh (0-684-80614-2). Networking available. DDC: 973.

Minimum requirements: For Windows, Windows 3.1 or Windows 95; 16 MB RAM. For Macintosh, MacOS 7.X (OS 8.X recommended); 32 MB RAM.

Building on the strengths of its print American history resources, Scribner has produced an interesting and useful CD-ROM that contains information on the full range of the American experience. It is designed to be useful to both student and scholar, and should benefit both.

The core of the product is the full text of several standard reference works: *Dictionary of American History, Encyclopedia of American Social History, The Presidents: A Reference History*, and supplements nine and 10 of *Dictionary of American Biography*. In addition, the work contains the texts of 75 historic public documents from the Mayflower Compact to the Warren Report. Six hundred images have also been incorporated to enhance the text.

Scribner uses Netscape as its search engine, making the use of the CD-ROM self-evident for experienced Internet users. By pointing and clicking, readers can access the database in several ways. The Outline of Contents provides the tables of contents of all source materials. Research Ideas groups articles thematically under such topics as Civil Rights, The Frontier, and Travel and Communication. Time Line groups entries chronologically by decade, and Photo Gallery provides direct access to the images. In addition, a Search feature allows the reader to search by keyword. Because Netscape is the primary search engine, users can print, download, and navigate as if using a Web page. Surprisingly, the publisher has not taken advantage of the use of Netscape to link out to Web sites—everything is contained on the CD-ROM.

Like any such product, there are some minor problems with this CD-ROM. A few of the images seem to take a long time to load, the order of display of the keyword search results is not clear, and at least one hyperlink was not accurate (the Civil War Battle of Spotsylvania). Some articles are dated, especially those in the original *Dictionary of American History* that have not been revised by the supplements, although half the entries of the *Encyclopedia of American Social History* were updated especially for the CD-ROM. Although the price is somewhat steep for a single CD-ROM, it is less than one-third the combined price of its print equivalents. Despite its minor annoyances, this product is well conceived and executed and should become a useful reference tool in many academic and public libraries.

Thomas Jefferson: A Biographical Companion. By David S. Brown. 1998. 266p. bibliog. illus. index. ABC-CLIO, $45 (0-87436-949-5). DDC: 973.4.

Most of us venerate Thomas Jefferson for his political leadership and for his role in formulating early American thought, but the wealth of information about him is contradictory and confusing at times. David Brown, a professor of history whose specialty is the period so heavily influenced by Jefferson, has compiled this guide to help readers understand the times in which Jefferson lived and worked and reconcile the images of the enlightened sophisticate and the parochial slaveholder.

Arranged alphabetically, the nearly 200 entries present overviews of topics (Anglophobia, impressment, sectionalism), events (elections, the publication of the Mazzei Letter, Shays' Rebellion), and people (the Adams Family, Maria Cosway, John Locke) that affected Thomas Jefferson and vice versa. Although these brief articles probably do not offer the Jefferson scholar new information, the reader less familiar with the subject can learn a great deal in a short time. Simply scanning the illustrations, for example, shows Jefferson's pragmatic "autocopier," his design for a macaroni machine, and an ad he placed after a slave named Sandy ran away with his shoemaker tools and a white horse. Reading the entries on James Callender (a pamphleteer who first "broke" the story of Jefferson's relationship with Sally Hemmings), the Tertium Quid (a divisive faction of the Republican Party), and the Yazoo Lands (a fraudulent land deal) suggests that politics then was no nobler than today.

In addition to the brief articles, there are selected primary sources that enhance the understanding of this remarkable man and his times. Included are Jefferson's draft of the Declaration of Independence (with the parts stricken by Congress in italics), letters to friends and family showing many of his interests and concerns, and his first inaugural address. A six-page chronology includes personal and political events, and it, as well as the index and the cross-references, helps direct the reader to relevant articles. The bibliography is extensive, but without annotations; it is probably overwhelming to the nonspecialist audience alluded to in the preface.

Its attractive format and easy readability will make this volume useful to anyone who wants to know more about Thomas Jefferson and the republican citizenry he endorsed. Although it is arranged like a reference book, it is one that many will want to peruse at leisure, so some libraries might want circulating copies, too. Recommended for high-school, public, and academic libraries, this is the second title in the publisher's Biographical Companions series. The first was published last year and dealt with Benjamin Franklin ($45, 0-87436-931-2).

War and American Popular Culture: A Historical Encyclopedia. Ed. by M. Paul Holsinger. 1999. 479p. bibliog. illus. index. Greenwood, $89.50 (0-313-29908-0). DDC: 973.

Holsinger, a professor of history at Illinois State University, has attempted to pull together in one volume "many of the most significant representations in popular culture that deal with this nation's various wars." He admits that though entries span American history from about 1565, his book is "undeniably tilted" toward the past 60 years. The popular culture forms he examines include novels, short stories, poems, songs, plays, movies, radio and television, paintings, photographs, cartoons, toys, comic books, dime novels, slogans, and posters.

The book is arranged chronologically, in chapters from "Colonial Wars, 1565–1765" to "The United States Military Since 1975." A generally clear and cogent historical summary of the issues surrounding each war forms an introduction to each chapter, after which appears an alphabetical list of signed entries. Numbers of entries in each chapter range from five for "Indian Wars East of the Mississippi" to more than 130 for "World War II." Treatment length runs from around a half-page to more than a page. The level of writing, analysis, and readability is high.

Examples of topics include: from the Civil War, the autobiography *Mary Chestnut's Civil War*, the song "Maryland, My Maryland," Matthew Brady Studios, Herman Melville, and Memorial Day; and from World War II, G.I. Joe cartoons, the song "God Bless America," the books *Gravity's Rainbow* and *Guadalcanal Diary*, the television series *Hogan's Heroes*, Bob Hope, Randall Jarrell, the Jeep, and the slogan "Kilroy Was Here." Bibliographic references appear at the end of each entry as well as after chapter introductions, but their numbers have been limited by space considerations. A black-and-white "photo essay" contains examples of paintings, postage stamps, and posters. The volume concludes with an index.

The study of popular culture is growing. Besides the advantages of its browsability and nostalgic subject matter, this book will serve as an important starting point for those who wish to begin exploration of this interdisciplinary field. Although titles such as *Encyclopedia of American Social History* (Scribner's, 1993) and *Encyclopedia of Social History* [RBB My 15 94] include discussions on popular culture, only *War and American Popular Culture* provides detailed examinations of representations of war. Recommended for academic and large public library collections.

The Spanish-American War: A Historical Dictionary. By Brad K. Berner. 1998. 592p. bibliog. Scarecrow, $85 (0-8108-3490-1). DDC: 973.8.

As the poet and Spanish-American War participant Carl Sandburg once said, "it was a small war edging toward immense consequences." This short (eight-month) war crowned the U.S. as a major imperial power and sent the vanquished European power Spain into retreat and self-analysis. A new military made its debut in the U.S. with a frightening fire-power deadliness. And a new term, *yellow journalism*, was coined for the war fever that was drummed by the media. The war's centennial was commemorated last year. With this title Scarecrow has issued its eighth in a series called Historical Dictionaries of War, Revolution, and Civil Unrest.

Beginning with a chronology, the dictionary seeks to add to the literature by examining the concepts, events, personalities, and weaponry of this "splendid little war." The introduction by the author, a history professor, provides a survey of the major events. A sampling of the A–Z entries includes *armored cruiser, black powder, black American volunteer soldiers, "embalmed beef" controversy, Maine newspaper coverage* (referring to the disastrous voyage of the *Maine* to Cuba), and *yellow press*. Since this war was the debut of the all-steel navy, all naval ship entries contain data on specifications, giving their launched and commissioned dates, displacement, armor, and armament. There are numerous biographical entries, covering such individuals as Clara Barton, Stephen Crane, Theodore Roosevelt, Miguel de Unamuno, and Booker T. Washington. Few entries take up more than a page, but liberal cross-references refer researchers to other entries related to the topic. A 25-page bibliography arranged by broad subject rounds out the volume.

For public and academic libraries with very little literature on this aspect of American history, this volume would make a fine addition. Smaller libraries that have purchased *Historical Dictionary of the Spanish American War* (Greenwood, 1996) may find they have sufficient coverage.

The New Encyclopedia of the American West. Ed. by Howard R. Lamar. 1998. 640p. bibliogs. illus. maps. Yale, $60 (0-300-07088-8). DDC: 978.

This revision of *The Readers Encyclopedia of the American West* (T. Y. Crowell, 1977, 1985) expands on its predecessor. Significant revisions, updating and expanding the text were made to articles by either the original 200 contributors or the editor, with such editorial attention being noted at the end of the articles. The inclusion of articles by 100 new contributors expands the work considerably, as do many additional clear black-and-white illustrations. Articles are initialized by their contributors, whose institutional affiliations and areas of expertise are provided at the end of the volume.

The New Encyclopedia seeks to "provide up-to-date, authoritative information about the American frontier and the West for general readers and students [in] a single volume." The more than 2,400 entries cover (though in regrettably dry, pedantic language) the history of any person, place, thing, or idea that has influenced life in the American West from the early days to the present. Though there is neither an index nor a table of contents, the alphabetical arrangement by topic allows for easy access. Broader topics, such as the Native American populations, and people of prominence in the westward expansion, such as Thomas Jefferson, are given more space than, for example, Calamity Jane or Deadwood, South Dakota. Cross-referencing, denoted by related topics set in small caps when they appear within the text of articles, is instrumental in enabling in-depth research and in making important connections. Each article is followed by *see also* references and brief bibliographies, when more in-depth works exist. The articles are generally evenhanded and objective, in line with the stated goal of providing a "unique source for topics, events, people, and places that have affected the complex, ever-changing, and endlessly fascinating story of the frontier."

The volume is large but easy to work with, enhanced by its well-placed illustrations that serve to break up the small, daunting-looking, columnar print. The running heads facilitate access, and the single-volume format is easier to use than the four-volume formatting of the cumbersome *Encyclopedia of the American West* [RBB D 1 96], published by Macmillan. In its review of the Macmillan set, the Board noted that *The Readers Encyclopedia of the American West* had a greater number of biographies and a unique article on Indian languages, and these features remain in the revised edition. Students of topics western will find in *The New Encyclopedia of the American West* both a time-tested and a current source of information. Recommended for public and academic libraries.

California ResourceLink. [CD-ROM]. 1999. ABC-CLIO, $49; network (unlimited use) $199 (1-57607-137-5). DDC: 979.4.
Florida ResourceLink. [CD-ROM]. 1999. ABC-CLIO, $49; network (unlimited use) $199 (1-57607-143-X). DDC: 975.9.
New York ResourceLink. [CD-ROM]. 1999. ABC-CLIO, $49; network (unlimited use) $199 (1-57607-142-1). DDC: 974.7.
Texas ResourceLink. [CD-ROM] 1999. ABC CLIO, $49; network (unlimited use) $199 (1-57607-144-8). DDC: 976.4.

System requirements: PC: *Windows 95/98/NT 4.0; Pentium-compatible processor; 16 MB RAM (32 MB recommended); 30 MB hard disk space*. Macintosh: *System 7.5.3 or later; 68040 or faster processor, including Power Macintosh; 16 MB RAM (32 MB recommended); 30 MB hard disk space).*

ABC-CLIO has a growing reputation for reference works that tie together other sources. They are now venturing into the CD-ROM field, and this series marks another advance for them. The advantages of CD-ROMs are obvious: hyperlinks and search engines. With these products the user can build a list of related sources, edit and print them, or even export them.

All four discs have the same kind of information and format. Each contains about 600 resources (photographs, maps, documents, biographies, organizational profiles, quotations, statistics, court cases, background information, etc.), mainly of historical importance, although references may be as recent as 1997 (the O. J. Simpson murder trial on the California disc). Coverage is a bit spotty. For instance, the only reference to Ft. Lauderdale is as the hometown of a hockey player. The one picture of San Antonio is so general that it is hard to distinguish it from any other large city. The historical pictures are actually better than current ones (maybe because of copyright issues). Biographies (some quite obscure) range in length from a few lines to lengthy entries; most start with major achievements and then give a detailed narrative of the person's life in chronological sequence. Hard-to-find information that is located on these CD-ROMs includes legal documents and tables.

The software is easy to install and uses Acrobat Reader (which is embedded onto the CD-ROM in case the user doesn't have the program already). The actual use of the CD-ROM is a little clunky. Basically, the user can either start a new file of resource links or go directly to the Search mode. Resources are listed according to topic: Culture, Economics, Government, Law, Population, Society. For each topic the user can choose Biographies, Documents, Events, Glossary, Images, Maps, Organizations, Quotes, or Tables. (Tables require an extra step to view.) The user can search using keywords, limiting the results by topic and type of information if desired. In each case, the user sees a preview of the resource. Once out of the Search mode, the user gets a list of each resource that was found. Then the user can delete those files that are not of interest and examine the remaining ones full screen.

For the price, this series is a nice addition to school and some public libraries. Like other ResourceLink CD-ROMs, they would be useful for students who are writing reports. Don't expect inclusiveness or the highest quality, but build on the browsing features of these products. Forthcoming titles in the series include Georgia, Illinois, Indiana, Kentucky, Ohio, and Virginia.

Index to Type of Material

ALMANAC
   Almanac of World War I. 100
   Gay & Lesbian Almanac. 43
   World Almanac for Kids, 1999, The. 32

ATLAS
   Atlas of American Migration. 42
   Atlas of Global Change, The. 65
   Book of the World, The. 95
   National Geographic Satellite Atlas of the World, The. 96
   People and the Earth. 42
   Reader's Digest Children's Atlas of the World, The. 96

BIBLIOGRAPHY
   A to Zoo. 26
   American Historical Fiction. 27
   Building an ESL Collection for Young Adults. 28
   Children's Book Awards Annual, 1998. 31
   Children's Books about Religion. 28
   Children's Literature. 28
   Children's Nonfiction for Adult Information Needs. 29
   Fiction Sequels for Readers 10 to 16. 29
   Guides to Collection Development for Children and Young Adults. 28
   Harlem Renaissance, The. 30
   Library Resources for Singers, Coaches, and Accompanists. 30
   Sequels in Children's Literature. 29
   World Historical Fiction. 27

BIOGRAPHICAL DICITONARY
   African Biography. 96
   American National Biography. 96
   Biographical Dictionary of British Prime Ministers. 102
   Biographical Encyclopedia of Mathematicians. 63
   Black Authors and Illustrators of Books for Children and Young Adults. 86
   Business Leader Profiles for Students. 50
   Contemporary African American Novelists. 88
   Contemporary Southern Writers. 87
   Dictionary of World Biography. 97
   Encyclopedia of British Women Writers, An. 89
   F. Scott Fitzgerald Encyclopedia, An. 89
   Femme Noir. 79
   Heroes and Pioneers. 98
   Jane Austen Encyclopedia, A. 90
   Leaders of the Civil War. 109
   Mammoth Book of British Kings and Queens, The. 103
   Notable Black American Men. 98
   Notable Black American Scientists. 98
   Oscar Wilde Encyclopedia, The. 91
   Outlaws, Mobsters and Crooks. 54
   Oxford Composer Companion to J.S. Bach. 76
   People of the Holocaust. 101
   Science Fiction Writers. 91
   Scientists and Inventors. 98
   Scientists, Mathematicians, and Inventors. 63
   Scribner Encyclopedia of American Lives, The. 99
   Shapers of the Great Debate on Immigration. 48
   Significant Contemporary American Feminists. 43
   Songwriters. 78
   Susan B. Anthony. 43
   Thomas Jefferson. 110
   Tycoons and Entrepreneurs. 98
   Villains and Outlaws. 98
   Who Was Who in the Napoleonic Wars. 101
   Who's Who in British History. 103
   Women Filmmakers and Their Films. 81
   Women in Horror Films, 1930s. 82
   Women in Horror Films, 1940s. 82
   Women under the Third Reich. 104

CD-ROM
   American Multimedia Archive, The. 108
   California ResourceLink. 111
   CensusCD+Maps. 41
   Compton's Interactive Encyclopedia. 4
   DISCovering Nations, States, and Cultures. 94
   Encarta Africana. 105
   Encyclopedia Americana. 4
   Encyclopedia of World Biography on CD-ROM. 97
   FedLaw EasySearch. 53
   Florida ResourceLink. 111
   Funk & Wagnalls Multimedia Encyclopedia. 5
   Grolier Multimedia Encyclopedia. 5
   McGraw-Hill Multimedia Encyclopedia of Science and Technology. 62
   New York ResourceLink. 111
   ResourceLink: American Government. 47
   ResourceLink: Twentieth-Century American History. 47
   Scribner's American History and Culture on CD-ROM. 110
   Texas ResourceLink. 111
   Twayne's English Authors on CD-ROM. 89
   Twayne's United States Authors on CD-ROM. 89
   Twayne's World Authors on CD-ROM. 89
   World Book. 6

CHILDREN AND YOUNG ADULTS
   African Biogrpahy. 96
   American Immigration. 42
   Ancient Greece and Rome. 100
   Bioethics for Students. 36
   Chemical Elements. 64
   Colonial America. 109
   Dinosaurs of the World. 65
   DK Children's Illustrated Encyclopedia. 32
   DK Nature Encyclopedia. 63
   DK Science Encyclopedia, The. 63
   DK Ultimate Visual Dictionary of Science. 63
   Endangered Species. 49
   Ethics and Values. 36
   Explorers. 95
   Great Misadventures. 93
   Heroes and Pioneers. 98
   Junior Worldmark Encyclopedia of World Culture. 44
   Kidbits. 32
   Kingfisher Children's Encyclopedia, The. 32
   Kingfisher First Animal Encyclopedia, The. 66
   Literary Lifelines. 86
   Lives and Works. 87
   New Book of Popular Science, The. 22
   North America in Colonial Times. 107
   Outer Space. 64
   Outlaws, Mobsters and Crooks. 54
   Oxford American Children's Encyclopedia. 33
   People of the Holocaust. 101
   Peoples of the Americas. 107
   Peoples of the World. 45
   Scholastic Encyclopedia of the United States at War. 110
   Scientists and Inventors. 98
   Technology in Action. 68
   Tycoons and Entrepreneurs. 98
   Under the Microscope. 69
   Understanding the Holocaust. 101
   Villains and Outlaws. 98
   Voices of the Holocaust. 101
   Wildlife and Plants of the World. 66
   World Almanac for Kids, 1999, The. 32
   World War II. 102

CHRONOLOGY
   American Years, The. 108
   Chronology of World History. 92
   Famous First Facts. 22
   History of the Internet. 26
   Wars of the Americas. 55

DICTIONARY
   African American Quotations. 34
   AIDS Dictionary, The. 71
   Arthurian Name Dictionary, The. 103
   Canadian Oxford Dictionary, The. 60
   Cassell Dictionary of Classical Mythology. 39
   Cassell Dictionary of Science, The. 61
   Cassell Dictionary of Slang, The. 61
   Collins Musicals. 78

Collins Opera and Operetta. 78
Columbia Dictionary of Quotations from Shakespeare. 90
Dictionary of Architecture, A. 75
Dictionary of Celtic Mythology. 40
Dictionary of Historical Allusions and Eponyms. 32
Dictionary of Languages. 59
Dictionary of Modern American Usage, The. 60
Dictionary of Philosophy. 34
Dictionary of Space Technology. 72
Dictionary of Television and Audiovisual Terminology. 79
Dictionary of Theories, Laws, and Concepts in Psychology. 36
Doubleday Christian Quotation Collection, The. 39
Encyclopedic Dictionary of Conflict and Conflict Resolution, 1945-1996. 92
From Aristotle to Zoroaster. 99
Historical Dictionary of Judaism. 40
Historical Dictionary of School Segregation and Desegregation. 57
Historical Dictionary of Taoism. 41
Historical Dictionary of the Green Movement. 53
Historical Dictionary of Women's Education in the United States. 57
Hutchinson Dictionary of Ancient & Medieval Warfare. 54
Illustrated Dictionary of Architecture. 76
International Dictionary of Modern Dance. 82
Key Concepts in Language and Linguistics. 59
Lexicon of Labor, The. 49
McGraw-Hill Illustrated Telecom Dictionary. 57
Multicultural Dictionary of Literary Terms, The. 85
New Dickson Baseball Dictionary, The. 83
New Palgrave Dictionary of Economics and the Law, The. 52
Nineteenth-Century European Art. 75
Oxford Dictionary of Slang, The. 61
Oxford Dictionary of Twentieth Century Quotations, The. 85
Oxford Dictionary of Twentieth-Century Art. 75
Penguin Dictionary of Architecture and Landscape Architecture, The. 23
Pronouncing Shakespeare's Words. 90
Random House Webster's Quotationary. 34
Spanish-American War, The. 111
Tap Dance Dictionary, The. 82
Who's Who in Opera. 78
World War II. 102

DICTIONARY—THESAURUS
Scholastic Children's Thesaurus. 60
Scholastic First Dictionary. 60
Scholastic Treasury of Quotations for Children. 60

DIRECTORIES
Complete Directory for People with Rare Disorders, 1998-99, The. 68
Free or Low Cost Health Information. 68
Global Links. 47
Hollywood Stunt Performers. 80
Hoover's MasterList of Major International Companies, 1998-1999. 52
Internet Resources and Services for International Business. 31
Plunkett's Employers' Internet Sites with Careers Information. 51
Plunkett's Entertainment & Movie Industry Almanac. 81
Political Market Place USA. 48
Princeton Review Guide to Performing Arts Programs, The. 79
Storytellers. 58

ENCYCLOPEDIA
ABC-CLIO World History Companion to Capitalism. 49
ABC-CLIO World History Companion to Utopian Movements. 49
Academic American Encyclopedia. 1
American Desk Encyclopedia, The. 31
American Heritage Encyclopedia of American History, The. 108
American Musical Film Song Encyclopedia, The. 78
American Science Fiction Television Series of the 1950s. 27
Ancient Greece and Rome. 100
Archaeology of Prehistoric Native America. 106
Beacham's Encyclopedia of Popular Fiction. 85
Bioethics for Students. 36
Cambridge Encyclopedia of Human Growth and Development, The. 69
Clowns and Tricksters. 58
Columbia Guide to the Cold War, The. 109
Companion to California Wine, A. 73
Conflict in the Former Yugoslavia. 104
DK Children's Illustrated Encyclopedia. 32
Encyclopedia Americana. 2
Encyclopedia of AIDS. 68
Encyclopedia of American Activism. 48
Encyclopedia of American Communes, 1663-1963. 50
Encyclopedia of American Government. 46
Encyclopedia of American Literature. 87
Encyclopedia of American Poetry. 88
Encyclopedia of American Women and Religion. 37
Encyclopedia of Animal Rights and Animal Welfare. 36
Encyclopedia of Arabic Literature. 92
Encyclopedia of Asthetics. 35
Encyclopedia of Bilingualism and Bilingual Education. 56
Encyclopedia of Birds. 67
Encyclopedia of China. 104
Encyclopedia of Chinese Film. 79
Encyclopedia of Christianity, The. 38
Encyclopedia of Comparative Iconography. 74
Encyclopedia of Conflicts since World War II. 94
Encyclopedia of Contemporary French Culture. 104
Encyclopedia of Country Music, The. 77
Encyclopedia of Cults, Sects, and New Religions, The. 37
Encyclopedia of Fable. 58
Encyclopedia of Family Life. 44
Encyclopedia of Fishes. 67
Encyclopedia of Folklore and Literature. 84
Encyclopedia of Genetics. 66
Encyclopedia of Global Population and Demographics. 42
Encyclopedia of Greco-Roman Mythology. 40
Encyclopedia of Guerrilla Warfare. 54
Encyclopedia of Hell. 39
Encyclopedia of Historians and Historical Writing. 93
Encyclopedia of Housing, The. 55
Encyclopedia of Hurricanes, Typhoons, and Cyclones, The. 65
Encyclopedia of Infectious Diseases. 71
Encyclopedia of Mammals. 67
Encyclopedia of Native American Economic History, The. 51
Encyclopedia of Native American Shamanism. 70
Encyclopedia of Parenting Theory and Research, The. 73
Encyclopedia of Political Anarchy. 46
Encyclopedia of Political Revolutions, The. 93
Encyclopedia of Popular Music, The. 77
Encyclopedia of Religion in American Politics. 47
Encyclopedia of Reptiles & Amphibians. 67
Encyclopedia of Russian and Slavic Myth and Legends. 40
Encyclopedia of Small Business. 73
Encyclopedia of Student and Youth Movements. 57
Encyclopedia of Television News. 33
Encyclopedia of the Novel. 86
Encyclopedia of the Persian Gulf War. 105
Encyclopedia of the Solar System. 64
Encyclopedia of the Vatican and Papacy. 38
Encyclopedia of the Vietnam War. 105
Encyclopedia of Urban America. 45
Encyclopedia of Warrior Peoples and Fighting Groups. 54
Encyclopedia of Women and World Religion. 37
Encyclopedia of Women in American Politics. 47
Encyclopedia of Women in Aviation and Space. 72
Encyclopedia of World Cities. 46
Encyclopedia of World Literature in the 20th Century. 84
Encyclopedia of World Religions, The. 38
Facts On File Encyclopedia of Science, Technology, and Society, The. 62
Gale Encyclopedia of Medicine, The. 71
Gale Encyclopedia of Native American Tribes, The. 109
Global Encyclopedia of Historical Writing, A. 94
History of the Mass Media in the United States. 41
Horse Encyclopedia, The. 72
International Encyclopedia of Science and Technology, The. 62
International Encyclopedia of the Stock Market. 51
Junior Worldmark Encyclopedia of World Cultures. 44
Kingfisher Children's Encyclopedia, The. 32
Language and Communication. 59
Legends of the Earth, Sea, and Sky. 39
Macmillan Encyclopedia of World Slavery. 44
Medieval England. 103
Music in the 20th Century. 76
Native American Literatures. 88
Native Americans. 106
Natural Resources. 49
New Book of Knowledge, The. 2

New Book of Popular Science, The. 22
New Encyclopedia of the American West, The. 111
Nueva Enciclopeda Cumbre. 33
On the Air. 80
Oxford American Children's Encyclopedia. 33
Oxford Companion to Canadian Literature, The. 88
Oxford Companion to Classical Civilization, The. 100
Oxford Encyclopedia of World History. 93
Pacific War Encyclopedia, The. 101
Q is for Quantum. 64
Routledge Encyclopedia of Philosophy. 34
Sciences of the Earth. 65
Sci-Fi Channel Encyclopedia of TV Science Fiction, The. 81
Shengold Jewish Encyclopedia, The. 40
Simon and Schuster Encyclopedia of Animals, The. 67
Travel Legend and Lore. 95
War and American Popular Culture. 110
World Book Encyclopedia, The. 3
World Encyclopedia of Comics, The. 76
World Encyclopedia of Contemporary Theatre, Volume 5. 82
World War II in Europe. 102

FILMOGRAPHY
Animated Short Films. 28
Feature Films, 1950-1959. 29
Film Cartoons. 28
Guide to Latin American, Caribbean, and U.S. Latino-Made Film and Video. 27
Reel Middle Ages, The. 81
Science Fiction Serials. 30
Universal Silents, The. 31

GAZETTEER
Columbia Gazetteer of the World, The. 95

GUIDE
Film Festival Guide, The. 79
Reference Guide to Russian Literature. 91

HANDBOOK
Consumer's Guide to Herbal Medicine, The. 69
Dun and Bradstreet/Gale Industry Reference Handbooks: Computers and Software. 50
Dun and Bradstreet/Gale Industry Reference Handbooks: Pharmaceuticals. 50
Dun and Bradstreet/Gale Industry Reference Handbooks: Telecommunications. 50
Genealogical Encyclopedia of the Colonial Americas. 99
Girl Pages, The. 43
Handbook to Life in Ancient Egypt. 100
Johns Hopkins Family Health Book. 71
Medicinal Plants of the World. 70
PDR for Herbal Medicines. 70
Weddings. 57
Wellness Nutrition Counter, The. 73

ONLINE DATABASE
Alt-HealthWatch. 67
CQ Researcher, The. 22
Grove Dictionary of Art Online, The. 74
InfoTrac LifeCenter. 25
Literature Resource Center. 83
New Book of Knowledge Online, The. 26
Poem Finder on the Web. 84
What Do I Read Next? Online. 24
World Book Online. 24

STATISTICAL COMPILATION
China Marketing Data and Statistics 1998. 52
Comparative Guide to American Elementary and Seconday Schools, The. 56
Education Statistics on the United States. 56
Statistical Portrait of the United States, A. 46

THESAURUS
Cambridge French-English Thesaurus, The. 61

Subject Index

ACTIVISM
Encyclopedia of American Activism. 48

ACTORS
Femme Noir. 79
Hollywood Stunt Performers. 80
Women in Horror Films, 1930s. 82
Women in Horror Films, 1940s. 82

AERONAUTICS
Encyclopedia of Women in Aviation and Space. 72

AESTHETICS
Encyclopedia of Asthetics. 35

AFRICA
African Biography. 96
Encarta Africana. 105

AFRICAN AMERICANS
Contemporary African American Novelists. 88
Encarta Africana. 105
Harlem Renaissance, The. 30
Notable Black American Men. 98
Notable Black American Scientists. 98

AIDS
AIDS Dictionary, The. 71
Encyclopedia of AIDS. 68

ALLUSIONS
Dictionary of Historical Allusions and Eponyms. 32

ALTERNATIVE MEDICINE
Consumer's Guide to Herbal Medicine, The. 69
Medicinal Plants of the World. 70
PDR for Herbal Medicines. 70

AMPHIBIANS
Encyclopedia of Reptiles & Amphibians. 67

ANARCHISM
Encyclopedia of Political Anarchy. 46

ANIMAL RIGHTS
Encyclopedia of Animal Rights and Animal Welfare. 36

ANIMALS
Kingfisher First Animal Encyclopedia, The. 66
Simon and Schuster Encyclopedia of Animals, The. 67
Wildlife and Plants of the World. 66

ARCHAEOLOGY
Archaeology of Prehistoric Native America. 106

ARCHITECTURE
Dictionary of Architecture, A. 75
Illustrated Dictionary of Architecture. 76

ART
Oxford Dictionary of Twentieth-Century Art. 75
Nineteenth-Century European Art. 75
Grove Dictionary of Art Online, The. 74

ASIAN AMERICANS
Asian American Literature. 87

ASTRONAUTICS
Dictionary of Space Technology. 72

ASTRONOMY—OUTER SPACE
Outer Space. 64

BASEBALL
New Dickson Baseball Dictionary, The. 83

BILINGUALISM
Encyclopedia of Bilingualism and Bilingual Education. 56

BIOGRAPHICAL DICTIONARY
Scientists, Mathematicians, and Inventors. 63

BIRDS
Encyclopedia of Birds. 67

BUSINESS
Business Leader Profiles for Students. 50
Dun and Bradstreet/Gale Industry Reference Handbooks: Computers and Software. 50
Dun and Bradstreet/Gale Industry Reference Handbooks: Pharmaceuticals. 50
Dun and Bradstreet/Gale Industry Reference Handbooks: Telecommunications. 50
Encyclopedia of Small Business. 73
Internet Resources and Services for International Business. 31

INTERNET
Internet Resources and Services for International Business. 31

CALIFORNIA
California ResourceLink. 111

CANADA
Canadian Oxford Dictionary, The. 60

CAPITALISM
ABC-CLIO World History Companion to Capitalism. 49

CAREERS
Plunkett's Employers' Internet Sites with Careers Information. 51
Plunkett's Entertainment & Movie Industry Almanac. 81

CARTOONS
Animated Short Films. 28
Film Cartoons. 28

CHEMICAL ELEMENTS
Chemical Elements. 64

CHILDREN AND YOUNG ADULTS
DK Student Atlas. 96
New Book of Knowledge Online, The. 26

CHILDREN'S LITERATURE
Children's Book Awards Annual, 1998. 31
Children's Books about Religion. 28
Children's Literature. 28
Fiction Sequels for Readers 10 to 16. 29
Guides to Collection Development for Children and Young Adults. 28
Sequels in Children's Literature. 29
Storytellers. 58

CHINA
Encyclopedia of China. 104

CHINA—MARKETING
China Marketing Data and Statistics 1998. 52

CHRISTIANITY
Encyclopedia of Christianity, The. 38

CITIES
Encyclopedia of Urban America. 45
Encyclopedia of World Cities. 46

CIVIL RIGHTS
Civil Rights in America. 48

CIVIL WAR
Leaders of the Civil War. 109

COLD WAR
Columbia Guide to the Cold War, The. 109

COMICS
World Encyclopedia of Comics, The. 76

COMMUNES
Encyclopedia of American Communes, 1663-1963. 50

115

Subject Index

COMPANIES
Company Profiles for Students. 50
Hoover's MasterList of Major International Companies, 1998-1999. 52

CONFLICT
Encyclopedic Dictionary of Conflict and Conflict Resolution, 1945-1996. 92

CONFLICTS
Encyclopedia of Conflicts since World War II. 94

CONSTITUTION
Constitution and Its Amendements, The. 53

CULTS
Encyclopedia of Cults, Sects, and New Religions, The. 37

CULTURE
DISCovering Nations, States, and Cultures. 94
Junior Worldmark Encyclopedia of World Cultures. 44
Peoples of the Americas. 107
Peoples of the World. 45

DANCE
International Dictionary of Modern Dance. 82
Tap Dance Dictionary, The. 82

DEMOGRAPHICS
Encyclopedia of Global Population and Demographics. 42

DINOSAURS
Dinosaurs of the World. 65

DISASTERS
Great Misadventures. 93

DISEASES
Encyclopedia of Infectious Diseases. 71

EARTH SCIENCES
Atlas of Global Change, The. 65
Sciences of the Earth. 65

ECOLOGY
People and the Earth. 42

ECONOMICS
New Palgrave Dictionary of Economics and the Law, The. 52

EDUCATION
Comparative Guide to American Elementary and Seconday Schools, The. 56
Education Statistics on the United States. 56
Historical Dictionary of Women's Education in the United States. 57
Princeton Review Guide to Performing Arts Programs, The. 79

ENDANGERED SPECIES
Endangered Species. 49

ENGLAND
Who's Who in British History. 103

ENGLISH AS A SECOND LANGUAGE
Building an ESL Collection for Young Adults. 28

ENTREPRENEURS
Tycoons and Entrepreneurs. 98

ENVIRONMENT
Environmental Disasters. 55
Historical Dictionary of the Green Movement. 53

ETHICS
Ethics and Values. 36

EXPLORERS
Explorers. 95

FAMILY
Encyclopedia of Family Life. 44

FBI
FBI, The. 55

FICTION
Beacham's Encyclopedia of Popular Fiction. 85
Encyclopedia of the Novel. 86

FISHES
Encyclopedia of Fishes. 67

FLORIDA
Florida ResourceLink. 111

FOLKLORE
Clowns and Tricksters. 58
Encyclopedia of Fable. 58
Encyclopedia of Folklore and Literature. 84

FRANCE
Encyclopedia of Contemporary French Culture. 104

GAYS & LESBIANS
Gay & Lesbian Almanac. 43

GENEALOGY
Genealogical Encyclopedia of the Colonial Americas. 99

GENETICS
Encyclopedia of Genetics. 66

GEOGRAPHY
Columbia Gazetteer of the World, The. 95

GIRLS
Girl Pages, The. 43

GOVERNMENT
Global Links. 47

GOVERNMENT, U.S.
Encyclopedia of American Government. 46
Federal Agency Profiles for Students. 50
Government on File. 47
ResourceLink: American Government. 47

HARLEM RENAISSANCE
Harlem Renaissance, The. 30

HEALTH
Alt-HealthWatch. 67
Complete Directory for People with Rare Disorders, 1998-99, The. 68
Free or Low Cost Health Information. 68
Informacion de Salud para los Consumidores. 69
Johns Hopkins Family Health Book. 71

HELL
Encyclopedia of Hell. 39

HISTORIANS
Encyclopedia of Historians and Historical Writing. 93
Global Encyclopedia of Historical Writing, A. 94

HISTORY, ANCIENT
Ancient Greece and Rome. 100
Dictionary of World Biography. 97
From Aristotle to Zoroaster. 99
Handbook to Life in Ancient Egypt. 100
Oxford Companion to Classical Civilization, The. 100

HISTORY, BRITISH
Arthurian Name Dictionary, The. 103
Biographical Dictionary of British Prime Ministers. 102
Mammoth Book of British Kings and Queens, The. 103
Medieval England. 103
Who's Who in British History. 103

HISTORY, U.S.
American Heritage Encyclopedia of American History, The. 108
American Multimedia Archive, The. 108
American Years, The. 108
Colonial America. 109
North America in Colonial Times. 107
ResourceLink: Twentieth-Century American History. 47
Scholastic Encyclopedia of the United States at War. 110
Scribner's American History and Culture on CD-ROM. 110

HISTORY, WORLD
Chronology of World History. 92
Oxford Encyclopedia of World History. 93

HOLOCAUST
People of the Holocaust. 101
Understanding the Holocaust. 101
Voices of the Holocaust. 101

HORSES
Horse Encyclopedia, The. 72

HOUSING
Encyclopedia of Housing, The. 55

ICONOGRAPHY
Encyclopedia of Comparative Iconography. 74

IMMIGRATION
American Immigration. 42
Shapers of the Great Debate on Immigration. 48

Subject Index

INTERNET
History of the Internet. 26
Internet Resources and Services for International Business. 31

JUDAISM
Historical Dictionary of Judaism. 40
Shengold Jewish Encyclopedia, The. 40

KINGS AND QUEENS
Mammoth Book of British Kings and Queens, The. 103

LABOR
Lexicon of Labor, The. 49

LANGUAGE
Language and Communication. 59

LANGUAGE, ENGLISH
Canadian Oxford Dictionary, The. 60
Dictionary of Modern American Usage, The. 60
Scholastic Children's Thesaurus. 60
Scholastic First Dictionary. 60

LANGUAGE, FRENCH
Cambridge French-English Thesaurus, The. 61

LANGUAGES
Dictionary of Languages. 59
Key Concepts in Language and Linguistics. 59

LAW
FedLaw EasySearch. 53

LITERARY TERMS
Multicultural Dictionary of Literary Terms, The. 85

LITERATURE
Literary Lifelines. 86
Literature Resource Center. 83

LITERATURE, ARABIC
Encyclopedia of Arabic Literature. 92

LITERATURE, CANADA
Oxford Companion to Canadian Literature, The. 88

LITERATURE, RUSSIAN
Reference Guide to Russian Literature. 91

LITERATURE, U.S.
Encyclopedia of American Literature. 87

LITERATURE, WORLD
Encyclopedia of World Literature in the 20th Century. 84

MAMMALS
Encyclopedia of Mammals. 67

MATHEMATICIANS
Biographical Encyclopedia of Mathematicians. 63

MEDIA
History of the Mass Media in the United States. 41

MEDICINE
Gale Encyclopedia of Medicine, The. 71

MIDDLE AGES
Medieval England. 103

MIGRATION
Atlas of American Migration. 42

MOTION PICTURES
Encyclopedia of Chinese Film. 79
Feature Films, 1950-1959. 29
Film Festival Guide, The. 79
Guide to American Cinema, 1930-1965. 80
Guide to American Cinema, 1965-1995. 80
Guide to Latin American, Caribbean, and U.S. Latino-Made Film and Video. 27
Reel Middle Ages, The. 81
Science Fiction Serials. 30
Universal Silents, The. 31
Women Filmmakers and Their Films. 81

MUSIC
Encyclopedia of Country Music, The. 77
Encyclopedia of Popular Music, The. 77
Library Resources for Singers, Coaches, and Accompanists. 30
Music in the 20th Century. 76

MUSICALS
American Musical Film Song Encyclopedia, The. 78
Collins Musicals. 78

MUSICIANS
Oxford Composer Companion to J.S. Bach. 76

MUTUAL FUNDS
Weiss Ratings' Guide to Mutual Funds. 51

MYTHOLOGY
Cassell Dictionary of Classical Mythology. 39
Dictionary of Celtic Mythology. 40
Encyclopedia of Greco-Roman Mythology. 40
Encyclopedia of Russian and Slavic Myth and Legends. 40
Legends of the Earth, Sea, and Sky. 39

NAPOLEONIC WARS
Who Was Who in the Napoleonic Wars. 101

NATIVE AMERICANS
Encyclopedia of Native American Economic History, The. 51
Encyclopedia of Native American Shamanism. 70
Gale Encyclopedia of Native American Tribes, The. 109
Native American Literatures. 88
Native Americans. 106

NATURAL RESOURCES
Natural Resources. 49

NATURE
DK Nature Encyclopedia. 63

NEW YORK
New York ResourceLink. 111

NUTRITION
Wellness Nutrition Counter, The. 73

OPERA
Collins Opera and Operetta. 78
Who's Who in Opera. 78

OUTLAWS
Villains and Outlaws. 98

PAPACY—VATICAN
Encyclopedia of the Vatican and Papacy. 38

PARENTING
Encyclopedia of Parenting Theory and Research, The. 73

PERSIAN GULF WAR
Encyclopedia of the Persian Gulf War. 105

PHILOSOPHY
Dictionary of Philosophy. 34
Routledge Encyclopedia of Philosophy. 34

PHYSICS
Q Is for Quantum. 64

PHYSIOLOGY
Cambridge Encyclopedia of Human Growth and Development, The. 69
Under the Microscope. 69

PICTURE BOOKS
A to Zoo. 26

PIONEERS
Heroes and Pioneers. 98

PLANTS
Wildlife and Plants of the World. 66

POETRY
Encyclopedia of American Poetry. 88
Poem Finder on the Web. 84

POLITICS, U.S.
Encyclopedia of Religion in American Politics. 47
Encyclopedia of Women in American Politics. 47
Political Market Place USA. 48

POPULAR CULTURE
War and American Popular Culture. 110

POPULATION
CensusCD+Maps. 41
Encyclopedia of Global Population and Demographics. 42

PRESIDENTS
Thomas Jefferson. 110

PRIME MINISTERS
Biographical Dictionary of British Prime Miniters. 102

PSYCHOLOGY
Dictionary of Theories, Laws, and Concepts in Psychology. 36

QUOTATIONS
African American Quotations. 34

Subject Index

[Quotations cont.]
- Doubleday Christian Quotation Collection, The. 39
- Oxford Dictionary of Twentieth Century Quotations, The. 85
- Random House Webster's Quotationary. 34
- Scholastic Treasury of Quotations for Children. 60

RADIO
- On the Air. 80
- Radio Programs, 1924-1984. 30

READERS' ADVISORY
- American Historical Fiction. 27
- Children's Nonfiction for Adult Information Needs. 29
- What Do I Read Next? Online. 24
- World Historical Fiction. 27

RELIGION
- Encyclopedia of American Women and Religion. 37
- Encyclopedia of Religion in American Politics. 47
- Encyclopedia of Women and World Religion. 37
- Encyclopedia of World Religions, The. 38

REPTILES
- Encyclopedia of Reptiles & Amphibians. 67

REVOLUTION
- Encyclopedia of Political Revolutions, The. 93

SCIENCE
- Cassell Dictionary of Science, The. 61
- DK Science Encyclopedia, The. 63
- DK Ultimate Visual Dictionary of Science. 63
- Facts On File Encyclopedia of Science, Technology, and Society, The. 62
- International Encyclopedia of Science and Technology, The. 62
- McGraw-Hill Multimedia Encyclopedia of Science and Technology. 62
- New Book of Popular Science, The. 22

SCIENCE FICTION
- American Science Fiction Television Series of the 1950s. 27
- Sci-Fi Channel Encyclopedia of TV Science Fiction, The. 81
- Science Fiction Serials. 30
- Science Fiction Writers. 91

SCIENTISTS
- Notable Black American Scientists. 98
- Scientists and Inventors. 98

SEGREGATION
- Historical Dictionary of School Segregation and Desegregation. 57

SHAKESPEARE
- Columbia Dictionary of Quotations from Shakespeare. 90
- Pronouncing Shakespeare's Words. 90

SLANG
- Cassell Dictionary of Slang, The. 61
- Oxford Dictionary of Slang, The. 61

SLAVERY
- Macmillan Encyclopedia of World Slavery. 44

SOLAR SYSTEM
- Encyclopedia of the Solar System. 64

SONGWRITERS
- Songwriters. 78

SPACE
- Dictionary of Space Technology. 72

SPANISH LANGUAGE
- Nueva Enciclopeda Cumbre. 33

SPANISH-AMERICAN WAR
- Spanish-American War, The. 111

STATES
- State Constitutions of the United States. 53

STOCK MARKET
- International Encyclopedia of the Stock Market. 51

STRESS
- Stress A-Z. 72

STUDENTS
- Encyclopedia of Student and Youth Movements. 57

TAOISM
- Historical Dictionary of Taoism. 41

TECHNOLOGY
- Facts On File Encyclopedia of Science, Technology, and Society, The. 62
- International Encyclopedia of Science and Technology, The. 62
- McGraw-Hill Multimedia Encyclopedia of Science and Technology. 62
- Technology in Action. 68

TELECOMMUNICATIONS
- McGraw-Hill Illustrated Telecom Dictionary. 57

TELEVISION
- American Science Fiction Television Series of the 1950s. 27
- Dictionary of Television and Audiovisual Terminology. 79
- Encyclopedia of Television News. 33

TEXAS
- Texas ResourceLink. 111

THEATRE
- World Encyclopedia of Contemporary Theatre, Volume 5. 82

THIRD REICH
- Women under the Third Reich. 104

TRAVEL
- Travel Legend and Lore. 95

TRENDS
- Statistical Portrait of the United States, A. 46

UTOPIAN MOVEMENTS
- ABC-CLIO World History Companion to Utopian Movements. 49

VIDEOS
- Guide to Latin American, Caribbean, and U.S. Latino-Made Film and Video. 27

VIETNAM WAR
- Encyclopedia of the Vietnam War. 105

WARFARE
- Encyclopedia of Guerrilla Warfare. 54
- Encyclopedia of Warrior Peoples and Fighting Groups. 54
- Hutchinson Dictionary of Ancient & Medieval Warfare. 54
- Wars of the Americas. 55

WEATHER
- Encyclopedia of Hurricanes, Typhoons, and Cyclones, The. 65

WEDDINGS
- Weddings. 57

WESTERN UNITED STATES
- New Encyclopedia of the American West, The. 111

WINE
- Companion to California Wine, A. 73

WOMEN
- Encyclopedia of American Women and Religion. 37
- Encyclopedia of Women and World Religion. 37
- Encyclopedia of Women in American Politics. 47
- Women under the Third Reich. 104

WOMEN'S MOVEMENT
- Significant Contemporary American Feminists. 43
- Susan B. Anthony. 43

WORLD WAR I
- Almanac of World War I. 100

WORLD WAR II
- Pacific War Encyclopedia, The. 101
- World War II. 102
- World War II in Europe. 102

WRITERS
- Asian American Literature. 87
- Black Authors and Illustrators of Books for Children and Young Adults. 86
- Contemporary African American Novelists. 88
- Contemporary Southern Writers. 87
- Encyclopedia of British Women Writers, An. 89
- Jane Austen Encyclopedia, A. 90
- Lives and Works. 87
- Oscar Wilde Encyclopedia, The. 91
- Science Fiction Writers. 91
- Twayne's English Authors on CD-ROM. 89
- Twayne's United States Authors on CD-ROM. 89
- Twayne's World Authors on CD-ROM. 89

YUGOSLAVIA
- Conflict in the Former Yugoslavia. 104

Title Index

A to Zoo. 26
ABC-CLIO World History Companion to Capitalism. 49
ABC-CLIO World History Companion to Utopian Movements. 49
Academic American Encyclopedia. 1
African American Quotations. 34
African Biogrpahy. 96
AIDS Dictionary, The. 71
Almanac of World War I. 100
Alt-HealthWatch. 67
American Desk Encyclopedia, The. 31
American Heritage Encyclopedia of American History, The. 108
American Historical Fiction. 27
American Immigration. 42
American Multimedia Archive, The. 108
American Musical Film Song Encyclopedia, The. 78
American National Biography. 96
American Science Fiction Television Series of the 1950s. 27
American Years, The. 108
Ancient Greece and Rome. 100
Animated Short Films. 28
Archaeology of Prehistoric Native America. 106
Arthurian Name Dictionary, The. 103
Asian American Literature. 87
Atlas of American Migration. 42
Atlas of Global Change, The. 65
Beacham's Encyclopedia of Popular Fiction. 85
Bioethics for Students. 36
Biographical Dictionary of British Prime Ministers. 102
Biographical Encyclopedia of Mathematicians. 63
Black Authors and Illustrators of Books for Children and Young Adults. 86
Book of the World, The. 95
Building an ESL Collection for Young Adults. 28
Business Leader Profiles for Students. 50
California ResourceLink. 111
Cambridge Encyclopedia of Human Growth and Development, The. 69
Cambridge French-English Thesaurus, The. 61
Canadian Oxford Dictionary, The. 60
Cassell Dictionary of Classical Mythology. 39
Cassell Dictionary of Science, The. 61
Cassell Dictionary of Slang, The. 61
CensusCD+Maps. 41
Chemical Elements. 64
Children's Book Awards Annual, 1998. 31
Children's Books about Religion. 28
Children's Literature. 28
Children's Nonfiction for Adult Information Needs. 29

China Marketing Data and Statistics 1998. 52
Chronology of World History. 92
Civil Rights in America. 48
Clowns and Tricksters. 58
Collins Musicals. 78
Collins Opera and Operetta. 78
Colonial America. 109
Columbia Dictionary of Quotations from Shakespeare. 90
Columbia Gazetteer of the World, The. 95
Columbia Guide to the Cold War, The. 109
Companion to California Wine, A. 73
Company Profiles for Students. 50
Comparative Guide to American Elementary and Seconday Schools, The. 56
Complete Directory for People with Rare Disorders, 1998-99, The. 68
Compton's Interactive Encyclopedia. 4
Conflict in the Former Yugoslavia. 104
Constitution and Its Amendements, The. 53
Consumer's Guide to Herbal Medicine, The. 69
Contemporary African American Novelists. 88
Contemporary Southern Writers. 87
CQ Researcher, The. 22
Dictionary of Architecture, A. 75
Dictionary of Celtic Mythology. 40
Dictionary of Historical Allusions and Eponyms. 32
Dictionary of Languages. 59
Dictionary of Modern American Usage, The. 60
Dictionary of Philosophy. 34
Dictionary of Space Technology. 72
Dictionary of Television and Audiovisual Terminology. 79
Dictionary of Theories, Laws, and Concepts in Psychology. 36
Dictionary of World Biography. 97
Dinosaurs of the World. 65
DISCovering Nations, States, and Cultures. 94
DK Children's Illustrated Encyclopedia. 32
DK Nature Encyclopedia. 63
DK Science Encyclopedia, The. 63
DK Student Atlas. 96
DK Ultimate Visual Dictionary of Science. 63
Doubleday Christian Quotation Collection, The. 39
Dun and Bradstreet/Gale Industry Reference Handbooks: Computers and Software. 50
Dun and Bradstreet/Gale Industry Reference Handbooks: Pharmaceuticals. 50
Dun and Bradstreet/Gale Industry Reference Handbooks: Telecommunications. 50
Education Statistics on the United States. 56
Encarta Africana. 105
Encyclopedia Americana. 2, 4.
Encyclopedia of AIDS. 68

Encyclopedia of American Activism. 48
Encyclopedia of American Communes, 1663-1963. 50
Encyclopedia of American Government. 46
Encyclopedia of American Literature. 87
Encyclopedia of American Poetry. 88
Encyclopedia of American Women and Religion. 37
Encyclopedia of Animal Rights and Animal Welfare. 36
Encyclopedia of Arabic Literature. 92
Encyclopedia of Asthetics. 35
Encyclopedia of Bilingualism and Bilingual Education. 56
Encyclopedia of Birds. 67
Encyclopedia of British Women Writers, An. 89
Encyclopedia of China. 104
Encyclopedia of Chinese Film. 79
Encyclopedia of Christianity, The. 38
Encyclopedia of Comparative Iconography. 74
Encyclopedia of Conflicts since World War II. 94
Encyclopedia of Contemporary French Culture. 104
Encyclopedia of Country Music, The. 77
Encyclopedia of Cults, Sects, and New Religions, The. 37
Encyclopedia of Fable. 58
Encyclopedia of Family Life. 44
Encyclopedia of Fishes. 67
Encyclopedia of Folklore and Literature. 84
Encyclopedia of Genetics. 66
Encyclopedia of Global Population and Demographics. 42
Encyclopedia of Greco-Roman Mythology. 40
Encyclopedia of Guerrilla Warfare. 54
Encyclopedia of Hell. 39
Encyclopedia of Historians and Historical Writing. 93
Encyclopedia of Housing, The. 55
Encyclopedia of Hurricanes, Typhoons, and Cyclones, The. 65
Encyclopedia of Infectious Diseases. 71
Encyclopedia of Mammals. 67
Encyclopedia of Native American Economic History, The. 51
Encyclopedia of Native American Shamanism. 70
Encyclopedia of Parenting Theory and Research, The. 73
Encyclopedia of Political Anarchy. 46
Encyclopedia of Political Revolutions, The. 93
Encyclopedia of Popular Music, The. 77
Encyclopedia of Religion in American Politics. 47
Encyclopedia of Reptiles & Amphibians. 67

119

Title Index

Encyclopedia of Russian and Slavic Myth and Legends. 40
Encyclopedia of Small Business. 73
Encyclopedia of Student and Youth Movements. 57
Encyclopedia of Television News. 33
Encyclopedia of the Novel. 86
Encyclopedia of the Persian Gulf War. 105
Encyclopedia of the Solar System. 64
Encyclopedia of the Vatican and Papacy. 38
Encyclopedia of the Vietnam War. 105
Encyclopedia of Urban America. 45
Encyclopedia of Warrior Peoples and Fighting Groups. 54
Encyclopedia of Women and World Religion. 37
Encyclopedia of Women in American Politics. 47
Encyclopedia of Women in Aviation and Space. 72
Encyclopedia of World Biography on CD-ROM. 97
Encyclopedia of World Cities. 46
Encyclopedia of World Literature in the 20th Century. 84
Encyclopedia of World Religions, The. 38
Encyclopedic Dictionary of Conflict and Conflict Resolution, 1945-1996. 92
Endangered Species. 49
Environmental Disasters. 55
Ethics and Values. 36
Explorers. 95
F. Scott Fitzgerald Encyclopedia, An. 89
Facts On File Encyclopedia of Science, Technology, and Society, The. 62
Famous First Facts. 22
FBI, The. 55
Feature Films, 1950-1959. 29
Federal Agency Profiles for Students. 50
FedLaw EasySearch. 53
Femme Noir. 79
Fiction Sequels for Readers 10 to 16. 29
Film Cartoons. 28
Film Festival Guide, The. 79
Florida ResourceLink. 111
Free or Low Cost Health Information. 68
From Aristotle to Zoroaster. 99
Funk & Wagnalls Multimedia Encyclopedia. 5
Gale Encyclopedia of Medicine, The. 71
Gale Encyclopedia of Native American Tribes, The. 109
Gay & Lesbian Almanac. 43
Genealogical Encyclopedia of the Colonial Americas. 99
Girl Pages, The. 43
Global Encyclopedia of Historical Writing, A. 94
Global Links. 47
Government on File. 47
Great Misadventures. 93
Grolier Multimedia Encyclopedia. 5
Grove Dictionary of Art Online, The. 74
Guide to American Cinema, 1930-1965. 80
Guide to American Cinema, 1965-1995. 80
Guide to Latin American, Caribbean, and U.S. Latino-Made Film and Video. 27
Guides to Collection Development for Children and Young Adults. 28
Handbook to Life in Ancient Egypt. 100
Harlem Renaissance, The. 30
Heroes and Pioneers. 98
Historical Dictionary of Judaism. 40
Historical Dictionary of School Segregation and Desegregation. 57
Historical Dictionary of Taoism. 41
Historical Dictionary of the Green Movement. 53
Historical Dictionary of Women's Education in the United States. 57
History of the Internet. 26
History of the Mass Media in the United States. 41
Hollywood Stunt Performers. 80
Hoover's MasterList of Major International Companies, 1998-1999. 52
Horse Encyclopedia, The. 72
Hutchinson Dictionary of Ancient & Medieval Warfare. 54
Illustrated Dictionary of Architecture. 76
Informacion de Salud para los Consumidores. 69
InfoTrac LifeCenter. 25
International Dictionary of Modern Dance. 82
International Encyclopedia of Science and Technology, The. 62
International Encyclopedia of the Stock Market. 51
Internet Resources and Services for International Business. 31
Jane Austen Encyclopedia, A. 90
Johns Hopkins Family Health Book. 71
Junior Worldmark Encyclopedia of World Cultures. 44
Key Concepts in Language and Linguistics. 59
Kidbits. 32
Kingfisher Children's Encyclopedia, The. 32
Kingfisher First Animal Encyclopedia, The. 66
Language and Communication. 59
Leaders of the Civil War. 109
Legends of the Earth, Sea, and Sky. 39
Lexicon of Labor, The. 49
Library Resources for Singers, Coaches, and Accompanists. 30
Literary Lifelines. 86
Literature Resource Center. 83
Lives and Works. 87
Macmillan Encyclopedia of World Slavery. 44
Mammoth Book of British Kings and Queens, The. 103
McGraw-Hill Illustrated Telecom Dictionary. 57
McGraw-Hill Multimedia Encyclopedia of Science and Technology. 62
Medicinal Plants of the World. 70
Medieval England. 103
Multicultural Dictionary of Literary Terms, The. 85
Music in the 20th Century. 76
National Geographic Satellite Atlas of the World, The. 96
Native American Literatures. 88
Native Americans. 106
Natural Resources. 49
New Book of Knowledge Online, The. 26
New Book of Knowledge, The. 2
New Book of Popular Science, The. 22
New Dickson Baseball Dictionary, The. 83
New Encyclopedia of the American West, The. 111
New Palgrave Dictionary of Economics and the Law, The. 52
New York ResourceLink. 111
Nineteenth-Century European Art. 75
North America in Colonial Times. 107
Notable Black American Men. 98
Notable Black American Scientists. 98
Nueva Enciclopeda Cumbre. 33
On the Air. 80
Oscar Wilde Encyclopedia, The. 91
Outer Space. 64
Outlaws, Mobsters and Crooks. 54
Oxford American Children's Encyclopedia. 33
Oxford Companion to Canadian Literature, The. 88
Oxford Companion to Classical Civilization, The. 100
Oxford Composer Companion to J.S. Bach. 76
Oxford Dictionary of Slang, The. 61
Oxford Dictionary of Twentieth Century Quotations, The. 85
Oxford Dictionary of Twentieth-Century Art. 75
Oxford Encyclopedia of World History. 93
Pacific War Encyclopedia, The. 101
PDR for Herbal Medicines. 70
Penguin Dictionary of Architecture and Landscape Architecture, The. 23
People and the Earth. 42
People of the Holocaust. 101
Peoples of the Americas. 107
Peoples of the World. 45
Plunkett's Employers' Internet Sites with Careers Information. 51
Plunkett's Entertainment & Movie Industry Almanac. 81
Poem Finder on the Web. 84
Political Market Place USA. 48
Princeton Review Guide to Performing Arts Programs, The. 79
Pronouncing Shakespeare's Words. 90
Q Is for Quantum. 64
Radio Programs, 1924-1984. 30
Random House Webster's Quotationary. 34
Reader's Digest Children's Atlas of the World, The. 96
Reel Middle Ages, The. 81
Reference Guide to Russian Literature. 91
ResourceLink: American Government. 47
ResourceLink: Twentieth-Century American History. 47
Routledge Encyclopedia of Philosophy. 34
Scholastic Children's Thesaurus. 60
Scholastic Encyclopedia of the United States at War. 110
Scholastic First Dictionary. 60
Scholastic Treasury of Quotations for Children. 60
Science Fiction Serials. 30
Science Fiction Writers. 91
Sciences of the Earth. 65
Scientists and Inventors. 98
Scientists, Mathematicians, and Inventors. 63
Sci-Fi Channel Encyclopedia of TV Science Fiction, The. 81
Scribner Encyclopedia of American Lives, The. 99
Scribner's American History and Culture on CD-ROM. 110
Sequels in Children's Literature. 29
Shapers of the Great Debate on Immigration. 48
Shengold Jewish Encyclopedia, The. 40
Significant Contemporary American Feminists. 43

Simon and Schuster Encyclopedia of Animals, The. 67
Songwriters. 78
Spanish-American War, The. 111
State Constitutions of the United States. 53
Statistical Portrait of the United States, A. 46
Storytellers. 58
Stress A-Z. 72
Susan B. Anthony. 43
Tap Dance Dictionary, The. 82
Technology in Action. 68
Texas ResourceLink. 111
Thomas Jefferson. 110
Travel Legend and Lore. 95
Twayne's English Authors on CD-ROM. 89
Twayne's United States Authors on CD-ROM. 89
Twayne's World Authors on CD-ROM. 89
Tycoons and Entrepreneurs. 98
Under the Microscope. 69
Understanding the Holocaust. 101
Universal Silents, The. 31
Villains and Outlaws. 98
Voices of the Holocaust. 101
War and American Popular Culture. 110
Wars of the Americas. 55
Weddings. 57
Weiss Ratings' Guide to Mutual Funds. 51
Wellness Nutrition Counter, The. 73
What Do I Read Next? Online. 24
Who Was Who in the Napoleonic Wars. 101
Who's Who in British History. 103
Who's Who in Opera. 78
Wildlife and Plants of the World. 66
Women Filmmakers and Their Films. 81
Women in Horror Films, 1930s. 82
Women in Horror Films, 1940s. 82
Women under the Third Reich. 104
World Almanac for Kids, 1999, The. 32
World Book. 6
World Book Encyclopedia, The. 3
World Book Online. 24
World Encyclopedia of Comics, The. 76
World Encyclopedia of Contemporary Theatre, Volume 5. 82
World Historical Fiction. 27
World War II. 102
World War II in Europe. 102